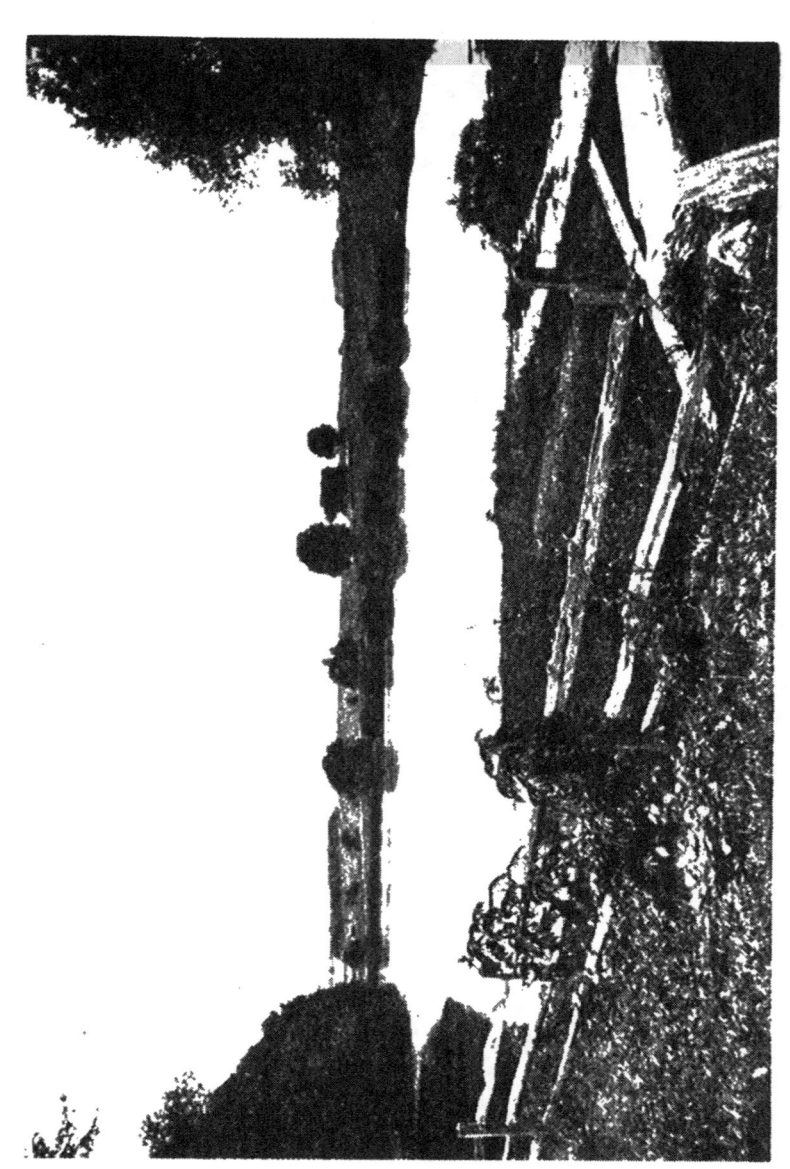

A VIEW NEAR BRYN MAWR, LOWER MERION, PA.
Plantation of Rowland Ellis.

MERION IN THE WELSH TRACT

WITH SKETCHES OF THE

TOWNSHIPS OF HAVERFORD AND RADNOR

HISTORICAL AND GENEALOGICAL COLLECTIONS CONCERNING THE WELSH BARONY IN THE PROVINCE OF PENN-
SYLVANIA, SETTLED BY THE CYMRIC
QUAKERS IN 1682.

BY

THOMAS ALLEN GLENN

*Member of the Historical Society of Pennsylvania, Genealogical Society of Pennsyl-
vania, Historical Society of Montgomery County, Pennsylvania Society,
Sons of the Revolution, Historical Society of Chester County,
Colonial Society of Pennsylvania, Etc.*

CLEARFIELD

Originally Published
Norristown, 1896

Reprinted
Genealogical Publishing Company
Baltimore, 1970

Reprinted for
Clearfield Company, Inc. by
Genealogical Publishing Co., Inc.
Baltimore, Maryland
1992, 1994, 1999, 2001

Library of Congress Catalogue Card Number 74-91971
International Standard Book Number: 0-8063-0429-4

Made in the United States of America

To
The Memory of
The First Welsh Planters
In the Province of Pennsylvania
Is Dedicated
This Humble Record of
Their Lives, their Lineage
and the
Country which they settled.

CONTENTS.

	PAGE
The Passing of the Cymry	1
The Great Welsh Tract or Barony in the Province of Pennsylvania, 1682 to 1700	21
The Merioneth Adventures: Dr. Edward Jones and John ap Thomas and Company	56
Rees John William, of Merion, otherwise Rees Jones, and his Descendants	73
Cadwallader Morgan, Minister among Friends	87
John and William ap Edward, of Merion, sons of Edward ap John, of Cynlas	89
Descent of Edward Rees (alias Price), ancestor of the Price Family of Merion, Lowry Lloyd and other settlers, from the Lloyds of Glanllyn and Gwern y Brechtwn, Merionethshire, North Wales, G. B	92
Roberts, of Pencoyd, Lower Merion	98
Hugh John Thomas, of Merion	111
The Owen Family, of Merion, in Pennsylvania, and Allied Lines	112
The Bevan Family, of Treverigg, Glamorganshire, and Merion, Pennsylvania	154
Social and Domestic Affairs in Wales and in the Welsh Tract in Pennsylvania	187
Bryn Mawr and Rowland Ellis	205
Ellis Lewis and His Descendants	235
The Humphreys Family	241
Cadwalader, of Merion, and afterwards of Philadelphia, Pennsylvania	252
Wynnewood and the Wynnes	261
Roberts of Merion and Blockley	280
Roberts	284
Notes on the Walker and Thomas Family, of Radnor	287
The Parry Family, of Radnor	291
John ap Thomas and the Jones Family, of Merion, Descended from Him	294
The Herbert and Awbrey Families of Wales, and their Descendants in Merion Township in the Province of Pennsylvania. Rees and Martha (Awbrey) Thomas	305
Dr. Edward Jones and His Descendants	315
Hugh Roberts of Merion and Chestnut Hill	323
Lloyd, of Dolobran—The Pedigree of the Family and an Account of Some of the American Descendants	336
The Brooke and Morgan Families	355
The Merion Meeting	364
Robert and Thomas Lloyd, of Bryn Mawr	375
Some Notes on the Warner Family, of Blockley	381
Appendix	384
Index	387

LIST OF ILLUSTRATIONS

[Not including Coats of Arms or Signatures. The Pennsylvania views are from photographs made especially for this work by Mr. Rolfe.]

	PAGE
A view near Bryn Mawr, Lower Merion, Pa., Plantation of Rowland Ellis . . . . To face	Title
Tyddin y Garreg, Llangelynin, Merionethshire, the property of Lewis Owen, 1678, and the Meeting Place of Friends from 1664 to 1700	16
Earliest Line Stone in Haverford Township	38
Ancient Mile Stone, with Penn's Arms, on the old Gulph Road	50
Bala Lake (Llyn Tegid), Merionethshire	56
Glanllyn, near Bala, purchased by David Lloyd, 1504	74
Gwern y Brechdwn (alias Brechtwn or Brychdwn), Home of the Lloyds, Merionethshire	96
The Roberts House, Pencoyd and Bala, Lower Merion, Pa., Oldest Portions by John Roberts about 1684	102
Fron Gôch, Home of Robert Owen, near Bala, Wales	120
Marriage Certificate of Robert and Rebecca Owen, 1678–9	126
The Owen House, near Wynnewood, Pa	128
Will of Robert Owen, 1697	136
Friends Meeting House erected by John Bevan upon his estate of Treverigg (sketch by Miss Bell)	160
Bryn Mawr, near Dôlgelly, built by Rees Lewis. The Birthplace of Rowland Ellis, 1650	206
Effigy of Meuric, of Nannau	213
Dôlgelly Church, near Bryn Mawr, Merionethshire, Wales	214
Pedigree in Handwriting of Rowland Ellis	220
Harriton (Bryn Mawr), built by Rowland Ellis, afterwards the Residence of Charles Thomson, Secretary of the Continental Congress	228
Wynnestay (alias Wynnstay), built by Jonathan Wynne about 1701 . . .	276
Gateway at Raglan, Wales	306
Residence of Benjamin Brooke, at Gulph Mills	356
The Morgan House, Radnor, Pa	360
The Merion Meeting	365
The Merion Meeting in 1829	368
The Radnor Meeting, Pa	370

PREFACE.

The following work, the scope of which is amply set forth on the title-page, was undertaken, at the suggestion of several of my valued friends, in order to preserve in a convenient shape some part of my collection of historical and genealogical material relating to the early Cymric Quaker planters of the Province of Pennsylvania. The compilation of such notes, and the necessity of considerable additional research, not only in this country but also in Wales, has, indeed, occupied much more time than I at first intended to spare from my other duties for this purpose. It is true that a large amount of data on the subject was collected by me some years since; but bearing in mind the sage advice of a certain excellent old Roman, to wit, "*Nonum prematur in annum*," I have, by delaying publication, been able to add to the pages of this book much that may prove of interest and value. Some questions, however, long mooted, I regret to say, remain yet undetermined, despite exhaustive inquiry.

Although the following chapters are not more than a series of historical and genealogical sketches, yet their arrangement is not without a preconcerted purpose. In the introductory article I have attempted to illustrate the general characteristics of the race from which the early Welsh settlers of Pennsylvania sprang, and the causes which led to their removal to that Province. Following this, I have endeavored to give a clear and concise account of the proposed Barony and its political history, and also to mark the final abandonment of that plan of government. Here will be found the dates of settlement of the three original townships, Merion, Radnor and Haverford, and rolls of the companies of planters that peopled them. In the chapter on the Merioneth Company of Adventurers, a detailed account of the genesis of Lower Merion, formerly old "Merioneth Town," is presented. Following these articles will be found biographical sketches and genealogies of many of the first settlers. The former show the character and useful and sober lives of the founders of Lower Merion, whilst the latter tell us from what ancestry these earnest men and women derived their superior qualities.

Scattered through the genealogies will be found valuable items of township and state history. The pedigrees included in this work are drawn from unquestionable sources and may be relied upon as correct in all the essential points. No genealogy has been printed in these pages that has not been proved beyond question by original family documents and public records. In all cases the authorities are given for each definite statement. No responsibility, however, is assumed for errors which may be discovered in records of *descendants* of early settlers where such information is stated to have been furnished by another person or derived from printed books, but such communications and type matter were carefully transcribed and verified where possible. It is not practicable, or within the scope of this book to give at length all of the various descendants down to the present generations, but in every case enough data has been furnished to enable any descendant to insert, on a separate page, his or her line, if desired.

The importance of the early Welsh emigration to Pennsylvania, and the excellent results following the infusion of Cymric blood into the veins of late generations of Pennsylvanians, cannot well be overestimated. In the municipal government of Philadelphia, during the Colonial period and the first half of the present century, the descendants of the Welsh Friends bore a distinguished part. A score of the earlier Mayors were of Cymric lineage, and of these I may name Edward Roberts and Robert Wharton as the best known. Of the Judges of the various Courts, and of the most eminent of the members of the Bar of this city and state, down to the present day, a very large proportion trace to the settlers of Merion, Radnor or Haverford.

Preface.

It is a curious fact, well worthy of remark, that the entire medical history of Philadelphia, beginning with Dr. Thomas Wynne, Dr. Griffith Owen and Dr. Edward Jones, proceeding with Dr. Lloyd Zachary, Dr. Thomas Cadwalader, Dr. Cadwalader Evans, Drs. Thomas and Phineas Bond, Dr. John Jones, Dr. Judah Foulke, and continuing through a long line to the most celebrated physicians and surgeons of our own day, is directly traceable, through ancestry or influence, to Welsh blood. Of the Revolutionary worthies descended from the Cymric Quakers we have spoken briefly elsewhere. In letters, in science and in art, some of the descendants of these early Colonists have acquired especial fame. It is also worthy of note that very much has been accomplished in the Historical Society of Pennsylvania by men of Cymric lineage, and the Council of that body has seldom been without a representative of some Merion settler.

It is proper, here, that I should thank all of those persons who, by their kind assistance, good advice and timely suggestions, have considerably lightened the burden of this undertaking. Of these I must mention first my friend, and for many years co-laborer in this field, Howard Williams Lloyd, Esq., of Germantown. Especial thanks are also due to Allen Evans, Esq., Haverford, for considerable and kindly interest in the furtherance of this work; to Frederick D. Stone, L. D., and John W. Jordan, A. M., of the Historical Society of Pennsylvania; P. S. P. Conner, Esq., Charles E. Cadwalader, M. D., of Philadelphia; Rowland Evans, Esq., of Haverford; Louis S. Kite, Esq., Joseph Fornance, Esq., of Norristown, Pa.; Charles J. Wister, Esq., of Germantown; and Joseph I. Doran, Esq., Francis M. Brooke, Esq., and Hon. Samuel W. Pennypacker, of Philadelphia.

THOMAS ALLEN GLENN.

Ardmore, Lower Merion, Pa.
January 8th, 1896.

ERRATA AND ADDENDA.

[Especial care has been exercised to avoid errors, either of a clerical or typographical nature, and if any are found, other than here noted, they will not, it is believed, be of a serious nature. No attempt, however, has been made to attain absolute uniformity in the orthography of the names of Welsh places, because they differ so remarkably in various documents that such a task would not only be extremely laborious but prejudicial to a proper understanding of the various references. "*Gwern y Brechdwn*," for example, will be found in four different forms taken from as many authorities, nor do the official ordinance maps of Wales conform, in this respect, to the practice of the inhabitants or to public archives. The dates were carefully verified by correcting the proofs from the original records, but it may be noted that public documents often differ from each other and from family records and printed books, in this particular.] The following were noted whilst this work was going through the press:

Page 4, line 12, for "*Harliaen*" read "*Harleian*."
" 10, " 5–6, for "*thirteenth*" read "*fourteenth*."
" 33, " 33, "*Marchnant*," so in record, but should be "*Mochnant*."
" 34, " 20, "*Techla*," so in record, but should be "*Telcha or Tylcha*."
" 36, " 26, "*Dalserey*," so in record, but should be "*Dolserey*."
" 115, under cut, for "*Argen*" read "*Argent*."
" 148, line 17, for "*Sidney, M. C. Farnum*," read "*Mary, m. C. Farnum*."
" 209, line 22–23, for "*revision*" read "*reversion*."
" 215, " 31, "*Trawvynydd*" is more correctly written "*Trawsvynydd*."
" 237, *foot note, strike out* "*Note B, p. 10*."
" 240, *foot note, strike out* "*mentioned on page 11*."
" 242, " 7, for "*Wynnwood*" read "*Wynnewood*."
" 243, "*Ednowain ap Bradwen*" is referred to indifferently in the Welsh records as "*Ednowain*" and "*Ednowen*." Both spellings are here given following references, but "*Ednowain*" is nearer correct
" 245, line 3, for "*Callwyn ap Tagno*" read "*Collwyn ap Tangno*."
" 245, " 10, for "*Llwyn*" read "*Llyn*."
" 245, " 17, for "*fourth*" read "*third*."
" 246, " 24, for "*Llwyngrill*" read "*Llwyngwrill*," *but the former is from a record.*
" 249, Foot Note, "*Montgomery Collections*" *refers to Montgomeryshire Collections of the Powysland Club.*
" 268, line 34, "*Pierreepoint*" is more correctly written "*Pre-poynt*."
" 281, " 10, for "*789*" read "*1789*."

MERION IN THE WELSH TRACT.

THE PASSING OF THE CYMRY[1].

"Their Lord they will praise, their speech they shall keep,
Their land they shall lose—except wild Wales."

In Robert Proud's history of Pennsylvania may be found the following brief note relative to those settlers in the Province who were natives of the Principality of Wales:

"Among those early adventurers and settlers, who arrived about this time, were also many from Wales, of those who are called Ancient Britons, and mostly Quakers—Divers of those early Welsh settlers were persons of excellent and worthy character; and several of good education, family and estate. They had early purchased of the Proprietary, in England, forty thousand acres of land. Those who came at present took up so much of it in the West Side of the Sculkil River, as made the three townships of Merion, Haverford and Radnor, and a few years afterwards their number was so much augmented as to settle the three other townships of New-town, Goshen and Uwchland. After this they continued still increasing, and became a numerous and flourishing people."

It is of the three townships first named, and their founders, that these pages will principally speak.

In education, industry and practical ability the Welsh planters had no superiors and few equals among the early colonists. All their national pride and all their personal interests impelled them to undertake those enterprises from which their fellow settlers seemed to shrink. This was due

---

[1] Regarding the word Cymric, as applied to the Welsh, see infra.

to their hereditary instincts. No people ever landed upon Pennsylvania soil so well equipped by birth and fortune to cope with those perilous emergencies so frequently arising in a new country as the Cymric Friends.

They were no pauper class subsisting or depending upon the charity of the Proprietor or any other philanthropist, but a body of self-reliant and resolute men with ample fortune in their hands, seeking, amid the primeval forests of Pennsylvania, a home of liberty, where undisturbed by priest or sheriff they could worship God after their own fashion.

Of these Welsh Quakers it has been remarked, and truly, that they were not only the first ministers, but the first statesmen, the first lawyers and the first physicians of Pennsylvania.

One of them, Dr. Thomas Wynne, presided over the first Assembly. The Deputy Governor, Thomas Lloyd, the Register General, Thomas Ellis, the third Attorney General and the first Deputy Surveyors, besides a large proportion of the earlier Justices and members of the Council and Provincial Assembly, were men of Welsh blood.

At home these colonists had been persons of consideration and influence in their several counties.

For the most part they had been freeholders or heirs to comfortable estates.

The existing conditions, therefore, which induced such men to emigrate to a wild and almost unknown country must indeed have been extraordinary.

To fully understand what these conditions were, and also the peculiarities of the people who founded the "Great Welsh Tract" or "Barony" in the Province of Pennsylvania, whose descendants have always been distinguished, not only in our own state, but over the entire United States and in England, on the bench, at the bar, in arms, and in letters, or in the halls of Assembly, it is necessary that we should examine the character of the Welsh race, their history, records, and their national traits.

Of Britain, prior to the landing of Cæsar, we know nothing of certainty. The island was inhabited by a number of valiant but half-savage woad-tattooed tribes[1], and was occasionally visited by traders from the continent. That period extending from the Roman invasion, back to the reign of a certain British Princeling, Brute by name, a period variously estimated at eleven to thirteen hundred years B. C., is known in history as "the doubtful age." Even the ancient Welsh Bards did not attempt, for all those centuries, a further record than the bare genealogy of their Kings. With the invasion of Cæsar, therefore, in the year 55 B. C., commences the authentic history of Britain and of the Welsh.

The Romans found the land subdivided amongst tribes, consisting each of many communities. Each tribe was ruled by a Prince or so called King, and each hamlet or community by a Lord or Chief, whilst the whole nation was occasionally united in times of war, under the doubtful authority of an Over-King or elected ruler.

The ancient Britons were always, it is claimed, a religious people. Long before the Roman invasion there existed their Druid Priests, the exponents of a religious belief which, although not perfect, had as its fundamental principles great truths analogous to those of the Christian creed. The basis of this religion of barbarian Britain was a strict adherence to truth, a spirit of exact justice, and a policy, perhaps we may say love, of peace. They recognized one Supreme Being only, whom they worshipped in the open air, under the great spreading oaks of the forest, and they venerated the ever surviving mistletoe as a symbol of eternal life. Their belief called for a strict and inflexible morality, and of it a learned writer has remarked that "it comprehended all the leading principles that tend to spread liberty, peace and happiness among mankind, and was no more inimical to Christianity than the religion of

---

[1] In ancient times Europe was inhabited by the Keltic nation, until they were driven, by the hardier tribes of Teutonic origin, to the extreme west, where the ranges of rugged hills guarding the Atlantic has protected this race from extinction. Cym or Cyn, meaning in their language "first," was the root of their name of Cymry, the name by which the inhabitants of Wales, claiming descent from the first tribe of these Kelts, still call themselves. The name " Welsh" is the Teuton word " Welsch," or the stranger. These Britons who were driven to the west coast were so called—hence, Wales.

Noah, Job, or Abraham." It is now considered by many historians more than doubtful that the Druids practiced those human sacrifices of which they are accused by Roman writers, and for which we have only the unchallenged word of the conqueror.

At this early period the Britons had their Bards, who were similar to those of mediæval days and more modern Heralds-at-Arms. The duty of these persons was to record the descent of the Princes and Lords of Britain, and at the death of a ruler his heir was presented with a copy of his genealogy from their "authentic books." The earliest of these "authentic books" now in existence is in the Harliaen collection in the British Museum, and was copied from a volume, then ancient, in the ninth century of the Christian era. Although, after the conquest, the Britons adopted the faded tinsel of the Romans, and invented a pedigree for their first ruler, Brute, to Æneas of Troy, yet their proud ancestry, and the lofty achievements which were attributed in the songs of the early Bards to the British race, inspired each succeeding generation with a love of brave exploits, a contempt of danger, and a lofty patriotism, which could not be crushed out even by four centuries of the iron heel of Imperial Rome, the Saxon or Danish axe, or the mace of the steel-clad Norman man-at-arms; yet back of all their fierce joy of battle was the inherent love of peace and home. And it was in defence of his liberty and his hearth that the Briton could fight best.

Cæsar approached Britain at a place since called Romney, near Deal. Although vigorously opposed, the Romans were able, at a great cost of life, to effect a landing. Having driven the Britons back into the country, Cæsar made a temporary truce and returned to Gaul.

In the spring of the following year he made a second attempt to conquer the island, taking with him 20,000 men. He landed at the same place, and after hard fighting against Caswallon, brother of Lud, king of Britain, was able to advance a short distance into the interior. After several terrific battles, Cæsar again arranged a truce upon condition of the payment of a specific tribute, and returned to Rome. It was not, however, until 43 A. D. that another attempt was made to reduce Britain. In that year a large army, under the command of Aulus Plautius, proceeded to the island, and was soon followed by Claudius, then Emperor of Rome.

The hardy Britons, although outgeneraled, were not easily subdued. Many years of carnage followed.

One by one the native Princes yielded to Roman arms and Roman discipline. Sullenly and reluctantly they surrendered their land and their government, to receive the same back as a fief from their conquerors. But the conquered districts were not to be entirely trusted. The great revolt of Boadicea is believed to have caused the death of over 70,000 Romans, and it was not until the year A. D. 85, under Julius Agricola, that the entire island, including a part of what is now known as Wales, was made tributary to Rome.

Under Honorius the Roman legions, including as many of the native Briton fighting men as they could gather, were withdrawn to protect Rome against the Goths. No sooner had this occurred than the Picts, who were wild tribes inhabiting Scotland, poured down upon the defenceless inhabitants. An appeal to Rome brought troops supplied by Stilicho in 396, and again in 418 the island was for the last time invested by a Roman army. They remained only long enough to drive the Picts back beyond the Roman wall, and then departed, to return no more. With the last of these Roman soldiers went many of those Romans who had not intermarried with the Britons or become natives by residence of many successive generations.

Left to their own resources the British and Roman citizens took into their service, as mercenaries, some bands of Saxons who were renowned as sea rovers, or Vikings. The reward for their services seems to have been lands upon the east coast.

Here begins a new chapter of Britain's history. The Saxons had not heretofore been friends; they were now acknowledged enemies. The rich lands of the islanders was a fair prize better worth the winning than good wages only for hard blows. "If," said the Saxons, "we must keep the Picts out of Britain, it would be well to gain what we can of the land, else we shall have our trouble for naught." They had easily driven the northern savages back to their highlands, and the conquest of a people defeated by such wild hordes seemed likely to be a brief affair. But the ancient military spirit of the Briton was not entirely extinct. It is true that the enlistment of their younger men by the Romans had reduced their strength; but now a new generation had grown up, and the Saxons found their first advances met by a brave resistance. As time went on the old training to arms revived, and after the first victories the fighting was more equal. Reinforcements of Angles, Jutes and Saxons were met by new generations of islanders. Greater personal strength, long continued exposure to hardships and superior numbers, however, gave, in the end, the victory to the invaders.

Step by step, and foot by foot, fighting desperately for each farm and village, the Briton retreated towards the west coast. But the conquest was not a brief one, and it was not until the eighth century that the stubborn Welsh consented to do homage to Saxon England, nor was that homage then of a servile kind; for we learn that the Cymric Princes sat in the frequent Parliaments which were held by the early English Kings, particularly those which mark the reign of the great and good Athelstan.

Little of moment, except wretched intestine broils, now disturbed the land until the Norman conquest rolled to the confines of Wales. The Britons had in early times accepted the Christian religion, to which they devoted themselves with a singular piety. In their belief, however, they were still swayed by the old teachings of the Druids and never accepted in their entireness the doctrines or dogmatic rules insisted upon by the Roman See.

At the death of Rhodri Mawr, which occurred in the year 876, the Principality had, unhappily, been divided into three districts, Powys, Gwynedd (or North Wales) and South Wales.

The Lords of these Provinces, left without a head, were torn by petty jealousy and were frequently at strife. Such was the state of affairs when the Normans set about to conquer the last bit of British ground yet remaining free and independent. A chain of mighty fortresses, erected by the Conqueror, served to keep the Welsh beyond the Marches and for a time in submission. These castles were garrisoned by an unrelenting and cruel soldiery. "From his earldom of Chester," says an old chronicler, "Hugh the Wolf harried Flintshire into a desert." " Robert of Belesme slew the Welsh like sheep, conquered them, enslaved them, and flayed them with nails of iron."

Under cover of the Lord Marchers, a band of Norman Free Lances obtained a royal grant to make conquest of Wales. Several towns were quickly seized and Rhys ap Tewdwr, Prince of South Wales, fell, fighting against Bernard Newmarché in Brecknock, at a place, to this day, called "Fynan Pen Rhys." Some of these adventurers were far-sighted enough to ally themselves with the native families, and in time became sympathizers with their adopted countrymen. Among these are found the names of Awbrey, Puleston, Gamage and Tuberville. Of the latter robber knight it is told that when Paine Tuberville encamped before the Castle of Coity, Morgan, the Lord thereof, came out to the Normans, leading his fair and only daughter, Sara, by one hand and having his sword drawn in the other. "This," said the Welsh Lord, "is no quarrel of our men, and therefore it is not right that we should shed their blood therein; but let your sword and mine, Tuberville, determine which of us shall have these goodly lands and the Lordship of Coity. If, however, you are free to wed, and will marry my daughter, so coming into possession honestly, then there is no further strife between us." Then Tuberville, putting up his sword, took the heiress of Coity by the hand, "and there was much feasting for many a day within that country."

For a time it seemed as if the last corner of ancient Britain had at last been conquered. On every side the Welsh were girt about by Normans, and within petty family strife made all concerted action impossible. At this dark hour there kindled into flame the smouldering embers of that lofty patriotism for which the Britons had so long been noted and admired. And as the glow of patriotic fire spread over hill and valley, out of each hendre and hamlet a most wonderful flood of song burst forth from all the Bards in Wales.

The Welsh had always been poetical and musical. "In every house," says the learned and curious Du Barri, "strangers who arrived in the morning were entertained until eventide with the talk of maidens and the music of the harp." Their poetic fancy took grotesque forms, but nothing can be more delightful than the descriptive verses of their earlier poets. "The maiden was clothed in a robe of flame-colored silk, and about her neck was a collar of ruddy gold in which were precious emeralds and rubies. Her hair was of brighter gold than the flower of the broom, her skin was whiter than the foam of the sea wave, and fairer were her hands and her fingers than the blossoms of the wood anemone amid the spray of the meadow fountain. The eye of the trained falcon was not brighter than hers. Her bosom was more snowy than the breast of the white swan, her cheek was redder than the reddest roses; whoso beheld her was filled with her love. Four white trefoils sprang up wherever she trod."

But side by side with such singing there rang out the stern, fierce call to arms. In these wild odes and war songs, the same that their savage woad-tattooed ancestors had chanted ages before, "amid the red desolation of forgotten wars," you can hear still the tinkle of armor, the clang of shield on shield, the tramp of the gathering tribesmen, and the mad rush of the Welshman's furious battle line.

Down through the ages that have passed, preserved as if in some wondrous mirror, you can see the desperate charge of the white-tuniced Briton, bare-breasted, against the Norman man-at-arms in mailed panoply. You can hear yet the clash of arms, the shouts of the combatants, and the crunch of mace and sword on limb and brain-pan. There is in this wild poetry, an awful reek of the joy of battle; of the love of slaughter.

"The dread eagle is wont to lay corpses in rows, and to feast with the leader of wolves, and with hovering ravens glutted with flesh, butchers with keen scent of carcasses." "Better the grave," sings a Bard, "than the life of a man who sighs when the bugles call him forth to the squares of battle." But amid this mighty tumult of song there rose up the great Llewellyn, to unite, under a clear head and steady hand, the shattered fortunes of wild Wales. "The sound of his coming is like the roar of the wave as it rushes to the shore, that can neither be stayed nor hushed."

Although it was proclaimed that the dead Arthur and his famous knights would wake from their long sleep and join Llewellyn in his struggle for liberty, and that the "Saxon sheep" and "Norman dogs" would be driven into the eastern seas, there were some who doubted the success of the Cymric arms. But all were strong believers in the ultimate survival of the British race.

"Think you," said King Henry to a Welsh chieftain who came over to the English camp, "that your people of rebels can withstand my army?" "My people," replied the chieftain, "may be weakened by your might, and even in great part destroyed, but unless the wrath of God be on the side of its foe it will not perish utterly. Nor deem I that other race or other tongue will answer for this corner of the world at the last day, save the people and tongue of Wales." Llewellyn, however, was successful. After a severe struggle the English granted to the Welsh charters of certain concessions, and for a time peace and comparative liberty was restored.

In the reign of Edward I. the rights of the Cymry were again encroached upon, and there rose up then another and mightier Llewellyn, who was to fall beneath the spear of a foot soldier amid the broom heath of Builth, for the cause of liberty, and whose brother David's head rotted for many a year on the grim spiked stones of Temple Bar. But the policy of Edward and his successors was rather to win Wales by politics than by arms. Prominent chiefs of that nation were given important duties, and many invited to join the forces of the Plantagenet in the French and Scottish wars.

Fresh acts of oppression toward the inhabitants on the Marches caused another uprising at the close of the thirteenth century. Owen Glendower, a Merionethshire Lord who was descended from the great Llewelyn, and also from Edward I., placed himself at the head of this revolt. After many weary years of fighting, after Owen had been acknowledged Prince of Wales by the French king, and on the eve of treaties with the English Henry, the last great Welsh patriot and leader passed away. Contrary to general expectation, little punishment was inflicted upon those engaged in this rebellion.

England had now learned that the Welsh might be conquered by kindness, but not by force. A period of prosperity, despite the War of the Roses, now continued in Wales until the accession of the Tudor Henry VII., himself of British stock, under whose rule the Welsh, who had done so much on the stricken field of Bosworth, to win the English Crown for his family, enjoyed special privileges.

During the reign of Henry VIII., an event occurred which had much to do with the subsequent emigration of the Welsh Quakers to Pennsylvania. This was the destruction of the monasteries. It is generally supposed that the Welsh church, as established in early times, and differing somewhat in form and belief from that of Rome, was left intact at the Reformation. This, however, is an error. Of all those rich and magnificent convents and abbeys which had been founded and endowed with broad lands and fat livings by the earlier Welsh Princes, there was not left one stone upon another. It is even believed that the church buildings themselves were in some cases partially destroyed, and it is certain that the lands were sold to the Welsh gentry for what they would bring. Such, indeed, was the fate of the Abbey of Marcella, near Bala, in Merionethshire, which were disposed of to the ancestors of the present Price family of Rhiwlas, who moved thither from

Denbighshire[1], bringing with them many other families, kinsmen or tenants, for their new estates. Under the old rule of monastery and church land, the revenues derived from the church properties were almost sufficient for their support without the necessity of large direct taxes upon the parishioners. The new churchmen who occupied the livings were, however, wholly dependent for their livelihood upon the collection of tithes, which were in many cases exorbitant. Nor were these High Churchmen at all times satisfied with the exact sums due them, but often insisted upon the payment of excessive and dishonest rates. During the Civil War a large number of the Welsh on this account joined Cromwell's army, and of these were many of the ancestors of the Cymric Quakers of Pennsylvania; upon the restoration of Charles II. those who had been prominent in the war, and subsequently joined Friends, were the greatest sufferers under the rule of the Cavalier and High Church parties. The introduction of the Quaker faith into Wales was due principally to a curious incident.

In the time of Cromwell many of the Welsh parishes were supplied with Non-Conformist ministers. This was true of the large Parish of Wrexham, in Denbighshire, where one Morgan Floyd (or Lloyd) was appointed "priest.[2]" In the year 1653 this minister, having heard much of the teachings of Friends throughout England, sent two of his congregation to the north "to trie the Quakers" and make a report of their belief and doings.

George Fox, in his journal, best informs us how this mission resulted: "When these triers came down among us the power of the Lord overcame them, and they were both of them convinced of the truth. So they stayed some time with us and then returned into Wales, where afterwards one of them

---
[1] There was quite a large exodus from Denbighshire to the immediate neighborhood of Bala after the fall of the monasteries and sale of church lands in that vicinity. Among those who settled in Penllyn at that time were the families of Owen, of Fron Goch, and the ancestors of John Cadwalader, of Philadelphia.

[2] "Priest" was the general name applied by Friends to clergymen who conducted religious services for pay, contrary to the express command of Christ to his Disciples. It was also the usual title of any regularly ordained minister.

departed from his convincement, but the other, whose name was John ap John, abode in the truth, and received a gift in the ministry to which he continued faithful."

Of these two members of Morgan Floyd's congregation, the one who received "a gift of the ministry" is closely connected with the early history of this Commonwealth. Of him a late member of the Historical Society of Pennsylvania has said[1]:

"*John ap John* was the direct agent, under Providence, in bringing about the changes which resulted in the settlement so largely by Welsh emigrants of the Township of Merion and the vicinity of Philadelphia. But of this man, the apostle of Quakerism in Wales, there has been a degree of ignorance which is surprising. So far as I could discover, when I began this investigation there had been nothing known of him in Pennsylvania other than what is noted in the journal of George Fox and of Richard Davies, of Cloddeau cochion. All knowledge of his later years seemed to be lost, and at a time when "testimonies" and memorials of deceased Friends were so general no such record of this man appears. Did he fall away from his faith in his later years, as his companion had so early done, or did he join the followers of Fox who came to the New World? If so, how is it that we have no record of his home, and how is it that no man knows his sepulchre?

"Impressed by this strange and anomalous ignorance, I devoted a considerable part of last summer to an investigation of the subject, which happily led to results of a gratifying character. I visited Plas Ifa, the home of John ap John, who, I learned, like Morgan Lloyd, belonged to a good Welsh family, a yeoman living on his ancestral estate. Plas Ifa is near the vale of Llangollen, not far from Ruabon, into which parish it is quite probable that the estate extended. Though a yeoman, he was evidently an evangelical preacher. George Fox says of him in his journal, that John ap John had once

---

[1] Address of J. J. Levick, M. D., before the Historical Society of Pennsylvania.

been a preacher in Beaumaris. It is probable he was one of the lay preachers selected by Morgan Lloyd and his associates, to the former of whom he had been known from his childhood.

"The old house, Plas Ifa, is nearly gone and a new one has been built on the original site. The place has evidently been the home of a well-to-do country gentleman. In the garden were bits of carved timber taken from the old house, and in one room of the house one of the rafters showed more of this carved work, which my friend Palmer said was not of later date than the fifteenth century. The view from Plas Ifa in John ap John's time must have been beautiful; it certainly is so now. Before it is the beautiful vale of Llangollen, the Berwyn mountains on one side, near by the dancing waters of the Dee, while between these are highly-cultivated fields of grass and grain with well-trimmed hedges intervening, making the whole look like one vast highly-cultivated garden. There was everything to tempt to rest and ease here; but as Fox has said of John ap John, the power of the Lord was upon him, and he had received a gift in the ministry, to which he remained faithful. And so from this peaceful home he went forth on his apostolic mission. First he went to his own personal friends and neighbors, the men of Wrexham, Ruabon, Corwen, Llangollen, Bala, and Dôlgelly. They knew the integrity of the man, and the Power which had melted his heart, under his preaching, melted theirs. In the year 1657, Fox passed into Wales, beginning at Cardiff aud Swansea, and going so far north as Beaumaris. In this journey he had as his companion John ap John, a companion in every way helpful to him, helpful as speaking the Welsh language, to which, as they do now, so then, the Welsh people loyally adhered, helpful as a fearless servant of the same Divine Master."

We may well stop here and inquire what manner of men these were who listened to, and accepted, the teachings of George Fox, and of their countryman, John ap John.

They were without any exception, the descendants of the ancient Britons whose history we have attempted to sketch.

They were the male representatives of those who had for centuries fought for liberty and independence; of those who later as soldiers, in the pay of England, had won their spurs at Agincourt and Poitiers; and the men, or the sons of men, who had fought bravely under Cromwell in the Civil War. Only here and there was there a strain of English blood; but where such a strain existed, it was from a stock that had made England mistress of land and sea. Such a transformation from fighting stock to peaceful Quaker is unique in history.

"To the superficial observer," says an authority,[1] "it would seem impossible that, even after the long lapse of centuries, the descendants of these warlike men should accept and become identified with the peaceful doctrines and manners of the Quakers; and yet to the earnest student of human nature, the transition seems not only possible but eminently proper and natural. To a simple-hearted people there was much in the simplicity of Quakerism to commend it, while the direct dependence of the individual upon God and his independence of man accorded with what had been the sentiment of their race for generations. But when to this, and far more than all this, was added the conviction that to them the call of their God was in this field of service, they did not hesitate because of the sacrifices it required, or the danger to which it exposed them. They were of the blood of heroes to which the blood of martyrs is closely akin, and they brought to bear in this warfare the earnestness of purpose, the devotion to duty, and the fearless courage which had characterized their forefathers on other fields." Under the Protectorate, the Quakers had to submit to the scorn and persecution of the Puritans; but their cruelest sufferings were to come after the Restoration of the Stuarts.

In Besse's "Sufferings of Friends," and in many other works and unprinted memorials, may be found full and touching accounts of the frightful persecution of the Welsh Quakers. These persecutions were more cruel because the participants

---
[1] J. J. Levick, M. D.

were of a class well born and tenderly nurtured. Special acts were passed to prevent the spread of Quakerism, and they were forbidden to meet together, and compelled to take the oath of allegiance and supremacy, which on account of their belief they particularly scrupled to do, although they were quite willing to solemnly affirm their loyalty to the King and their abjuration of Popery.

All persons not attending their parish church were heavily fined, as were those who attempted to preach the Quaker faith. They were frequently dragged before Justices, often their kinsmen who had been Royalists during the late war, and who had now an opportunity to reap a petty revenge. It was of an occasion like this that old John Humphrey speaks: "The Court was astonished and mad with fury because they could not make them bow to their wills when so many had obeyed their commands and bowed to the Image they had set up and taken Oath upon their knees. Their anger was kindled against these faithful sufferers, and *they Commanded them to be Chain'd in Irons*, which was immediately done by the goaler in Presence of the Court, linking them two and two, and binding their hands on their backs, thus conveyed them from thence to the goaler's House, where they remained all night in that Posture." They were then driven many miles along muddy roads, and beaten with the flats of swords, and imprisoned for a long time.

At another place several persons were condemned to death as traitors, because they refused to take the oath—the men ordered to be drawn and quartered and the woman burnt, a sentence which fortunately was never carried out.[1]

Owen Humphrey and some friends, accused of non-attendance at their parish church, were shut up in a filthy hog-pen for days, and their servants not suffered to come near them or give them proper food or clothing. Some were con-

---

[1] This was under an obsolete act of Parliament, which, owing to the exertions of Hugh Roberts, Cadwalader Thomas, Robert Owen, Thomas Lloyd and others, was repealed.

fined for years in Bala or Dôlgelly jail, within sight of their homes, and others so heavily fined as to almost ruin them.

To show how cruel was the temper of the times, and how the officials had to be bribed to prevent the imprisonment or execution of innocent persons, the following letter is given :

DOLGELLEY, ye 25th of the 4mo. 1681.

My dear Friend John ap Thomas:

These in haste may let thee understand that the persons undernamed are outlawed and the Deputy Sheriff hath writts against them. Many of them are dead, those that are alive wish them to look to themselves untill such times as friends shall come together to confer in their behalfe, that soe friends in their liberty may order some considerable gratuity to the Deputy Sheriffe for his Kindnesse. Beside those undernamed Elizabeth Williams is particularly to look to herself. There is a writt out of the Exchequer against her as the Deputy Sheriffe informs me. Ye names are as followeth, vizt. :—

William Prees. de Llandervol, Litter Thomas, de eadem (or of ye same), John Davies, de ead', Lodovicus ap Robt. de ead', Thomas ap Edward, de Llanvawr, Thomas Williams, de ead', Elizabeth Thomas, de ead' widdow, Robt John Evan, de ead', Griffith John, de Gwerevol and Elizabeth his wife, Hugh Griffith of the same & Mary his wife, Maurice Humphrey Morgan of the same.

This is att present from thy dear friend a.id desires to Excuse my brevity. LEWIS OWEN.

All of the above were afterwards linked in some way with the settlement of Pennsylvania; and on the earlier writs we read other names equally familiar to us.

Here is one of the writs suppressed by John ap Thomas during the time that he held the position of High Constable:

MERIONETH, SS.

To Lewis Morris Keeper of his Majts goale for ye sd County & to Richard Price & Joseph Hughes.

WHEREAS I have apprehended Cadwalader ap Thomas ap Hugh, Robert Owen, Hugh ap Robert, John David, John Robert David & Jonett John, spinster.

By virtue of his Ma'ties writt issued out of the last great sessions & unto me directed & delivered (I) therefore do will

TYDDIN Y GARREG, LLANGELYNIN, MERIONETHSHIRE.
The Property of Lewis Owen, 1678, and Meeting Place of Friends from 1664 to 1700.

and require you to receive into your custody the bodyes of the said Caddw'r ap Tho ap Hugh, Robert Owen, Hugh Roberts, John David, Jo^n Robert David & Jonett John and them safely to convey to the common geole of the sd County and them in safe manner to be kept in ye sd geole whom I doe hereby commit, there to remain for the next great sessions to be held for ye sd county on Monday of ye sd sessions then and there to answer such matters . . . as shall be objected agt them on his Ma'ties behalfe this omitt you not at yr perill given under my hand & seale of office the fourth day of May Anno R. R. Caroli . . . Angliae & vicessimo sexto Annoq do 1674. OWEN WYNNE, ESQ., *Sheriff.*

Another old paper of 1675 gives the names of twenty-eight persons of Penllyn, Merionethshire, who were fined for attending a meeting :[1]

[1] The names of those that unlawfully met together att Llwyn y Braner, within ye Parish of Llanvawr, upon ye 16th day of May, Being Sunday, 1675, Oathes being made they were present formerly in unlawful Meetings within Three months. First conviction on the Oathes of Owen Dd. and Thomas Jones, Second conviction, and warrant for the double fine, on the Oath of Robert Evans.

10. S	John David, Jon. and his wife of Cilltalgarth.
10. S	Hugh Robert, and his wife of the same.
10. S	Cadr. Thomas, of the same.
10. S	Robert David, of the same.
10. S	Robert Owen, of vron goch.
10. S	Ellen Owen.
10. S	John Thomas ap Hugh, of llaythgwm.
10. S	John ap Edward, of nanlleidiog.
10. S	Evan ap Edward, of Cynlas.
10. S	Peter Owen, of betts y Coed.
10. S	Robert John, of penmaen.
10. S	Margaret John, of the same.
10. S	Hugh John Thomas, of nanlleidiog. sonne and daughter.
10. S	Litter Thomas, of llaethgwm.
10. S	Jane Moris, of penmaen.
10. S	Edward Griffith, of llaethgwm.
10. S	Edward Reese, of llantgervel.
10. S	John James, of llanddervel.
10. S	Wm. Morgan, of llanecill.
10. S	Owen David, of Cilltalgarth.
10. S	John Williams, of the same.
10. S	Annes verch David, wid. of Penmaen.

At the bottom of the foregoing document is the following in the handwriting of John ap Thomas:

"Evan Owen ye son of a widdow, called Gainor, whose late husband was Owen ap Evan of Vron Goch, was convicted by Oath to be present at a meeting, though but 9 or 10 years old."

MERIONETH, SS.

To the high and pettie Constables of the Sayd County and to the Churchwardens and Overseers of the poore of each parish within the sd County.

WHEREAS by late Act of parlam^t made the two & twentieth Yeare of the reigne of our said august Lord the King that now is (was) Instituted An Act to prevent and suppress seditious Conventicles, it is among other things enacted that if any person of the age of sixteen years or upwards, being a subject of this Realme, at any time after the tenth day of May next shall be present at any assembly, conventicle, or meeting under colour or pretence of any exercise of Religion in any other manner than according to the Litargie and practice of the Church of England, in any place within the Kingdom of England, dominion of Wales or towne of Berwick on Tweede, at which Conventicle meeting or Assembly there shall be five persons or more assembled over and beside those of the same household. And whereas wee the justices of the peace subscribed have been informed by the corporall oathes of Owen david and Thomas Johnes, of Penmaen, in the Parish of Llanfawr, and by notorious evidence and circumstance of the fact that on the sixteenth day of May instant the persons in the schedule annexed—being twenty-eight, assembled together in a house called by the name of Llwyn y branar in the township of pen maen within the parish of llanfawr in the sd countie under colour or pretence of Religion not according to the litargie and practise of ye Church of England,—contrarie to the sd Act. These therefore in his Ma'ties name (we) chardge and command you all & eyther of you y^t immediately upon sight hereof you levie by way of distresse and sale of goods and Chattels the sum appearing at each person's name mentioned in the schedule annexed, and the sum soe levied to pay in open court at the next generall Sessions of the year to be holden for the countie of Merioneth that we may distribute and pay the same as by Act of parlament we are ordered and required to doe; and of your proceeding therein you are to give an account to his Ma'ties justices of the peace att their next generall sessions of the yeare to be holden in this County, and there this our warrant dated at llanfawr under our hands and seales this twentieth day of May Anno Regni Caroli di Anglae vicessimo sextimo Annoq dom 1675.

         HUMPHREY HUGHES.
         JOHN WYNNE.

What, it has been asked, was the faith which took so deep a root in the hearts of these Welshmen that they were willing to suffer such great privation and imprisonments, to be branded as outlaws, to be driven with swords miles along terrible roads, to be shunned by kinsmen and neighbors, and finally to leave for ever the beautiful hills and valleys of Wales to seek a home in the wilderness among savages and wild beasts, that they might practice it unrestrained. George Fox, himself, has left us upon record[1] a short and clear account of this primitive and simple faith, and we shall give it in his own words:

"Whereas many scandalous Lies and Slanders have been cast upon us to render us odious, as that we do deny God and Christ Jesus and the scriptures of Truth, this is to inform you that all our Books and Declarations which for these many years have been published to the world do clearly testify the contrary. Yet notwithstanding for your satisfaction we do now plainly and sincerely declare That we do Own and Believe in God, the only Wise, Omnipotent and Everlasting God, who is Creator of all things, both in Heaven and on Earth and the Preserver of all that He hath made; who is God over all blessed forevermore! And we do Own and Believe in Jesus Christ his beloved and only begotten Son, in whom he was well pleased; who was conceived by the Holy Ghost and born of the Virgin Mary, in whom we have Redemption through his Blood, even the forgiveness of Sins; who is the Express Image of the invisible God, the First-born of every Creature by whom were all things created that are in Heaven and that are in Earth visible and invisible whether they be Thrones or Dominions or Principalities or Powers. All things were created by Him. And we do Own and Believe that he was made a sacrifice for sin who knew no sin, neither was guile found in his mouth. And that he was crucified for us in the Flesh without the Gates of Jerusalem and that He was buried and Rose again the third day by the power of his Father for our justification. And we do Believe

---

[1] Journal of George Fox.

that he ascended up into Heaven and now sitteth at the right hand of God. This Jesus who was the Foundation of the Holy Prophets and Apostles is our Foundation and we do believe that there is no other Foundation to be laid, but that which is laid, even Christ Jesus who we believe tasted Death for every Man and shed his Blood for all Men and who is the propitiation for our Sins and not for ours only but also for the sins of the whole world. According as John the Baptist testified of him when he said Behold the Lamb of God that taketh away the sins of the world: John 1: 29. We believe that He alone is our Redeemer and Saviour even the Captain of our Salvation."

By the year 1681 the persecution against Non-Conformists had scarcely abated, nor had there been any marked cessation of it during all those years, despite the short reign of the Declaration of Indulgence, and the repeal of the more severe acts relating to the oath of allegiance. It was, therefore, with great thankfulness, and hearts yearning for peace and rest, that the Cymric Quakers heard that William Penn had secured in the New World an asylum for the persecuted, and thence, after a short space of preparation, they journeyed, to found there for their children, and children's children, the great Commonwealth of Pennsylvania; bringing with them to their new home their religion, their language, and their honor. Here, truly, in their Townships of Merion, Haverford, and Radnor, "they continued, still increasing, and became a numerous and flourishing people."

THE GREAT WELSH TRACT OR BARONY IN THE PROVINCE OF PENNSYLVANIA, 1682 to 1700.

"Within which all causes, quarrels, crimes, and disputes might be tryed and wholly determined by officers, magistrates and juries of our language."

The early Welsh Quakers were orderly and cautious in their dealings. Although the promises held out by William Penn were liberal, and although Friends throughout the Principality, as well as in England, reposed great confidence in the Proprietor, and had every faith in his project, yet they deemed it only prudent, before removing to the Province, to have a definite understanding with him, and to obtain, if possible, an agreement that the plantations which they proposed to purchase should be laid out adjacent to each other, so as to constitute a separate settlement or Barony, wherein they might perpetually enjoy that liberty of worship which they were seeking, and be governed by persons elected by themselves, of their own religion, language[1], and blood.

The conference with the Proprietor for this purpose appears to have been held in London in the latter part of the year 1681, and was conducted on behalf of the Welsh Nation by Dr. Griffith Owen, Dr. Edward Jones, Dr. Thomas Wynne, John ap Thomas, Charles Lloyd, John ap John, Richard Davies, Edward Prichard, and others. The names of some of these persons are attached as attesting witnesses to the Charter of Charles II., showing that they were close companions of the Founder.

William Penn had long professed a kindliness towards the Cymric Friends, and appears to have anticipated, or at

---

[1] It must not be supposed, however, that the Cymric Friends spoke only in the Welsh tongue. Several conversed and wrote fluently in English and Latin. They, however, desired, with pardonable pride, to preserve the ancient British Language, which marked them as a peculiar and historic people.

least hoped for, a considerable and important emigration from the Principality.

In illustration of this it may be observed that the Founder, in a letter to one Robert Turner, written in 1681, says: "This day my Country was confirmed to me under the Great Seal of England, with large powers and privileges, by the name of Pennsylvania; a name the King would give it in honor of my father. I chose New Wales, being as this, a pretty hilly country, but Penn being Welsh for a head, as Pen Manmoire in Wales, and Penrith in Cumberland, and Penn in Buckinghamshire, the highest land in England, they called this Pennsylvania, which is the high or head woodlands; for I proposed, when the Secretary, a Welshman, refused to have it called New Wales, Sylvania, and they added Penn to it; and though I much opposed it, and went to the King to have it struck out and altered, he said, 'twas past, and would take it upon him; nor could twenty guineas move the Under Secretary to vary the name."

It has indeed been claimed that the Proprietor himself was of Cymric origin, and as the story has lately been revived, and especially as it originated in Merion, it may not be out of place to repeat it here as it was told by Jonathan Jones to the old annalist Watson.

It seems that one Hugh, David, who emigrated from Wales in the early years of the Province, happening to be on the same ship with the Governor in the year 1700, they being both conversing on the deck, Penn, observing a goat gnawing a broom which was lying near by, called out: "Hugh, dost thou observe the goat? See what hardy fellows the Welsh are, how they can feed on a broom; however, Hugh, I am a Welshman myself, and will relate by how strange a circumstance our family lost their name: My (great?) grandfather was named John Tudor, and lived upon the top of a hill or mountain in Wales; he was generally called John Penmunnith, which in English is John on top of the hill; he removed from Wales into Ireland, where he acquired considerable property. Upon his return into his own country he was addressed by his old friends and neighbors, not in their former way, but by the name of Mr. Penn. He afterwards removed to London, where he continued to reside, under the name of John Penn; which has since been the family name."

Honest Hugh David, who afterwards lived near Gwynedd, prepared some verses embodying the above story, it being his intention to present them to Thomas Penn upon his arrival in 1732, but was deterred from so doing by the chilling reception extended to him by the Governor, for after being properly introduced he was addressed by the great man in just three sentences, which were: "How dost do?" "Farewell," "The other door."

Of course Hugh hastened out to Merion to tell his kinsman Jonathan Jones all about it and you may be sure that few Welshmen troubled this pompous son of Penn afterward. The lines, it is true, were rather crude, and hardly a fair example of Welsh poetry. The third verse ran thus:

> "From Anglesie, an Isle in rich Array,
> There did a Prince the English Sceptre Sway;
> Out of that Stem, I do believe no less,
> There sprung a Branch to rule this Wilderness."

This much at least of the old tale, which for a long time was discredited, is true. Hugh David was on the ship "Canterbury" with the Governor, and that he was intimately acquainted with Penn, and was probably employed by him in some clerical capacity, is evident from several circumstances, and especially from the fact that it is a matter of record that whilst on shipboard Penn promised him fifty acres of land under an old concession then obsolete[1].

It also appears from recent researches that Penn's ancestors came from the Marches of Wales, and that they had probably not always borne the name of Penn. That the arms of the family are the same as those used by the older English Penns proves simply nothing at all, because they were first displayed by the Admiral after he had become rich, and there is nothing

---

[1] See minutes Board of Property, Pennsylvania Archives, wherein may be found the petition of this Hugh David to the above effect.

at present to prove that they were ever formerly used by the family. But be these circumstances as they may, it is certainly true that the Proprietor was ready to offer extraordinary inducements to Welsh settlers, and that he had a large and intimate acquaintance among them, and seems to have agreed entirely with the views of those leaders who had been selected to arrange with him the details concerning the establishment of a Cymric Barony in Pennsylvania.

The fatal mistake made by the Welsh upon this occasion was that there seems to have been nothing at all reduced to writing, and that they allowed themselves to be persuaded by the Founder that the powers given to him in his Charter, and the general Articles of Concession to all colonists, which papers were signed by the Welsh Patentees, would be sufficient, with his personal promise, to protect them, and enable them to carry out the plan they had in view.

There can certainly be no reasonable doubt that by his Charter Penn and his successors were empowered to erect Baronies. It is equally clear that under the English laws there would appertain thereto the ancient rights of Court Baron, Frank Pledge, and other Feudal privileges and customs.

In England, in early times, the system of Baronial government was opposed to individual freedom and equal justice. Those in the Barony were subject, without any appeal, or personal rights bound to be respected, to the Lord thereof. At the great Manor House was held the Court Baron, and here the Lord or his Steward received homage, recovered fines, held the view of Frank Pledge, or levied the tithes. If the Lord held criminal jurisdiction, executions might be ordered without any appeal being permitted or indeed possible. And such executions were entirely within the law of the realm. The tenants in the Barony held by service and were bound to gather the crops of their Lord, to haul his wood, and to till his land. In addition to this military service was a possibility ever present. No man there, then, was a freeholder. By degrees, however, all this was changed. The exact tithes to be paid, the fines, the reliefs and the services that a Lord could claim, came to be defined by law. The possession of land, on payment of certain rents or taxes, came to be a right that might be bought and sold, and the Foreman of the manor, or Reeve of the Barony, was an officer elected by the tenants or land holders, and was their representative, the Lord's Bailiff acting only as his master's agent in collecting the rents and taxes due, and such Bailiffs acted only under the direct supervision of the Reeve. In time it came that the petty officers were also chosen by the people, each freeholder having his vote. In early times the Lord's tenants were not amenable, except for treason, whilst within the Barony, to any other authority than their Feudal Lord, provided he held criminal jurisdiction; but later this was so much changed that not only might they be reached by process of common law, but they held the right to have a voice in the general government of the country and vote for representatives in Parliament. But these privileges did not detract from their right to decide their own petty disputes among themselves, to fix their own local ordinances, and to levy their own taxes for the purposes for which they were intended to be imposed. It was a modification of the Old English Barony that the Welsh proposed to establish in Pennsylvania. Probably their scheme of government may have been more like a large Borough than a Feudal Barony, but the latter was of course the only form which they could legally select, on account of the area covered and the probable small and scattered population.

The plan proposed, and which was subsequently attempted to be carried out in part, was to elect a certain number of Justices or Chief Men, the Chief Justice or Foreman to act as Reeve of the Barony. These Justices were to determine all minor disputes coming under the head of civil suits. Sitting as a Court *in banc* they could inflict penalties in criminal cases. They might also levy, upon approval by vote, such taxes as were required for the support of the Baronial government, and have a general supervision over that territory, which included the Townships of Radnor, Haverford and Merion.

The Barony being constitutionally a part of the Province, the inhabitants held it their right to be represented in the Provincial Assembly, and they considered that the entire vote of the Barony should be placed in one county, viz.: Philadelphia, in which the Tract lay. At first they seem to have imagined that the Barony should be permitted to elect its own Delegates to the Assembly; but this having quickly been found impracticable, they were content to cast their votes as above described, and for a time at least to rest satisfied with exercising only those rights which seemed to them clearly indisputable. They insisted, however, upon refusing to serve upon juries in Philadelphia or elsewhere, or to bear any part of the taxes of the county in which they were included. Such were the plans submitted by the Welsh to the Proprietor, and approved by him.

William Penn, no doubt, was entirely honest in his intentions; but he was naturally sanguine, and moreover was desirous of the ultimate success of his colony. This is not surprising. He had at stake not only a large amount of money, but also his personal reputation. Failure meant ruin. These reasons led him to make many promises, given in good faith it is true, but which circumstances entirely beyond his control subsequently prevented him from fulfilling.

There can be no question of his purpose to keep his word with the Welsh. His warrant, given in 1684, to Thomas Holmes, the Surveyor General, clear and concise as it is, can not be mistaken. In it he says:

"Whereas divers considerable persons among ye Welsh Friends have requested me y^t all ye Lands Purchased of me by those of North Wales and South Wales, together with ye adjacent counties to y^m, as Herefordshire, Shropshire and Cheshire, about fourty thousand acres, may be lay^d out contiguously as one Barony, alledging y^t ye number allready come and suddenly to come, are such as will be capable of planting ye same much wth in ye proportion allowed by ye custom of ye eountry, & so not lye in large useless vacancies. And because I am inclined and determined to agree and favour y^m wth any reasonable Conveniency and priviledge: I do hereby charge thee and strictly require thee to lay out ye sd tract of

Land in as uniform a manner as conveniently may be, upon ye west side of Skoolkill river, running three miles upon ye same, & two miles backward, & then extend ye parallel wth ye river six miles and to run westwardly so far as this ye sd quantity of land be Compleately surveyed unto y^{ou}.—Given at Pennsbury, ye 13th 1st mo. 1684."

Holmes thereupon issued an order to one of his Deputy Surveyors, David Powell[1] (a Welshman), dated 2d month 4th, 1684, directing him " to survey and sett out unto the said purchasers the said quantity of land, there, in manner as before expressed, and in method of townshipps lately appointed by the Governor att five thousand acres for a townshipp," which directions were only partially carried out.

The warrant of the Proprietor was issued on account of complaints from the Welsh Friends already arrived, that they were compelled to have the tracts which they had purchased in Wales, divided, part being surveyed to them near Philadelphia, and part in what they afterwards called Goshen, and some of it in the lower counties of New Castle, Kent and Sussex, now Delaware, and that already lands were being surveyed to the English within the bounds of their proposed Barony. In order to understand fully this state of affairs it is necessary to explain the plan pursued by the Welsh in obtain-

---

[1] The following is a copy of an original paper endorsed " D. Powels Acct of ye Welch Purchasers in Genl," but unfortunately lacks any date.

"An account of the purchasers concerned in the Welsh Tract granted by the Generall wart by wich the said tract was Laid out and such Lands as hath bin Laid out by warts Dulie Executed within the same and ist of ye ould England Parishes.

"Charles Lloyd and Margaret Davis, 5000 acres; Richard Davis, 5000; William Jenkins, 1000; John Poy, 750; John Burge, 750; William Mordant, 500; William Powell, 1250; Lewis David, 3000; Morris Llewlin, 500; Thomas Simons, 500; John Bevan, 2000; Edward Prichard, 2500; John Ap John and Thomas Wyn, 5000; Edward Joanes and John Thomas, 5000; Richard Davis, 1250; Richard ap Thomas, 5000; Mordicia Moore, in Right of ——, 500; John Millinton, 500; Henry Right, 500; Daniell Med——, 200; Thomas Ellis, 1000; Thomas Ellis for B. Roules, 250; Thomas Ellis, on acct Humphrey Thomas, 100; David Powell, 1000; John Kinsy, 200; David Meredith, 250; David Davis, 200; Thomas John Evan, 250; John Evans, 100; John Jormon, 50; David Kinsy, 200; Evan Oliver, 100; Samuell Mills (Miles), 100; Thomas Joanes, 50; David Joanes, 100; John Kinsy, 100; Daniell Hurry, 300; Henry Joanes, 400; John Ffish, 300; John Day, 300; Burke and Simson, 1000; The whole Complnt 50000 acres."—*Pennsylvania Magazine.*

ing title to the various plantations upon which they proposed to settle.

After they were satisfied that they were entirely safe, as they supposed, in proceeding with their arrangements for a settlement in Pennsylvania, they banded themselves into several Companies of Adventurers, selecting some prominent persons among them as Trustees, who took out a patent in their own names for the whole amount of land the Company subscribed for. This system was necessary in order to obtain a " First Choice " of land, and was a scheme doubtless settled upon at the London conference, with the approval of the Proprietor, in order to carry out successfully the proposed plan of a Barony.

The following is a copy of the Patent to John ap John and Dr. Thomas Wynne for the 5000 acres purchased by them. As this patent agrees in verbiage with the other Patents granted by Penn to the Welsh, we give it here at length :

This Indenture, made the Fifteenth Day of September in the year of our Lord One thousand six hundred Eighty and one, and in the ccciith yeare of the Reigne of King Charles the Second over England, *Between* William Penn of Worminghurst in the county of Sussex Esqre of the one part and John ap John of the parish of Ruabon County of Denbie yeo : &. Thomas Winn of Caerewis in ye County of Flint, Chirurgion of the other part, Whereas King Charles the Second by his Letters Patent under the greate Seale of England bearing date the fourth day of March in the Three and Thirtieth yeare of his Reign for the Consideration therein mentioned *Hath* given and granted unto the said William Penn his heirs and assigns All that Tract or part of Land in America with the Islands therein conteigned and thereunto belonging as the same is bounded on the East by the Delaware River from Twelve Miles Distance Northward of Newcastle Towne to the Three and fortieth Degree of Northerne Latitude and Extendeth Westward five Degrees in Longitude and is bounded on the South by a Circle drawn att Twelve Miles distance from Newcastle aforsaid Northwards and Westwards to the beginning of the fortieth Degree of Northern Latitude and then by a straite Line Westward to the Limit of Longitude above mentioned together with divers great powers, Authorities, Royalties, Franchises and . . . . and hath erected the said Tract of Land Into a Province or Signory by the Name of Pensylvania in order to the establishing of a Colony and plantation in the same and hath thereby also further granted to the said William Penn his heires and assigns from tyme to tyme power and Lycense to assign alien grant demise or enfeoffe such parts and parcells of the said province or Tract of Land as hee or they shall think fitt to such person or persons as shall be willing to purchase the same in fee simple fee Tayle for Terme of Life or Yeares to be holden of the said William Penn his heires and assignes as of the Seignory of Windson by such services customes and Rents as shall seame fitt to the said William Penn his heires or assignes and not immediately of the said King his heires and successors notwithstanding ye statute of Quia Emptores terrarum made in the Reigne of King Edward the first. *Now this Indenture Witnesseth* that the said William Penn as well for and in consideration of the summe of One hundred pounds sterling moneys to him in hand paid by the said John and Thomas the Recipt whereof hee the said William Penn doth hereby acknowledge and thereof and of every part thereof doth acquit and discharge the said John and Thomas their Executors Administrators etc of the Rents and Services hereinafter reserved.

Hath aliened granted bargained sold and confirmed and by these presents doth alien grant bargain release and confirm unto the said John and Thomas in their actuall possession (now being by vertue of a Bargain and sale to them thereof made for one whole year by Indenture bearing date the day next before the Date of these presents and by force of the statute for transferring of uses into possession) and to their heires and assignes The full and just proportion and quantity of Five thousand Acres to bee alloted and set out in such places or parts of the said Tract or province in such manner and at such time or times as by certaine Concessions or Constitutions bearing date the Eleventh day of July last past And signed sealed and Executed by and between the said William Penn on the one part and the said John and Thomas and other purchasers of Lands within the said Tract or Province of the other part are agreed lymited and appointed or hereafter to bee Signed Sealed and Executed by and betweene the same parties shall be agreed lymited and appointed And allsoe all the estate right Title and interest of him the said William Penn of

in and to the said Five thousand Acres *to have and to hold* the
said Five thousand Acres and every part and parcell of the
same to them the said John and Thomas their heires and assignes as of the said signory of Windsor. *Yielding and paying*
therefor yearely unto the said William Penn his heires and assignes the Chief or Quitt Rent of one shilling for every hundred acres of the said Five thousand Acres att or upon the
first day of March for ever in lieu and stead of all services and
demands whatsoever. And the said William Penn for himself
his heires and assignes doth covenant and agree to and with
the said John and Thomas their heires and assignes in manner
and form following. That is to say that hee the said William
Penn his heires or assignes shall and will by and before such
time or tymes as for that purpose are limited and appointed
and by such Constitutions or Concessions made or hereafter
to bee made as aforesaid Cleare acquitt and Discharge the
said Five thousand Acres soe to be sett out as shall be therein
appointed and every part of the same of and from all manner
of Tithes and Claymes of any Indian or Native of the said
Tract or Province. *And* allsoe that they the said John and
Thomas their heires and assignes shall and may quietly and
peaceably have hold and enjoy the said Five thousand Acres
and every part thereof according to the true intent and meaning of these presents without the Lett, Disturbance or Inter-
ruption of him the said William Penn his heires or assignes or
any other person or persons whatsoever Claiming or to claim
from by or under him them, or any of them. *And further* that
hee the said William Penn his heires or assignes shall and will
from time to time make doe and execute all such further and
other Act or Acts thing or things Conveyances and assurances
whatsoever as by or in pursuance if or according to the true
intent of such concessions or constitutions soe made or to bee
made as aforesaid shall be agreed or appointed for the better
conveying and assuring of the said Five Thousand Acres to
them the said John and Thomas and their heires to the use of
them and their heires and Lastly it is the true intent and
meaneing of all the parties to these presents for the better
preserveing and secureing the Title of the said Five thousand Acres. And the said John and Thomas do themselves
their heires and assignes Covenant promise and agree to and
with the said William Penn his heires and assignes that they
the said John and Thomas their heirs and assignes within Six
months after such time as a publike Register shall be appointed and settled within the said Tract or Province shall and

will cause and these presents or sufficient memorandums of the same bee entered and Inrolled in the said Register in such manner and sort as shall for that purpose ordained and appointed. *In Witness* whereof the said partys to these P'sents have to these P'sents Indentures interchangeably set their hands and seales dated the day and yeare first above written.
  Witnesses:
HARBERT SPRINGETT.   WILLIAM PENN [Seal]
MARK SRVANER.
I. S. WINTON.

This instrument is endorsed " William Penn to John ap John and Tho. Wynn for 5000 acres in Pensilv^a Sept. 15th 1681," and below, " Record & Penn will pay me for it." Recorded in the Office for the Recording of Deeds for the City & County of Philadelphia in Book H No. 9, page 330 etc the 29th day of December 1758.

On the back of this ancient document, which Charles Morton Smith, Esq., of Philadelphia, has kindly placed in my hands, is the following in the handwriting of John ap John, setting forth that:

" Here is An Account of what I John ap John have sould out of my part of this deed and what remains still in my hands. First I paid William Penn by ye hands of Richard Davies and his soun David Davies ye sum of Fifty pounds Stl. and for which I have their recets, and I have disposed of ye land as followeth:—

To Thomas Taylor I sold	500 acres.
To John Roberts[1] I sold	500 acres.
To Treial Reider I sold	400 acres.
To Mary Fouk— I sold	200 acres.
To Richard Davies[2]	250 acres.
To Owen Parry sold	150 acres.
reserved for myself	500 acres.

[1] This was John Roberts, of Pen y Clwyd, in Denbighshire, millwright, aged 60 years. Nearly all of his tract was laid out in Merion, and was situate just north of Ardmore Station on the Pennsylvania Railroad, in the Valley of the Mill Creek. Here he erected in 1683 the first grist mill in the Province of Pennsylvania. He married in Pennsylvania, 1691, Elizabeth Owen, aged 16 years, daughter of Owen Humphrey, of Llwyn du Merionethshire, and was the grandfather of John Roberts, the noted Tory of Revolutionary times.

[2] This person may not have been identical with Richard Davies, the celebrated minister among Friends.

> Be it remembered also yt I rebought from Trial Reder aforsd 400 acres
> So wt. remains for me unsold is 900 acres."

It would seem from this paper that our old friend John ap John[1] intended to remove to Pennsylvania; but it is evident that he did not do so, for we find that he died "at the house of his son-in-law, John Miller, of Whitehugh, England, on the 16th day of the ninth month, 1697, as has been but recently learned by a careful examination of the papers at Devonshire House Meeting, where in the return from Staffordshire of answers to the queries for 1698, 'What Public Friends deceased this year?' it is answered, 'none save our antient Friend John ap John,' whose death is recorded as above and his interment at Basford, a hamlet adjoining Whitehugh. In the year 1712, Friends in North Wales were desired by the Yearly Meeting to collect books and manuscripts relating to the services of 'our ancient and faithful friend, John ap John,' and to send them up to the second day's meeting. If this was done, no record of it can be found now."

A partial list of the grantees under this Patent is as follows:

Thomas Taylor, of Denbighshire; John Roberts, of Pen y Clwyd, Denbighshire, Millwright; Tryall Rider, of Wrexham, Flax Dresser; Mary Fouk, of Denbighshire; Richard Davies, Owen Parry, of Dynunllo Issa, Denbighshire, yeomen; Isaac Wheeldon (or Wheelen,) of Lanroost, Denbighshire; Owen Foulke, of Bettws y Coed, Caernarvonshire, Tanner. It is believed that Tryall Rider did not come to Pennsylvania, but died in Wrexham.

---

[1] As to the 2500 acres, one-half of the Patent, belonging to Dr. Thomas Wynne, the same was surveyed in various parts of the Province, and after Dr. Wynne's decease his only son and heir petitioned the Board of Property of Philadelphia, stating that a large part of the tract was as yet unlocated and desiring a warrant of survey for the same, which was accordingly granted him and the same laid out in Blockley adjoining the Merion line. This land lay near the present Christ Church Hospital property, and southeast of Bala, on the Schuylkill Valley Railroad. The house which Jonathan Wynne built here is still standing, and described elsewhere in this work.

The Great Welsh Tract. 33

The date of the first deed is 25th of Fifth-month, 1681, to Isaac Wheeldon and Owen Foulke, and that of John Roberts, 7th of Fifth-month, 1682.

The principal Patentees, besides John ap John and Dr. Thomas Wynne, that is to say those who were acting as Trustees for Companies of Adventures, were:

Charles Lloyd, of Dolobran, Montgomeryshire, gentleman, and Margaret Davies, widow,	5000 acres.
John Bevan, of Treverigg, Glamorganshire, gentleman,	2000 acres.
John Thomas, of Llaithgwm, Merionethshire, yeoman, and Dr. Edward Jones, of Bala,	5000 acres.
Richard ap Thomas, of Whitford Garne, Flintshire,	5000 acres.
Richard Davies, of Clodion cochion, gentleman,	5000 acres.
Lewis David, of Llandewy Velfry, Pembrokeshire, gentleman,	3000 acres.

Considerable other land was taken up by individuals on their own account, and 10,000 acres, additional to the 40,000, was reported to be held by Welshmen, or persons from the Marches of Wales, before 1684. Not all of this land was, however, surveyed in one tract, as we have observed, but some in Goshen and elsewhere. Considerable tracts were held within Haverford, Radnor, and Merion, by English purchasers, and some by the Swedes.

The grantees under the Patent to Charles Lloyd and Margaret Davies had their deeds executed in Wales, 24th April, 1683, and 29th June, same year, that to Joseph Harris being the only one bearing the latter date. They were:

John Humphrey[1], of Llanwthin, Montgomeryshire, yeoman,	312½ acres.
Thomas Morris, of Marchnant Issa, Montgomeryshire, yeoman,	156¼ acres.

---

[1] John Humphrey was late of Llwyn du, Merionethshire, and was brother to Owen Humphrey of that place. He had removed to Montgomeryshire, near to his cousins, the descendants and kinsmen of John Powell, of the Parish of Llanwddyn, his maternal grandfather. All of the above named grantees were cousins to John Humphrey.

Thomas Jones,[1] of Parish of Llanwthin, Montgomeryshire, yeoman, 156¼ acres.
Edward Thomas, of Llanwith, Montgomeryshire, yeoman, 312½ acres.
Margaret Thomas, of Garthblch, Montgomeryshire, widow, 156¼ acres.
John Rhytherch, of Parish of Hirnant, Montgomeryshire, yeoman, 156¼ acres.
Joseph Harris, "late of Wallbrook, Middlesex, London," 1250 acres.

This made just half of their purchase, the balance passing to Thomas Lloyd, brother of Charles, and the Deputy Governor of Pennsylvania, by deed 6th June, 1683. Of this land and another tract which he purchased in Merion, Thomas Lloyd sold 442 acres and upwards to Robert Owen, and 125 acres to Edward Rees, by deeds dated 1691.

The grantees under the John Bevan Patent were:

Charles Bevan, of Treverigg, Glamorganshire, his brother, Edward Richard, of Treverigg, Glamorganshire, tailor, Katharine Prichard, of Techla, Llantresaint, Glamorganshire, spinster, Elizabeth Prichard, of same place, Mathew and David Jones, and Ralph Lewis.[2]

Edward Richard died without issue, and his land descended to his brother, Lewis Richard, who by deed resold to John Bevan. Katharine and Elizabeth Prichard, of Techla, were kinswomen to John Bevan (cousins), but not related to Edward Richard it seems. Elizabeth died, and her sister re-

---

[1] The original deed of Charles Lloyd and Margaret Davies to this person is in the possession of Rowland Evans, Esq., of Haverford, Lower Merion, who owns a part of the original tract, situate on the North side of Montgomery Avenue, near Haverford station. The country seats of A. J. Cassatt, John C. Wallace, Frederick Sylvester, Esquires, and Col. A. Loudon Snowden, adjoin, or are part of this plantation. Mr. Evans has placed the old deed, and also his title papers, at my disposal for the purposes of this work. The very perfect Brief of Title prepared by him recites the Patent of Penn to Charles Lloyd and Margaret Davies, dated 15 and 16 September, 1681, and deed of same parties, dated 24 April, 1683, to said Thomas Jones. The will of Thomas Jones, otherwise Thomas John Thomas, is dated 25 May, 1701, proved 1723, wherein he bequeaths unto his "cousin Benjamin Humphreys, of Merion, my house and Plantation in Merion," containing 156 acres. He was descended from John Powell, of Llandwddyn, and in this way was first cousin once removed of Samuel Humphrey, of Llwyn du, who was father to the Benjamin Humphreys in question, to whom he was therefore second cousin.

[2] See elsewhere in this volume.

sold their joint purchase to John Bevan. Part of this tract, that reserved by John Bevan for his own use, lay partly in Merion, and now constitutes the Morris and other properties, just south of Wynnewood station[1]. The balance was surveyed in Haverford township.

A very full account of the grantees under the purchase made by Dr. Edward Jones and John ap Thomas is given further on, so it is not necessary to mention them particularly here, further than to say that they were the first settlers in Merion township. Richard ap Thomas is referred to elsewhere. His purchase caused him considerable loss.

Richard Davies was the celebrated minister among Friends. The grantees under his patent are given in the accompanying table. (See next page.)

The following is a copy from an original paper endorsed "Richd Davies Purchase & Alienation of 5000 acres ℔ Rowl^d Ellis," in the collection of the Historical Society of Pennsylvania.

"Richard Davis's purchases 5000 acres as by the originall deed doth apeer, sold & subdivided to ye severall purchasers hereafter named.

"Names first purchasers in England:

"To *Rowland Ellis*, 1100 acres, as by deed apears, whereof, 600 is taken up & setled att Merion; 483 acres att Goshen in ye Welch tract laid out & both entered in ye Survey^r Generall's Office; 17 acres Lyberty land.

"To *John Roberts*, 150 acres, taken up in the Township of Merion, & in's own possession.

"To *Richard Humphrey*, 156¼ acres, taken up in ye Township of Radnor—he died, John Humphrey's Executor, did assign right thereto William Tho.

"To *Evan Jno. William*, 156¼ acres, laid out Goshen in ye Welch Tract—he died by's will bequeathed the same to

---

[1] A portion of the original tract remained in the family until a few years since, when it was sold by the father of Walter Bevan, now of Rosemont. (See Bevan Genealogy.) This tract of land is situate directly back of the residences of Isaac Clothier, Esq., and William P. Henszey, Esq., of Wynnewood, on the south side of Lancaster avenue. The old Bevan home is still standing.

The Richard Davies Company.

Date—1682.	Grantee.	Residence.	Profession.	Acres.
19-20 June	Richard Miles	Llanvihangel Velgyen Parish, Mer.	Weaver	100
" "	John Evans	Nantmele Parish, Rad.	Gentleman	350
" "	James Price	Mothvery Parish, Carmarthen	Gentleman	300
30-31 July	Richard Humphrey	Llan Glynin, Mer.	Gentleman	156¼
19-20 June	Margaret James	Newchurch Parish, Rad.	Spinster	200
" "	Roger Hughes	Llanishangell Rhydrython, Rad.	Gentleman	250
" "	David Meredith	Llanbister Parish, Rad.	Weaver	100
30-31 July	Ellis Maurice	Dolgynecha, Mer.	Gentleman	180
" "	Lewis Owen	Gwanas, Mer.	Gentleman	78
" "	Rowland Owen	Gwanas, Mer.	Gentleman	183
19-20 June	Richard Corne	Langunllo Parish, Rad.	Glover	50
" "	Thomas Jones	Glascombe, Rad.	Gentleman	100
" "	Richard Cooke	Langunllo Parish, Rad.	Glover	100
" "	John Lloyd	Dissart Parish, Rad.	Glover	100
30-31 July	John Roberts	Llangian Parish, Caernarvon	Gentleman	150
19-20 June	Edward Jones	St. Harmon Parish, Rad.	Gentleman	250
30-31 July	Evan John William	Llanglynin, Mer.	Gentleman	156¼
31 "	Evan ap William	Llanvachreth, Mer.	Gentleman	156¼
31 "	David Evan	Llanvachreth, Mer.	Gentleman	156¼
19-20 June	Ellis Jones	Nantmele Parish, Rad.	Weaver	100
30-31 July	Rowland Ellis	Bryn Mawr, Mer.	Gentleman	1100
19-20 June	Evan Oliver	Glascombe Parish, Rad.	Gentleman	200
30-31 July	Ellis Pugh			161
19-20 June	David James			100
" "	David Kinsey	Nantmele Parish, Rad.	Carpenter	100
30-31 July	Edward Owen	Late of Dalserey, Mer.	Gentleman	
	Petter Edwards			100

Evan ab William, by's will bequeathed ye same to's son *Philip Evan*, it being laid out (as by patent doth appear) in ye Welch tract—ye s^d Philip died without issue—brother *David Evan* possess ye same.

"To *Lewis Owen, Rowland Owen, Ellis Maurice, Ellis Pugh*, 625 acres, sold to *Thomas Ellis* their title & interest therein—ye sd quantity was taken up together in Merion—he dec'd, Executor's sold ye same to Joh: William.

"To *James Price*, 300 acres, he sold same to *David Price*, ye sd David to *Henry Rees*, the present possessor thereof—in ye Township of Radnor.

"To *John Evans*, 350 acres—out of's said tract he sold 100 acres to *John German* now deceased—his widow in possession. Another p^t thereof he sold vizt. 100 to *John Roberts*, the sd John sold the same to *John Morgan*, who has it in possession—the remaining p^t ye s^d *John Evans* hath in's possession all in Radnor.

"To *Richard Corn*, 50 acres deceased, his son *William Corn* convey'd's right therein to *John Evans* as by deeds doth appear, & being posses'd thereof, lying in Radnor.

"To *Edward Jones*, 250 acres, one *James Morgan* purchased's right to ye s^d quantity. Late deceased's son & heir John Morgan now possessor.

"To *Ellis Jones*, 100 acres, he assigning's right & title therin to *William David*, the said William to *John Morgan* the possessor thereof.

"To *Roger Hughes*, 250 acres: he selling one moety thereof, vizt. 125 acres to *Tho. Parry* the s^d Parry assigning over's right to *Richard Moore*, ye other half ye s^d Roger sold to *David Meredith* [torn] now in his possession.

"To *Richard Cook*, 100 acres, taken up for him in Radnor.

"To *John Lloyd*, 100 acres, laid out for hime likewise.

"To *David James*, 100 acres, deceased—his daughter Mary James Executrix of ye s^d father sold ye title & interest therin to *Stephen ab Evan*, present possessor.

"To *Margaret James*, 200 acres, *Samuel James* in right of's wife the said Margaret possesseth ye same.

"To *Richard Miles*, 100 acres, settles thereon.

"To *Thomas Jones*, by his heirs the title thereof was made to *William Davies* the possessor.

"To *Evan Oliver*, 200 acres, deceased, his heirs sold ye s^d quantity to ye sd *William Davies* the possessor.

"To *David Kinsey*, 100 acres, the Execut^ors of the deceased Kinsey, sold the sd. tract to *James James*, & ye s^d James to *Lewis Walker* who possesseth ye same.

"To *Petter Edwards*, 100 acres: he sold's title and interest to *Thomas Parry*, and the said Parry to *Tho. Rees*, ye present possessor.

"The whole subdivided among ye above named first purchasers in England comes 5000: whereof 2656 accers & ¼ is laid out in ye Township Radnor, the remainder of ye property hath been laid p^t in Merion the rest where the [torn] lives in ye Welch tract.

"Here followeth some acc more of lands taken up in ye said Township part whereof by purchase & part rent land—

"*David Mredith*, 250 acres, purchased as by patent doth appear.

"*Samuel Miles*, 100 acres, formerly took up att Rent, sometime after paid for as doth appear.

"*John Evans*, 100 acres, took up att rent, in his possession.

"*William Davies*, 150 acres, formerly took up att Rent.

"*Stephen ab Evan*, 100 acres, hath taken up likewise att Rent: all by orders in Radnor Welch tract."

Of the planters who constituted Lewis David's Company we will speak at length on a future page.

There has been considerable doubt as to the exact date of the founding of the three original townships, in the Great Welsh Tract, so that the following statement, drawn from unquestionable authorities, may possibly settle all doubts.

The first settlement in Merion was made by Dr. Edward Jones, Edward Reese, William ap Edward, and a few others from near Bala, Merionethshire, in the latter part of August, 1682, they having sailed from Liverpool in the ship "Lyon," Captain John Compton, Master, which arrived in the Delaware River on the 13th day of the sixth month, that year. Dr. Jones and his companions arrived at Philadelphia from Upland, the landing place, a few days after, and in about a week obtained a warrant of survey for their joint purchase "on Scoolkil River." Their plantations were called by them "The Town of Merioneth," which soon after was changed to plain

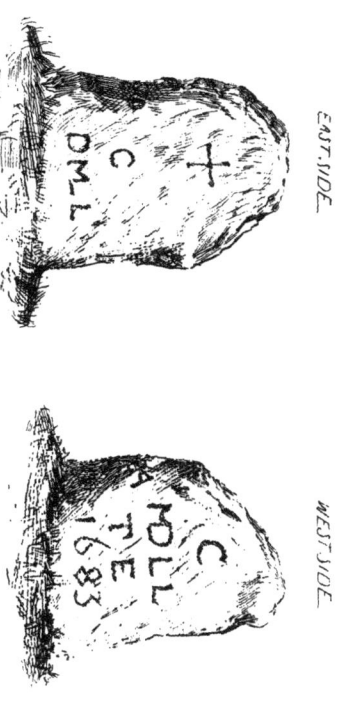

EARLIEST LINE STONE IN HAVERFORD TOWNSHIP, 1683.

The Great Welsh Tract.

"Merion," probably at the time of Powell's survey in 1684, but it was referred to as Merioneth at least as late as 1698.

The Haverford and Radnor purchasers were later arrivals, and the first evidence we have of a settlement in the former township is an ancient line-stone on line between the properties of Hannah Llewellyn and Haverford College, on the north side of Cobb's Creek, near the spring-house of Edwin Johnson.

Samuel M. Garrigues[1], Civil Engineer, of Bryn Mawr, Pa., writes me under date of August 6th, 1895, regarding this landmark, as follows:

"I discovered this stone when making a survey of this line on October 12, 1889. By reference to Smith's map of early grants and patents you will notice a tract in name of John & Morris Llewellyn. This is the tract now owned in part by Hannah Llewellyn, a descendant of Morris Llewellyn. David Llewellyn owned part of the Ellis patent. This land is now owned by Haverford College. The part of the Ellis patent on south side of tract is now owned by Edwin Johnson.

"This old line stone was a common corner of lands of Thomas Ellis on south, David Llewellyn on west and Morris Llewellyn on east. I have understood that Morris Llewellyn was a deputy surveyor for Wm. Penn, and he probably made the survey of this line and set the stone, cutting the marks thereon. It is the oldest land-line monument I have ever seen or heard of in this neighborhood, and about as early as possibly could be under the Penn title.

"The survey was made 2–1, 1683, and very few if any surveys were made in Delaware county prior to that date."

The first settlement in Haverford[2] Township was therefore made prior to the 2d of the first month (March), 1683, and

---

[1] The Garrigues family have been long identified with Lower Merion. They are of French origin. Jean De La Garrigui was the common ancestor of the different branches; he served in Holland as a Lieutenant in the French Army in 1550, after which, on account of his bravery on several occasions, he obtained a company from Henry IV., and afterwards became a noted soldier. [See note on Garrigues family of Merion in Appendix.]

[2] It is a fact worth noting that in many early documents Haverford Township appears as "Harford," which was a common way at that time of spelling the name of Hereford, a county on the Marches of Wales. This spelling occurs in the Colonial Records as late as 1689 and perhaps later, and in deeds. Holmes's Map of 1681-2 mentions it as "Haverford"; but this map was really not issued until 1687, or not so soon. It has been very generally understood that Haverford was

Radnor was established about the same time. Although it may be conceded that Dr. Edward Jones and Company were the first Welshmen in the Barony as permanent settlers, having, as we have seen, arrived some months before Penn, yet they were not the first of Cymric birth to land at Philadelphia. That honor must be accorded to one Thomas Sion (John) Evan, from the Comot of Penllyn, near Bala, who arrived in Pennsylvania in April of 1682. He was not at that time a Friend, but afterwards joined the Society, after he had finally settled in Radnor Township.

This fact appears from an interesting letter, written about 1708, to a certain Hugh Jones, of Bala, in Wales. It appeared in its original language in a Welsh periodical of London, 1806, and again in the *Gwyliedydd* at Bala in 1833, and in the latter year the following translation appeared in the *Cambrian Magazine*. By a curious error, the signature is given as "Hugh Jones." An examination of the will of Thomas Sion (John) Evan, "of Radnor in Pennsylvania," dated 31st 1st mo., 1707, proved at Philadelphia 23d September, 1707, informs us that the writer of this letter was called John, not Hugh; but it is

named after Haverford West, in Wales, and that "Harford" was a corruption thereof. There is, however, upon record at Philadelphia a deed executed in Wales, and by Welshmen, in which both places are mentioned. This document is dated 19 August, 1686, and is between Richard Davies, of Welshpool, Gentleman, of the first part, Thomas Ellis, of the township of *Harford, in Pennsylvania*, yeoman, Francis Howell, of Parish of Llanrilio, yeoman, Morgan David, of (Littlenew?) Castle Parish, Carmarthen, Pembroke, husbandman, Francis Lloyd, *of the Town and County of Haverford West*, shoemaker, James Thomas, of Llanboyden Parish, Carmarthen, yeoman, of the second part, and William Howell, of the township of *Harford, in Pennsylvania*, carpenter, and Ellis Ellis, of the township of *Harford*, husbandman, of the third part, recites a second patent to Richard Davies for 1250 acres, of which 500 acres are already laid out "*in Harford Township in Pennsylvania*," of which 500 acres he transfers 410 acres to the parties of third part for use of parties of second part who have paid £32 for the same. The land to be divided into shares with the "approbation of Henry Lewis, of *Harford, Pennsylvania*, carpenter, George Painter, of *Harford*, yeoman, John Beevan, of *Harford*, yeoman (should have been of Merion), and David Powell, of Philadelphia, surveyor, or any two of them.—(Deed Book C, 2.) Gabriel Thomas, in his history of Pennsylvania, printed in 1698, says: "Besides there are several Country Villages, viz, Dublin, *Harford*, Merioneth, and Radnor in Cambry." Some of the Welsh described themselves as "of Haverford" at an early date, and it seems reasonable to suppose, as a probable explanation, that some of the settlers at first called their plantations "Haverford," and that subsequently the entire township, called at first Harford, assumed the former name. To avoid confusion we have referred to the township as Haverford, irrespective of dates, throughout this work.

probable that he called himself Jones, as did his father. Thomas left, as his letter states, his farm of three hundred acres to his two sons John and Joseph, in equal shares; to his daughter Elizabeth £50; to his wife (Lowry) £6 per annum, and right to reside on the farm. He appoints as "Guardians and Overseers" his friends Rowland Ellis, Sr., Joseph Owen, and Rowland Ellis, Jr. The Thomas Lloyd mentioned " of Penmaen," a township in the parish of Llanvaur, Merionethshire, was a Bard of note before he joined the Friends. There are excellent verses of his published in the *Gwyliedydd* for March, 1824, on the subject of his conversion.[1]

MY DEAR KINSMAN, HUGH JONES,
    I received a letter from you, dated May 8, 1705; and I was glad to find that one of my relatives, in the old land of which I have heard so much, was pleased to recollect me. I have heard my father speak much about old Cymru; but I was born in this woody region—this new world.

    I remember him frequently mentioning such places as Llan-y-Cil, Llan-uwchlyn, Llan Vair, Llan Gwm, Bala, Llangower, Llyn Tegyd, Arènig Vawn, Vron-Goch, Llaethgwm, Havod Vadog, Cwm Tir-y-naint, and many others. It is probably uninteresting to you to hear these names of places, but it affords me great delight even to think of them, altho- I do not know what kind of places they are; and indeed I long much to see them, having heard my father and mother so often speak in the most affectionate manner of the kind hearted and innocent old people who live in them. . . And now my friend, I will give an account of the life and fortunes of my dear father from the time he left Wales to the day of his death. He was at St. Peters fair, at Bala (July 10th 1681) when he first heard of Pennsylvania; three weeks only after this, he took leave of his neighbors and relations, who were anxiously looking forward to his departure for London on his way to America. Here (in London) he waited three months for a ship; and at length went out in one bearing the name of "William Penn." He had a very tempestuous passage for several weeks; and when in sight of the river Delaware, owing to adverse winds and a boisterous sea, the sails were torn, and the rudder injured. By this disaster they were greatly disheartened, and were obliged to go back to Barbadoes, where

---

[1] This letter was printed by the author in *Pennsylvania Magazine*, in 1889.

they continued three weeks, expending much money in refitting their ship. Being now ready for a second attempt, they easily accomplished their voyage, and arrived safely in the river Delaware on the 16th of April, being thirty weeks from the time they left London.

During this long voyage he learned to speak and read English tolerably well. They now came up the river 120 miles, to the place where Philadelphia is at present situate. At that time, as the Welsh say, there was "na thy nac ymogor" (neither house nor shelter) but the wild woods, nor any one to welcome them to land. A poor look out this, for persons who had been so long at sea, many of whom had spent their little all. This was not the place for them to remain stationary. My father therefore went alone where chance led him, to endeavor to obtain the means of subsistence. He longed much at this time for milk. During his wanderings he met with a drunken old man, who understood neither Welsh nor English, and who, noticing the stranger, by means of some signs and gesticulations invited him to his dwelling, where he was received by the old man's wife and several sons, in the most kind and hospitable manner: they were Swedes: here he made his home, till he had a habitation of his own. As you shall hear, during the summer of 1682 our governor William Penn Esq., arrived here, together with several from England, having bought lands here. They now began to divide the country into allotments, and to plan the city of Philadelphia, (which was to be more than two miles in length) laying it out in streets and squares, &c. with portions of land assigned to several of the houses. He also bought the freehold of the soil from the Indians, a savage race of men, who have lived here from time immemorial, as far as I am able to understand. They can give no account of themselves, not knowing where or whence they came here, an irrational set, I should imagine, but they have some kind of reason too, and extraordinary natural endowments in their peculiar way; they are very observant in their customs, and more unblameable, in many respects, than we are. They had neither towns nor villages, but lived in booths or tents. In the autumn of this year (1682) several from Wales arrived here: Edward ab Rhys,[1] Edward Jones, of Bala,[2] William ab Edward,[3] and many others.

---

[1] Edward Rees, or Price.
[2] Dr. Edward Jones, who settled in Merion.
[3] William ap Edward, in a deed executed in Wales 1st April, 1682, for land in Pennsylvania, is described as "of Ucheldri in co. Merioneth, yeoman."

By this time there was a kind of neighborhood here, although as neighbors they could little benefit each other. They were sometimes employed in making huts beneath some cliff, or under the hollow banks of rivulets, thus sheltering themselves where their fancy dictated. There were neither cows nor horses to be had at any price. "If we have bread we will drink water and be content," they said; yet no one was in want, and all were much attached to each other; indeed much more so, perhaps, than many who have every outward comfort this world can afford.

During this eventful period, our governor began to build mansion houses at different intervals, to the distance of fifty miles from the city, although the country appeared a complete wilderness. The governor was a clever, intelligent man, possessing great penetration, affable in discourse, and a pleasant orator; a man of rank, no doubt, but he did not succeed according to his merit, the words of the bard Edward Morys might be applied to him:

> "Ni chadwodd yr henddyn o'i synwyr vriwsionyn:
> Mi giliodd i ganlyn y golud."

At this time my father, Thomas Sion Evan, was living with the Swedes, as I mentioned before, and intending daily to return to Wales; but as time advanced, the country improved. In the course of three years several were beginning to obtain a pretty good livelihood, and my father determined to remain with them. There was, by this time, no land to be bought within twelve miles the city, and my father having purchased a small tract of land[1] married the widow of Thomas Llwyd, of Penmaen.

> "Chwi glywsoch son yn Nyfryn Clwyd,
> Am domas Llwyd o Ben Maen."

He now went to live near the woods. It was now a very rare but pleasing thing to hear a neighbor's cock crow.

My father had now only one small horse, and his wife was much afflicted with the tertian ague. In process of time however the little which he had prospered, so that he became possessed of horses, cows, and every thing else that was necessary for him. . . . During the latter years of his life he kept twelve good milch cows. He had eight children[2], but I was

---

[1] In Radnor Township.

[2] Five appear to have died young; one of them, "Rowland Johns, son of Thomas John Evan," died 1698.

the eldest. Having lived in this manner twenty-four years, he now became helpless and infirm and very subject to difficulty of breathing at the close of his day's labour. He was a muscular man, very careful and attentive to his worldly occupations.

About the end of July . . . years ago he became sick, and much enfeebled by a severe fever, but asthma was his chief complaint.

Having lived thus five weeks indisposed, he departed this life, leaving a farm each for my brother[1] and self, a correspondent portion for my sister[2], and a fair dower for my mother. My sister married Risiart ab Thomas ab Rhys, a man whom I much respected prior to his marriage, and still regard. My brother and I continue to live with our mother, as before, endeavoring to imitate our father in the management of his affairs; but we are in many respects unequal to him. Our mother is 73 years old. . . . Do send some news; if you should have anything remarkable to mention I shall be glad to hear it. I must conclude my letter.

your Kinsman

Here is a passage from another letter which will serve to show to what dangers and hardships the first Welsh colonists were exposed, and as such it has perhaps an historic interest. It occurs in an epistle from Thomas Jones, of Merion, to his "loving cousin Robert Vaughan." After referring to his brother Cadwalader, who had made successful voyages to Jamaica, Barbadoes, and elsewhere, "and who, through mercy, hath escaped well and not been taken hitherto, considering how troublesome it is," he says:

"I suppose thou hast had an account of that Owen Roberts and his company were taken by the French. . . . They were taken about the 12th day of the 5 month within a few days' sail (less than a week) good wind, of the Capes or mouth of the Delaware, being all alive and pretty well and hearty, and were carried by them, some to Martinico, and the rest to Guardalupa, islands belonging to the French. And so from thence to Monsterat and Antigo, islands belonging to the English, and so from thence here, where they arrived at Philadelphia about ye 7th of 8th month last, excepting nine of the

---

[1] Joseph, born 2d mo. 28th, 1695.
[2] Elizabeth, born 11th mo. 8th, 1691.

servants that were pressed on board a ship (or man of war) at Monsterat. The names of them that came from your neighborhood are Humphrey Williams, Cadder John, Robert Arthur, Hugh Griffith, and James Griffith. The other three came from Llun and one from Dolgelley. Two died, a young maid related to Rowland Ellis, at Antigo, and Morris Richard, the Tailor, at sea, coming hither. There were several of them weakly on their arrival, and Edward Thomas' child dyed att that time. One, Thomas Owen also that came then and lived with Edward Roberts (remember my love to him, my schoolfellow, and old acquaintance, if thou dost remember it and hast opportunity) dyed also on the 2d mo. Owen Roberts went to Antigo in the 2d month last, and writt from thence that he heard nothing of the servants. There was a great storm or hurricane, and it is feared they are lost."

The Welsh, upon their arrival in Pennsylvania, found considerable trouble awaiting them. They had been led to suppose, not only that their Tract would be laid out in one place, but that it would be surveyed to them in the immediate vicinity of Philadelphia, and that communication therewith, for market and other purposes, would be easy, and facilitated by the building of free roads and the establishment of convenient ferries. These were of the greatest importance to them because they expected to derive their principal income either from planting, or by milling interests, both of which occupations they were well prepared to undertake.

That they did undertake these enterprises under the most discouraging circumstances possible for the Provincial government to offer, and turned them into successful industries, is unquestionably true, and only proves the superiority of the Cymric colonists over many other settlers.

They were, upon their arrival in the Province, not long in concluding that purchasing land from William Penn in England was one thing, whilst getting a warrant of survey for it in a habitable place from the Proprietor's agents, swayed as they were by petty prejudice and partialities, was quite another matter.

To obtain a warrant of survey at all was the work of the utmost difficulty, accomplished only after days of attendance at the Land Office, and this was true even after Penn had arrived and issued his "General Warrant" to his Surveyor-General. They were forced, therefore, to choose between accepting their land in the lower counties or on the west side of the Schuylkill River, which was then considered in the extreme wilderness, and they were quick to choose the latter location.

These lands, comprising what are now the Townships of Merion, Haverford and Radnor, possessed, indeed, many natural advantages. There were amongst other desirable features, an abundance of excellent streams, plenty of good timber and fine building stone; and the fair, rolling country, reminding the colonists of their native Wales, had much to commend itself to their eyes. Still, they were, at first, disappointed. They had relied upon William Penn, and he had sorely disappointed them; nor did this feeling wear off as years rolled by. Had it not been for his personal assurances they would have hardly ventured to face the wilderness, even to escape bitter persecution.

Hugh Roberts, writing to Penn some years after regarding the Keith controversy, touches upon this subject. He says:

"MY DEAR FFRD W. P.

"I am greatly trubled with many more that thee hast lost the government of this cuntry, I can truley say it is a great disappointment unto us, (I mean ye Welsh) for I can truley say that many of us had never cam here, but becaus of the love & unity & confidence we had in thee, not questioning but the Lord god had an eminent hand in ordering thee this cuntry, & yet I doe not question but it was so, though som may now thinke otherwise dear ffrd we have wanted thee here very much, for great hath been the truble & exercise of many of us, upon the account of the devision & separation that hath hapned amongst us which was jefley ocationed by G. K : well Let me & others writ unto thee w^t we will, I think thee canst hardly believe that he is gon as bad as he is I need not mention many of his actions, for I do belive thee hast heard a great-el alredy, but this I can truley afirm thee (whether thee willt belive soe or no), that I never so a man (under any profesion) in mor pasion & bitternes of spirit and mor redy to carp & to discover the weakness of ffrds, than he is & not onely so but he will endevour to put many things to frds charg, when they are very clear.

"And further my dear frd, it is well known unto thee that many of our ffrds in England, had hard thougts of thee & we, because of our removal from that to this cuntry and I doe not thinke but they had som cause, for here cam som peopel that had not a right end in their removals som for fere of persecution some that were discontented with their brethren where they were, and others that promised to themselves to be great in the world I belive all these meet with great disapointments & som of them cam back unto England, others of you did send very bad reports, both of the cuntry & ffrds, for they were not contented with ffrds here, no more than they were in their native Land, & so when som ffrds in England heard & perceved these things, some were redy to conclud that they had not mist in their first thoughts of us, but for all this I know here is many hundreds that cam here in the integrety of their harts & in a true sence of what they did, and never to this day had cause to repent nor repin, though they were very hard put to in the outward, & not oneley so, thorow the great goodnes of the Lord our god have keept our places in the truth hitherto, blessed be his worthy nam sayth my soul."

We should not judge the Proprietor harshly because of his inability to accomplish all that he had undertaken to perform. As we have observed, difficulties which he had not foreseen, or which, if he had, could not have entirely controlled, prevented him at many times from asserting the extraordinary authority bestowed upon him, through his charter, by the crown. To obtain his Province had cost much money and considerable political influence. The King was constantly in debt. Those who desired such a thing as Penn asked for, even when it was in settlement of an old claim, were expected to pay dearly for the favor. Courtiers and court servants, secretaries and members of Parliament, through whom the King had to be reached, all held their services at a certain arbitrary price. To obtain settlers and the necessities of colonial establishment, cost more money and additional influence, whilst the maintenance of the Provincial Government during the first years, together with personal expenses, necessitated the negotiation of large loans from several persons. Penn was, therefore, in a great measure compelled to yield somewhat to the various interests of those to whom he was indebted, and to their followers and dependents. To oppose their wishes openly would have been to encourage financial ruin, personally, and the dissolution of that project upon which he had set his heart. It was also necessary that he should, in some measure, give heed to the voices of those of other races who had purchased his land.

That there was considerable opposition, by the settlers of other nationalities, to the Welsh having their own way, is not surprising, and is indeed extremely clear when we consider that the Cymric force of character and ability began to be felt from the start; and it was only a question of time, in the opinion of the other colonists, when those of British lineage would have control of the Provincial government; which object they did indeed almost achieve within a quarter of a century after their arrival.

The first serious difficulty between the Welsh and the government, of which we have any record, was a dispute concerning the encroachment upon the Tract made by one Charles Ashcome, a Deputy Surveyor, who laid out certain parcels of lands to English settlers, within the bounds of the Barony.

This occurred in the year 1687. On the 13th of the Third-month of that year, "David Powell, Hugh Roberts, Griffith Owen, Edward Jones, William Edwards, Price Jones (Rees John William) and Rowland Ellis appearing before the Commissioners in ye behalf of Welsh Friends, the minute of Council was read to them w'ch ordered that ye Surveyor-General should make returns of the land Surveyed by Charles Ashcome in the Welsh Tract for Thomas Barker and Company, 4000 acres—being asked if the Welsh consented, they answered No! and prayed that the 4000 acres should not be Confirmed unto Barker."

On the 25th of the Fifth-month of the same year, the same question having arisen relating to Barker's land, it was recorded that " we, the Proprietary Deputies, having taken into consideration the request to us made by several persons—concerning in a Tract of Land, about forty thousand acres, which was laid out by virtue of a warrant from the Proprietary and Government bearing date ye 13th day of the first month 1684, for the purchase of North and South Wales and adjacent Counties of Herefordshire and Cheshire, where they set forth yt after the Legal Executors of the said warrant several Incroachments have been made within ye bounds of ye said Tract—by other than had in Right—It was found that what land had been so surveyed there was by Charles Ashcome, Deputy, without Authority of Surveyor General. Against which Incroachments the persons concerned in the said Tract have craved Justice from us that their rights might be maintained according to the true Intent and meaning of the aforsaid Warrant granted therin."

The bounds of the Tract as given by the said general warrant were then recited, and persons warned not to trespass, and all surveys made before the date of the warrant annulled. Although the Welsh at this time scored a signal victory by the friendly assistance of the acting Commissioners at the time —viz., William Markham, Thomas Ellis and John Goodson— yet those subsequently in power were not so easily convinced of the Cymric rights or so ready to uphold them.

The next trouble occurred under Governor John Blackwell. This man seems to have taken the greatest pleasure in snubbing the Welsh or any other colonists who asked anything of him, either right or wrong. He was ably seconded in this course by several members of his Council, who were either so puffed up with the honor of serving in office that they were ready to obey the slightest wish of the Governor, or else were bought for the purpose of running the government to suit Blackwell's constituents. The matter in question was the Chester County line dispute, which had been under discussion before.

In a Council held 25th of First-month, 1689, Thomas Lloyd appeared, and said " he understood some thing had been moved about adding ye Welsh Towns or Tracts to the

County of Chester, and if anything was proposed desired they would give him an opportunity to speak." " The Governor told him *no such thing was yt brought before them ;* But that if any such thing were *wherein it should be found requisite to hear them*, they should have notice thereof."

That Blackwell was a most adroit politician can not for a moment be denied. The petition of the Justices of Chester County was already before him, prepared by his confidants at his suggestion. It was to be presented that afternoon, and was to be acted upon immediately. Its main purpose was to cut off from Philadelphia County the votes of some sixty Welshmen who had previously voted there, and who, if left alone would elect persons to the Council and Assembly opposed to Blackwell's policy. It was, indeed, a political move worthy of the present day.

In the afternoon this petition of the Justices of the County of Chester was presented. It is scarcely worth while to give this paper, at length, here. It provided for placing the townships of Radnor and Haverford, which the Council held were then in Philadelphia County, but which the Welsh maintained were part of a separate Barony and only for election purposes in the latter county, into Chester. The matter came up for argument the next day, Thomas Lloyd and John Eckley appearing for the Welsh interests in spite of threats on the part of the Governor and his friends. In the discussion that followed, on the part of the Government, "'twas asserted that the Welsh Inhabitants had Deneyed themselves to be any part of the County of Philadelphia, refusing to bear any share of Charges or serve in office or on Juries, and the like, as to the County of Chester. That the pretence thereof was they were a distinct *Barony wch they might be yet that several Baronies might be in one and ye same County*." The Welsh protested that a Barony ought not to be divided. Thomas Lloyd said that "the Proprietor had given them grounds it should be made a County Palatinate." The Governor asked "if any such thing had been past; nothing appeared." Lloyd then asked for a further hearing, which request was seconded by

ANCIENT MILE-STONE, WITH PENN'S ARMS, ON THE OLD GULPH ROAD, NORTH OF BRYN MAWR.

Samuel Carpenter, but was vigorously opposed by Griffith Jones, a Welshman in the pay of the Governor. The matter was settled, therefore, to the satisfaction of the Councils, the Welsh protesting, and the townships of Haverford and Radnor were declared to be in Chester County.

At the election which followed the Welsh of these townships, to the number of sixty, insisted upon casting their votes for their candidate, Eckley, with the inhabitants of Philadelphia, which was reported by the Sheriff on the 1st of Second-month, 1689, and continued a subject for debate for a long time, finally resulting in an order for another election.

Up to this time, however, the Cymric Friends had been able to maintain entire the bounds of their Tract, and had prevented the attempted encroachments of those of English or other nationalities. Under the utmost discouragements they had built up their three townships, so that they were garden spots compared with other parts of the Province. They had built mills; and finding that Penn held the milling rights, as Lord of the Province, had succeeded in having one of their number appointed as the Governor's miller, or miller in chief. At their own private expense they had built good roads, and the Surveyor General had marked them with stones bearing Penn's arms, and had charged the Welsh with the expense thereof. They had established a good ferry over Schuylkill, and they had had their boat seized and the ferryman arrested; and, again persisting, they had gotten into serious complications because they claimed the right to cross rivers upon their own boats or to swim over if they so chose. Their settlements, and the fine lands which they had selected, were naturally viewed with envy by those who were not so industrious or so fortunate.

Accordingly a persistent and finally successful effort was made in 1690 and 1691 to break up the last remnant of Baronial authority which the Cymric colonists possessed. A general attack upon the lands adjacent to, or in, the three townships, and not yet taken up, was skillfully planned. Such a proceeding was, of course, vigorously opposed by the Welsh.

The fight lasted for some time, and it would be tedious to give here all of the details; the petitions, votes, decisions and appeals. On the 13th of the Tenth-month, 1690, Griffith Owen and others defined their position in a dignified and ringing address to the authorities.[1] "We," they said, "the Inhabitants of the Welsh Tract in the Province of Pennsylvania in America, being descended of the Ancient Britains, who always in the Land of our Nativity, under the Crown of England, have enjoyed that Liberty and privilege as to have our bounds and limits by ourselves within which all causes, quarrels, crimes, and titles were tryed, and wholly determined by officers, magistrates, jurors, of our own language, which were our equals. Having our faces towards these Counties, made motion to our Governor that we might enjoy the same here,—to the Intent we might live together here, and enjoy our Liberty and Devotion, which thing was soon granted us before we came into these parts."

After a very lengthy discussion, it was finally agreed that if the Welsh would at once purchase and pay quit rent for the entire Barony from 1684, that they might retain the same in one tract, the titles of so called trespassers to be void. On the 2d of the Third-month, 1691, "This being the day appointed for the Welsh Friends to give their answer to the Commissioners— there appeared in behalf of the Welsh: Griffith Owen, Hugh Roberts, Robert Owen, John Bevan, with many others. The Welch Friends answer is, that they are willing to pay hence forward Quit Rent for the whole 40,000 acres, but not since Date of Survey, the which answer not being Satisfactory or Direct to the purpose of the proposition, Resolved that the lands already laid out in the said Tract unto other purchasers be confirmed unto them."

Shortly after, the Welsh, having reconsidered the matter, agreed to pay the entire back rents of the whole tract; but the Commissioners made answer that it was too late, that the matter had been settled.

---

[1] There are several versions of this address, each differing slightly from the other. Two separate petitions are among the Penn papers.

The Great Welsh Tract. 53

Between this and 1700 several attempts were made by the Welsh to regain their lost advantage, but without success, and the Barony became a name only; but the three townships continued to be known as the "Great Welsh Tract in The Province of Pennsylvania," until so late a period as the Revolutionary War, and even early in the present century was so described in titles to the lands therein, and in wills. The first tax list of Philadelphia County, made in 1693, gives the taxables in the Barony, but is not complete; therefore, the following list of persons in Merion, Haverford and Radnor, who subscribed to the Susquehanna Land Company, in 1696, although it omits some names, is given in preference, as it also shows the prosperity and comparative wealth enjoyed by the Welsh at this early day, as proven by the considerable amounts they were able to invest in a scheme, the success of which was somewhat uncertain.

An account of those who subscribed for the purchase of lands on the Susquehanna River in 1696[1]:

IN MARION TOWNSHIP.

	L.	S.	D.
John Bevan,	25		
Hugh Roberts,	20		
John Roberts,	20		
Cadwalader Morgan,	15		
Robert David,	15		
Griffith John,	10		
Edw[d] Rees,	15		
Edw[d] Jones,	10		
Rees Jones,	6		
Wm. Edward,	6		
Hugh Jones,	5		
Robert Owen,	8		
John Roberts, of Wayne Mill,	5		
Thomas ⎫ Robert ⎪ Evan ⎬ Jones,	20		
Cadwal[d] ⎭			

---
[1]Penn Papers, Historical Society of Pennsylvania.

	L.	S.	D.
David Hugh,	5		
Jn°. Humphrys,	10		
Margret Howell,	10		
Dan Thomas (erased),	8		
Rees Thomas,	8		
David Havord,	10		
Thomas Howell,	5		
Dan[ll] Thomas,	5		
Ellis Pugh,	5		
Robert Lloyd,	2	10	
Edw[d] Jones, Glov. [er.],	5		
Edw[d] Griffith,	3		
Thomas David,	1	10	
Peter Jones,	5		
James Thos., Sen.,	5		
James Thos., Junr.,	5		
Evan Harry,	5		
Joshua Owen,	5		
Benj[a] Humphrys,	5		
Tho. Jones, Senr.,	2	10	
David William,	4		
Jno. Owen,	5		
John William,	2	10	
Abell Thomas,	2	10	
Kath. David,	5		
Sarah Evans,	5		
Phillip Price,	5		

IN HAVERFORD AND RADNOR TOWNSHIPS.

	L.	S.	D.
William Lewis,	10		
David Lewis,	5		
William Jenkins,	10		
Jno. Lewis,	5		
David Lawrence,	5		
Morrice LLewellen,	10		
Ellis Ellis,	5		
William Howell,	6		
Dan[ll] Humphrey,	10		
Henry Lewis,	5		
Sam[ll] Lewis,	5		
William Row,	5		
Lewis David,	5		

		L.	S.	D.
Jno. Evans,	. . . .	6		
David Meredith,	. . .	10		
John Jarman,	. . . .	2	10	
David Evan,	. . . .	8		
Richard Orms,	. . . .	10		
David Morice,	. . .	5		
Tho. Jno. Evan,	. . . .	5		
Henry Rees,	. . . .	2	10	
Jno. Evan Edwd,	. . .	2	10	
Thomas Parry,	. . .	2	10	
Evan Prothero,	. . . .	8		
Hugh Sam^{ll},	. . . .	2	10	
Owin Evan,	. . . .	2	10	
Dan^{ll} Chivers,	. . . .	2	10	
Rees Henton,	. . . .	10		
Wm. David,	. . . .	2	10	
Richd Moor,	. . . .	2	10	
Sam^{ll} Miles,	. . . .	6		
Wm. David,	. . . .	5		
John Morgan,	. . . .	2	10	
Tho. Owen,	. . . .	3		
David James,	. . . .	5		
Wm. Thomas,	. . . .	2	10	
Eliza. Jones,	. . . .	2	10	

IN CHESTER COUNTY.

John Symcock,	. . . .	20		
Jonathan Hoys,	. . .	20		
Geo. James,	. . . .	5		
Wm. Hues, Sr.,	. . .	10		

The total, which, taking into consideration the then actual purchasing value, say about $10,000 or more of our money, was certainly a very respectable amount for settlers, many of whom had been only a few years in the country, to invest in speculation.

THE MERIONETH ADVENTURERS: DR. EDWARD JONES AND JOHN AP THOMAS AND COMPANY.

"These men, like the oak, faced the tempest."

That quaint old map of the Province of Pennsylvania, claiming to be issued in the year 1681, by Captain Thomas Holmes, a person who held the lucrative but somewhat vexatious office of Surveyor General, but which was not really finished until the year 1687, fails, through some unaccountable oversight, to designate any township of Merion, although Radnor and Haverford, settled subsequently, are particularly marked out. On the west side of the Great Welsh Tract, however, may be found located along the southwest bank of the River Schuylkill, and a short distance above the Falls, a Cymric settlement briefly noted as belonging to "Edward Jones & Company, being 17 families."

Although the old Surveyor was evidently very much mistaken, or else, for various reasons intentionally misled, regarding the number of adventurers with their families actually established on this land, in 1682, or even the year the work was published, yet the situation of the several plantations, which together formed the early Provincial Town of Merioneth, is correctly given.

This little colony, called at first "Merioneth," after the Welsh county of that name, and containing much less than the five thousand acres usually credited to it, was the genesis of that larger and prosperous Merion Township of colonial days, which was afterwards divided into the Upper and Lower divisions of the present time[1].

---

[1] Upper Merion, meaning near and above the present Bryn Mawr, is mentioned before 1700.

BALA LAKE (LLYN TEGID),
Merionethshire.

Merioneth, or as it was originally called in the Welsh tongue, Meirioneth, is one of the most ancient shires in Wales, and in the Cymric language signifies the earth, land, or possessions of Merion. It was so called, some writers assert, from being once the territory of a Welsh chieftain named Merion, who is said to have flourished during the eighth or ninth century of the Christian era. So much for a name, so old that its origin is lost amid the traditions of a dim past. Even as Bala is now a principal place in our own Merion, so in North Wales it is one of the chief towns.

It was from the immediate neighborhood of this ancient and picturesque Cymric village that the settlers on the land, which now lies north of the Pennsylvania Railroad, near Philadelphia, chiefly came. The Welsh Bala is in the parish of Llanykil, in the hundred of Penllyn, is seventeen miles from Dôlgelly, and lies at the northeast end of Bala Lake, called in the Cymric tongue, Llyn Tegid, or Pemblemere. This charming sheet of water extends in a southwesterly direction from the town for the distance of four miles, and is three-quarters of a mile wide; being by far the largest body of water in the Principality. The River Dee, the sources of which are in the range of lofty mountains to the south, called Arran Fowddy, flows through the lake. At one end of the mere and facing the town, is a high and round mound of earth, a miniature hill, probably part of some ancient monument or fortification. On this tumulus for generations, in the early morning, have gathered the women of the neighborhood attired in their quaint native costume, to knit and gossip throughout the day. Lord Lyttleton says he saw here the prettiest girls he ever beheld.

This region abounds in wild and beautiful scenery, and is full of interest to the student of Welsh history. On a high bank, or rather craggy rock, on the southern bank of the picturesque River Lloir, are the remains of a famous old Castle, called Castell Carn Dochan, the theatre of many bloody conflicts, and on the other side of the stream, to the northeast, is Caer Gai. This venerable and romantic pile once belonged, it is claimed, to Cai Hir ap Cymyr, Spencer's Timon, the foster-father of King Arthur, who is said to have been educated near this spot.

> " Here Timon dwelt,
> His dwelling is full low in valley green,
> Under the foot of Arans mossy hoar,
> From whence the River Dee as silver clean,
> His tumbling billows rolls with gentle roar."

The site of Caer Gai was originally a Roman camp, and many curious tiles, and a coin, bearing the device of the Emperor Gratian, have been found in the vicinity.

Nearly due north of Bala is the parish of Llanvawr (or Llanfor), comprising the townships of Tre'r Llan, Rhiwaedog Uwch Avon, Rhiwaedog Is Avon; Nant Lleidiog, Penmaen, Ciltalgarth (or Kiltalgarth), Garth, Ucheldref, and Llawry Bettws; including also (at the present time) the church lands or ecclesiastical divisions of Trinity and Fron Gôch[1].

The Township of Llaethgwm, which was formerly within Llanvawr, is now in Llandderfel. Llanvawr, or as the name is now usually spelled by the natives, " Llanfor," is only about one mile from Bala, and has been of much interest to antiquarians. The Britons, under their aged Prince Bard, Llywarch Hên, had a terrific battle with the Strathclydes on the hill of Rhiwaedog, near the home of Llywarch, and the Prince, though defeating his enemies with great slaughter, having lost most of his friends and his last remaining sons in the fight, retired to a hut or cave at Aber Ciog, now called Dôl Giog, where, during the remainder of his days, his harp discoursed mournfully his country's woes. Here he composed some of the most beautiful verses to be found in Welsh poetry. Of an elder son he declares that he was dutiful, meeting death fearlessly; but of his youngest boy, who fell, leading a desperate charge on the crimsoned slope of Rhiwaedog, he says that he deserves a crown of pure gold.

---

[1] This is the modern name for an " Ecclesiastical Division," and is not to be confused with the farm or manor lands of Fron Gôch, which are near by and partly in same parish. See account of the Owen family, of Merion, on another page of this book.

Old Llywarch died, it is said, about the year 634, and lies buried in Llanfor church-yard, where many of his kindred and descendants, some of them ancestors to the first Merion settlers, sleep their last sleep.

" Of lordly lineage, 'neath fair woodbine laid,
The church-yard trees are sepulchres of kings."

East of Bala Lake, and south of the town, lies the parish of Llangower. Northeast of the lake extends Llandderfel, including within its uncertain boundaries the township of Trev Llan, Nant Ffreiar (the foaming brook), Tref Gynlas (Cynlas), Selwern, Crogan, Dôl Drewyn, Llaethgwm and Caergeliog. This parish formerly embraced ecclesiastically several other townships. Indeed there is so much confusion in this respect that it is almost impossible to determine to what parish a certain township belonged at any given period. In Llandderfel (Llanddervel) is the estate or farm of Gwern y Brechtwn, or Owl's Brindle Bush, belonging to the Lloyds, ancestors to the Foulke Family, of Gwynedd, Edward Price, or Rees, Hannah, wife of Rees John William, of Merion, and other early settlers of Pennsylvania. Fron Gôch, the home of the Owen Family, of Merion, and the Evans Family, of Gwynedd, was mostly in Llandderfel, although partly, for church purposes, in Llanfor Parish. Other large estates are: Rhiwlas, Plasynghrogen, once belonging to another family of Lloyd, and Palau, formerly the property of still another race of that name.

Southwest, at the very limit of Llyn Tegid, stretches Llanuwchllyn, called anciently Llanuwchllyn Tegid, and containing the townships of Pen Aran, Tref Prys, or Brysg, Pennant, Llivr, Tref Gastell and Cynllwd.

The above described five parishes are all in the old hundred of Penllyn, and are within five miles of Bala. In this part of Merionethshire the townships were often named after the chief estate which they contained; these estates were divided into farms of various sizes, each one of which was usually known by some name derived either from a peculiarity of the locality, a tradition, or the mere idle fancy of some farmer, landlord or tenant.

Two of the most considerable persons amongst the residents of this locality in the year 1681 were John ap Thomas and Doctor Edward Jones, the leaders of the Merion Company.

"John ap Thomas, of Llaithgwm, Commott of Pennllyn in the County of Merioneth, gentleman," as the old manuscript records name him, became a member of the Society of Friends in the year 1672. Hugh Roberts, his neighbor and friend from his childhood, says of him: "In the year 1672 he came to Friends' Meeting and was thoroughly convinced of God's truths, and he gave up in obedience to the Heavenly Father's call, though it was a time of great suffering; the first two meetings he was at he was fined £15, for which the informer took from him two oxen, and a horse that was valued to be worth £11, and returned nothing back.

"The appearance of Truth was so precious to him that he did not only make profession of it, but was also willing to suffer for its sake, which he did valiantly. When this faithful man first came among us it was the hottest time of persecution that we ever underwent. The chief informer being a cunning, subtile man, seeing that the high constables and petty constables were something backward to execute his warrants, intended to have been the high constable so that he might make a quick despatch.

"Most of the great men, being willing to assist John ap Thomas in what they could, this good man went to one of the Justices that was moderate, and requested that he might accept of him to be the high constable, which was granted. So the informer went on and informed against Friends, and when he got a warrant he brought it to the high constable according to his orders; so he received his warrant, time after time, and would tell the informer to go about his business, that he was responsible for them.

"Among other manuscripts which have been preserved by the descendants of John ap Thomas are the original records of the sufferings of himself and other Friends, these memoranda having been made by him at the time of their occurrence. They show, beside the one already given, that in many instances he had property taken from him for tithes, for refusing to swear. Among them is the following: In the year 1674, about the 20th day of the Fourth-month, Harry Parry, parson of Llanthervol, he and his men came to the ground of John ap Thomas and demanded lambes tithes; and when the said John ap Thomas was not free to give him tithes he sent his men abroad to hunt for the lambs, and at length they found them in one end of the barn where they used to be every night, and they took out the best 5 out of 21 for tithes; and for the tithe corn they took of the corn I cannot tell how much."

Edward Jones, of Bala, a skillful physician, was born about 1645. Joining the Society of Friends he suffered the same cruel persecution as his neighbor John ap Thomas. Both men were loved and trusted by their kinsmen and acquaintances in Wales, many of whom were reckoned the greatest families in these parts. It was, therefore, only natural that the Quakers of Penllyn, having their faces turned toward Pennsylvania, should have selected such men as these for the leaders and trustees of the Company of Adventurers which they set about to organize. In order to secure the advantages and privileges of a first choice offered by Penn to purchasers of lots of 5000 acres or more, the Penllyn Friends decided to have John ap Thomas and Dr. Edward Jones take out a patent for that quantity of land, which they agreed to apportion, subsequently, among themselves.

Arrangements having accordingly been made, and the purchase money, being one hundred pounds, duly forwarded to the Proprietor, by the hands of Richard Davies, the patent therefor (termed a "Lease and Release") was signed by the Founder and dated the 16th and 17th day of September, 1681, and the full amount of five thousand acres of land, to be laid out in the Province of Pennsylvania was duly transferred to

John ap Thomas, of Llaethgwm, yeoman, and Edward Jones, of Bala, "chirurgeon," who were to act as trustees. The conditions of this purchase, regarding town lots, liberty lands, head lands, etc., was precisely similar to those accompanying other patents in the Welsh Tract. This company was also, it would seem, party to the specific agreement with the Proprietor regarding the proposed Welsh Barony.

Seventeen Friends had contributed toward the purchase money, and each was to have his just proportion of the land patented. The amounts which each man contributed, and his proportion of quit rent, are mentioned in the following quaint old list taken from the original document formerly in the possession of a descendant of one of these early Welshmen[1].

---

[1] In a patent from William Penn, bearing date 3d day of the Eleventh-month (January), 1703, confirming to the sons of John ap Thomas their father's Pennsylvania estate, the 16th and 17th of September, 1681, are recited as the dates of the original grant; and of John ap Thomas's 1250 acres, one-half are named as in the Township of Merion, County of Philadelphia, and the other 612½ acres in the Township of Goshen, in the County of Chester.

"An Indenture where several are concerned," bearing date "the first day of April, in the four and thirtieth year of our sovereign Charles Second," recites the conveyance of five thousand acres, by William Penn, to John ap Thomas and Edward Jones. It states that there have been two severall Indentures ye one of bargain and sale for one year, bearing date ye 16th day of September in the three and thirtieth year of his majesty's reign; the other . . . bearing date ye 17th day of the same month and year, both made between William Penn and John ap Thomas and Edward Jones; that for and in consideration of the sum of One hundred pound of good and lawful money of England to him in hand paid by Jne ap T. & Edw. Jones he did grant . . . the full portion of five thousand acres of land, . . . ye first, within ye tract of land in the Province, in such manner . . . as by certain concessions bearing date ye 11th day of July then last past; paying one shilling for every hundred acres of ye said Five Thousand upon the first day of March forever. . . .

It then recites that others than John ap Thomas and Edward Jones have contributed towards this £100 of purchase-money, and that the said J. T. and E. J. are as Trustees, they being personally responsible for the amounts to which they have individually subscribed . . . that for the £25 which John ap Thomas has subscribed he shall have 1250 acres, and Edward Jones in like proportion; and that the residue of the land is to be of equal goodnesse. And should John ap Thomas happen to die before ye said Edward Jones that E. J. should take no benefit of survivorship.

Signed A. D. 1682,
by DAVID DAVIES,
(for his loving friend in Edward Jones absence).

"An account of wt sum of money every ffriend in Penllyn hath Layd out to buy land in Pensylvania & wt quantity of Acres of Land each is to have and wt sum of Quit Rent falls upon every one."

	Pounds.	Acres.	Quit Rent.
John Tho'	25. 0s. 0d.	1250.	12s. 6d.
Hugh Robt.	12. 10. 0.	625.	6. 3.
Edd Jones	6. 5. 0.	312½.	3. 1½
Robt. David	6. 5. 0.	312½.	3. 1½
Evan Rees	6. 5. 0.	312½.	3. 1½
John Edd	6. 5. 0.	312½.	3. 1½
Edd Owen	6. 5. 0.	312½.	3. 1½
Will Edd	3. 2. 6.	156¼.	1. 6⅓
Edd Rees	3. 2. 6.	156¼.	1. 6¼
Will Jones	3. 2. 6.	156¼.	1. 6⅓
Tho Rich	3. 2. 6.	156¼.	1. 6⅓
Rees John W.	3. 2. 6.	156¼.	1. 6⅓
Tho. Lloyd	3. 2. 6.	156¼.	1. 6⅓
Cadd Morgan	3. 2. 6.	156¼.	1. 6⅓
John Watkin	3. 2. 6.	156¼.	1. 6⅓
Hugh John	3. 2. 6.	156¼.	1. 6⅓
Gainor Robt.	3. 2. 6.	156¼.	1. 6⅓
	£100. 0. 0.	5000.	£2. 10

The tract purchased was immediately deeded by the trustees to those interested. The deeds were probably executed at Bala, but certainly in Wales, and the Merionethshire residence, and the occupation or profession of each grantee is impartially set forth. The conveyances were recorded at Philadelphia[1] in Deed Book C. I., and are as follows:

1682. ACRES.

1 April, John Thomas, Llaithgwm Parish, Llanvawr, yeoman, 1250

1 " Edward Jones, Bala, chyrurgion, 312½

28 Feb., Hugh Roberts, township of Ciltalgarth, yeoman, 625

18 May, Robert David, Gwern Evel Ismynydd, yeoman, 312½

---

[1] It is of course understood that these deeds do not contain any description, or locate the land purchased, as it was necessary to obtain a warrant of survey in Pennsylvania, and have the various tracts laid out to the purchasers.

1682.		ACRES.
18 "	Evan Rees, Penmaen, Grocer,	312½
18 "	John ap Edwards, Nantlleidiog, yeoman,	312½
1 April,	Edward Owen, late of Doleysorre, gentleman,	312½
1 "	William ap Edward, Ucheldri, yeoman,	156¼
1 "	Edward Rees, Kiltalgarth, yeoman,	156¼
1 "	William John, Bettws, yeoman,	156¼
1 "	Thomas Richard, Nantlleidiog, yeoman,	146¼
1 "	Rees John William, Llanglynin, yeoman,	156¼
1 "	Thomas Lloyd, Llangower, yeoman,	156¼
1 "	Cadwallader Morgan, Gwernefel, yeoman,	156¼
1 "	John Watkins, Gwernefel, "Batchiler,"	156¼
18 Mar.	Hugh John, Nantlleidiog, yeoman,	156¼
1 April,	Gainor Robert, Kiltalgarth, spinster,	156¼

The witnesses to these deeds were: Daniel Jones, Robert Owen (of Fron Gôch), William John, Rees Evan, Thomas John, William ap Edward (to his brother's deed), Griffith Evan, John Lloyd, Robert Lloyd. Of the above named grantees, several never landed upon Pennsylvania soil.

John ap Thomas, who had for many years been an invalid, died in England just as he was about to sail for the New World, 3d of Third-month, 1683, and was buried at Havod Vadog, Penllyn, but his wife, Katherine Robert, as she was usually called, after the Cymric custom, came hither with her grown-up children, and settled upon her husband's lands. Her house, called "Gelli Yr Cochiaid"—"the grove of the red partridges"—lay due north of Narberth Station. An account of this family, some members of whom still hold the land, will be found upon another page. Evan Rees sold out his interest in the company, but his son, Rees Evan, of Penmaen, came out to Merion in later years. Thomas Lloyd, of Llangower (son of John Lloyd, of that place), died in Wales, leaving his lands in Pennsylvania to his nephew, John Roberts, who was the son of his brother, Robert Lloyd. This farm, in Merion, afterwards passed into the hands of John Roberts, of Pencoyd. Edward Owen had a deed for another tract of land which was surveyed for him on Duck Creek, New Castle

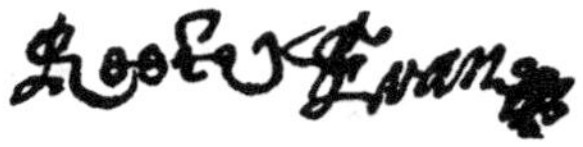

County, where he settled, having sold his Merion plantation to his brother, Dr. Griffith Owen. He was the son of Robert Owen, of Dolserey, near Dôlgelly, Merionethshire, and Jane, his wife, daughter of the celebrated antiquary Robert Vaughan, of Hengwrt. Edward Owen was direct in descent from Lewis Owen[1], Baron of the Exchequer of North Wales, who was murdered, in 1555, in the woods at Dinas Mowdry, in Merionethshire.

William John, alias Jones, died either on shipboard or directly after his arrival in Merioneth. His nuncupative will was proved First-month 1, 1685, at Philadelphia[2], he being "late of Merionethshire." He mentions his son, John Williams, and daughters, Alice, Katherine and Gwen Williams. He also refers to his deceased wife, Ann Reynolds. Hugh Roberts and John Roberts are executors.

Thomas Richard, alias Prichard, of Nantlleidiog, is believed to have died in Wales. Katherine Robert, who was a sister to Hugh Roberts, and daughter of Robert Pugh, was married, soon after her arrival, to John Roberts, from Caernarvonshire, and much concerning her will be found under Roberts, of Pencoyd, and Roberts, of Chestnut Hill.

Regarding the social standing of this particular body of colonists, little can be said beyond that stated elsewhere concerning the Welsh settlers as a class. They were for the most part of a rank known now as "gentlemen farmers"; well educated, and the penmanship, not only of the men, but of the women and children also, was remarkably good. Very many of these persons were free-holders in their native country, and their fathers, uncles or near kindred are frequently found as such; others, it appears, resided upon leased lands; many upon the estate of Colonel Roger Price, of Rhiwlas, to whom some of them were distantly related. Sometimes these Merionethshire families had lived upon the same farms for many generations, and had therefore become much attached to their

---

[1]See pedigree elsewhere. This family of Owen is not to be confused with the Owen family of Merion, whose genealogy is given on another page.

[2]Will Book A, p. 34.

old homes and surroundings; in such cases it must have been hard for them to leave for ever their friends and kindred, and prepare for their home in the New World. Dr. Edward Jones was, it would seem, one of the most active of the party, and no sooner did he finish the business of conveying the lots held by John Thomas and himself to their respective owners, than he departed with his family and such Friends as were ready, to Pennsylvania. He arrived some time before Penn, in August, 1682. The good ship "Lyon," John Compton, Master, must be accorded the honor of bringing this first body of Welshmen hither. This vessel arrived at Philadelphia, or rather in the Delaware, 13th of Sixth-month (August), 1682. On board were: Dr. Edward Jones, his wife Mary and children; William ap Edward, wife Jane, and two daughters by his first wife; Edward Rees and family and probably William John and Cadwallader Morgan. The balance of the company arrived at intervals during the next few years, the first comers bringing powers of attorney from them to occupy their land.

It has been stated that there were in all forty on the "Lyon"; but it is presumed that many of these were servants. Regarding the voyage, the arrival of the "Lyon" passengers, and the preparations made by them to settle, the following letter from Dr. Edward Jones to his friend John ap Thomas, gives us much information :

"*These ffor his much esteemed friend John ap Thomas, of Llaithgwm neer Bala in Merionethshire, North Wales, to be left with Job Boulten att the Boult and tun in Lumber Street, London, and from thence to William Sky, Butcher, in Oswestrie, to be sent as above directed and via London—with speed.*

"My endeared fr'd and brother my heart dearly salutes thee, in a measure of ye everlasting truth dear fr'd hoping that these few lines may find thee in health or no worster yn I left thee.

"This shall lett thee know that we have been aboard eleaven weeks before we made the land (it was not for want of art but contrary winds) and one we were in coming to Upland, ye town is to be buylded 15 or 16 miles up ye River. And in all this time we wanted neither meate, drink or water though several hogsheds of water run out. Our ordinary allowance of beer was three pints a day for each whole head and a quart of water; 3 biskedd a day & some times more. We laid in about half hundred of biskedd, one barrell of beere, one hogshed of water—the quantity for each whole head, & 3 barrells of beefe for the whole number—40—and we had one to come ashoare. A great many could eat little or no beefe though it was good. Butter and cheese eats well upon ye sea. Ye remainder of our cheese & butter is little or no worster; butter & cheese is at 6d per lb. here if not more. We have oatmeale to spare, but it is well, yt we have it, for here is little or no corn till they begin to sow their corn, they have plenty of it. The passengers are all living, save one child, yt died of a surfeit. Let no frds tell that they are either too old or too young, for the Lord is sufficient to preserve both to the uttermost. Here is an old man about 80 years of age; he is rather better yn when he sett out, likewise here are young babes doing very well considering sea diet. We had one tun of water, and one of drinke to pay for at Upland, but ye master would faine be pd for 13 or 14 hogsheds yt run out by ye way, but we did not, and about 3 quarters of Tunn of Coales we p'd for; we laid in 3 Tun of Coales and yields no profit here. We are short of our expectation by reason that ye town is not to be built at Upland, neither would ye Master bring us any further, though it is navigable for ships of greater burthen than ours. Y^e name of town lots is called now Wicoco; here is a Crowd of people striving for ye Country land, for ye town lot is not divided, & therefore we are forced to take up ye Country lots. We had much adoe to get a grant of it, but it Cost us 4 or 5 days attendance, besides some score of miles we traveled before we brought it to pass. I hope it will please thee and the rest yt are concerned, for it hath most rare timber, I have not seen the like in all these parts, there is water enough beside. The end of each lot will be on a river as large or larger than the Dye at Bala, it is called Skool Kill River. I hope the Country land will within this four days [be] surveyed out. The rate for surveying 100 Acres [was] twenty shilling, but I hope better orders will be taken shortly about it. . . . The people generally are Swede, which are not very well acquainted. We are amongst the English which sent us both venison and new milk, & the Indians brought venison to our door for six pence ye quarter. And as for ye land we look upon it (as) a good and fat soyl generally producing twenty, thirty, and fourty fold. There are stones to be had enough at the falls of the Skool Kill, that is where we are to settle, & water enough for mills, but thou must bring Mill stones and ye Irons that belong to it, for Smiths are dear. Iron is about two and thirty or fourty shillings per hundred; steel about 1s. 6d. p.l. Ye best way is to make yn picken axes when ye come over, for they cannot be made in England, for one man will work with ym as much as two men with ours. Grindle Stones yield good profit here; ordinary work men hath 1s. 6d. a day. Carpenters 3 or four shillings a day; here are sheep, but dear, about twenty shillings a piece. I cannot understand how they can be carried from England. . . Taylors hath 5s. & 6s. a day. . . I would have you bring salt for ye present use; here is coarse salt, sometimes two measures of salt for one of wheat, and sometimes very dear. Six penny and eight penny nails are most in use, horse shoes are in no use, good large shoes are dear; lead in small bars is vendible, but guns are cheap enough. . . . They plow, but very bungerly, & yet they have some good stone. They use both hookes and sickles to reap with. . . . Time will not permit me to write much more for we are not settled. I (send) my dear love and my wife's unto thyselfe and thy dear wife and the rest of my dear friends, H. Ro.; Rich. P. Evan Rees; J. ap E. Elizabeth Williams E. & J. Edd; Gainor R.; Ro. On.; Jo Humphrey; Hugh J. Tho.; and the rest of fr'ds as if named.

I remaine thy Lo' friend & Bro. while I am,

Edd Jones.

My wife desires thee to buy her one Iron Kettle 3s. or 3s. 6d; 2 paire of shoes for Martha, and one paire for Jonathan, let them be strong and large; be sure and put all ye goods in cases if they be dry they keep well, otherwise they will get damp and mouldy. . . .

this is ye 2nd letter, Skool Kill River,
Ye 26th of ye 6mo., 1682.

This plot of land or "country lot" which Dr. Jones thus particularly describes, is mentioned, as we have observed, in Holmes's map of 1682. It was bounded south by "The Liberty Lands of Philadelphia City" and lands of Charles and Thomas Lloyd[1], John ap John[2], Richard Davies[3], and John Bevan[4]; and by the Liberty Lands and the Schuylkill River,

[1] Of Dolobran, Montgomeryshire.
[2] Of Rhuabon, Denbighshire.
[3] Of Welch Poole, Montgomeryshire.
[4] Of Treverig, Glamorganshire.

north by William Sharlow, and west by said Lloyd's land and that of John Roberts[1]. The commencement of the tract was at short distance above Falls of Schuylkill, and extended westward and northward for several miles along the river shore, and back to almost, if not quite, the present Montgomery avenue, near the Merion Meeting-House, whilst below it overlapped that line. Dr. Edward Jones was soon followed by other members of the company.

The experience of these first arrivals must indeed have been a trying one, judging from the following account of their hardships during the first year, written in an ancient Bible belonging to one of them. This old manuscript says: " In the fall of 1682 William ap Edwards with his family Edw. Jones, Ed. Rees, Robert Davis and many others settled on the west side of Schuylkill Six or seven miles distant from the city, there dug caves, walled them and dwelt therein a considerable time where they suffered many hardships in the beginning the next season being wet and rainy about (at the time of) their barley harvest they could not get their grain dry to stack before it swelled and it began to sprout rendering it unfit for bread. They were in their necessities supplied by the natives (Indians) with venison and wild fowl. Their first cows to milk were obtained from New Castle, Del. (then Pennsylvania), and divided among the neighbors, and not having inclosures for them they were obliged to tie them with rope of grape vine some to a tree or stake driven into the ground, there being plenty of grass and sweet weeds. The Lord blessed them and enabled them to bear their difficulties for a time and blessed their labor with great success in raising grain and every support they could wish for."

Indeed, this little colony of Welshmen were so thrifty that a traveler writing in 1708 speaks of them as the best planters in the province; certainly a great compliment. This excellence was, it would seem, in a great measure due to their education. They were, without doubt, the best informed people

---

[1] Of Penn y Clwyd, Denbighshire; he is not to be confused with John Roberts, of Llyn, Caernarvonshire, who called his farm Pencoid.

at that time in Pennsylvania; and among them were several men of considerable learning, not only in English and Welsh branches but in the Classics. Well educated themselves, they intended that their children should be so. Schoolmasters of acknowledged ability were invited from Wales, the first of whom, perhaps, was John Cadwalader, then a youth, who afterwards rose to rank and importance among the colonists. Cadwalader, who soon gave up teaching in Merion for a merchant's life in Philadelphia, was followed by others of like ability, and thus the natural intelligence of this people was fostered and preserved. By ten years after the first Welshmen had planted themselves on Pennsylvania soil, a considerable change had taken place in this portion of the " Great Welsh Tract."

Not a few from old Merionethshire had joined them, some had returned, and many had been laid at rest forever under the shade of the virgin forest they came to clear away. Among the most important neighbors by 1692 were John Humphrey, Thomas Jones (his cousin), Robert Owen, John Roberts, Rowland Ellis, Griffith John, Joshua Owen, John Owen, Thomas Lloyd, Robert Lloyd, Frances Howell, Frances Lloyd, James Thomas and Morris Llewellyn, all of whom we shall speak of elsewhere. A few of these were grantees of the Lloyd Tract, of which Charles Lloyd of Dolobran and Margaret Davies were the patentees. In the years that followed the descendants of these men were among the most distinguished Pennsylvanians of their day.

The changes in titles, in so small a tract of land as old Merioneth Town, were considerable, because the colonists were constantly buying or selling. The following, from the Board of Property books, although rather incomplete, shows the difference between the landholders in Merion in 1682 and 1701, a period of nineteen years.

In 1701, " 22nd 10br," the Board of Property having convened at Philadelphia, it was stated that in pursuance of an order of the Board issued the 1st instant " for taking some Measures to regulate the Welsh Tract, some of the Chiefs of that Nation in this Province having met and concerted the

Methods to be taken in order to the Regulations aforesaid,—
It was agreed, "That in as much as the Welsh Purchasers of
the Propr'ry were, by large Quantities of acres in one Pair by
Deeds, granted to one or two Persons only, under which several other Purchasers had a Share; the Gen'l Deeds of one
Purchase should be first brought in with an acc't of all other
Persons who had a Share in such Purchase, also an account in
whose possession the Respective Lands of every under Purchase now are"—"and accordingly the Propr'ry Deeds to John
ap Thomas and Edward Jones for 5,000 acres was brought in
(to the Board) with all such necessary acc'ts." These accounts
show that there had been a very considerable change in the
ownership of the Merion Company's tract since 1682. The
proportion of acres originally surveyed in Merion was held in
1701 as follows, the amount held in Goshen being also given:

	MERION.	GOSHEN.
Hugh Roberts,		67
Robert Roberts,	200	
Owen Roberts,	200	
Edward Rees,	205¼	
Dr. Edward Jones,	151¼	353
Edward Jones, Jr.,	158⅛	158⅛
Robert David,	274¼	234½
Richard Walter,	100	
Richard Rees, alias Jones,	137½	75
Cadwallader Morgan,	202½	
John Roberts, Pencoid,	76½	230
Hugh Jones,	768¼	
Griffith John,	194	
Robert William,		76¼
Ellis David,	151½	
Thomas Jones, ⎫ left them by their		
Robert Jones, ⎬ father, John	612½	612½
Cadwallader Jones, ⎭ ap Thomas,		
John Roberts, cordwainer, Goshen,		78¼

It will be noticed that the landholders have increased from
fifteen to nineteen.

There are some strangers. Richard Walter is one of them.
Ellis David is another. John Roberts, cordwainer, who had

sold his inherited land in Merion to John Roberts, gentleman, holds under this patent but in Goshen, as does Robert William, another new comer. Griffith John, sometimes called Griffith Jones, has purchased 194 acres in Merion. He was first cousin of Robert Owen, of Merion, and a very prominent person. Of twelve of the original members of the Merion Company we have not spoken. Of these twelve, three—John Thomas, Dr. Edward Jones and Hugh Roberts—are mentioned very fully elsewhere in this book. Of some of the remaining members, Rees John William, John and William ap Edward, Edward Rees, Cadwallader Morgan and Hugh John Thomas, biographical sketches are given in the pages immediately following.

REES JOHN WILLIAM[1], OF MERION, OTHERWISE REES JONES, AND HIS DESCENDANTS.

Rees ap John ap William, or Rees John William as he was usually called, following the peculiarities of Welsh nomenclature, was a son of John, who was a son of William[2]. His children assumed as a surname that of Jones, being the given name of their grandfather anglicized. John William, the father of Rees, was born about the year 1590. In 1661 he was living in the Parish of Llangelynin, in Merionethshire, and was a sufferer on account of his religious belief, being one of the Christian people called Quakers. He is believed to have had but three children, Evan John, Rees John and Margaret. The latter was doubtless the Margaret John William whose certificate of removal, dated 27th of Fifth-month, 1683, is recorded in Radnor (Pa.) Meeting books. Evan John was probably the oldest son; he died soon after arriving in the colony. The record of his burial in Merion Meeting book is as follows: "Evan John William abt the 10th of the Eleventh month, 1683." He left a son, Robert John or Jones, who was identified with Gwynedd.

Rees John, in the year 1682, having determined to leave his old home and remove to Penn's infant colony, became a purchaser of land in the Welsh Tract. The conveyance to him is recorded at Philadelphia, in Deed Book C, page 1, 234,

---

[1] This sketch of Rees John William was prepared by Howard Williams Lloyd, Esq., of Germantown, a descendant.

[2] There is reason to suppose that he is identical with one William ap Humphrey.

under date of Fourth-month 21, 1684. The date of the deed is April 1, 1682, for 156¼ acres; price, £3, 2s. 6d. The grantors are John Thomas, of Llaithgwm, County Merioneth, yeoman, and Edward Jones, of Bala, County Merioneth, chyrurgion. The grantee is called Rees John Williams, of Llanglynin, County Merioneth, yeoman. The witnesses are John Lloyd, Griffith Evan, Robert Lloyd, Reece Evan and William John.

In 1684, being a member in good standing of the religious Society of Friends, he applied to his Quarterly Meeting for a certificate of removal. It being in the quaint form used in those early times, it is here given in full:

To o^r Deare frinds in the Province of Pennsylvania in America. Dearly beloued frinds.

These are to certifie yo^u that o^r honest and Antient frinde Rees John of Iscregenan in the County of Merioneth, o^r brother and companion in Bonds & great Psecutions, hath stood and continued faithfull to trueth and to his Principles valiently from the Begining of trueth appearance in that part of the said County, where he lived, he was plaine, serious, and honest, and his wife Hanah likewise a good honest plaine Louing tender-hearted woman, Serviceable and faithfull in her place and Calling, we recomend them unto yo^u in the tender loue, hoping that their removal & Cominge over to yo^u will be to the mutuall Comfort & Consolation of yo^u and them, likewise, Soe pray & ernestly wish yor Brotheren & Sisters in trueth, whose names are vnd^r written.

Dated att o^r Quarterly meeting near dogelley the 4th of ye 2nd month 1684.

Rowland Owen
Humphrey Owen

Owen Humphrey
Owen Lewis
Hugh Rees
Reece Evan
Rowland Ellis
Rowland Owen

Richard Jones
Ellis Davies
Ellis Moris
John William
Lewis Owen
Humphrey Owen
David Jones
Kathrine Price
Jane Robert
Ellin Ellis
Agnes Hugh
& others.

GLANLLYN, NEAR BALA.
Purchased by David Lloyd, 1504.

Rees John William.

Having set sail on the ship "Vine of Leverpoole," William Preeson, Master, Rees John, his wife Hannah, and their sons Richard and Evan, and one daughter Lowry, arrived in Philadelphia the 17th of Seventh-month, 1684, from "Dolyserne near dolgules" (Dôlserau, Dôlgunuchaf and isaf, places near Dôlgelly, Merionethshire).

Hannah, wife of Rees John, was of a good family, a woman of character, and interested in the religious society of which she was a member. She was a daughter of Richard ap Griffith ap Rhys. He had assumed the surname of Price, and at the time of his death was a resident of the Parish of Llanfawr, County Meroneth. He was a member of Penllyn Meeting, held near Bala. His name appears often signed to papers issuing from that meeting, such as certificates of removal, etc. His name is the first of those signed to that of Cadwalader Morgan, of "Gwernfell" (Gwernevel Llanycil-Bala), who was one of Richard Price's sons-in-law and a purchaser of land in the Welsh Tract. To show the sincerity of these Quaker worthies in their religious belief, the will of Richard Price is here given in full.

Lloyd of Gwern y Brychdwn.

Extracted out of the District Registry attached to the Probate Division of Her Majesty's High Court of Justice at St. Asaph:

Let all such unto whom this may concern, know that whereas I Richard Price, of Glanlloidiogin in the Parish of Llanfor in the county of Merioneth, husbandman, being . . . and weak in body but of good and perfect memory, blessed be the Lord, do make and ordain this my last Will and Testament as followeth, my body soul and spirit I have given up unto the Lord, with which I have glorified God, which all are the Lords and have long been given up unto him, and now I do commend my body, soul, and spirit unto my Saviour and Redeemer's hands, for all is his, and I die in the Lord, in whom I lived and moved and had my being, a true and real Protestant Christian and a member of the true reformed Church in

the St. Jesus as was in the Apostles days before Apostacy was, of which Church Christ Jesus was and is the holy head and husband, mediator Redeemer, and Saviour, and no pope nor false Christian, by whom I have been a great sufferer, for bearing a true testimony unto the holy name of my God, In whom I trust. Likewise I do give and bequeath unto my eldest son Edward Price, the sum of five pounds if by him demanded within the space and term of five years after the day of my decease. I do also give and bequeath unto my eldest daughter Jane the now wife of Cadwalader Morgan the sum of two pounds, and also unto my daughter Hannah, the now wife of Rees John William, the like sum of two pounds, and I do also give and bequeath unto my Grandchild William John, the sum of twenty shillings to be paid unto him at his being of the age of twelve years with the lawful use from the time of my decease if he be then alive, otherwise to his sister Catherine by Father and Mother. I do also give and bequeath unto my Grandchild Catherine John being both the children of John William, the like sum of twenty shillings, to be paid unto her at her being of the age of twelve years with the lawful use from the time of my decease if she be then living, otherwise unto my aforenamed grandchild. I do bequeath and declare that it is my will that the sum of Ten Shillings be paid into the hands of Rees Evans, to be disposed of to such use and concerns of truth as shall be judged most convenient by the monthly meeting of friends of truth (by the world called Quakers) in Penllin, Merionethshire. I do also nominate and appoint my dear son Thomas ab Richard to be my sole and only Executor of this my last Will and Testament, to enjoy the residue of my Estates these legacies being by him paid, and for the better enabling him so to do, I give and bequeath unto him all my temporal estate, moveable and immoveable revoking and disannulling all other will or wills heretofore by me made. As Witnesseth my hand and seal this six and twentieth day of the eleventh month commonly called January Anno Domi, 1685.
     The mark and seal of
          RICHARD PRICE [seal]

Signed, sealed in the presence and sight of Edward Nicholas, Thomas ap Robert, Lowry vch Thomas, Rees Evans, Cadwalader Elis.

(Proved 1686.)

Thomas ap Richard, the son and sole executor, renounced all his right and title to the executorship, and administration (with the will) was granted to Edward Nicholas[1], of Kynlas, near Bala, yeoman, one of the deceased's relations. Bondsmen—Thomas Richard, of Llanllidrog, Llandderfel, and Thomas Edward, of the same place.

From this interesting document[2] is gathered the fact that Edward Price, the eldest son, assumed the same surname as that of his father, while Thomas, the youngest son, adhered to the ancient Welsh mode of taking his father's given name for his surname. Edward Price had removed to Pennsylvania some years previous to the date of his father's death, while Thomas ap Richard remained at his old home in Wales. Many of the early settlers in Merion brought with them carefully preserved copies of manuscript pedigrees showing their descent from the ancient tribes of Wales, the Welsh taking a special pride in matters of this kind. Edward Price, after being in his new home some years, and desiring to know something of his family, he having neglected to bring with him such account, wrote over to a friend in Wales for it. Parts of it are now hard to decipher. It, as much as can be made out, is given here:

My old friend Edward Prees (alias Price) hath w . . . (written) in his letter to Thomas Lloyd, Requesting to send

---

[1] Edward Nicholas, who was a relative of Richard Price, and a resident of the township of Cynlas, Parish of Llandderfel, was born in 1647, and baptized on the 28th day of September of that year. (Llandderfel Parish Registers.) He doubtless was a son of Nicholas ap Edward, who was assessed for land of the value of XXs in the Parish of Llanycil-Bala in the Subsidy List for 1636, "Yeare Anno R's Caroli nunc Anglie," &c., &c., "duodecimo 1636." Thomas Edward, of Cynlas, one of the bondsmen named above, was a son of Edward ap John, of Cynlas, who was buried March 1, 1667. (Llandderfel Parish Registers.) He (Thomas ap Edward) was a brother to John ap Edward, Evan ap Edward and William ap Edward, emigrants to the Welsh Tract. (See infra.) They, as well as Edward Nicholas, were probably descended from Rhirid Flaidd, Lord of Penllyn, temp. 1072 to 1133. The descent of Nicholas ab Edward was as follows: "Nicholas ab Edward ab Watkin of Garth Llwyd in Llanddervel (Watkin buried 22 February 1610-11 at Llanddervel) ab Edward ab John Wynn of Dôl Derlwyn, in the same parish ab Ieuan ab Maredydd fifth son of Tudor ab Goronwy ab Howel y Gadair of Cadair Benllyn, ab Gruffydd ab Madog ab Iorwerth ab Madog ab Rhirid Vlaidd (Flaidd) Lord of Penllyn. (Arms vert a chevron inter three wolf's heads erased Argent, langued gules.)"—History of Powys Fadog, Vol. VI., p. 84.

[2] It will be remarked that the legacies in this and other wills, to one of the sons (the eldest) and to the daughters, are insignificant. This was because they had doubtless all been provided for at the time of their marriage, or at age. Edward Price, the eldest son, was also called Preese (ap Rees), or Rees, the name of his grandfather.

him some intelligence of his Pedigree. I know but a little thereof at this time but give him this much while he stays for more.

Edward Price son of Richard, son of Griffith son of Re . . (Rees) . . . . (I Know) no more than this of his Father's side these were own . . . . (ers) of that Land where you have seen William ap Robert . . . (live) . . . and the name of that land is Tyddin Tyfod, (alias . . . . . . And the mother of Rees Prichard, was Mary the D . . (aughter of) . . . Thomas son of Robert, David Lloyd the son of D(avid) . . . . . Vaughan son of Griffith son of Evan Son of . . . . . Madock, the son of Ierwith the son of Madock . . . . Flidd (Rhirid Flaidd) of Glan y LLyn (alias) Lake's Bank . . . . these followed further by Ann, John Vaughan of . . . . Mein y (alias) Stone Pen that comes over. The mother of Mary the daughter of Thomas Lloyd of Gwern y Brychdwyn (alias Owlars Brindle Bush), was Catharine the daughter of Robert, the son of Griffith the son of Côch, or Red the son of Ddu (black Evan) the son of David, the son of Einion, the son of Canwrig Vaughan, the son of Canwrig, the son of Heilin, the son of Tyvid, the son of Tago, the son of Ystwyth, the son of Marchwyth, the son of Marcheithian of the fifteen tribes of Gwynedd (alias) North Wals, from the Lord Is Aled. The mother of Catherine vch Robert or daughter of Robert, was Margaret the daughter of Cadwalader, son of Rees Lloyd of Cydros. Linealy descending from Enion Ardudwy, the mother of Robert, the son of Griffith, was marred the daughter of Tudor the son of Ewan Lloyd of the Upper Plasin Llanfair (alias) Mary's Church Dyffryn (or Valley Clywd). The mother of Griffith, the son of Evan, the son of Côch (or Red) . . . . was Gwenhwyfir the daughter of Thomas David . . . . . . (or having one eye) of the Court in Fenel Hill. Lineally . . . . (descend)ing from the Lady Dulas (alias) Gray. The mother . . . (Thom)as the son of Robert Lloyd of Gwern Brychdwyn . . . . . the daughter of Raynold the son of Griffith the . . . . . of Upper Branas, the mother of Richard Griffith . . . . (Gwen)llian the daughter of Rees of the House where . . .wen Lived[1]. *For John Harry.*

This pedigree was probably prepared about the year 1690, certainly prior to 1700. Glan y LLyn, or Glanyllyn Tegid, is

---

[1] The above transcript was made from a copy in the possession of Gilbert Cope, of West Chester.

situated on the banks of Lake Bala. It was purchased by David Lloyd, of Llanuwchllyn, from Jenkin ab Rhys ab Howel, 19 Henry VII., 1504. It is now a shooting-box, and in the possession of Sir Herbert Lloyd-Watkin-Williams-Wynn, Bart. Gwern y Brychdwyn is an old-fashioned farm-house situated in the northern part of the parish of Llanderfel; near by is the farm called Tyddin Tyfod. By the alliance of Robert Lloyd, of Gwern y Brychdwyn, in the township of Nant Freuer (Foaming Brook), with one of the daughters of the house of Branas Uchaf (Upper Branas) Llandrillo, a strain of English royal blood is introduced, as follows:

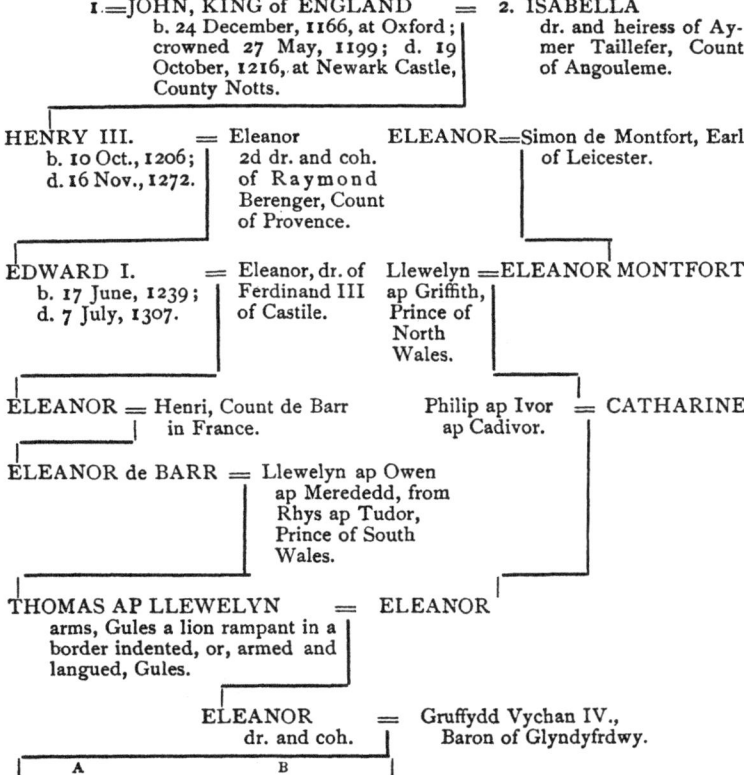

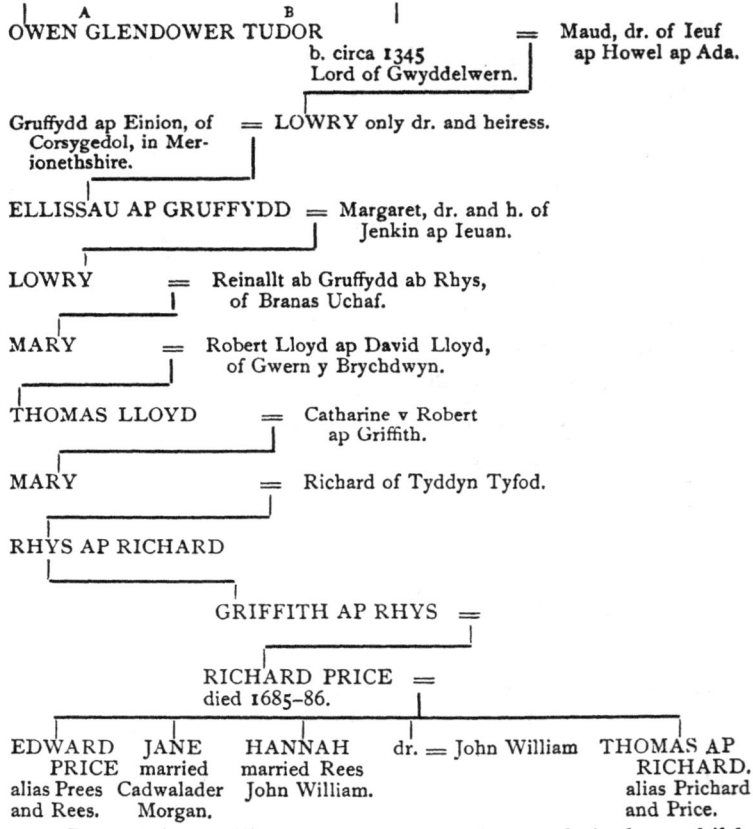

Rees John William, his wife Hannah, and their three children, Richard, Lowry and Evan Jones, settled on their farm as laid out to them in Merion. The following children were born to Rees and Hannah, in Pennsylvania—Jane, Ninthmonth 15th, 1685; John, Fourth-month 6th, 1688; Sarah, Seventh-month 25th, 1690; Edward,
Margaret, Sixth-month 20th, 1697; Katharine, a twin with John, died in infancy. Rees John William died on Eleventh-month 26th, 1697, 1698, and was buried at Merion, in the burial ground belonging to the Meeting. Richard Jones, the eldest son, had left to him one hundred acres, being the home plantation, he then being under age.

Rees John William.

"To Evan Jones and John Jones, one hundred and fifty acres of land taken up at Goshen." The will is dated "this four and twenty day of ye eleventh month, 1697-8."

ye mark of Rees ⸺ John William.

Proved March 4, 1702-3, Register of Wills office, Philad^a. Book B, page 282.

Hannah Jones, the widow, married for her second husband Ellis David, of Goshen, widower, at Merion Meeting, Second-month 22, 1703. They resided in Goshen, where he died in 1720, and was buried there on the 17th of First-month. They had no children. He left issue by his first wife. Again left a widow, Hannah married, for a third time, Thomas Evans, of Gwynedd, on Tenth-month 14th, 1722. He died, Tenth-month 12th, 1738, aged 87, at Goshen. She survived him until Ninth-month 29th, 1741, when she departed this life, aged 85, making the year of her birth 1656.

A Genealogical Sketch of the Children of Rees John and Hannah his wife.

I. RICHARD JONES—b. 1679, d. 7-16-1771, aged 92, at Goshen. Married twice.
    1st. 4th-month-6-1705, Jane Evans, b.   d. 2-27-1711, at Merion.
        CHILDREN—Reece, b. 2-4-1706, m. 1-23-1731—2 Amy Cock.
        Ann, b. 11-11-1707, m. ⸺ Goodwin.
        Hannah, b. 11-8-1709—10.
    2d. 1718, Rebecca Vernon, widow of Thomas Garrett, she d. 12-23-1748.
        CHILDREN—Rebecca, b. 7-21-1719, m. William Rettew.
        Deborah, b. 7-13-1721, m. John Cheyney.
        Nehemiah, b. 7-21-1723, m., had Robert and Rebecca.

II. LOWRY JONES—b. 1680-1, d. 11-25-1762, aged over 80, at Philad^a. Married twice.
    1st. 8th-month (Oct), 11-1698, at Merion. Robert Lloyd, b. 1669, d. 3d-month-29-1714, at Merion.
        CHILDREN—Hannah, b. 9-21-1699, d. 1-15-1763. 1st m. 9-3-1720, John Roberts, d. 1721. 2d, m. 9-22-1722, William Paschall, d. 1732. 3d m. 4-6-1734, Peter Osborne, d. 1765.
        Gwen, b. 8-20-1701, d. 1783, unmarried.

Sarah, b. 5-19-1703, d. 7-5-1739, m. 10-5-1729, at Merion, Gerard Jones, d. 3-21-1765.
Gaynor, b. 2-5-1705, d. 9-3-1728, m. 3-26-1727, at Merion, Mordecai James, d. 12-15-1776.
David, b. 4-27-1707, d. ———, m. Anna ———. Removed to North Carolina.
Rees, b. 4-25-1709, d. 2-5-1743, m. 12-12-1735, at Philad., Sarah Cox, d. 11-4-1775.
Robert, b. 8-25-1711, d. 8-27-1786, m. 6-21-1735, at Gwynedd, Catharine Humphrey, d. 10-13-1782.
Richard, b. 1-15-1713—14, d. 8-9-1755, m. 9-24-1736, at Darby, Hannah Sellers, d. 4-12-1810, had Samuel, d. in infancy, Isaac, Hugh.

2d. 12-month-13-1716—17, at Merion. Hugh Evans, b. 1682, d. 4-6-1772, in Phila.

CHILDREN—Ann, b. 1-23-1718, d ———, m. 1-8-1744—5, Samuel Howell.
Susanna, b. 11-25-1719—20, d. 5-4-1801, m. 5-30-1740, Owen Jones, d. 10-10-1793.
Abigail, believed to have died unmarried.

III. EVAN JONES—b. 1682—3, d. 1708, "buried at Merion, 7th day of 2d month, aged about 25 years." Unmarried.
In his will, dated 1st-month-28-1708, proved October 1, 1708, at Philad[a]., he leaves a legacy to Merion Meeting.

IV. JANNE JONES—b. 9-15-1685, d. 8-27-1764, buried at Goshen, m. David Davis, son of Ellis David, b. 10-14-1754.

CHILDREN—Hannah, b. 5-1-1710, m. 1732, John Ashbridge.
Richard, b. 3-3-1712, d. 1735.
Ellis, b. 10-24-1713, m. 1741, Lydia Ashbridge.
Sarah, b. 7-20-1715, m. 1737, Aaron Ashbridge.
Jonathan, b. 6-4-1717, m. 1742, Esther Haines.
Amos, b. 3-26-1719, m. 1745, Ann Pratt.
Susanna, b. 4-25-1721, m. 1741, Thomas Hoopes.
Jane, b. m. 3-16-1745, Joseph Pratt.
Priscilla, b. m. 4-8-1749, Joseph Ashbridge.

V. CATHERINE JONES—b. 4-6-1688, d. infancy.

VI. JOHN JONES—b. 4-6-1688, d. 12-30-1774, m. 4-9-1713, at Gwynedd. Jane Edward, d. 5-11-1758
(Removed to Gwynedd, and known as John Jones, carpenter.)

CHILDREN—Hannah, m. William Foulke.
Catherine, d. infancy.
Margaret, d. 1745.
Priscilla, m. 3-20-1740, Evan Jones, of Merion.
Evan, m. Hannah Lawrence.
Jesse, m. Mary ———.
Katharine, d. 1741.
Jane, d. 1806.
Benjamin, d. infancy.
Ruth, d. infancy.

VII. SARAH JONES—b. 7-25-1690, d. 3-28-1758, m. twice.
   1st. 8-2-1712, at Merion. Jacob Edge, b. 3-8-1690, d. 2-7-1720.
      CHILDREN—Hannah, b. 6-18-1713, m. 9-18-1736, John Lea.
         Jane, b. 9-3-1715, m. 2-26-1739, Thomas Parke, and m. 8-10 1763, James Webb.
         Abigail, d.   1781, unmarried.
         Sarah, d.   1728, infancy.
   2d. 11-10-1721—2, Caleb Cowpland, b.   1690, d. 10-12-1757, at Chester.
      CHILDREN—David, b. 10-31-1722.
         Jonathan, b.   1724—5.
         Agnes, b. 6-4-1727.
         Caleb, b. 3-15-1730.
         Grace, b. 12-18-1732—3, d. 10-17-1756.
VIII. EDWARD JONES—believed to have died in infancy.
IX. MARGARET JONES—b. 6-20-1697, d.   Married twice.
   1st. 10-16-1716, at Merion. Thomas Paschall, b. 7-22-1693.
      CHILDREN—Margaret, m. Samuel Mather, John Watson, Daniel Lewis.
         Thomas, m. Ann Chandler, d. without issue.
         Hannah, m. Isaac Roberts.
   2d. 1-61729- 30, George Ashbridge, d.   1748.

HOWARD WILLIAMS LLOYD.

COATES, TOWNSEND, TROTH AND OSBORNE BRANCHES.

I. ROBERT LLOYD, born in Wales, 1669; died in Merion, 1714 (see another page), married in Merion, 1698, LOWRY JONES, daughter of REES JOHN WILLIAM, of Merion (see preceding article), and had issue, an eldest daughter.

II. HANNAH LLOYD, born in Merion, Pennsylvania, 1699; married first, John Roberts, son of John Roberts and Elizabeth Owen, daughter of Owen Humphrey (see Roberts and Humphreys). She married secondly, William Paschall, son of Thomas Paschall and Margaret Jenkins; and thirdly, Peter Osborne.

By her first husband she had: 1, John Roberts, b. 6mo. 15th, 1721.

By her second husband she had five children: 1, Hannah; 2, Margaret; 3, Joanna; 4, Elizabeth; 5, Sarah, m. Henry Troth.

By her third husband she had four children: 1, Lydia; 2, Peter; 3, Charles; 4, Ann.

III. SARAH PASCHALL, fifth daughter of William Paschall and Hannah Lloyd, daughter of Robert, of Merion, and Lowry Jones, his wife, married 5th of 5th month, 1751, at Pikeland Meeting, Henry Troth, and had by him: 1, William; 2, Samuel, m. Ann Dixon, widow; 3, Henry; 4, Elizabeth; 5, John; 6, Sarah.

III. PETER OSBORNE, second child of Peter Osborne and Hannah Lloyd, married, at Wilmington, Delaware, 8 month 7th, 1763, Elizabeth Stevens, and had issue: 1, Hannah; 2, Lydia; 3, Sarah; 4, Elizabeth, m. Peter Henri; 5, Ann; 6, Susan.

IV. SAMUEL TROTH, second son of Henry Troth and Sarah Paschall, married, 10th month 2d, 1783, Ann Dixon, widow, and had: 1, Elizabeth; 2, Sarah Paschall; 3, Ann B.; 4, Henry; 5, Mary; 6, Samuel F.

IV. ELIZABETH OSBORNE, fourth daughter of Peter Osborne and Elizabeth Stevens, married, 18 December, 1789, in Second Presbyterian Church, Philadelphia, Peter Henri, son of Pierre Henri and Henrietta his wife, and had : 1, Henrietta, m. Henry Troth; 2, Eliza; 3, Peter.

V. HENRY TROTH, fourth child of Samuel Troth and Ann Dixon, married, 11 month 29th, 1816, Henrietta Henri, and had issue: 1, Anna, m. George Morrison Coates; 2, Eliza Henri, m. Joseph P. H. Coates; 3, William Paschall, m. first, Emma M. Thomas, secondly, Clara G. Townsend; 4, Henrietta M., m. Edward Y. Townsend; 5, Louisa; 6, Henry Morris; 7, Edward; 8, Samuel, now (1895), of Philadelphia.

VI. ANNA TROTH, eldest daughter of Henry Troth and Henrietta Henri, married 10 month 1, 1840, George Morrison Coates, of Philadelphia, descended from Thomas Coates, a prominent Colonial merchant of Philadelphia who settled in the Province of Pennsylvania in 1684. George Morrison Coates and Anna, his wife, had four children: Henry Troth Coates, of Philadelphia, m. Estelle B. Lloyd, also descended from Robert Lloyd; 2, William Morrison, m. Anna Morris Lloyd, sister of Estelle; 3, Joseph H., m. Elizabeth G. Potts; 4, Samuel H., died infant.

VI. ELIZA H. TROTH, second daughter of Henry Troth and Henrietta Henri, married 4th month 10th, 1844, Joseph P. H. Coates, brother to George Morrison Coates, and had: 1, George M., m. Laura Lloyd, sister to Estelle; 2, Edward H., m. first, Ella M. Potts; secondly, Florence Earl Nicholson, widow.

VI. WILLIAM P. TROTH, third son of Henry Troth and Henrietta Henri, married first, 1845, Emma M. Thomas, second 1860, Clara G. Townsend.

By his first wife he had: 1, Helen, m. Charles Ridgway; 2, Anna Coates, m. Henry S. Harper, and have Alice.

By his second wife he had: 1, Emily S.; 2, Henrietta; 3, Alice Gordon, m. John R. Drexel, of Philadelphia; 4, Lillian S.; 5, Mabel, d. infant.

VI. HENRIETTA M. TROTH, fourth child of Henry Troth and Henrietta Henri, married, 1850, Edward Y. Townsend, and had: 1, Henry T., m. Maria J. Potts; 2, John W., m. May Sharp.

THE KITE BRANCH.

I. JAMES KEITE (Kite), born in England; married, first, Mary, daughter of William[1] and Ann Warner, about 1680. They had four children. Mary, died January 1st, 1686. He married secondly, Martha Medlicott, widow of Daniel, of Merion, March 13, 1698, and died September 6th, 1713.

DESCENDANTS OF JAMES AND MARY (WARNER) (KEITE).[2]

II. JAMES JR., b. October 10, 1682; Abraham, b. October 19, 1685, m. Mary, daughter of Thomas and Elizabeth Peters, July 9, 1708, d. October, 1748; John, d. May 25, 1701; Grizzel, m. Samuel Lewis, February 26, 1706.

---

[1] William Warner was born in Blockley Parish, Worcestershire, England, and was son of John Warner. He came to Pennsylvania before Penn, and settled in what was afterward known as Blockley Township, Philadelphia, near Fifty-Second street and old Lancaster road. See Warner family on another page.

[2] William Kite, of Germantown, is descended from Thos. Kite and Mary Brentnal. Their son Benjamin Kite had Thomas, the minister among Friends, who was the father of William, of Germantown, Philadelphia.

III. ISAAC, eldest son of Abraham, m. April 2, 1749, Catherine, daughter of Anthony and Mary Tunis, d. 1781; James, son of Abraham, m. August 30, 1741, Martha Wynne; John, son of Abraham, m. Mary, daughter of John Roberts, November 10, 1745; Thomas, son of Abraham, m. Mary, daughter of John and Susanna Brentnal, December 10, 1742, d. May 11, 1790; Elizabeth, daughter of Abraham, m. Thomas Bowell, November 16, 1737.

IV. ELIZABETH, daughter of Isaac and Catherine Kite, b. May 29, 1751, m. ―――― Summers; Isaac, son of Isaac and Catherine Kite, b. December 24, 1754, m. Sarah Sellers,[1] 1784, d. September 21, 1823; Mary, daughter of Isaac and Catherine Kite, b. March 22, 1757, m. 1778, Richard Pearce; Anthony, son of Isaac and Catherine Kite, b. January 21, 1760, m. February 7, 1778, Deborah Roberts; Deborah, daughter of Isaac and Catherine Kite, b. November 20, 1762, m. July 24, 1793, Robert Henvis, d. September 17, 1842; Hannah, daughter of Isaac and Catherine Kite, b. ――――― 1763; Catherine, daughter of Isaac and Catherine Kite, b. ―――, m. Osman Henvis, d. May 20, 1793.

V. HANNAH, daughter of Isaac and Sarah Kite, b. August 24, 1784, m. Benj. Hobson, August 28, 1807, d. February 7, 1865; Mary Pearce, daughter of Isaac and Sarah Kite, b. March 30, 1787, m. William E. Wright, December 20, 1806, d. April 14, 1844; Isaac, Jr., son of Isaac and Sarah Kite, b. August 20, 1789, m. Rachel Jarden, April 6, 1812, d. July 21, 1825; Joseph Sellers, son of Isaac and Sarah Kite, b. March 9, 1792, m. first Julian Jarden 1812, m. secondly Jane Morgan 1833, d. October 13, 1862; William, son of Isaac and Sarah Kite, b. November 11, 1797, d. April 3, 1830; Benjamin, son of Isaac and Sarah Kite, b. August 6, 1799, d. March 3, 1824; Paschall, son of Isaac and Sarah Kite, b. March 20, 1803.

VI. JOSEPH JARDEN, son of Joseph Sellers and Julian Kite, b. November 12, 1815, m. Harriet Pfiel, d. ――――; Elizabeth Marple, daughter of Joseph Sellers and Julian Kite, b. June 12, 1817, m. Dr. W. W. Watson, May 25, 1837; Ann Eliza, daughter of Joseph Sellers and Julian Kite, b. September 17, 1819, m. Jacob Snyder, June 14, 1843, d. May 5, 1846; William Leinav, son of Joseph Sellers and Julian Kite, b. March 10, 1823, m. Rachel Dutton; Charles Pitman, son of Joseph Sellers and Julian Kite, b. January 21, 1826, m. Elizabeth Dutton, October 21, 1851; Isaac Fletcher, son of Joseph Sellers and Julian Kite b. October 26, 1827, m. Julia R. Glenn, April 15, 1852; Alexander Jarden, son of Joseph Sellers and Julian Kite, b. January 28, 1830, m. Josephine Hare, November 19, 1850; Thomas Mason, son of Joseph Sellers and Jane Kite, b. November 14, 1834, m. Emma Jane Widener, ―――, d. December 28, 1870; Samuel Nevin, son of Joseph Sellers and Jane Kite, b. March 16, 1836; Henry Berrell, son of Joseph Sellers and Jane Kite, b. April 26, 1839, m. Mary Evans.

VII. WILLIAM WILKINS, son of Dr. W. W. and Elizabeth M. Watson, b. August 6, 1843, m. Amanda Carr, October 20, 1870; John M., son of Dr. W. W. and Elizabeth M. Watson, b. March 29, 1845, m. Annie L. Stokes, May 1, 1873.

VII. JOSEPH SELLERS, son of Charles P. and Elizabeth Kite, b. June 7, 1852, m. Amanda Cresson, March 17, 1879; Martha Klapp, daughter of Charles P. and Elizabeth Kite, b. June 29, 1858; Frank Watson, son of Charles P. and Elizabeth Kite, b. January 17, 1861, m. Fannie Brunker, November 16, 1881.

---

[1]Sarah Sellers, b. February 28, 1760, wife of Isaac Kite, was the daughter of Joseph Sellers (son of Samuel, b. April 5, 1726, d. December 12, 1790), by Hannah his wife, daughter of William Paschall (b. July 22, 1693), by Hannah his wife, daughter of Robert Lloyd, of Merion, and Lowry his wife, daughter of Rees John William. [See preceding genealogy.] [For notices of other members of the Kite Family, see Appendix.]

86   *Merion in the Welsh Tract.*

VII. LOUIS STANWOOD, son of Isaac F. and Julia R. Kite, b. March 31, 1857, m. Abby M. Hovey, daughter of Franklin S. Hovey, April 24, 1884.

VII. CHARLES HARE, son of Alex. Jarden and Josephine Kite, b. November 30, 1851, m. Emma Morris, November 15, 1876, d. June 24, 1877; Joseph Sellers, son of Alex. Jarden and Josephine Kite, b. February 22, 1854, m. Mary Jahke, June 3, 1889; Mary Williams, daughter of Alex. Jarden and Josephine Kite, b. April 19, 1856; Florence Jarden, daughter of Alex. Jarden and Josephine Kite, b. July 22, 1858, m. Alban H. Reid, July 8, 1886; Alex. Clarence, son of Alex. Jarden and Josephine Kite, b. May 3, 1861; Annie E. J., daughter of Alex. Jarden and Josephine Kite, b. July 27, 1863; Jane Bell, daughter of Alex. Jarden and Josephine Kite, b. February 18, 1865, m. O. S. Johnson, April 12, 1887; Elizabeth Watson, daughter of Alex. Jarden and Josephine Kite, b. July 22, 1868; Virginia Briscoe, daughter of Alex. Jarden and Josephine Kite, b. January 20, 1871.

VIII. BESSIE KENTON, daughter of William W. and Amanda Watson, b. August 28, 1871, m. Jas. H. Milhouse, November 11, 1891; William W. Jr., son of William W. and Amanda Watson, b. July 10, 1878.

VIII. MABEL CRESSON, daughter of Joseph S. and Amanda Kite, b. February 1, 1880; Charles Clement, son of Joseph S. and Amanda Kite, b. April 10, 1883; Elizabeth Dutton, daughter of Joseph S. and Amanda Kite, b. August 30, 1888; Josephine Warder, daughter of Joseph S. and Amanda Kite, b. December 13, 1891.

VIII. CHARLES PITMAN, son of Frank Watson and Fannie Kite, b. September 11, 1882; Robert B., son of Frank Watson and Fannie Kite, b. January 6, 1884; Edith B., daughter of Frank Watson and Fannie Kite, b. March 22, 1891.

VIII. ELSA GLENN, daughter of Louis Stanwood and Abby M. Kite, b. October 26, 1886; Alan Mansfield, son of Louis Stanwood and Abby M. Kite, b. June 15, 1888.

VIII. CHARLESEMMA, daughter of Charles Hare and Emma Kite, b. November 3, 1877.

VIII. JOHN H. J., son of Joseph Sellers and Mary J. Kite, b. August 23, 1890; JOSEPH SELLERS, Jr., son of Joseph Sellers and Mary J. Kite, b. June 25, 1892.

VIII. JOSEPHINE HARE, daughter of Florence J. Kite and Alban H. Reid. b. October 17, 1889; Alban Elwell, son of Florence J. Kite and Alban H. Reid, b. January 21, 1894.

VIII. WILLIAM CURTIS, son of Jane B. Kite and O. S. Johnson, b. January 17, 1888; Mildred Kite, daughter of Jane B. Kite and O. S. Johnson. b. August 28, 1890; Gertrude Bell, daughter of Jane B. Kite and O. S. Johnson, b. August 28, 1892.

IX. MARION KENTON, daughter of Bessie K. Watson and J. H. Milhouse, b. April 3, 1893; Helen, daughter of Bessie K. Watson and J. H. Millhouse, b. February 23, 1895.

CADWALLADER MORGAN, MINISTER AMONG FRIENDS.

Cadwallader Morgan, a yeoman, and Minister among Friends, from the township of Gwernevel Ismynydd, in the Comôt of Penllyn, Merionethshire, arrived in Pennsylvania some time in the early fall of 1683. Like others of the Merioneth Company, he had suffered from harsh persecutions.

His certificate of removal was given him from the Penllyn Meeting, and was dated Fifth-month 8th, 1683. It speaks of him as a man of exceptional worth, and of great service within the religious society of which he was a member. His wife, Jane, daughter of Richard Price[1], is said to have accompanied him to his new home in the wilderness. They settled in Merion, a short distance from Pencoyd, on the Schuylkill River, upon the plantation which Cadwallader had purchased from John ap Thomas and Dr. Edward Jones[2]. It appears that he was very highly esteemed in Merion on account of his blameless life and savory ministry, and remembered for many a year after his decease.

Eleanor Evans, of Gwynedd, who knew him personally, has left the following testimony of record concerning him:

"Cadwallader Morgan, a native of Merionethshire, was one of the first settlers in Merion. Tho' he held no great share of the ministry, he had an excellent talent at advice & teaching in his conversation, his discourse was so instructive that some who had the advantage of hearing him relate his ex-

---

[1] See Rees John William and Edward Rees.
[2] By deed 7th of Seventh-month, 1687 (Deed Book E 1, p. 586, etc.), Cadwallader Morgan conveyed his original tract of 156 acres to "John Roberts, gentleman," of Merion, but in 1701 held 202½ acres under the Merion Company's patent.

perience of his spiritual travel have reaped benefit therefrom 30 or 40 years after his death. He had much to say in favor of Watchfulness & keeping the mind trusty upon God. He lived and died in Merion"[1].

Cadwallader Morgan's eldest son, Morgan Cadwallader, was born in Wales, on the 23d of Sixth-month, 1679, and also became a minister, but being a confirmed invalid, he died young, and unmarried. Edward Cadwallader, the second son, who was born in Wales, on 22d of Sixth-month, 1682, died before his father, also, presumably, unmarried. Cadwallader Morgan died in 1711. His will was signed on the 10th of September, 1711, and proved at Philadelphia, on the 10th day of October, of the same year[2].

He mentions in it Elizabeth, wife of his "brother Lewis Morgan," and his "brother John Morgan," to whom he leaves £40. The balance of his estate is devised to "Edward Evan, 2nd son of my son-in-law Robert Evan[3]," "my son-in-law Hugh Evan[4]," and "Elizabeth Thomas, daughter of my son-in-law, Abell Thomas[5]," Robert Evan and Abell Thomas are executors, whilst his friends, Edward Jones, John Roberts, David Jones and Thomas Jones, are appointed to act as overseers. The witnesses were: Robert Roberts, Moses Roberts, Thomas Jones.

David Jones, one of the overseers, was probably identical with David Jones, of Blockley, of whom we shall have occasion to speak elsewhere in these pages.

John Morgan, the brother of Cadwallader, settled, it is believed, in Radnor.

---

[1] Eleanor Evans was wife of John Evans, of Gwynedd, Pa., and daughter of Rowland Ellis.
[2] Will Book C, page 259, Philadelphia.
[3] Of Gwynedd, Pa.
[4] Of Gwynedd, Pa.
[5] Abell Thomas resided in Merion for a time, but he held, on 16th of Twelfth-month, 1701, 76½ acres in Goshen in right of the John ap Thomas and Edward Jones purchase. [Board of Property Books.]

JOHN AND WILLIAM AP EDWARD, OF MERION.
SONS OF EDWARD AP JOHN, OF CYNLAS.

I. EDWARD AP JOHN, of the township of Cynlas, Llanddervel Parish, Penllyn, Merionethshire, was the father of the above named colonists. He was buried in Llanddervel Church yard March 1, 1667[1]. According to the record in an old Bible belonging to a descendant, he "was a free-holder of about £24 per annum[2]—a man of good repute and careful to bring up his children in the fear of the Lord, according to the Church of England." Documents in Wales show him to have been a kinsman, probably a first cousin, of Edward Nicholas, of Cynlas (born 1647), who was son of Nicholas ap Edward, of the same township, and a descendant of Rhirid Flaidd, Lord of Penllyn[3]. The name of Edward ap John's wife has not been definitely ascertained. He left surviving him, so far as known, four sons: 1, John ap Edward, b. Wales; m. first Katherine, d. Robert ap Hugh; m. second, Jane, d. John ap Edward; 2, William ap Edward, b. Wales; 3, Evan ap Edward, b. Wales; 4, Thomas ap Edward, b. Wales; of Llanllidrog, liv. there 1686.

II. JOHN AP EDWARD, son of Edward ap John, of Cynlas, had a deed from Dr. Edward Jones and John ap Thomas, dated 18 April, 1682, for 312½ acres of land, which were surveyed to him in Merion. He arrived in August, 1682. John ap Edward was an enterprising man, and no doubt had acquired considerable property prior to his removal from Nantlleidiog Township to Pennsylvania. He was a member of the Society of Free Traders, of London, and the head-land claimed by him indicates that he brought with him at least four servants. He died soon after his arrival, in 1683. His will is dated 16th of Eighth-month, 1683, and proved at Philadelphia the same year[4]. By this document he leaves his plantation of 312½ acres in Merion, to his eldest son, Evan, and to his other sons, Edward, "that quantity or proportion of land due me for the bringing over of servants by the laws or concessions of Pennsylvania aforesaid, that is to say two hundred acres." The names of his children, who probably took the surname of Edwards, were as follows: 1, Elizabeth, b. Wales, 18th Twelfth-month, 1671; 2, Sarah, b. Wales, 8th Eleventh-month, 1673; 3, Evan, b. Wales, 2d of Second-month, 1677; 4, Edward, b. Wales, 5th of Eighth-month, 1681.

---

[1] Register of the Parish Church, of Llandderfel (Llanddervel), Penllyn.

[2] This sum doubtless represented the rent land he held at the assessed value. At that day, as at this, farm lands were assessed at a rate much under their exact value, and the lands above rated probably produced Edward ap John a handsome revenue. They appear to have been in the family for many centuries.

[3] See a former page.

[4] Will Book B, p. 270, Philadelphia.

II. WILLIAM AP EDWARD, son of Edward ap John, of Cynlas, resided upon a rented farm in the township of Nantlleidiog. in Penllyn. before his removal to Pennsylvania, but is sometimes described as "of Cynlas," prior to that event. He married first, about 1671, Katherine, daughter of Robert ap Hugh, of Llwyndedwydd, near Bala, Merionethshire, and sister to Hugh Roberts (i. e., Hugh ap Robert, or Hugh, the son of Robert), who also removed to Pennsylvania and became a member of the Provincial Council. (See article on Hugh Roberts.) The wife of Robert ap Hugh (alias Robert Pugh) was Elizabeth, daughter of William Owen, of Llanvawr Parish, Penllyn. Katherine died in Wales, 1676, and William ap Edward married secondly, 1681, Jane, daughter of John ap Edward, of near Bala. William ap Edward and family early joined the Quakers, and came to Pennsylvania on the ship, "Lyon," which arrived in August, 1682. He was a member of the Company of Merioneth Adventurers, and, by deed, dated 1 April, 1682, under the designation of "William ap Edward, of Ucheldri, yeoman," became the purchaser of 156¼ acres of land, a part of which was surveyed to him in Merion, and part in Goshen. This land he disposed of soon after, and having purchased from other members of the company their right to the entire amount of Liberty land belonging to the purchasers under the Edward Jones and John ap Thomas Patent, which parcel of land he had surveyed to him in Blockley Township, and for which with the overplus thereunto belonging, and another lot, he had a patent in 1702[1]. This land, late the George Estate, is situate at Overbrook station, on the Pennsylvania Railroad, and now forms a part of "Overbrook Farms," in the Thirty-fourth ward of the city of Philadelphia. William ap Edward died in 1714. His will was signed 29 December, 1714; proved, 29 January, 1714-15, at Philadelphia[2]. He had issue by his first wife[3]: 1, Elizabeth, b. Wales, 14th Third-month, 1672; m. Thomas Lloyd[4]; 2, Katherine, b. Wales, 29th Eleventh-month, 1676; m. but d. s. p.

By his second wife he had: 1, Sarah, b. 29th Eighth-month, 1685; m. Thomas Lawrence[5], S. David; 2, Edward, b. 7th Twelfth-month, 1689; 3, Ellen, b. 19th Fourth-month, 1691; m. Henry Lawrence; 4, Mary, b. 11th Eleventh-month, 1694; m. Richard Preston.

III. EDWARD, only son of William ap EDWARD, born in Merion or neighborhood, 7th of 12th, 1689, died 1749[6], the surname of WILLIAMS, "a name assumed according to the custom in Wales." He inherited, under his father's will, the Blockley plantation, "unto him and his heirs forever."

---

[1]Patent William Penn, by his Commissioners, to William Edward, for two tracts of land in the Liberties of Philadelphia; one of them containing 186 acres, 3 qrs., 24 ps., and the other of them containing 20 acres and 5 ps. Recorded Third-month 8th, 1702, in Patent Book A, vol. 2, page 239, etc. See also Minute Books Board of Property, Harrisburg, Penna.

[2]Will Book D, p. 25, etc.

[3]The account of the issue of William ap Edward by both as here given is derived from family records. See also Penna. Magazine.

[4]Thomas Lloyd was of Merion and resided a mile north of the present Bryn Mawr station, Pennsylvania Railroad. He was a brother to Robert Lloyd of the same place.

[5]Thomas Lawrence was the son of David Lawrence, whose wife was a daughter of Thomas Ellis, by his first wife. It does not, however, seem certain that David Lawrence was not married twice. See Thomas Ellis.

[6]His will is dated 3d September, 1749, proved February 21, 1749. Will Book I, p. 225, etc., Philadelphia. He mentions children as above, and leaves his estate to his son, Joseph Williams. Speaks of his property at "Gwineth" (i. e., Gwynedd), and leaves his wife, Eleanor, one brass pot, his large boiler, clothes-press in the parlor, and his white mare and colt and new blue plush side-saddle.

John and William ap Edward.

He married Eleanor, daughter of David Lawrence, and had issue: 1, Joseph, b. ———— ; 2, Daniel, b. 12th 2d month, 1717[1]; 3, Sarah, b. 13th 4th month 1720, m. Joshua Humphreys[2]; 4, Edward, b. 24th 7th month, 1722, m. Hannah Garrett; 5, Jane, b. 21st 7th month, 1732, m. Evan Thomas[3].

IV. JOSEPH WILLIAMS, son and heir to Edward Williams, died intestate, leaving issue, three daughters, viz.: 1, Rebecca, m. Amos George; 2, Eleanor, m. Joseph Bond; 3, Sarah, m. Edward George. Eleanor Bond died intestate, leaving issue, three children: Samuel, Robert, and Hannah Bond who m. Aaron Hackney. The aboved named Amos George died intestate, 1790, leaving children by the said Rebecca: Joseph, Richard, Ann, Hannah, Elizabeth, Jane, William and Amos.

---

[1] It is claimed that this person was the founder of Williamsport.

[2] This was Joshua, son of Daniel Humphrey (alias Daniel Samuel), of Haverford, son of Samuel Humphrey, son of Humphrey ap Hugh, of Llwyndu, ap David ap Howell ap Gronwy ap Einion.

[3] Probably son of Edward Thomas, of Merion. They had children, Edward, Eleanor, Joseph and Jonathan.

ARMS OF LLOYD OF GLANLLYN AND GWERN Y BRECHTWN[1].

Vert, a chevron between three wolves' heads erased, argent.

DESCENT OF EDWARD REES (ALIAS PRICE), ANCESTOR OF THE PRICE FAMILY, OF MERION, LOWRY LLOYD AND OTHER SETTLERS, FROM THE LLOYDS OF GLANLLYN AND GWERN Y BRECHTWN, MERIONETHSHIRE, NORTH WALES.—*G. B.*

[From Visitations of Wales by Lewis Dwnn, Deputy Herald, Harleian, MS. 2288; MS. pedigrees in Pennsylvania, etc.]

RHIRID FLAIDD, Lord of Penllyn; = GWENLLIAN, dau. of Ednyfed, temp. Henry II. and Richard I.   Lord of Broughton.

MADOG, of Rhiwaedog, Lord of Penllyn.	= ARDUN, dau. Philip ap Uchtrydd, Lord of Cyfeiliog.	RHIRID VYCHAN.	EINION, slain 1261.
IORWERTH, of Penllyn, Lord of that Cantref.	= GWERFYL, dau. of Pasgen ap Gwyn ap Gruffydd, Lord of Cedigfa and Deuddwr.		GWRGEN Y GWYN LLWYD, of Rhiwaedog; he had Anne, who m. David Lloyd, whose dau. Maud m. David Gôch of Penllech, who was direct male ancestor of Robert Owen of Fron Gôch and Merion, d. 1697. See Owen genealogy.
MADOG AP IORWERTH, Lord of Penllyn; he presented a petition to the Prince of Wales, at Ken- A	= EVA, dau. of Griffith ap Einon ap Griffith (not of Cors y Gedol).	GRUFFYDD. IORWERTH VYCHAN.	GWENLLIAN, m. Llewelyn ap Ithel, of Awlhairn.	MAUD, m. Gronwy ap Tudor, ap Gronwy, ap Ednyfed Vychan.

[1] It will be noted that the last syllable of this word is spelled in a slightly different way in another part of this book. Either style, the pronunciation being identical, appears to be correct. At least a dozen ways of writing it have been noted. In this work the spelling used originally by the particular authorities or documents cited in the different chapters, has been closely followed, irrespective of appearances and an apparent lack of uniformity; and this applies to all Welsh names which appear on the pages of this work.

sington, 33 Edw. I., 1305, praying that he might enjoy certain lands and the Bailiwick of " Unius Cantr. in Penllyn and Ardudewey," which the King had granted him.

| SIR GRUF- FYDD AP MADOC, Knt., of Llan Uwch Lyn Tegid. | = JANET, dau. of Cynfelyn, ap Dolphin, Lord of Manofon; but, according to Harl. MS. 2288, he m. Alice, dau. Bleddyn Vychan. | GRONWY, m. Eva, dau. Llewellyn, ap Einion of Llwdiarth. | GWERFYL, m. Iorwerth, ap Hwfa, of Dudeleston. | MARGARET. | GWENLLIAN. |

| GWENLLIAN, dau. and heir of Ievan, ap Howell, descended from Collwyn, ap Tangno, Lord of Llyn. | = SIR IEVAN AP GRUFFYD, Knt., of Llanuwchllyn, and Cefn Treflaith in Llanstundwy; died probably 1379; he was one of the jury of an inquisition held at Bala, upon the next Friday after the Festival of the Assumption, 48 Edw. III. [S. R. Meyrick's notes to Dwnn], Sept. 1374. The date upon his tomb is MCCCLXX; but a figure appears to have been chipped off. He lies in effigy within the church of Llanuwchllyn, near Bala, in Penllyn. | = ANNESTA, dau. of Llewelyn ap Einion, ap Meiler Grûg, Lord of Tref Gynon. | HOWELL, Y GADER, of Gader Penllyn; m. Mali, dau. of Goronwy Lloyd. | RHYS, ancestor of Jones of Llandyrnog. |

OWEN, of Cefn Treflaith.

A   B

A			B
IEVAN VYCHAN, of Llanuwchllyn, in the Comôt of Penllyn, and held other lands in Nant y Friar, in Llanderfel.	=	ANNE, dau. of Sir Griffith Vaughan, Knight Banneret, at Agincourt; and Lord of Burgedin, Garth, and Garth Fawr. He was knighted 1415; beheaded at Pool Castle, 1447, being then very aged.	RHYS, of Cyn Llwyd; he had Ievan ap Rhys.

DAVID AP IEVAN VYCHAN, of Llanuwchllyn.	=	GWENHWYFAR, dau. of David Lloyd, ap Howell; descended from Rhirid Flaidd, Lord of Penllyn.	HOWELL.

DAVID LLOYD, ap David, of Llanuwchllyn and Llanderfel Penllyn. He purchased the demesne lands of Glanllyn Tegid, 19 Henry VII., 1503-4.	= m. 1st, ANNESTA, dau. of Griffith ap Ievan.	= m., 2d, LOWRY, dau. of Howell Vaughan ap Howell ap Gruffyd of Llwydiarth.	RHYS, of Tref Brysg.

ROBERT LLOYD, of Nantfreur, in Llanderfel, Penllyn. He was the owner of Gwern y Brechtwn, which was a part of his father's estate. [Vide MS. Robert Vaughan, of Hengwrt; and Dwnn II., p. 232.] He died prior to 1592.	= MARY dau. of Reynold ad Griffith, of Upper Branas.	HOWELL VAUGHAN, of Glanllyn; living 13th Sept., 1568.	WILLIAM VAUGHAN, of Llanrhiadr, in Morchnant.	LLEWELYN. — Owen. — Mallt. — Catherine. — Annesta.

THOMAS, ap Robert Lloyd, born circa, 1515-20; died May, 1612; buried within the Church of Llanderfel, 21 May, that year. "Thomas Lloyd, gen.	= CATHERINE, dau. of Robert ap Griffith, ap Evan; derived from Marchweithian, Lord of Isaled.	ROBERT, ap Robert Lloyd; he had Ellis, who had Foulke, who had Thomas Foulke, of Llanderfel.	EVAN, ap Robert Lloyd.	OWEN AP ROBERT, died 1601.	FOULKE. ap Robert Lloyd; died prior to 1591.	JOHN, ap Robert Lloyd; he had Morgan, who had Thomas, b. 1614.

| A
erosus paterfamilias fuit in ecclesia p'ochia de Llandrvell XXI May dieque domino in Albus Ano Dni. 1612. [Llandderfel Reg.] He is called, of Gwern y Brechtwn, gentleman.

ROBERT LLOYD, who had John Lloyd, of Gwern y Brechtwn. Some of the first settlers are believed to have come from this line.

EVAN, ap Thomas Lloyd of Nant y Friar; born circa 1555; died May, 1640. " Evanus ap Thomas Lloyd, P. F. Sepult fuit XVI May in Cemeterio 1640." [Llandderfel Reg.]

= DORO- THEA EVANS. " Dorothea Verch Evan, uxor Evan ap Thomas Lloyd. Sepulto fuit decimo octavo die February dieque Jovis Ao. 1619. [Llandderfel Reg.]

THOMAS, ap Thomas Lloyd. Foulke ap Thomas Lloyd.

MARY = RICHARD of Tyddin Tyfod.

RHYS, ap = Richard, of Tyddin Tyfod; alias Rees Prichard.

THOMAS, ap Evan Lloyd, born circa 1578-80. High Sheriff of Mer. 1623; died Nov. 1649; m. Catherine, dau. Wm. David, of Llanderfel, and had Foulke ap Thomas Lloyd, baptized 14 April, 1623; who had Edward Foulke Lloyd, alias Edward Foulke, settled at Gwynedd, Pa., 1698.

GWEN. JANE.

JOHN, ap Evan Lloyd.

ELLEN.

GRFFITH = ap Rhys, of Tyddin Tyfod.

RICHARD PRICE (alias ap = Rees, or Prees), of Tyddin Tyfod; d. 1686, and will proved at St. Asaph Registry, 1686; dated 26 January (11-mo.) 1685.

EDWARD REES (alias Prees, alias Price), of Merion, 1682.

JANE, m. Cadwallader Morgan, of Merion. See Cadwallader Morgan.

HANNAH; m. Rees John William (alias Prees Jones), of Merion. See Rees John William.

dr. = John William.

THOMAS PRICE; he remained in Wales; of Tyddin Tyfod, living 1686.

Edward Rees, alias Prees, or Price, by which last name his descendants called themselves, and by which he was frequently designated, came to Merion with Dr. Edward Jones, in August, 1682. His father was Richard Price—i. e., Richard ap Rees, or Richard Prees (or Rhys), of Tyddin Tyfod, Merionethshire, who died 1685-6, and whose will, dated 26th January, is given on another page. Edward Rees, as we shall call him, was a prominent man in Merion. He was one of the founders of the Merion Meeting, and in 1695 donated the ground upon which the meeting-house now stands, the lot being a part of his plantation, purchased by deed 1682, and which extended along both sides of the old Lancaster road, now Montgomery Avenue. His house stood, and still remains, in the field to the northwest of the Meeting, whilst a fine old Colonial residence was erected by one of his descendants, almost opposite, on the south side of Montgomery Avenue. The property, it is believed, after remaining for two centuries in the possession of his descendants, has lately passed, by will, to another family. In his old age, in company with Benjamin Humphrey, he paid a visit to his old home in Wales. The will of Edward Rees is dated 28 November, 1728, and was proved at Philadelphia 6 January, 1727-8, Will Book E, p. 91, etc. He mentions his son, "Rees Prees," grandson, Edward, and cousins, Peter, David and Jane Evans, etc. He married first in Wales, Mably, daughter of Owen ap Hugh, brother of Thomas ap Hugh, gentleman, of Wern Fawr, Merionethshire, son of Hugh ap Ievan ap Rhys Gôch ap Tudor ap Rhys ap Ievan Gôch, of Cwm Pen Aner, in the Parish of Cerrig y druidion, Denbighshire, lineally descended from Marchweithian, the Lord of Isaled. (See a future page.) She died 1699;

MARCHWEITHIAN.
Gules, a Lion Ramp., *Argent*.

GWERN Y BRECHDWN.
Home of the Lloyds, Merionethshire.

buried at Merion, Eighth-month 23d. Edward Rees married secondly, in Pennsylvania, Rebecca Humphrey, daughter of Samuel Humphrey, son of Humphrey ap Hugh (living 1662), son of Hugh ap David, ap Howell ap Gronwy ap Einion. By his second wife he had no issue. By his first wife he had: 1, Rees Prees (alias Price), b. Eleventh-month 11th, 1678; 2, Catharine, bur. at Merion, Eighth-month 23d, 1682; 3, Jane, b. Ninth-month 11th, 1682; m. first, Jonathan Hayes; secondly, —— Maries.

Rees Price, born 1678, in Penllyn, married first, at Radnor, Tenth-month 6th, 1705, Sarah Meredith; secondly, at Haverford, Tenth-month 9th, 1718, Elizabeth Ellis, daughter of Ellis Ellis, deceased, of Haverford (and Lydia Humphrey, his wife, daughter of Samuel, as above); thirdly, at Haverford, Third-month 10th, 1737, Ann Scotharn (widow), of Darby. He had issue: 1, Edward; 2, John; 3, Ellis; 4, Mary, m. Rees Harry, son of David, of Plymouth; 5, Margaret[1]; 6, Jane.

---

[1] Margaret, daughter of Rees Price, of Merion, married, first, —— Paschall, and secondly, at Philadelphia, William Montgomery, of New Jersey, descended from the Montgomery Family of Brigend, Scotland. [See History of Montgomery Family, by Thomas H. Montgomery.] William Montgomery and Margaret Price, his second wife, had issue one son, who was ancestor to the present Montgomery family of Bryn Mawr and Philadelphia. The late Richard R. Montgomery, Esq., of Bryn Mawr, was a direct descendant, therefore, of Rees Price, of Merion. Margaret's first husband, Paschall, was not a Friend, and she was disowned by the Society for marrying out of Meeting; but after his death, having made the necessary acknowledgment, was received back into membership, and married Montgomery, who at that time was a Friend. Rees Price in his will leaves a bequest to her children by Paschall. It may be noted here that there was another Rees Price, who was among the first settlers in Radnor, and who died about the beginning of the eighteenth century, who should not be confused with Rees Price, of Merion, son of Edward, to whom he was not related in any way.

THE ARMS OF COLLWYN, LORD OF LLYN.
Sable, a chevron, between three fleurs-de-lys, argent.

ROBERTS, OF PENCOYD, LOWER MERION.

[This genealogy is compiled from a pedigree by Lewis Dwnn, Deputy Herald, for Wales (by patent under seal of Clarencieux and Norroy Kings at Arms), made out in the year 1588; from MS. pedigree by John Roberts, compiled about 1704; from MSS. in Harleian Collections, British Museum; from wills and deeds in Pennsylvania; from official records in Wales; and from papers now in possession of the author. Pencoyd does not appear to be excellent Welsh. John Roberts called his plantation Pencoid, which is better, but Coed seems to be the correct ending of this name.]

The first of this family in Pennsylvania was John Roberts, son of Richard Roberts, of Cowyns, in the parish of Llanengan, in Llyn Division, Caernarvonshire, North Wales, who was descended from Collwyn, Lord of Llyn. John Roberts was born in the year 1648, and at the age of twenty-nine he became a member of the Society of Friends.

It appears that he lived for a time near Dôlgelly, in Merionethshire, and it was probably his acquaintance with Quakers at that place which induced his removal to Pennsylvania in the year 1683.

Previous to his departure from Wales he purchased from Richard Davies, of Welshpoole, by Lease and Release dated 30-31 July, 1682, 150 acres of land to be laid out in the Province of Pennsylvania. In this deed he is described as "of the Parish of Llangian, in the county of Caernarvon, gentleman." Of this tract, which was surveyed to him in Merion, we will speak hereafter.

John Roberts arrived in Pennsylvania, in company with other Cymric Friends, on the 16th of Ninth-month, 1683, bringing with him a certificate of removal from Penllyn Meeting, which is recorded in the books of the Radnor, Merion and Haverford Meeting, and reads as follows:

Whereas John Robert in ye county of Carnarvon hath declared his intention in order to his removal to Pennsylvania in America we thought it convenient to certify in his behalf that he is one th^t owned and received the truth for these 6 years past. Hath walked since blameless in his conversation and servicable in his place—also that he is free from all contracts of marriage and matrimony to a certain knowledge of good reputation amongst his neighbors acquaintance and relations where he lived.

From the Mens Meeting at Penllan ye 18 of 5th month 1683.

RICHARD PRICE	EDWARD GRIFFITH
ROBERT OWEN	THOMAS PRICHARD
CADD ELLIS	DAVID JONES
EVAN REES	WILLIAM MORGAN
ROBERT EVAN	GRIFFITH JOHN
ELLIS DAVID	ROGER ROBERT
HUGH GRIFFITH	EVAN OWEN
MORRIS HUMPHREY	

It having been thought advisable by the Welsh Friends that the settlers should bring to the Meeting some account of themselves and their descent, we find the following entry in the minutes of Merion Meeting:

" MERION PREPARATIVE MTG.
" 11 mo. 5. 1704.

" John Roberts brought in an account to this meeting of his place of abode in his native country being Llun in Caernarvonshire, convincement and removal to this Country, marriage and other remarkable passages of his life, in order to be entered upon Record."

Unfortunately the record of this and similar narratives cannot now be found, but as duplicates were often retained by the family, the account in question has been preserved. The document of which we speak, the original of which, in the handwriting of the first John Roberts, is still in possession of his descendants, reads as follows:

"An account of *John Roberts* left to my Posterity.

"A short account of John Roberts formerly of Llyn, being son of Richard Roberts, and Grand-son of Robert Thomas Morris, who lived at Cowyns, in the Parish of Llanergan, and County of Carnarvon; my Mother, being Margaret Evans, daughter of Richard Evans of the Parish of Llangian and county aforesaid. Being convinced of God's Everlasting Truth about the year 1677, not by man nor through man, but by the Revelation of Jesus Christ in my own heart, being about thirty miles from any Friends or Meeting, in that time when I was convinced, but coming into acquaintance with Friends near Dollgelle and near Bala in Merionethshire I frequented their meetings while I abode in those parts, but by the Providence of God, in the year 1683 I transported myself with many of my friends for Pennsylvania where I and they arrived, the sixteenth day of the ninth month, One thousand six hundred and eighty-three, being then thirty-five years old; and settled myself in the place which afterwards I called Pencoid in the Township of Merion, which was afterwards called so by them, being the first settlers of it, having brought with me one servant man from my native land, and fixed my settling here I took to wife Gaynor Roberts, daughter to Robert Pugh (or ap Hugh) from Llyndedwydd near Bala in Merionethshire, her mother being Elizabeth William Owen, one of the first that was convinced of the Truth in that neighborhood. So leaving this account for our Offspring and others that desire to know from whence we came and who we descended from and when we came to settle unto this place where we now abide, being then a wilderness, but now by God's blessing upon our endeavors is become a fruitful field. To God's name be the Praise, Honor and Glory, who is worthy of it for ever and for ever more."

From the above interesting record it is possible to gather very considerable information regarding the family. The Robert Pugh mentioned was the father of Hugh Roberts, that celebrated Minister among Friends, and a member of the Governor's Council. William Owen was a free-holder in Llanvawr in 1636, a man of very considerable property, and of good family.

Regarding the direct male ancestry of John Roberts, the writer was unsuccessful, some time since, in obtaining enough information from Wales to establish the identity of Thomas Morris, who was, it will be observed, the great-grandfather of the first settler (John Roberts).

This was largely due to the missing wills in the Registry covering that portion of Caernarvonshire in which the family had dwelt for many generations.

Since then, however, chance has thrown in the author's way, certain documents and records which prove conclusively that Richard Roberts was a cadet of an ancient family holding the estates of Pencoed, or Penkoed, in Llyn, Caernarvonshire, a few miles from Cowyns, where Robert Thomas Morris lived, and it appears that Cowyns, although in another parish, was formerly a part of the Pencoed Estates[1].

The descent of John Roberts is as follows:

Collwyn ap Tangno was anciently Lord of that portion of the promontory of Llyn, in Caernarvonshire, which included among others the parishes of Llangian, Llanengan, Llanbedrog, and Llanarmon. These several parishes are on the Bay of Cardigan. Collwyn lived in the eleventh century, and was ancestor to most of the families in this part of Llyn. In

---

[1] It is greatly regretted that owing to the imperfect records referred to, it is impossible to give here details as complete as desired, but the following pedigree can be relied upon as correct in the essential points. The evidence connecting one generation with another has been conscientiously weighed, the dates of birth of each individual carefully estimated, and the title to the Llyn lands well considered. The reader will note that John Roberts called his land " Pencoid," after the principal possessions of his ancestors.

later years the Lordship of a great part of Llyn belonged to the Princes of North Wales and their descendants, among whom was Trahairn Gôch, who held the title to a considerable portion thereof in the fourteenth century. Notwithstanding this fact the immediate possessions of the descendants of Collwyn do not seem to have been disturbed. Down to the year 1700 there was scarcely a free-hold in the parishes mentioned not held by the posterity of this old Welsh Princeling.

Collwyn had a son, Meredith ap Collwyn, of Llyn, who had Gwrgan, who had Einion, who had Meredith, who had Howell, who had Griffith, who had Ievan, who had Rhys, who had Ievan, who had Griffith ap Ievan, who was father to Morris ap Griffith, who held the lands of Pencoed, near Plas Du, in the parish of Llanarmon, and other detached farms about the year 1500 and later[1]. This Morris ap Griffith had issue several sons, viz.: Griffith Morris, John Morris, William Morris, THOMAS MORRIS, Hugh Morris, Richard Morris, David Morris, Robert Morris and Meredith Morris. Thomas Morris had (besides a son Richard) a son Robert, called ROBERT THOMAS MORRIS, of Cowyns, who was father of Richard Roberts, who by Margaret his wife, daughter of Richard Evans, was father to John Roberts (born 1648), Richard Roberts and Anne Roberts. Both his brother, Richard, and his sister, Anne, appear to have removed with John Roberts to Pennsylvania in 1683.

John Roberts brought a servant with him from Wales, and engaged others after his arrival. His first business was to clear his 150 acres which had been surveyed to him along the Schuylkill, just above the Blockley line. Here he built a fine old mansion, yet standing, and now the home of his descendant, George B. Roberts, Esq., of Bala. This tract was directly

---

[1] The writer has in his possession a copy of a very curious and detailed pedigree of this family made out by a Welsh Herald during the reign of Queen Elizabeth. In it all of the various marriages, from Collwyn down, and the children of each generation, are given. It is, unfortunately, too voluminous to insert here. It appears that the elder sons married very early, whilst the line from which John Roberts came, being younger sons, married late in life, making quite a difference between the ages of the same generations. Thus, although Thomas ap Owen Griffith Morris died about 1625 or 1630, at an advanced age, yet his second cousin lived until 1675.

THE ROBERTS HOUSE,
Pencoyd and Bala, Lower Merion, Pa. Oldest Portions Built by John Roberts, about 1684.

westward of the land taken up by his wife, which extended to the Schuylkill River. He married, "at Friends Meeting-House in Lower Merion," the 20th day of the First-month, 1684 ("being first marriage at said meeting-house"), Gainor Roberts, daughter of Robert ap Hugh (or Pugh), of Llyndedwydd, near Bala, Merionethshire, Wales, and sister of Hugh Roberts, Provincial Councillor, of Pennsylvania.

John Roberts became a very prominent man in the Colony. He held the office of Justice of the Peace, and was elected to the Provincial Assembly. The old books of the Board of Property give us some interesting details concerning his real estate transactions. It seems that besides his 150 acres and the lot which his wife had for her share in the John ap Thomas and Dr. Edward Jones purchase, John Roberts bought in 1699, of one Andrew Wheeler, a Swede, a tract of land in Merion, and Liberties, "on the westerly side of the Schilckeel, by the Falls, Beginning at a hickory marked tree standing by ye Schilckeel, thence North 62°, West, by land late of said Andrew Wheeler, but sold to the Garretsons, 320 Perches, to another Hickory tree, by a Runn side next the land of John Roberts, from thence down by said Runn to a Spanish oake standing by the Schilckeel, and from thence down the several courses of the said Schilckeel, to the place of Beginning, Containing 60 acres[a] of Land," being a part of that 400 acres surveyed by Richard Noble for one Swan Loin, the 24th of Third-month, 1681, by virtue of a warrant from the Court at Upland, being dated First-month, 1677, pursuant to the petition of Lace Andreas in behalf of John and Andreas Wheeler for 300 acres. "And the said John Wheeler having died, the said Andreas is his sole heir." It will thus be seen that John Roberts' original purchase was almost surrounded by Swede holdings; the Wheelers on one side, and the Garretsons, afterwards called Garrett, on the other.

Some time before 1700 he purchased the land-rights of various servants brought here by Hugh Roberts, John Bevan,

---

[a] It proved to be 113 by resurvey in 1703.

and others, amounting altogether to 750 acres of land, which he afterwards sold to Owen Roberts, who, however, never paid for or claimed the same, so that John Roberts left it in his will to his son Robert.

By resurvey in 1703, the original purchase from Richard Davies proved to be but 130 acres. At the same time John Roberts held in Merion, under right of Patent John ap Thomas and Dr. Edward Jones, 108 acres, as per resurvey, and 262 acres in Goshen.

Part of this was land belonging to his wife, and part that purchased from Cadwallader Morgan and Hugh Jones, 1687. From Cadwalader Morgan he had 76½ acres, from Hugh Jones 76½ acres, and in right of his wife 153½ acres, being in all 306½ acres, which being resurveyed in 1703, showed an overplus of 33½ acres, but the tract under the Patent of Richard Davies proved 20 acres short, so that it was only necessary to have a patent for 13½ acres on this tract and 47 acres of the Wheeler tract. John Roberts died 6th June, 1724, and Gainor, his wife, 20th February, 1722, aged 69 years. They were both buried at the Merion Meeting. He had accumulated a very considerable amount of property, which he left to his son and daughter.

The following is a very full abstract of his will:

"Know all men by these Presents, That I John Roberts of the Township of Merion in the County of Philadelphia, in the Province of Pennsylvania, being weak in Body etc."

"To my only son and heir apparent, Robert Roberts, my house and Plantation with the Edifice and Building thereon, and all the Land belonging thereto, and all the Lands and Lots belonging to me in this Province whatsoever or wheresoever—Together with all my right Title and interest in and to the 750 acres of land which I sold to Owen Roberts verbally, at £6 per the hundred, some years since, but am not paid for it, to the only use and behoof of my said son Robert Roberts and his Heirs forever."

"To my daughter Elizabeth Roberts £200 and one half of all my household stuff, and all my personal estate.

"To my grandsons John, Alban, Rees, and Phineas the sum of £20.

Roberts, of Pencoyd.

"To my brother Richard, 40 shillings, also to his daughter Margaret 40 shillings.

"To my niece Margaret, my sister Annes' daughter, 40 shillings.

"To the disposal of Friends of the Monthly Meeting (Merion) to the use of poor Friends, £5, that is to say the principal to remain upon interest, and the interest thereof to be received and disposed of yearly."

Son Robert, and daughter Elizabeth, Executors, and his "Dear Friends Robert Jones, Robert Evans, and Thomas Jones to be overseers."

Dated 3d of Seventh-month, 1722. Proved at Philadelphia 31 August, 1724. The witnesses being Edward George, Gainor Jones, Thomas Jones. (Will Book D, page 397.)

John and Gainor Roberts had issue: 1, Robert, b. 15th Twelfth-month, 1685; 2, Elizabeth, b. 21st First-month, 1692; d. 9th September, 1746.

ROBERT ROBERTS, only son of John and Gainor, born in Merion, 15th Twelfth-month, 1685, died in the same township, 17th March, 1768. He married at Merion Meeting, 17th of Fourth-month, 1709, Sidney Reese, daughter of Reese Evan, of Penmaen, Merionethshire, Wales. Reese Evan was son of Evan Reese, of Penmaen (Fronween), who married a daughter of John ap Thomas, of Llaethgwm, "gentleman," died 1683, son of Thomas ap Hugh ap Evan ap Rees Gôch ap Tudor ap Rees ap Evan Gôch, of Bry-

LORD OF ISALED[1].
Gules, a lion rampant, argent.

ammer, in the parish of Cerrig y Druidion, and county Denbigh, descended from Marchweithian, Lord of Isaled, Merionethshire. [Gules, a lion rampant, argent., armed and langued

---
[1] From MS. pedigree or parchment dated 1682, in possession of a descendant.

Azure.] Sidney Roberts died 29 June, 1764, aged 74 years. They were both buried at the Merion Meeting. His will has been abstracted as follows:

Will of " Robert Roberts, of the Township of Merion in the Province of Pennsylvania, being antient and Infirm of Body." Dated 4th of Seventh-month, 1764. Proved at Philadelphia 26th March, 1768.

"Unto my eldest son John, and to his heirs forever the plantation where he now lives—containing 180 acres.

Bounded on the Northward by land late of Robert Evans decd. On the westward by land late of John Griffith decd. On the Southward by the Township Line Road to the Ford road, thence by the land I sold to Rudolph Latch, to the line of John Garret's Land. Thence North Eastward by Garret's land to a corner marked Hickory tree on the line of my mother's original purchase, and from thence by land of the said John Garrett, South 64° east 76 perches to a corner stone in the said Garrett's line, thence by the land herein given and devised to my son Phineas north 66° 30′ east 76 perches to a corner stone and north 41° east 34 perches to the River Schuylkill, thence up the several courses thereof to the line of the aforesaid Robert Evans land.

To son Phineas—the remaining part of the land my father bought of Andrew Wheeler, bounded Northward by the lines mentioned dividing this from my son Johns Land, westward by John Garretts land, southward by land heretofore granted to my said son Phineas, and on the eastward by the said Schuylkill river,—Containing 30 acres."

" To my daughter Sidney Paul £50."

Remainder of Personal estate to sons John and Phineas and son in-law John Paul. Witnesses: Richard George Jr. David Lloyd John Roberts Jr. (Will Book O, page 218, etc.)

Robert and Sidney Roberts had the following children: 1, John, b. 26th Fourth-month, 1710; 2, Alban, b. 17th Seventh-month, 1712; d. 6th October, 1727; 3, Reese, b. 17th Sixth-month, 1715; d. 24 October, 1755; 4, Phineas, b. 13th of Third-month, 1722; 5, Elizabeth, b. 21st Seventh-month, 1727; 19th October, 1727; 6, Sidney, b. 9th Third-month, 1729; m. John Paul.

JOHN ROBERTS, eldest son of Robert and Sidney, born in Merion, 26th of Fourth-month, 1710; died there 13th January, 1776. He married Rebecca, daughter of Jonathan Jones (born 21 Twelfth-month, 1709–10), at Merion Meeting-House, 4th of Third-month, 1733. Jonathan Jones was son of Dr. Edward Jones (by Mary, daughter of Dr. Thomas Wynne, Speaker of the Assembly). The mother of Rebecca, and wife of Jonathan Jones, was Gainor, daughter of Robert Owen, of Merion (see that family), Justice of the Peace and member of the Provincial Assembly, died 1697. Rebecca Roberts departed this life 8 December, 1779.

John Roberts had before his death given a large part of his lands to his sons:

His will was as follows:

"John Roberts of Merion in the County of Philadelphia, in the Province of Pennsylvania, yeoman, being Indisposed of Body. Provision for wife by Lease to his son Algernon, dated 1st Sept 1775."

To her also a portion of his household goods.

"Unto my son Algernon Roberts and his heirs forever, that part of my plantation my father bought of Joseph Abraham, situate in Blockley, bounded Northward by Merion Township line to the Ford Road, Southward by the line of David George's Land and Eastward by Morten Garrett's line and on the Northeastward by the middle of the New road on Algernon Roberts line—Containing 50 acres."

A lot in Plymouth to him also.

"To said Algernon and his heirs, the messuage and plantation and all that part of the Tract of land whereon we now live above the new Road, bounded Eastward by the said new Road, Northward by Thomas Norris and John Leacocks Land, Westward by Jacob Bealert's and William Stadleman's lands, and on the Southward by Blockley Township," Containing 100 acres (after his mothers decease).

Eldest son Jonathan Roberts 27 acres and 100 perches adjoining Schuylkill in Blockley, leased " by my father to William Denny Esq.

"and also as a token of my love a silver Tankard or other Plate he may choose to the value of £20."

"To my son Benjamin Roberts £50."

"To my son John Roberts £50; son Robert Roberts £50, and my Right and share in the Library of Philadelphia."

"To my son Edward Roberts £50."

"To my daughter Elizabeth Palmer, wife of John Palmer, £40."

"To my daughter Tacey Palmer £40."

"To my grandson John Roberts, the son of Benjamin, £10."

Loving brothers Owen Jones, Jacob Jones, and my friend and kinsman James L Jones the younger Trustees.

Dated October, 1775. Proved at Philadelphia 7th February, 1776. (Will Book Q, page 249, etc.)

Witnesses: John Roberts, Miller, Rees Price, Hugh Cully.

John and Rebecca Roberts had issue: 1, Jonathan, b. 30 March, 1734; 2, Gainor, b. 30 January, 1735; d. 12 June, 1761; 3, Alban, b. 7 September, 1738; d. 24 February, 1772; 4, Elizabeth, b. 18 August, 1740; m. Thomas Palmer; d. 24 October, 1782; 5, Mary, b. 5 July, 1742; d. 23 August, 1771; 6, Tacy, b. 2 September, 1744; d. 3d August, 1791; 7, Benjamin, b. 27 August, 1746; 8, John, b. 16 November, 1747; 9, Robert, b. 10 October, 1749, d. unm.; 10, Algernon, b. 24 January, 1751; 11, Franklin, b. 27 November, 1752 (N. S.), d. 15 December, 1774; 12, Edward, b. 1 January, 1755.

ALGERNON ROBERTS, born in Merion, 24th January, 1751; died there. He was Lieutenant Colonel of the Seventh Battalion, Philadelphia County Militia, 1777.

He married at Philadelphia, by Rev. M. Hultgreen, Swedish minister, 18th January, 1781, at Old Swedes' Church, Tacy Warner, daughter of Colonel Isaac Warner, of Blockley.

Colonel Warner, of the Seventh Battalion, Philadelphia County Militia, was descended from William Warner, of Draycott, Blockley Parish, Worcestershire, England (son of John Warner), who came to Pennsylvania about 1660. (See Warner.) They had issue:

1, Rebecca, b. 26 January, 1782.

2, Lydia, b. 3d December, 1783.

3, John, b. 5 March, 1787; d. 30th January, 1837. He m. first, 12 March, 1812, Sarah Jones (b. 21 August 1791, d. 4 May, 1823), and had issue: Mary Jones, b. 26 January, 1813; d. 1 March, 1819; William Warner, b. 4 March, 1815 (m. Emily Jones); Esther Jones, b. 14 June, 1817, m. William Howell (son of William Howell and Abigail, of Trenton); Tacy, b. 23 August, 1820, m. Samuel Mattson; Sarah, b. 12 April, 1823, m. Nathan T. Clapp, who died 30 September, 1891, issue: Frank Clapp.

John Roberts married secondly, 12 May, 1830, Lydia Pratt (b. 28 May, 1794), by whom he had no issue.

4, Isaac Warner, b. 15 March, 1789; d. 19 September, 1859. He m. first 20 March, 1817, Emily Thomas (b. 29 December, 1795; d. 4 March, 1825), and had: Rebecca, b. 15 December, 1817, d. 27 January, 1895, unm.; Mary, b. 2 April, 1819; m. Col. Owen Jones, of Wynnewood (descended from Dr. Edward Jones); Gainor, b. 18 March, 1821; Emily, b. 5 July, 1823, d. 25 November, 1824.

Isaac Warner Roberts, m. secondly, 22 February, 1827, Rosalinda Evans Brooke, daughter of George and Hannah Brooke (she was b. 1 July, 1800; d. 21 June, 1873), and had by her: Algernon, d. 5 November, 1868, unm.; and George B. Roberts, m. first Sarah Lapsley Brinton, secondly Miriam Pyle Williams.

5, Gainor, b. 23 January, 1791.

6, Ann, b. 19 May, 1793.

7, Elizabeth, b. 9 August, 1795; d. 30 January, 1837; m. Miles Carpenter.

8, Algernon Sidney, b. 29 March, 1798; d. 14 September, 1865. He m. 10 April, 1823, Elizabeth, daughter Captain Anthony Cuthbert, of Philadelphia (and Mary Ogden, his wife), (she was born 22 February, 1802; died 9 December, 1891), and had by her: Mary, d. 1 June, 1831; Anthony Cuthbert, d. 10 February, 1891, m. Ellen Chase; Algernon Sydney; Percival, m. Eleanor Williamson; Elizabeth Cuthbert;

Josephine, d. 3 October, 1835; Frances Anna; George Theodore, m. Sarah Cazenore Greene.

9, Edward, b. 29 June, 1800; d. 3 November, 1872; m. May, 1825, Mary Elizabeth Reford (b. 3 August, 1801; d. 15 August, 1862), and had: Elizabeth Reford, m. Lewis S. Ware; Anna Frances, b. 7 November, 1827, d. 13 October, 1890, m. Edward Browning (and had Edward Browning, of Philadelphia); William Lehman, unm.; Edward, b. 22 September, 1832, m. Martha Price Evans; Mary Warner, m. first Stephen W. Dana, secondly Roberts C. Eskens; Adelaide, m. Daniel Francis Shaw, M. D.; Clara, m. Gôffredo Galli; Albert, b. 1 April, 1841, d. 2 April, 1842; Howard, b. April, 1843, m. Helen Pauline Davis Lewis.

10, George Washington, b. 10 June, 1802.

11, Tacy, b. 9 February, 1805.

HUGH JOHN THOMAS, OF MERION.

Hugh John, the purchaser of 156¼ acres of the Merion Company's land in 1682, is described as of Nantleidiog, Penllyn, Merionethshire, yeoman. He was a fairly prosperous man, and a member of the Society of Friends. His land, near Mill Creek, ran to the Schuylkill River, and at one time he was engaged in milling. As we have seen his deed bore date of 18 March, 1682. He is also designated in various documents, Hugh John Thomas, which is to say, Hugh, the son of John Thomas, and Hugh Jones. Presuming Hugh John to have been born about 1655, his father, John Thomas, must have been born circa. 1625. His wife may have come over with him, but if so she died soon after—but no record remains concerning her. He married secondly in Merion, Fifth-month 16th, 1686, Margaret David, of Merion, who appears to have died soon after, for he married again Eleventh-month 18th, 1693, Ann Williams, of Radnor, Spinster, at Radnor Meeting, who died 1700. He then married, Ninth-month 22d, 1703, Margaret Edwards, of Merion; and having previously removed to Plymouth, after selling all his land in Merion, he died there in 1727, leaving issue: Hugh Jones, who died in Plymouth, 1739, unmarried, and Joseph Jones, born Fourth-month 12th, 1697, of whom nothing has been ascertained.

TRAHAIRN GÔCH.
Azure, a chevron between three Dolphins naiant embowed argent.

THE OWEN FAMILY, OF MERION, IN PENNSYLVANIA, AND ALLIED LINES.

I. TRAHAIRN GOCH AP MADOC, considered the head of this genealogy, is usually described as of Llyn in Caernarvonshire, and was descended from the Princes of South Wales, being a grandson of Rhys Glôff (the lame), Lord of Cymytmaen. He appears in ministers' accounts, being mentioned as father to David Gôch, and it is probable that he died prior to the 18th year of Edward II. [1325]. He was possessed of the lands of Penllech in the hundred of Cymytmaen, in the Cantref of Llyn, and also the district called Graianog, besides numerous other lands in different parts of Caernarvonshire. It was owing to his vast possessions in the Cantref Llyn, which, beside Cymytmaen, contained the Comôts of Dinlhayn and Canolog, that he acquired the title of "O Llyn."

ELYSTAN GLODRYDD.
Gules a lion regardant or.

He married Gwenervyl, daughter of Madog ap Meurig ap Madog ap Ioreth ap Cyndel ap Elystan Glodrydd, Lord of Fferyllwg. Trahairn Gôch assumed the arms of the Lords of Cymytmaen, from whom he descended, viz.: Azure, a chevron between three dolphins naiant embowed, argent. Trahairn had issue: David Gôch, of whom presently, Trahairn Gam, Ithel Talfrith, Madog, Meredydd.

II. DAVID GOCH seems to have been the eldest son of Trahairn Gôch. The custom of gavel-kind, however, gave him only a proportion of his father's vast possessions. We find, though, that he was powerful enough to make himself both feared and respected by his warlike and troublesome neighbors. His lands probably included a large part of Penllech; with parts of the Mills of Bodwda, Newith, and Vagheys in Cymytmaen; in the hundred of Issaph he was holder of extensive farms in the ville of Nouum Burgum and neighborhood[1].

The lands of Graianog also fell to his share.

David Gôch was besides lessee of certain crown lands in Caernarvonshire.

In an ancient MS., long preserved at Rûg, in Merionethshire (Harl. MS., 1974), consisting of transcripts of ministers' accounts, etc., relating to Wales, it appears that under the designation of "DAFYDD GOCH AP TRAHAERN," he was "firmar man. ii Neugolf," i. e., lessee of the manor of Neugolf, in the hundred of Cymytmaen, in the 18th year of Edward II. (1325), and that he was living on Friday, the 9th day of November, 1329.

He married Maud[2], daughter of David Lloyd, ap Cynveloc, ap Llewelyn. According to the Visitations of the Herald Lewis Dwnn and other MS., the latter was a son of Prince David, ap Llewelyn the Great. Prince David's mother was the Princess Joanna, a natural daughter of JOHN, KING OF ENGLAND, by Agatha, daughter of Ferrers, fourth Earl of Derby.

David Lloyd's wife was Anne, daughter of "Y gwyn Lloyd, of Rhiwaedog," ap Madog, ap Rhirid Flaidd, Lord of Penllyn.

---
[1] Records of Caernarvon.
[2] Dwnn II., 175.

David Gôch had issue:
- 1. David Vaughan, of Bodreeth and Penllech, living 1352, who had four sons all of them of age in that year[1].
- 2. Ievan Gôch, of whom presently.
- 3. Meredydd, who had issue.
- 4. John Carreg Bach, of Carreg. [Hist. Powys Fadog.]

III. IEVAN GOCH appears to have been the second son; he was a man of very considerable influence, and held large possessions in Caernarvonshire. It is difficult to determine definitely the date of his birth, but it must have been circa 1312, for we find that his nephew, David Meryne, son of his brother, David Vaughan, of Penllech and Bodreeth, was of age in or before 1352, in which year he died, leaving two infant sons.

Ievan Gôch was the second man on the jury for taking the extent of the hundred of Cymytmaen, at Nevyn, on the next Thursday after the Festival of St. James the Apostle, in the 26th year of Edward III. (1352). The record of which event being as follows[2]:

> KEM. *Extenta eisdem comoti facta apud Nevyn die Jouis Px' post f'm Sci Jacobi Apli Anno r' r' E. tertij a conq'vi vicesimo sexto p. Sacrm & examinacon cui' lt ten eisdem comoti tam libos qdm nati' os & p' ea ex'a i' ota p. Sacrm Xij libos & leg' ho' i' m ei d' m com vs.*
>
> *Ithell Duy*
> *Jeuan ap David Gôch*
> *Jos ap Mad*
> *David ap Jos Vaughan*
> *lli ap Blethin*
> *Jeuan ap Atha*
> *Griffvth ap Mad*

---
[1] Records of Caernarvon.
[2] Records of Caernarvon, Ad Walliam Spectantis, 26 Edw. III, E codice MS. to Harl. 696 et 4776.

Owen Family.

Ken ap Mad
Mad Cogh
David ap lli
Mad ap Md
Jeuan ap lower

He is generally described in MS. pedigrees of families descended from him, as of Penllech and Graianog; he resided near the former ville and within, probably, the bounds of the present parish of that name, but it cannot be ascertained that on the division of his father's lands, according to the custom of "gavel-kind," any great portion of David Gôch's possessions there (in this ancient ville proper) fell to his share. He was, however, holder of many lands in the hundred of Cymytmaen and elsewhere, a part of which had been his father's.

We find him in the year 1352, second owner of the Wele "Res ap Seisilth" in the ville of Bodreeth; he had a part of the Mills of Bodwrda, Newith and Vagheys, and was one of the heirs to the ville Tyndowet in the same comot. In the hundred of Issaph he appears as heir to his father in two farms in the ville of Nouum Burgum, near to the hamlet of Merghlyn; and was also heir to the Gavel called "Gavel David Gôch." In the hundred of Meney in Anglesea he seems to have been co-heir with one Einion ap Grono, probably his cousin, to the fourth part of the Wele called "Menoowe ap Moredik," in the ville of Pothamal[1].

An interest in the lands of Graianog also remained to him.

Ievan Gôch married Eva, daughter of Einion ap Celynin, of Llwydiarth in Montgomeryshire. This Einion, under the designation of "Anian ap Celynin," had a grant from John de Charleton, Lord Powis, of Weston, in the ville of Pennayrth, in Glasmeynoc, on the Thursday after the decollation of St. John the

EINION AP CELYNIN.
Sable, a he-goat, argen

---

[1] Records Caernarvon.

Baptist, 14th year of Edward III. (1340)[1]. There is but little information concerning Ievan Gôch, subsequent to 1352, so that the date of his death is uncertain.

His brother-in-law, Llweln ap Einion, of Llwydiarth, was living as late as 7 Henry V[2].

Ievan Goch had issue:

    1. Meredydd, who inherited part of his father's lands[3].

    1. 2. Madoc, of whom presently.

    3. Morfydd, who married Meredydd, of Evionyd; he held the Lordship of Gest in the 6th of Richard II[4].

IV. MADOC AP IEVAN GOCH, of Penllech[5], a younger son, was probably born in the parish of Penllech circa 1355–60. He is described in one MS. pedigree as "*MADG AB IEVAN GOCH O PENLLECH, hynau gwyr yr YSBYTY*" (i. e., ancestor to the gentlemen of Ysputty-Ievan) in Denbighshire[6], to which place he appears to have removed. Ysputty-Ievan is a parish in the union of Llan-Rwst, composed of the townships of Tir-Ievan and Tribrys in the cômot of Isaled in Denbighshire, and the township of Eidda, in the cômot of Nant Conway, Caernarvonshire.

Some idea of the time in which Madoc lived may be gathered from the fact that his brother-in-law, Meredydd, of Evionyd, was Lord of Gest, 6 Richard II.; that his uncle, Llewelyn ap Einion, of Llwydiarth, was living 7 Henry V., and that his sister's will was proved 1416[7]. Dwnn does not give the name of his wife, and only mentions one son: Deikws Ddu.

V. DEIKWS DDU AP MADOC[1], of Ysputty-Ievan, was born circa 1395. He married, according to the Herald

---
[1] Montg. Coll., Vol. IV.
[2] Ibid.
[3] Dwnn II., 175.
[4] Montg. Coll.
[5] Dwnn II., 278–9.
[6] Ibid. II., 175.
[7] MS. Rowland E. Evans. Note to Dwnn.

Owen Family.

Lewis Dwnn, Gwen, daughter of Ievan Ddu ap Meirig ap Madog ap Gwillim ap Madog Vychan ap Madog ap Maelog Crwm, Lord of the comôt of Llechwedd Issaf, and of Creuddyn, the Promontory of the Great and Little Orme's Head. Maelog lived circa. 1175, "as Sir Thomas William's Book averreth[2];" his (Maelog's) arms were argent, on a chevron sable, three angels or.

Only one son is mentioned: Einion ap Deikws Ddu.

VI. EINION AP DEIKWS DDU, of Ysputty-Ievan, was born circa 1430, and died in or before the year 1514. His second cousin, David Vaughan, of Penllech, is mentioned in ministers' accounts, Chapter House, Westminster, in 1481, as living that year.

Einion married[3] Morvydd, daughter of Matw ap Llowarch ap Gwyn ap Llewelyn ap Meredydd ap Llewelyn ap Llowarch ap Urien ap Tegwored ap Rotpert ap Asser ap Meredydd Gôch, of Llyn, son of Collwyn ap Tangno, Lord of Llyn.

Einion had three sons: Howell Gôch, of whom presently; Ievan[4], living 1514; David, living 1514.

COLLWYN AP TANGNO.
Sable, chevron between three fleur-de-lys, argent.

VII. HOWELL AP EINION was of Ysputty-Ievan, and was living 6 Henry VIII (1514)[5]. He married Mali (Mary), daughter of Llewelyn ap Ievan ap Iolyn ap Cynwrig ap Llowarch ap Cynddelw ap Ithel Velyn ap Llewelyn Eurdorchog, of Ial, in Flintshire[6].

---

[1]Dwnn's Visitations, II., 278–9.
[2]"Lyfe William Cynwal."
[3]Dwnn, II., 278–9.
[4]MS. R. E. Evans.
[5]Dwnn II., 278–9.
[6]Llewelyn Eurdorchog was the son of Coel, ap Gweryd ap Cynddelw ap Elgud ap Gwrisnadd ap Dwyng ap Llythyraur ap Tegawg ap Dyforfrath ap Madog ap Sanddef Bryd Angel ap Llywarch Hên, Prince of the Strath Clyde Britons, and so to Brute, the first King of the island of Britain.

The mother of Mali was Dyddgu, daughter of Einion Lydan, of Foelas in Ysputty, ap Tudor ap Cynwrig ap Cadwgan ap Einion ap Llowarch ap Heilin ap Tivid ap Tangno ap Ysdwyth ap Marchwysth ap Marchweithian, Lord of Isaled in Merionethshire.

Howell had two sons:
1. Griffith ap Howell.
2. David ap Howell[1], who had John ap David, who had Wm. Cynwal, Sir Rhys Cynwal, who was Vicar of Langwm in 1591; Thomas Cynwal, and Catharine.

LLEWELYN EURDORCHOG.
Azure, a lion rampant gardant his tail between his legs and reflected over his back, or, armed and langued gules.

VIII. GRIFFITH AP HOWELL AP EINION[2]

BLEDDYN LLOYD.
Sable, a hart argent, attired and unguled, or,

of Ysputty–Ievan, was born circa 1480 to 1495, or probably as late as 1500. He married Gwenllian, daughter of Einion ap Ievan Lloyd, ap Madoc ap Ierwerth ap Llewelyn Chwith, ap Cynwrig, ap Bleddyn Lloyd of Havod Un Nos in the parish of Llangerniw in the Lordship of Rhuvoniog, ap Bleddyn Vychan, ap Bleddyn ap Gwrn ap Rhaiad Vach, descended from Hedd Molwynog, founder of the 9th Noble Tribe of Wales, a native of Denbighshire. (Sable, a hart, argent, attired and unguled or.) The mother of Gwenllian was Gwenhwyfar, daughter of Gronwy ap David, ap Griffith ap Griffith Gethin ap Cynwrig ap Gronwy ap Ierwerth ap Casswallon ap Hwva ap Ithel Velyn ap Llewelyn Awdorcbog. The mother

---
[1] Dwnn.
[2] Dwnn II., 278–9.

of Gwenhwyfar was Anne, daughter of Griffith ap Llewelyn ap Ievan ap Rhys Gethin ap Griffith Vychan ap Griffith ap David Gôch, Lord of Penmanchno, Carnarvonshire. This David Gôch was the son of David ap Griffith, Prince of Wales, who was executed 1282, by Edward I., King of England, for high treason, being hanged, drawn and quartered.

ITHEL VELYN.
Sable, on a chevron between three goats' heads, erased, or three trefoils, slipped of the field.

David Gôch married Angharad, daughter of Heilin ap Sir Tudor, Knt., of Nant and Llangynhafel, whose wife was descended from the Norman family, of Clare, and also from Robert Fitz Roy, Earl of Gloucester, natural son of Henry I., King of England.

Rhys ap Ievan, ap Llewelyn Chwith, a brother of Iorwerth, ap Ievan above mentioned, and probably also Iorwerth, was Esquire to the body of Edward IV., and "was very unruly in the Lancasterian wars." Griffith ap Howell had issue:

1. David, married Elizabeth, d. Rhys of Gerrig y Druidion. (Kerrig y Druidion, Denbg.)
2. Edward, had issue.
3. Lewis, of whom presently.
4. Catharine, married Sir Robert ap Rhys ap Sion, of Ysputty-Ievan; their son, Robert m. Ellis d. of Nicholas Mootle of Aber Conway, their d. Mary m. her cousin Sir Ievan (Evan) Lloyd ap William Lewis.

IX. LEWIS AP GRIFFITH, third son, was born circa 1525, and it is probable that he resided in Ysputty-Ievan all his life. He died prior to 1601.

He married Ellen, daughter of Edward ap Evan, Esquire, of Llanwddyn Parish, Montgomeryshire, who was son of Evan ap Tudor ap Deio ap Evan Ddu. The wife of Edward ap Evan was Catharine, daughter of Griffith ap Llewelyn ap Einion, son of David ap Evan ap Einion, the celebrated Constable of Harlech Castle (descended from the house of Cors y Gedol), whose wife, Margaret Puleston, was a descendant of Edward I. (See Cors y Gedol, and Puleston in Dwnn.)

The mother of Edward ap Evan was Morvydd, daughter of Evan ap Morris; her mother being Gwenhwyfr, daughter of Griffith ap David. The children of Lewis ap Griffith were:

1. David Lewis, married Marsley, d. David ap Rhys of Lan Uvydd, and had issue a d. and heiress.
2. William Lewis; d. prior to 1601, married Margaret d. Lewis David of Ddyfryn Cloyd, and had issue, Sir (Rev.) Ievan (Evan) Lloyd of Landav, living 1601; who had issue, Edward and Margaret, both born before 1601.
3. Evan Lewis, married Gwen, d. "William Chwaer infam ag. Edward ap Hugh Prydydd."
4. Robert Lewis, of whom presently.
5. John Lewis, died young.
6. Cadwallader Lewis, issue.

X. ROBERT LEWIS, fourth son of Lewis ap Griffith, of the parish of Ysputty-Ievan in Denbighshire, was born circa 1555. He appears to have been the first of his family to remove to Merionethshire, where he settled upon a large farm on the Rhiwlas estate, near Bala, belonging to the Price family, who also came from Ysputty-Ievan. The Parish Register of Llandderfel contains the following entry, Rhiwlas being mostly within that Parish: "Robert Lowice 14th February Sepultuo, 1645." This would make him about ninety years old at the time of his death.

He married Gwervyl, daughter of Llewelyn ap David, of Llan Rwst, Denbighshire, descendant from David Gôch, of Penmanchno, and had by her six sons and six daughters: Cadwal-

DAVID GOCH OF PENMANCHNO.
Sable, a lion rampant, argent, in a border engrailed, or

FRON GÔCH.
Home of Robert Owen, Near Bala, Wales.

lader, Thomas, John, Evan, of whom presently, Hugh, Humphrey, Lowry, Margaret, Jane, Catharine, Ellen, Margaret.

XI. EVAN ROBERT LEWIS[1], fourth son of Robert Lewis, was born in the Parish of Ysputty-Ievan, in Denbighshire, circa 1585, and died at Fron Gôch, in the Parish of Llandderfel in the Comôt of Penllyn, Merionethshire, circa 1662.

One of the early manuscript pedigrees of this family states that Evan Robert Lewis "removed from Rhiwlas to Fron Gôch." Rhiwlas is the estate of the Price family, who, as we have stated, came from Ysputty-Ievan. I am inclined to think that at the time of his decease Evan held, under lease, lands on the Price estate, near Rhiwlas village, as well as the Fron Gôch place[2].

RHIRID FLAIDD.
Vert a chevron between three wolves' heads, erased argent.

The farm called Fron Gôch is situate partly in the township of Ucheldref in Llanfor Parish and partly in the Parish of Llandderfel. The farm lands of Fron Gôch have always paid tithes to both Llandderfel and Llanfor churches. The wife of Evan Robert Lewis was named Jane, and she was probably the heiress of Fron Gôch and descended from Rhirid Flaidd, Lord of Penllyn. They had issue: John ap Evan, Cadwallader ap Evan, died unm., Owen ap Evan of whom presently, Griffith ap Evan, and Evan ap Evan, ancestor of the Gwynedd settlers. (See Evans branch, under article on Rowland Ellis.)

XII. OWEN AP EVAN, of Fron Gôch[1], near Bala, in the comôt of Penllyn, third son of Evan Robert Lewis, was born probably prior to his father's removal from Rhiwlas, which event may have occurred subsequent to 1636. Owen

---

[1]Dwnn's visit, Wales, 1601. MS. pedigree of the Owen family. MS. pedigree of the Evans family, 1750-1797, Pennsylvania.
[2]Land titles, Penllyn, Mer.

ap Evan died at Fron Gôch prior to 6th of First-month, 1678. From records extant it appears that his wife's name was Gainor John[2], and that she was living and signed the marriage settlement and marriage certificate of her son, Robert Owen, 6th of First-month, and 11th day of the same, 1678, but appears to have died 14 December of the same year, and was buried at Llanfor church, the 16th, not, apparently, being in membership with Friends. Owen and Gainor had issue, five children:

1. Robert, b. circa 1657; m. Rebecca Owen.
2. Owen, supposed to have d. s. p.
3. Evan, who remained in Wales.
4. Jane, m. Hugh Roberts.
5. Ellin, m. Cadwalader Thomas ap Hugh.

XIII. ROBERT OWEN[3], son of Owen ap Evan, of Fron Gôch, and Gainor, born at Fron Gôch, Merionethshire,

---

[1] Owen ap Evan had several brothers (see charts), of whom John ap Evan was father of William John, of Gwynedd, and of Griffith John, of Merion, early settlers in Pennsylvania. Further on it will be noticed that Robert Owen in his will mentions his "cousin Griffith John," thus confirming the account given in the old manuscript from which the above statement is partly taken. Evan ap Evan, another son of Evan Robert Lewis, was father of the Evans brothers who settled at Gwynedd. The children of Griffith John called themselves "Griffiths," and those of William, "Williams." The descendants of Owen ap Evan assumed the surname of Owen.

[2] She is supposed to have been the daughter of John Lloyd, Esquire, of Gwern y Brychdwn, in the township of Nant y Friar (see another page), and if so, was baptized in Llandderfel church, 13 September, 1629. [Llandderfel Register.]

[3] There was another Robert Owen and Jane, his wife, of Dolsereu, near Dôlgelly, Merionethshire, who came to Pennsylvania in 1684, on the "Vine," and settled on Duck Creek, New Castle (now Delaware), where a son, Edward Owen, had previously located. Robert and Jane died in 1685. They had nine sons, all of age before their arrival here, of whom I can name only Lewis, who came with them, settled on Duck Creek and left descendants, Dr. Griffith Owen, who accompanied them, and died in Philadelphia; Edward, who remained on Duck Creek and left descendants, Robert Owen, eldest son and heir, who continued to reside on the Dolserey estate, and left issue. (Register of Dôlgelly Parish Church. See Appendix.)

Wales, circa 1657; died in Merion Township, Philadelphia County, Pennsylvania, Tenth-month 8th, 1697, and was buried in the ground of the Merion Friends' Meeting on the 10th of the same month. His brother-in-law, Hugh Roberts, says of him: " He was one that feared the Lord from his youth, being convinced of the truth when about seventeen years of age . . . traveling several times through his native country, Wales, where he was of good service: In 1690 he came into Pennsylvania, where he lived about seven years, visiting this and the adjacent provinces, and was also very useful in the meeting where he resided, . . . a man of peace, hating all appearance of contention, endued with wisdom and authority, yet merciful unto the least appearance of good in such as he had to do withal."

Regarding his earlier life in Merionethshire many particulars have been obtained. The following from " Besse's Sufferings of Friends," Vol. I., p. 755, is the first mention we have of him as a Quaker: "Anno 1674, on the 3d day of the month called May, John David, Robert David, Robert Owen, Cadwallader Thomas, and Hugh Roberts were taken by the Sheriff with a process and committed to Dolgelly Goale, being indicated at sessions some time before for their being absent from National Worship." " Robert Owen, of Vron Goch," was one of those Quakers fined for meeting at Llwyn y Braner, in the parish of Llanvawr, May 16, 1675, together with his two sisters, Elin, who afterwards married Cadwallader Thomas ap Hugh; and Jane, wife of Hugh Roberts. His younger brother, " Evan Owen ye son of a widdow called Gainor, whose late husband was Owen ap Evan of Vron Goch," was also present at a meeting, " though but 9 or 10 years old."

Robert was appointed one of the overseers of the will of John Thomas, of Llaithgwm, which document is dated 9th February, 1682, and was executed in Wales, but probated in Pennsylvania in the year 1688. He is described therein as " Robert Owen late of fron goch neer Bala in the County of Merionyth." Subsequent to this date, however, I find him still a resident of the parish of Llanddervel in Merionethshire[1]. On the 8th day of the Sixth-month (August), 1690, the Quarterly Meeting of Friends held at Tyddyn y Garreg, Merionethshire, granted a certificate of removal to this Robert Owen[2]. This certificate is of record in Book 1st, pp. 286–87 of the Merion, Radnor and Haverford Meeting, and is as follows:

To o^e Friends & Brothers in the Province of Pennsylvania.

These are to certifie, as occasion shall require, unto whom it may concern in the behalf of o^e dearly beloved friende & Brother Robt. Owen & Rebecca his wife & their dear & tender children. That they are faithful & beloved friends, well known to be serviceable unto Friends & brethren since they have (become convinced), of a Savory & Blameless conversation. Alsoe are psons Dearly beloved & Respected of all sorts. His testimony sweet & tender, reaching to the quicking seed of life, of a meek, quiet & gentle Behavior; we cannot alsoe but bemoan the want of his company, being he was near and dear unto us & seasonable in intention for Pennsylvania many months before his removal, now seeing it remaineth still on his mind, & in order therein unto finding his way clear & freedom in the truth according to the measure manifested unto him, wē thought it o^e duty to commend him unto you as o^e dear & faithfull friend & brother, and hereby desiring their faithfull services in the truth may increase & abound among you to their endless joy without end.

Att o^e quarty. Meeting att Tyddyn y Garreg in Merionethshire the eight of the six month in the year 1690.

Ellis Morris
Hugh David
Rowland Ellis
Jn. Evan
Hugh Rees

Rowland Owen
H Cumphrey Owen[3]

---

[1] Besse.

[2] He appears as a witness to sundry deeds executed in Merionethshire in 1682, and recorded in Philadelphia, 1684, in Deed Book C I, for land in Pennsylvania, viz.: "John Thomas, of Llaethgwm, Merioneth, yeoman," to "Edward Jones, of Bala Chyrurgeon," dated 1st April. "Edward Jones, of Bala, to Hugh Roberts, of the township of Ciltalgarth, yeoman," dated the last day of February.

[3] Humphrey Owen's signature does not appear of record on the original entry in the Merion, Radnor and Haverford records, but he is believed to have signed the original certificate.

Robert Vaughan	Ellin Ellis
Rees Thomas	Jane Robt.
Rees Evan	Margaret Robt.
David Jones	Ann Rowland
Evan Owen	Gainor Jones
Regnald (Rowland?)	Rowland Owen
Humphrey	Lewis Owen
Margaret David	Owen Lewis
Jonett Johnes	Griffitt Robt.
Elizabeth Jones	Evan Rees

Some time before this, 11th of First-month, 1678–9, Robert Owen had married, according to Friends' ceremony, Rebecca Owen, daughter of Owen Humphrey (or Humphreys), Esquire, a gentleman who "had a good and indefeisible estate of inheritance" called Llwyn-du, in the township of Llwyngwrill and parish of Llangelynin, Talybont, Merionethshire, which he had succeeded to in or about 1664[1]. The agreement concerning a marriage settlement was executed on the 6th of First-month, 1678, between Gainor John, mother of Robert Owen, and Owen Humphrey. The bond of this contract, "Owen Humphrey de Llwundu" to "Robt Owen de vron goch com^t Penllin, gener." (gentleman), dated as above, is extant. The witnesses were, Rowland Ellis, Edward Vaughan, John ap Thomas, Cadwallader Thomas.

The following is a copy of the marriage certificate, the original of which is still in the possession of a descendant, Mrs. Mary A. Haines, of Rosemont, Pennsylvania:

Be it Knowen by these p'esents unto all whom it may concern that upon the eleventh day of the first month 1678–9

---

[1] Owen Humphrey was the son of Humphrey ap Hugh, died circa 1664, ap David ap Howell ap Gronwy ap Einion; descended from the families of Llwydiarth, Nannau and Tal y Llyn, Herbert, and the English families of Stanley, Clifford, Mortimer, Strange, and from Edward III. See Humphrey.

Robt. Owen Eldest son of Owen ap Evan (deceased) late of Vron gôch in the comot of Penlin & in the County of Merioneth hath taken Rebeccah Owen first daughter of Owen Humphrey of Llwyn du in the Comt. of Talybont in the County aforsd to be his wife & that by the free Assent & consent of their parents & near relations & friends of the truth, And that according to the example & practice of primitive Christians followers of the truth. And the sd Rebeckah in like manere hath taken sd Robt. Owen to be her husband The day & yeare above written in the P'esence & sight of us the witnesses hereunder written.

Owen Humphrey her father
Cadd[r] Thomas[1]
Rowland Ellis[2]
Hugh Robert[3]
Humphrey Owen[4]
Rowland Owen[5]
Edward Vaughan
Ellis Rees[6]
Evan John[7]
Rees Evan
John Thomas
John Humphrey[8]
Humphrey Reynolds
John Howell[9]
Daniel Samuel[10]
Rees John[11]

John William
John Owen[12]
Joseph Samuel[13]
Richard Humffrey[14]
Elizabeth Thomas
Hannah (Prichard?)
Ellin Rees
Gwen Rees
Anne Owen
Elizabeth Owen
Gainor John
Lydia Samuel
Rebecca Samuel
Gobeithia
Elizabeth Owen.

After his coming to Pennsylvania his name is of continual occurrence as executor, administrator, or trustee, or as party to some agreement. He is described in one of these documents, dated 30th May, 1696, as "Robert Owen, of Merion-

---

[1] Father of John Cadwalader, and husband to Ellen Owen, sister to Robt. Owen.
[2] Nephew of Owen Humphrey, and cousin to Rebecca Owen.
[3] Husband of Jane, sister to Robert Owen.
[4] Brother of Rebecca.
[5] Brother of Rebecca.
[6] Father of Rowland Ellis.
[7] Son of John William ap Humphrey, of Llangelynin.
[8] Brother of Owen Humphrey.
[9] From Llanwddlyn, Montgomeryshire; cousin of Owen Humphrey.
[10] Alias Daniel Humphrey, son of Samuel Humphrey, deceased.
[11] Rees John William.
[12] Brother to Rebecca.
[13] Brother to Daniel.
[14] Brother-in-law to John Humphrey.

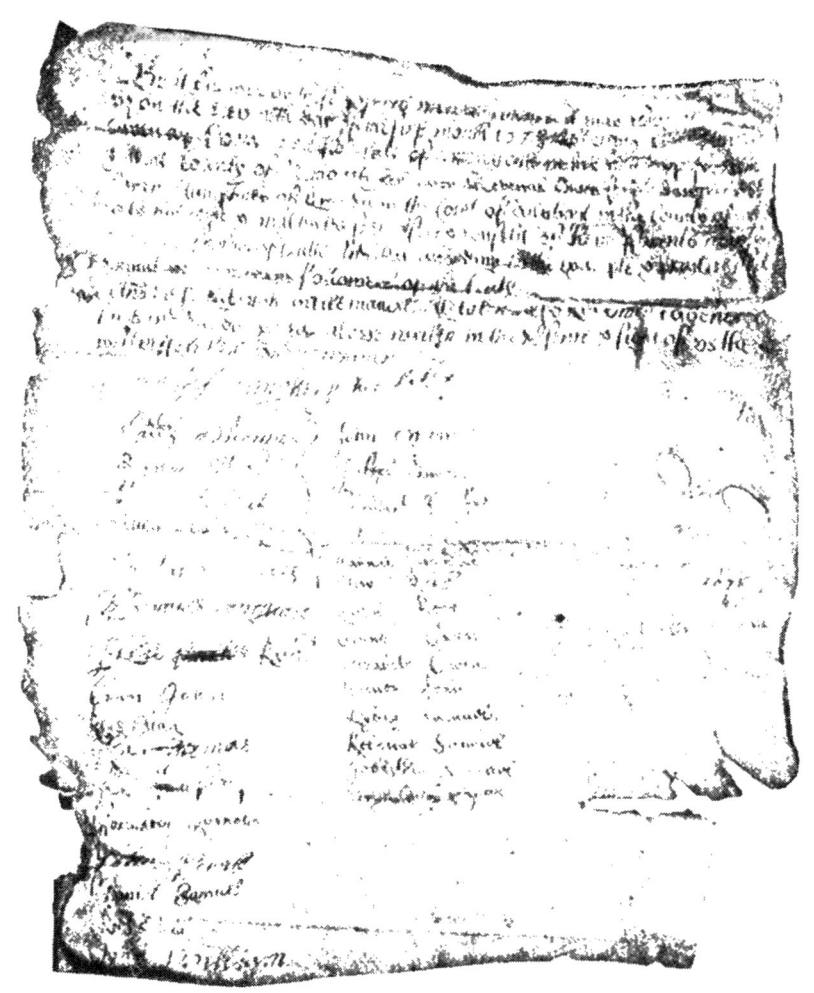

MARRIAGE CERTIFICATE OF ROBERT AND REBECCA OWEN, 1678-9.

eth, in the County of Philadelphia, in the Province of Pennsylvania, Yeoman," and is grantee in a deed from Thomas Lloyd[1], dated "the fifth day of the sixth month, Anno Dom. 1691," for a tract of land containing four hundred and forty-two acres, situate in "the Township of Merion," in Philadelphia County, the consideration being one hundred pounds. This "plantation," as it was then called, lay west of the present Wynnewood Station, on the Pennsylvania Railroad, and extended to near the present village of Ardmore. It was confirmed to Evan Owen, eldest son and heir to Robert, by patent[2] from Penn's Commissioners, dated 8th February, 1704, "Together with the Messuage or Tenement, Plantation, . . . Houses, Barns, Buildings, Gardens, Orchards, Woods, Underwoods, Ways, Waters, Meadows, Water-courses, Fishings, Fowlings, Hawkings, Huntings, Rights, Liberties." By a deed dated 31st December, 1707[3], "Evan Owen, of the Township of Merion, in the County of Philadelphia, and Province of Pennsylvania, yeoman, son and heir of Robert Owen, late of Merion, yeoman, deceased," conveyed this farm, devised to him by his father, to his brother-in-law, "Jonathan Jones, of Merion, yeoman." A manuscript by Owen Jones, grandson of Robert Owen, says[4], "He purchased a large tract of land about nine miles from the city of Philadelphia, in the township of Lower Merion. Here he built a large, commodious dwelling-house, and resided in it during the remainder of his life. He had children, viz., Gainor, Evan, Owen, Elizabeth, John and Robert, some of whom were born in Wales." This house is yet standing, and compares favorably with many of the modern dwellings erected near it. The date is carved on a corner-stone, "1695." Robert Owen was a Justice of the Peace for Merion, and by 1695 had, says this old manuscript, "gained the confidence of the people in general, which they manifested by making choice of him to repre-

---

[1] Deed Book E2, Vol. V., p. 174, etc., Philadelphia.
[2] Patent Book A, Vol. III., p. 241, Harrisburg, Pennsylvania.
[3] Deed Book E4, Vol. VII., p. 40, etc., Philadelphia.
[4] "Memoir of Charles J. Wister."

sent them in the Assembly of the Province of Pennsylvania (elected again, 1697), . . . which position he filled with much reputation. It pleased Divine Providence to remove his beloved wife in the year 1697 (died 8th mo. 23d, buried 25th), which severe trial he survived but a few weeks."

Robert, as already stated, outlived his wife—whom he had loved long and tenderly—but a short time, and was buried beside her. Among the eminent Friends whose bones lie near his, scarcely one has left a more stainless, and none a more honored, name. His will, dated "10th mo. 2d day, 1697," was probated May 16, 1705[1]. He left his plantation in Merion to his eldest son, Evan Owen, and speaks of his other children without mentioning their names. He appoints as overseers John Humphreys, Hugh Roberts, John Roberts, Griffith John, Robert Jones, Robert Roberts, Robert Lloyd, and Rowland Ellis, and appoints his "cousin Griffith John above named" as sole executor. The witnesses were Joshua Owen, Robert Jones, and Rowland Ellis. John Owen, described elsewhere as "ye 2nd son of Owen Humphreys of Llwyndu," in Merionethshire, and brother to Joshua, above named, subsequently acted as an appraiser. Robert Owen's important services as a minister among Friends must not be overlooked. He was one of the founders of the Merion Meeting, and a trustee thereof, as appears by a deed dated 20th Sixth-month, 1695, Edward Rees[2], of Merion, yeoman, to Robert Owen, Edward Jones, Cadwallader Morgan, and Thomas Jones, of Merion, yeoman, in trust, for one-half acre of land in Merion, "for the purposes of the Merion Meeting." As early as 28th June, 1692, Robert Owen, with Thomas Lloyd, Nicholas Waln, Dr. Griffith Owen, Hugh Roberts, John Symcock, William Byles, and others, the then ministers at or near Philadelphia, signed the communication of the Meeting of Friends in Philadelphia, to the Monthly Meetings of Friends in Pennsylvania, and East and

---
[1] Register of Wills' Office, Philadelphia.
[2] This was Edward Rees, alias Prees and Price, see elsewhere.

THE OWEN HOUSE,
Near Wynnewood, Pa.

Owen Family.

West Jersey, setting forth their displeasure and sorrow at the action of Keith, who was making himself obnoxious to Friends about this time. Perhaps the last documents, executed the year of his death, 1697, that in any way concerned Robert, are an agreement of his with one Evan Harry concerning the estate of Cadwallader Lewis, deceased, of which Robert Owen was appointed by the court administrator, " Letters of Attorney[1], Richard Davies of Cloodie Cochion, Welchpoole (Montgomeryshire), gentleman," to Robert Owen *et al.*, his "true and lawful attys.," date 1st mo. 8th, 1696–7, and a letter from him to Hugh Roberts, then traveling in Wales, dated 24th of Second-month, 1697. So far as can be ascertained at this late day, Robert and Rebecca Owen had but eight children; or, if there were others, their early decease in Wales renders their existence of little interest. Of these eight, the first four—Evan, Gainor, Elizabeth, and Jane—were born in Merionethshire, and are the "tender children" mentioned in the certificate of removal. The rest were born in Merion Township, Philadelphia County, Pennsylvania, as appears by the record of their births in the "Book of Births" of the Radnor Monthly Meeting, and there mentioned as children "of Robert and Rebeckah Owen." Their births are also noted in records of said Meeting as "Births in Merion Meeting." The eight were:

1. Gainor, b. 1681; m. Jonathan Jones.
2. Evan, b. 1683; m. Mary Hoskins.
3. Jane, b. 1685.
4. Elizabeth, b. 1687; m. *Jane Owen* David Evans.
5. Owen, b. 12 mo. 21st, 1690; m. Anne Wood.
6. John, b. 12 mo. 26th, 1692; m. Hannah Maris.
7. Robert, b. 7 mo. 27th, 1695; m. Susanna Hudson.
8. Rebecca, b. 1 mo. 14th, 1697; d. inft.; buried 9 mo. 21st, 1697[2].

---

[1] Exemplification Book 4, p. 677, Philadelphia.
[2] "Burials at Merion Meeting," Records of Radnor Monthly Meeting of Friends.

XIII. JANE, daughter of Owen ap Evan, of Fron Gôch, and Gainor, born at Fron Gôch, 1653–4; died in Merion Township, Philadelphia County, Pennsylvania, 7th mo. 1st, 1686, and buried 3d of same month. She married, in Merionethshire, 1672–3, " Hugh Roberts, of the township of Kiltalgarth, parish of Llanvawr, Merionethshire, yeoman." He was a prominent minister among Friends, and afterwards a Provincial Councillor of Pennsylvania. Their certificate of removal from the comôt of Penllyn, is dated "ye 2nd of 5 mo., 1683," and they settled upon about six hundred acres of land in Merion. All of their children, except Elizabeth, were born in the township of Kiltalgarth, but a record of their births has been preserved in the archives of the Merion, Pennsylvania, Monthly Meeting of Friends. They were as follows :

1. Robert, b. 11 mo. 7th, 1673; m. 1st Catharine Jones; 2ndly, Priscilla Johnes.
2. Ellin, b. 10 mo. 4th, 1675.
3. Owen, b. 10 mo. 1st, 1677; m. Ann Bevan.
4. Edward, b. 2 mo. 4th, 1680; m. 1st Susanna Painter; 2ndly, Martha Hoskins; 3rdly Martha Cox.
5. William, b. 3 mo. 26th, 1682; d. 1697 in Pennsylvania.
6. Elizabeth, b. 12 mo. 24th, 1683.

XIII. ELLIN, second daughter of Owen ap Evan, of Fron Gôch, and Gainor, born at Fron Gôch, circa 1660; died in Merionethshire prior to 1697. She married, subsequent to 16th May, 1675, Cadwallader Thomas ap Hugh, of the township of Kiltalgarth, in Llanvawr, Merionethshire. He was the son of Thomas ap Hugh ap Evan ap Rees Gôch ap Tudor ap Rees ap Evan Coch, of Bryammer, in the parish of Gerrig y drudion, Denbighshire, derived from Marchwerthian, Lord of Issallt, who

bore Gules, a lion rampt., arg., armed and langued azure. Cadwallader Thomas died prior to the 9th February, 1682, as appears by the will of his brother, John Thomas, of Laithgwn, "gentleman," dated as above, and proved in Philadelphia, 1688. Cadwallader had issue by Ellin, two sons and two daughters:
1. Thomas Cadwallader, living 9th Feb., 1682.
2. John Cadwallader, born prior to 1682; removed to Pennsylvania and became ancestor to the Cadwalader family of Philadelphia. He was a member of the Provincial Assembly, and his son, Dr. Thomas Cadwalader, was a Councillor. See Cadwalader Genealogy.
3. Elizabeth.
4. Katherine.

XIV. EVAN OWEN, eldest son and heir of Robert and Rebecca, born in Merionethshire, Wales, 1682–3; died at Philadelphia, Pennsylvania, 1727. Letters were granted on his estate to Mary, his widow, 27th October, that year. He married 10th mo. 11th, 1711, Mary, daughter of Dr. Richard Hoskins. The record of their marriage says, "Evan Owen, son of Robert, of Merion Township, Philadelphia County, yeoman, deceased, and Mary Hoskins, daughter of Richard, practitioner of physick, deceased. . . Philadelphia Meeting." The witnesses were Owen, John and Robert Owen, Gainor Jones, John and Martha Cadwalader, and forty-seven others. Evan Owen, having sold his Merion land to his brother-in-law, Jonathan Jones, removed to Philadelphia, and was admitted to the freedom of the city in April, 1717; neither he nor his brother Robert, who was admitted with him, gave any occupation. He (Evan) became a member of Common Council, 1717, and was appointed a Justice of the Peace of the Philadelphia County Courts, 1723, serving until his decease. He was Justice of Court of Common Pleas, Quarter Sessions, and Orphans' Court, commissioned 18th February, 1723. Became Associate Justice of the City Court and Alderman, 6th October, 1724. Justice of Orphans' Court from 5th December, 1724; was a Master of the Court of Equity, 1725; Treasurer of Philadelphia County from 1724 to his death. Became a member of the Provincial Assembly, 1725, and Provincial Councillor of Pennsylvania, 1726, being a Justice of the Court of Chancery the same year. While serving as a member of the Assembly, Evan Owen was, as we have seen, called to the Provincial Council, the Lieutenant-Governor expressing a desire to have another Quaker at the board, and Preston and Fishbourne, whose advice was asked, recommended him. He asked to be excused until the expiration of the sessions of the Assembly, but appears to have qualified, as there is a note to the minutes of the first meeting he afterwards attended, which was during Gordon's term, that he had qualified in Keith's time. Perhaps Evan's most important trust was as a Trustee of the Society of Free-Traders, who had purchased several thousand acres in Pennsylvania. The records of the Arch Street, Philadelphia, Monthly Meeting show the births of four children of Evan and Mary, and the death of one. They were:

1. Robert, d. 10 mo. 9th, 1712.
2. Robert, b. 10 mo. 12th, 1712; d. s. p.
3. Martha, b. 4 mo. 12th, 1714.
4. Esther, b. 9 mo. 18th, 1716; m. 1743, William Davis[1].
5. Aurelius, b. 1 mo. 1st, 1718; d. 5 mo. 2d, 1721.

XIV. GAINOR OWEN, daughter of Robert and Rebecca, born in Merionethshire, died in Pennsylvania. She married, 8th mo. 4th, 1706, Jonathan, son of Dr. Edward Jones, of Merion, by Mary, daughter of Dr. Thomas Wynne, of Bronvedog, near Caerwys, Flintshire. Gainor is described as being "much beloved by her neighbors, a friend to the poor." They had eleven children; surname Jones:

---

[1] Register of Christ's Church, Philadelphia.

Owen Family.

1. Mary, b. 14th 5 mo., 1707; m. Benjamin Hayes.
2. Edward, b. 7th 7 mo., 1708; d. unm.
3. Rebecca, b. 20th 12 mo., 1709; m. John Roberts.
4. Owen[1], b. 19th 9 mo., 1711; m. Susanna[2] Evans, and had a large family, for whose descendants see Dr. Edward Jones, of Merion, and the genealogy of Hannah Jones, who married Amos Foulke.
5. Ezekiel Jones, supposed by his father to have d. s. p.
6. Jacob, b. 14th 5 mo., 1713; m. Mary Lawrence.
7. Jonathan, b. 29th 4 mo., 1715; m. Sarah Jones.
8. Elizabeth, m. 1758, Jesse George.
9. Martha, b. 6th 3 mo., 1717.
10. Hannah, b. 28th 11 mo., 1718–9.
11. Charity, b. 4th 8 mo., 1720.

---

[1] He was Colonial Treasurer of Pennsylvania.
[2] Called "Ann" in one genealogy, which was probably a nick-name.

MARRIAGE CERTIFICATE JOHN AND SARAH [OWEN] BIDDLE, 1736.—Whereas John Biddle of the City of Philadelphia, in the Province of Pennsylvania, son of William Biddle of Mansfield, in the County of Burlington in the Province of New Jersey; and Sarah Owen, daughter of Owen Owen of the said city: Having declared their intentions of Marriage with each other before several Monthly Meetings of the People called Quakers at Philadelphia aforesaid, according to the good order us'd amongst them, and having consent of Parents, their proposal of Marriage was allowed of by the said Meetings: NOW these are to certify whom it may concern, that for the full accomplishing their said intentions, this Third day of the First month in the year of our Lord, One thousand seven hundred and thirty-six: They the said John Biddle and Sarah Owen appeared in a publick meeting of the said people of Philadelphia aforesaid, and the said John Biddle taking the said Sarah Owen by the Hand did in solemn manner openly declare that He took Her, the said Sarah Owen to be his Wife, promising with the Lord's assistance to be unto Her a Loving and Faithful Husband until Death should separate them: and then and there in the same assembly, the said Sarah Owen did likewise declare that she took Him, the said John Biddle to be her Husband, in like manner promising to be unto Him a Loving and Faithful Wife until Death should separate them: And moreover They, the said John Biddle and Sarah Owen (she according to the custom of Marriage assuming the name of her Husband), as a further confirmation thereof did then and there to these presents set their Hands, and we who hereunto subscribe our names being present at the solemnization of the said Marriage and Subscription as witnesses thereunto set our Hands the Day and Year above written.

Sam'l Preston	Sam'l Norris	Margaret Preston	Thos Cadwalader	Michael Biddle	Rebecca Evans	John Biddle
William Hudson	Sam'l Burge	Beulah Coates	Rees Roberts	Clayton Biddle	Mary Roberts jr	Sarah Biddle
Henry Cliffton	William Horne	Mary Emlen	R'd Brockden		Rebecca Scull	Owen Owen
John Jones	Edward Scull	Hannah Hudson	Cadwalader Foulke		Jonathan Jones	Ann Owen
Jonathan Corkshaw	Jacob Lewis	Phebe Morris	Mary Foulke		Gainor Jones	Mary Biddle
Anth'y Morris	Wm Shippen	Eleanor Bevan			Jane Wood	Penelope Whitehead
Dennis Rackford	Stephen Vidal	Hannah Lewis			Wm Biddle	Nicholas Scull
Daniel Cheston	Jos. Morris jr	Susanna Shippen				Abigail Scull
Isaac Griffit	Nicho: Scull	Hannah Cadwalader				Robert Owen
Isaiah Foulke	Jona'th Evans	Hannah Morris				Rebecca Owen
Ephraim Parker	Charles Jenkins	Elizabeth Dickenson				Tacy Owen
		Elizabeth Morris				Jane Owen
		Amy Lawrence				Martha Owen
		Sydney Evans				Mary Jones
		Sarah Evans}				Hannah Owen
		Ann Brockden				Rachel Owen
		Letitia Brockden				
		Mary Roathford				

MARRIAGE CERTIFICATE OF OWEN AND ANNE [WOOD] OWEN, 1714.—Whereas Owen Owen of Upper Dublin in the County of Philadelphia, and Province of Pennsylvania, Yeoman, and Ana Wood, daughter of John Wood of Darby in the County of Chester, and Province aforesaid, Yeoman, having declared their Intentions of Marriage with each other before Severall Monthly Meetings of the people called Quakers in Darby aforesaid, according to the good order used amongst Them, Whose proceedings therein after a Deliberate Consideration thereof, and having the Consent of Parents & Relations concerned; Nothing appearing to obstruct was approved of by the said Meetings. Now these are to Certifie all whom it may Concern That for the full accomplishment of their said Intentions this twenty third day of the first Month In the year of Our Lord One Thousand Seven Hundred and Fourteen, They, the said Owen Owen & Anne Wood appeared in a publick meeting of the said people for the purpose appointed at the Meeting house in Darby aforesaid, and the said Owen Owen Taking the said Anne Wood by the Hand, Did in a Solemn manner openly Declare that he Took her to be his wife, Promising to be unto her a Loving and ffaithful Husband till Death should Separate them. And then & there in the saic Assembly, The said Anne Wood Taking the said Owen Owen by the hand did in Like manner Declare that she Took him to be her Husband, Promising to be to him a ffaithful and Loving wife till itt should please the Lord by death to separate Them. AND Moreover, the said Owen Owen & Anne Wood (she according to the custom of Marriage assuming the name of her husband) as a ffurther Confirmation Thereof Did then & there to these present set their hands.

Owen Owen
Anne Owen

And we whose names are hereunto subscribed being amongst others present at the Solemnization of the said Marriage and Subscription in manner aforesaid, as witnesses Thereunto have sett our hands the Day and Year above written.

John Blunston	Josiah Hibberd	Rose Bethell	Owen Roberts	John Wood
Griffith Owen	Thomas Paschall	Anna Sellers	Anne Roberts	Rebecca Wood
John Smith	James Hunt	Margaret Blunston	John Cadwalader	Evan Owen
Rowland Ellis	Geo. Claypoole	Agnes Salkeld	Martha Cadwalader	John Owen
John Salkeld	Evan Harry	Margaret Paschall	Edward Roberts	Robert Owen
John Roberts	Edward Cadwalader	Jane Garratt	James Hunt	Joshua Owen
Caleb Pusey	Thomas Jones	Katherine Jones	John Jones	Evan Bevan
Edward Jones	John Bethell	Ellin Jones	Tho's Lloyd	Eliner Bevan
John Smith	Rob't Roberts	Phebe Pulford	John Blunston junr	Jonathan Jones
Thomas Worth	Rich'd Jones	Elizabeth Pulford	Obadiah Bonsall	Gainer Jones
Samuel Bradshaw	Hugh Evans	Phebe Blunston	Rich'd Parker	David Evans
Samuell Garrett	Owen Evans	Hannah Parker	William Smith	Eliz'a Evans
David Thomas	Moses Roberts	Sarah Hunt	Aubray Wood	George Wood
Benja. Cliffe	John Davids	Jane Jones	Joanna Paschall	William Wood
Josiah ffearne	John Marshall	Rachel Wharton	Sarah Thomas	Barbra Wood
John Worth	Thomas Paschall junr	Mary Wharton	Mary Smith	Mary ffawsitt
John Marshall	Evan Thomas	Hannah Clemison	Thos Worth	Benjamin Bonsall
Thomas Edwards	Job Harvey	Martha Bonsall	Eliz. Hallowell	Dabiel hiberd
		Rachall hiberd	Enoch Bonsall	Renakah Huntt
		Ellin Bonsall		John Wood junr
		Martha Parker		Barbra Bevan
		Anne Blunston		Abraham Wood

XIV. ELIZABETH OWEN, daughter of Robert and Rebecca, born in Merionethshire, Wales; died at Philadelphia, Pennsylvania, 22d 10th mo., 1753. She married David Evans, of Philadelphia, "gentleman," Deputy Sheriff of Philadelphia, 1714–21. His will is dated September 27, 1745. They had six children; surname Evans:

1. Evan, d. prior to 1762; issue, Sidney, David, Rebecca.
2. Rebecca, d. unm.
3. Sidney, m. 4 mo. 26th, 1759, Joseph Howell, of Chester.
4. Sarah, d. unm. Will d. 14 July, 1762; proved 21 December.
5. David, d. 11 mo. 18th, 1725.
6. Margaret, d. unm. 4 mo. 12th, 1734.

XIV. OWEN OWEN, second son of Robert and Rebecca, born in the township of Merion, Philadelphia County, 21st 12th mo., 1690; died at Philadelphia, 5th 8th mo., 1741. Will dated 4th 5th mo., 1741; proved 11th August, 1741. He married, 23d[1] 3d mo., 1714, Anne Wood, who died 2d mo. 4th, 1743. He was High Sheriff of Philadelpha from 4th October, 1726, and Coroner, 1729 to 1741. The *Pennsylvania Gazette*, August 6, 1741, says, " Yesterday died after a long illness, Owen Owen, Esquire; formerly High Sheriff, and for many years Coroner of this city and county." Owen and Anne had five children:

1. Robert.
2. Jane, m., 1760, Dr. Cadwallader Evans, who d. s. p., 1773.
3. Sarah, m. John Biddle; d. 1 mo. 1st, 1773. (See Biddle Branch.)
4. Tacey, m., 1744, Daniel Morris, of Upper Dublin, Pa.
5. Rebecca, d. unm., 10th December, 1755.

---

[1]Stated as 13th in one document.

...tt fifty pounds for ye towards ye maintenance & preferrment of my other children which summe I doe whereby referr to ye discret[i]on of my herein after named trustees for ye shareing & dividinge among the[m] as they find convenient & see cause

I doe constitute nominate & appoint my trustee & vnto[?] ... Cosen Edward Lloyd, Hugh Roberts, John Roberts, Griffith John, Robert Jones, Robert Roberts, Robert Lloyd, & Rowland Ellis to be trustees & overseers of this my will & testament, And doe hereby give full power & for my fore menc[i]oned friends to in my trusty to manage & dispose of me & estate according to ye true intent and meaning of this my will & testament, and to set & profitt & abrouation of my Children.

Lastly I doe nominate & appoint my well beloved Cosin Griffith John aforenamed to be sole Executr of this my last will & testament and doe hereby revoke & annull & make void all former wills by me heretofore made In witness whereof I have here vnto sett my hand & seal the second day of ye tenth month In ye year 1697

Signed sealed & published
in ye sight & p[rese]nce of

Jona: Owen
Humphrey Ellis
...

Robᵗ [seal]

XIV. JOHN OWEN, third son of Robert and Rebecca, born in Merion Township, Philadelphia County, 12th mo. 26th, 1692; died in Chester County, 1752. Will proved 23d January that year. He removed from Philadelphia to Chester in 1718. He married, 8th mo. 22d, 1719, Hannah, daughter of George Maris, Provincial Councillor and a Colonial Justice of Pennsylvania, the marriage being recorded as follows in the books of the Chester Monthly Meeting of Friends: "John Owen, son of Robert, of Merion, Philadelphia County, yeoman, deceased, and Hannah Maris, daughter of George of Chester, yeoman." The witnesses were Evan, Robert and Owen Owen, George Maris, Sr., and forty-four others.

John Owen was High Sheriff for the county of Chester, 4th October, 1729–31; 3d October, 1735–37; 4th October, 1743–45; 8th October, 1749–51. He was elected a member of the Provincial Assembly of Pennsylvania at periods extending from 1733–1748; was collector of excise for Chester, 1733–37, and for many years one of the trustees of the Loan Office of Pennsylvania. He had issue by Hannah, his wife—five children[1]:

1. Jane, m. Joseph West.
2. George, m., 1751, Rebecca Hains; d. at Philadelphia s. p., 1764. Will proved 28th September that year.
3. Elizabeth, m. James Rhoads.
4. Rebecca, m. 8 mo. 22d, 1754, Jesse Maris.
5. Susanna, m. Josiah Hibbard.

XIV. ROBERT OWEN, fourth son of Robert and Rebecca, born in Merion Township, Philadelphia County, 7th mo. 27th, 1695; died circa 1730. He married, 11th mo. 10th, 1716–17, Susanna, daughter of William Hudson, Mayor of Philadelphia and Justice of the Orphans' Court, by Mary, his first wife, daughter of Samuel Richardson, Provincial Councillor and a Justice of Pennsylvania. The following is an ab-

---

[1] For descendants, see "History of Maris Family, of Pennsylvania."

stract of the original record of their marriage certificate[1]: "Robert Owen, son of Robert, late of Merion, Philadelphia County, yeoman, deceased," and "Susanna Hudson, daughter of William, of the city of Philadelphia," at Philadelphia Meeting. The witnesses were William, Hannah, Samuel, William, Jr., John, Hannah, and Rachel Hudson, Evan, Mary, John, and Owen Owen, and fifty others.

Along with his brother Evan, the Councillor, Robert Owen was admitted to the "freedom of the city" in April, 1717, and continued to reside there until his decease. His widow married, 3d mo. 2d, 1734[2], John Burr, of Northampton, Burlington County, New Jersey, and died at Philadelphia, 3d mo. 4th, 1757[3].

Robert Owen is grantee in a deed[4] dated "24th May, in 4th year of the reign of our Sovereign Lord George, King of Great Britain, and in the year of our Lord 1718," for a lot of ground "fronting 28 feet on Walnut St., and in length to formly the 30 foot cartway under the bank of the Delaware, called King Street, 58 feet" and "with North and West, the Smithshop & ground of Robert Jones, Eastward by Samuel Carpenter's Warehouse."

Robert and Susanna had three daughters, whose births are thus noted in the original book of record of the Arch Street, Philadelphia, Monthly Meeting of Friends:

    1. "Mary Owen, daughter of Robert & Susanna Owen, was born in Philadelphia ye 3d day of ye $\frac{3}{mo}$: 1719." She d. young.

    2. "Hannah Owen, daughter of Robert & Susanna Owen, was born in Philadelphia ye 16th day of ye $\frac{3}{mo}$: 1720." She m. 1st, John Ogden; 2ndly, Joseph Wharton.

---

[1] Philadelphia (Arch Street) Friends' Monthly Meeting Records, Book A, p. 91, No. 188.
[2] Philadelphia (Arch Street) Friends' Monthly Meeting Records, Book A, p. 131, No. 259.
[3] She was born 12th mo. 17th, 1698-9.
[4] Deed Book F1, p. 251, etc., Philadelphia.

Owen Family. 139

 3. "Rachel Owen, daughter of Robert & Susanna Owen, was born in Philadelphia ye 19th day of ye $\frac{6}{mo}$: 1724." Living unm. 1740.

XV. Mary, first daughter of Jonathan and Gainor Jones, born in Merion Township, 14th 5th mo., 1707; married at Merion Meeting, 10th mo. 2d, 1737, Benjamin Hayes, son of Richard, of Haverford, "yeoman." They had one child:
  Elizabeth, b. 7th mo. 16th, 1738.

XV. REBECCA, second daughter of Jonathan and Gainor Jones, born in Merion Township, 20th 12th mo., 1709; married at Merion Meeting, 3d mo. 4th, 1733, John Roberts, son of Robert Roberts, of Merion. They had twelve children; surname Roberts[1]:

  1. Jonathan, b. 1 mo. 30th, 1734.
  2. Gainor, b. 11 mo. 30th, 1735-6.
  3. Alban, b. 7 mo. 7th, 1738.
  4. Elizabeth, b. 6 mo. 18th, 1740.
  5. Mary, b. 5 mo. 5th, 1742; d. unm.
  6. Tacy, b. 7 mo. 2d, 1744.
  7. Benjamin, b. 6 mo. 27th, 1746.
  8. John, b. 9 mo. 16th, 1747.
  9. Robert, b. 8 mo. 10th, 1749.
  10. Algernon, b. 11 mo. 24th, 1750-1.
  11. Franklin, b. 9 mo. 27th, 1752.
  12. Edward Roberts, b. 11 mo. 1st, 1755.

XV. JONATHAN JONES, fifth son of Jonathan and Gainor, born in Merion Township, 29th 4th mo., 1715; married at Merion Meeting, 11th mo. 8th, 1742, Sarah, daughter of "Thomas Jones, of Merion, deceased, yeoman," son of John Thomas, of Llaithgwm, Merionethshire, Wales, descended from Evan Côch, of Bryammer, Denbighshire. (See another page.) They had three daughters[2]:

---

[1] For descendants see Roberts, of Pencoyd, Merion, on another page.
[2] For genealogy of the Jones Family see another page.

1. Mary, b. 11 mo. 23d, 1744–5.
2. Gainor, b. 8 mo. 4th, 1742.
3. Katharine, m. Lewis Jones, of Blockley.

XV. HANNAH OWEN, second daughter of Robert and Susanna, born in Philadelphia, 3d mo. 16th, 1720; died January, 1791, in said city. Will dated 28th November, 1786; probate January, 1791[1]. She married first, 8th mo. 23d, 1740[2], John Ogden, of Philadelphia (widower), son of David Ogden, of Chester. John Ogden died 6th February, 1742, being then of the "Township of Myamensing and Passyunct, Philadelphia County." Will dated 31st January, 1742; probate 12th February, same year[3]."

Hannah married secondly, 6th mo. 7th, 1754, Joseph Wharton, of Walnut Grove, Southwark, Philadelphia. In her will, dated as above, Hannah leaves to her "son William Ogden," among other bequests, "my Silver Tankard," and directs that her executors "sell my Charriott, and apply the Amount of the same toward payment of my debts." She also mentions her grandfather, William Hudson, and her children by her second husband, Wharton. By her first husband, John Ogden, she had one son:

William Ogden, b. prior to 31st January, 1742; m. 1st, Marie Pinniard, 2ndly, Tacey David.

By her second husband, Joseph Wharton, she had a large family, the most distinguished of whom was Robert Wharton, Mayor of Philadelphia, Captain of the City Troop, etc. For an account of them and their descendants, see "History of Wharton Family," in PENNA. MAG., Vol. II.

XVI. WILLIAM OGDEN, only child of John Ogden, and Hannah, his 2nd wife, born in Philadelphia prior to 31 January, 1742; died in Camden, N. J., 13 May, 1818. He married 1st mo. 11th, 1769, Marie Pinniard, who died 7 mo.

---

[1] Will Book W, p. 65, Philadelphia.
[2] Philadelphia (Arch Street) Friends Monthly Meeting Records, Book A, p. 172.
[3] Will Book G, p. 31.

Owen Family. 141

14th, 1775[1]. He married 2ndly, Tacey[2], daughter of Benjamin and Ann David. Tacey died 11 Sept., 1809[3]. William Ogden had issue by his first wife:
1. Hannah, b. 17 Nov., 1770; bapt. in 3d Presbyterian Church of Philadelphia, 16 May, 1803.
2. Joseph, b. 7 mo., 1775; d. 10 mo. 20th, 1778.

He had by his second wife two children:
1. Ann, m. Hezekiah Niles, of Baltimore.
2. Robert Wharton, of Camden.

XVII. HANNAH OGDEN, eldest daughter of William by Marie (his first wife), born in Philadelphia County, 17th November, 1770; died at Philadelphia, 29th July, 1827; buried in the ground of the Third Presbyterian Church, Pine Street, said city. She married first, in Christ Church, 10th April, 1795, Captain William Duer, who was lost at sea, 1800–1[4]. She married, secondly, in Christ Church, 27th January, 1810, Samuel Cuthbert, "gentleman," son of Thomas. He died January, 1839. Hannah had by Captain Duer three children:
1. Mary Ann, b. 7 October, 1796; m. 5th May, 1825, Lewis Washington Glenn, son of James, of Maryland, and had issue—William Duer, d. s. p. in Cairo, Egypt, 1876; Edward[5], of Ardmore, Lower Merion; Hannah Cuthbert, m. A. W. North, who d. s. p.
2. Harriet, b. 4 November, 1798; d. unm. at Phila. 7th May, 1851.

---

[1] Believed to have been of French lineage.
[2] Registry of St. Paul's Church, Philadelphia.
[3] Friends' Records.
[4] Letters of administration granted on his estate, 25th November, 1801, to Hannah Duer. Sureties, William Ogden, "gentleman," and Robert Ralston, "merchant."
[5] Edward Glenn married 1st, Frances Stewart Van Osten, and had Harriet Duer, married C. C. Royce, and 2ndly Sarah Catherine, daughter of Thomas Hardy Allen, son of Captain Robert Allen, late officer in the English Army, and had: Thomas Allen Glenn, of Ardmore (who married Marie Therese, daughter of Edward Robins, of Philadelphia, and has: Edward Glenn, and William Duer Glenn) and Edna Glenn.

3. William, d. at Phila., 25th March, 1802.

By Samuel Cuthbert she had two daughters:
1. Frances Duer, d. infant.
2. Elizabeth Frances, d. unm.

THE BIDDLE BRANCH OF THE OWEN FAMILY, OF MERION.

I. JOHN BIDDLE, son of William, of Mount Hope, New Jersey, married, 3 March, 1736, Sarah, eldest daughter of Owen Owen, Esquire, High Sheriff and Coroner of Philadelphia County, second son of Robert Owen, of Merion (died 1697), and Rebecca, his wife. They had issue:

1. Owen m. Sarah Parke; issue.
2. Clement, b. 10 May, 1740; m. 1st Mary Richardson; 2ndly Rebekah Cornell.
3. Ann.
4. Sarah.
5. Lydia.

II. COLONEL CLEMENT BIDDLE, second son of John and Sarah, born in Philadelphia, 10 May, 1740; died 14 July, 1814. He married first, 6 June, 1764, Mary, daughter of Francis Richardson, of Chester. He married secondly, Rebekah, only daughter of Hon. Gideon Cornell, of Rhode Island, Lieutenant Governor and Chief Justice of that Colony. Clement Biddle was commissioned Deputy Quarter Master General for the "Flying Camp" and for the Militia of Pennsylvania and New Jersey, with the rank of Colonel, 8 July, 1776; Marshal of the Court of Admiralty of Pennsylvania, 10 November, 1780; Justice of the Court of Common Pleas and Quarter Sessions of the Peace for Philadelphia, 23 September, 1788.

Colonel Biddle was distinguished in many ways as a citizen, and his services as an officer in "the Continental Army during the Revolutionary War were such as to elicit the highest praise."

By his first wife he had issue:
1. Francis R., d. infant.

By his second wife he had:
1. Frances, b. 20 May, 1775; d. infant.
2. Thomas, b. 4 June, 1776; m. Christine Williams.
3. George Washington, b. 21 Feb., 1779; d. 1812.
4. Mary, b. 12 Jan., 1781; m. Gen. Thomas Cadwalader. See that family.
5. Rebecca Cornell, b. 7 Nov., 1782; m. Prof. Nathaniel Chapman, M. D.
6. Clement Cornell, b. 24 Oct., 1784; m. Mary Barclay.
7. Anne, b. 24 Dec., 1785; d. infant.
8. Lydia H., b. 12 May, 1787; d. 1826.
9. Sarah T., b. 21 Oct., 1789; d. young, unm.
10. Anne Wilkinson, b. 12 June, 1791; m. Thomas Dunlap.
11. John Gideon, b. 10 June, 1793; m. Mary Biddle.
12. James Cornell, b. 29 Dec., 1795.
13. Edward Robert, b. 7 Feb., 1798.

III. THOMAS BIDDLE, eldest son of Colonel Clement and Rebekah, was born 4 June, 1776; married, 12 February, 1806, Christine, daughter of General Jonathan Williams, and had issue:
1. Clement, b. 14 Sept., 1810.
2. Thomas Alexander, b. 22 Aug., 1814.
3. Henry Jonathan, b. 16 May, 1817.
4. Alexander, b. 29 April, 1819.
5. Jonathan Williams, b. 12 Aug., 1821.

III. REBECCA CORNELL BIDDLE, third daughter of Clement and Rebekah Biddle, born 7 November, 1782. She married, 1 September, 1808, Professor Nathaniel Chapman, M. D., of Philadelphia. They had issue:
1. Emily, b. 25 Aug., 1810; m. John Montgomery Gordon, of Virginia, 21 Nov. 1833.
2. John Biddle, b. 3 June, 1811; m. Mary Randolph.

Owen Family—Biddle Branch.

3. George William, b. 10 Dec., 1816.
4. Rebecca Biddle, b. 24 Feb., 1818; d. 1824.
5. Marie, b. 10 Dec., 1820; died.

III. COLONEL CLEMENT CORNELL BIDDLE, third son of Clement and Rebeckah, born 24 October, 1784; married Mary Searle, daughter of Hon. John Barclay, Mayor of Philadelphia, 1791[1]. Clement Cornell Biddle was Captain of the State Fencibles and Colonel of the First Regiment Vols., Light Infantry, of Pennsylvania, during the war of 1812. He was also President of the Philadelphia Savings Fund Society, and President of the Franklin Insurance Company of Philadelphia. He had issue:

1. John Barclay, b. 3 January, 1815.
2. George Washington, b. 11 January, 1818.
3. Chapman, b. 22 January, 1822.

III. ANN WILKINSON BIDDLE, seventh daughter of Clement and Rebekah, born 12 June, 1791; married 2 June, 1822, Thomas Dunlap, President of Bank of the United States. They had:

1. Sally Biddle, b. 19 March, 1823.
2. Julianna, b. 19 Oct., 1824.
3. Lydia Biddle, b. 1 Sept., 1826; d. young, unm.
4. Mary, b. 1 Dec., 1827; d. unm.
5. Rebecca Biddle, b. 10 Mar., 1829.
6. Nannie, b. 21 Nov., 1830; m. George Mecum Conarroe, Esquire, of Philadelphia.
7. Thomas, b. 23 Aug., 1832; m. Margaret A. Lewis, of New Haven, Conn., 10 July, 1856, and had: Nannie Biddle.

III. JOHN GIDEON BIDDLE, fourth son of Clement and Rebeckah, born 10 June, 1793; married 22 Aug., 1820, Mary, daughter of Hon. Charles Biddle, Vice President of the Supreme Executive Council of Pennsylvania. They had issue:
Ann Eliza, b. 20 March, 1822.

---
[1] From Ballyshannon, Ireland.

III. JAMES CORNELL BIDDLE, third son of Col. Clement and Rebecca, born 29 Dec., 1795; married Sarah Caldwell, daughter of Hon. Michael Keppele, 9 March, 1825. They had issue:
1. Thomas, b. 2 Jan., 1827.
2. Caldwell Keppele, b. 22 Jan., 1829.
3. Catherine Keppele, b. 1 Feb., 1831; m. William P. Tatham, 20 June, 1867.
4. Rebecca, b. 22 May, 1833; d. 1859.
5. James Cornell, b. 3 Oct., 1835.
6. Cadwalader, b. 28 Oct., 1837.

III. EDWARD ROBERTS BIDDLE, fourth son of Colonel Clement and Rebeckah, born 7 Feb., 1798.

IV. CLEMENT BIDDLE, first son of Thomas and Christine, born 14 September, 1810.

IV. THOMAS ALEXANDER BIDDLE, second son of Thomas and Christine, born 22 Aug., 1814; married, 1 July, 1845, Julia, daughter of John Cox, Esquire, and had:
1. John Cox, b. 21 April, 1846.
2. Henry Williams, b. 7 April, 1848; m. 25 Feb., 1873, Jessie Duncan, dau. Rear Admiral Thomas Turner, U. S. A., and has: Mildred Lee, Juliette.
3. Anna Sitgreaves, b. 31 Jan., 1850; m. Andrew A. Blair, of New York City, N. Y., 1872.
4. Alfred, b. 15 Dec., 1852.
5. William Lyman, b. 8 Oct., 1854.
6. Frances, b. 31 Oct., 1856.
7. Julia, b. 16 May, 1858.
8. Frances, b. March, 1862; d. infant.

IV. COLONEL HENRY JONATHAN BIDDLE, third son of Thomas and Christine, born 16 May, 1807; m. 1 June, 1854, Mary Deborah, daughter of Samuel Baird. He was Adjutant General of Penna. Reserves, and died from a wound received at Market Cross Roads, 30 June, 1862. He had:

1. Jonathan Williams, b. 1 Aug., 1855; d. 1877.
2. Lydia McFunn, b. 9 April, 1857; m. Moncure Robinson, Jr.
3. Spencer Fullerton Baird, b. 12 Jan., 1859.
4. Christine Williams, b. 28 Aug., 1860.
5. Henry Jonathan, b. 14 May, 1862.

IV. ALEXANDER BIDDLE, fourth son of Thomas and Christine, born 29 April, 1819; married, 11 October, 1855, Julia Williams, daughter of Samuel Rush, M. D., and had:

1. Alexander Williams, b. 4 July, 1856; m., 1879, Anne, dau. Hon. William McKennan, Judge U. S. C. C., and has: Pauline, Christine.
2. Henry Rush, b. 15 March, 1858; d. 1877.
3. Julia Rush, b. 25 July, 1859.
4. James Wilmer, b. 22 Nov., 1861.
5. Louis Alexander, b. 12 March, 1863.
6. Mariamne, b. 8 Nov., 1865.
7. Lynford, b. 26 Aug., 1871.

IV. JONATHAN WILLIAMS BIDDLE, fifth son of Thomas and Christine, born 12 Aug., 1821; married, 16 April, 1846, Emily, daughter of Dr. Charles Meigs, of Philadelphia, and had:

1. Christine, b. 14 Feb., 1847; m. Richard M. Cadwalader. (See that family.)
2. Charles Meigs, b. 10 Jan., 1849.
3. Williams, b. 16 July, 1850.
4. Mary, b. 7 Dec., 1851.
5. Thomas, b. 7 July, 1853.
6. Emily Williams, b. 15 March, 1855.

IV. EMILY CHAPMAN, first daughter of Dr. Nathaniel Chapman and Rebeckah Cornell Biddle, his wife, born in Philadelphia 25 August, 1810; married, 21 November, 1833, John Montgomery Gordon, of Virginia. They had issue:

1. Chapman, b. 2 Aug., 1834; d. young.
2. John Montgomery, b. 10 Aug., 1836; d. infant.

3. Susan Fitzhugh, b. 17 Jan., 1838; d. young.
4. Emily Chapman, b. 20 April, 1840; d. infant.
5. Rebecca Chapman, b. 3 Sep., 1842; m., 1867, Eugene Blackford, of Lynchburg, Va., and had: Emily Chapman, Eugene, William G., b. 1874.

IV. JOHN BIDDLE CHAPMAN, first son of Dr. Nathaniel Chapman and Rebeckah Cornell Biddle, his wife, born in Philadelphia, 3 June, 1811. He married Mary Randolph, of Virginia, and had:
1. Gabriella, m. Marquis de Potesdad.
2. Emily, m. Prince Joseph Pignatelli d'Aragon.

IV. GEORGE WILLIAM CHAPMAN, second son of Dr. Nathaniel Chapman and Rebeckah Cornell Biddle, his wife, born in Philadelphia 10 December, 1816; m. Emily, daughter of John Markoe, and had:
1. Mary Randolph, m. John Borland Thayer, and has: George C., Henry C., John B., Walter, Mary, Sidney, M. C. Farnum.
2. Elizabeth Camac, m. William Davis Winsor, and has Emily Chapman, m. William W. Philler, and Louise Brooks.
3. Henry Cadwalader, b. 17 Aug., 1845; m. Hannah Megargee.
4. Rebecca, m. James Davis Winsor, and has: Mary, Henry, James, Davis, Rebecca, Ellen.
5. George, b. 5 July, 1852; d. infant.

IV. JOHN BARCLAY BIDDLE, eldest son of Col. Clement Cornell and Mary, born 3 January, 1815, married 7 Nov., 1850, Caroline, daughter of William Phillips, and had:
1. Anna Clifford, b. 17 Sept., 1851; m. Clement Stocker Phillips, 1881.
2. Harriet, b. 8 Aug., 1852; m. 11 Oct., 1876, De Grasse Fox.
3. William Phillips, b. 17 Dec., 1853.
4. Clement, b. 11 Dec., 1854.

5. Elizabeth Rebecca, b. 9 Dec., 1856; m. 9 Dec., 1877, Samuel M. Miller, M. D., and has Charlotte Barclay, Marion Spencer, John Barclay.

6. Caroline, b. 16 March, 1860.

IV. GEORGE WASHINGTON BIDDLE, second son of Col. Clement Cornell and Mary, born 11 January, 1822; married Maria, daughter of William McMurtrie, of Burlington, New Jersey, and had:

1. George, b. 21 Aug., 1843; m. Mary Hosack, dau. Dr. F. Kearney Rodgers, of N. Y., and has: Dorothea Pendleton, Eleanor K., Constance Elizabeth.

2. Algernon Sydney, b. 11 Oct., 1847; m. 1879, 28 June, Frances, d. Moncure Robinson.

3. Arthur, b. 23 Sept., 1852; m. Julia Biddle, and had: Edith Frances, b. 1881, Julia Cox, b. 1882.

IV. COLONEL CHAPMAN BIDDLE, third son of Col. Clement Cornell and Mary, b. 22 January, 1822, Colonel 12 Reg. Penna. Vol., 1862. He married, 1849, Mary Livingston, daughter of Captain Walter Livingston Cochran, of New York, and had:

1. Mary C., b. 16 June, 1850.

2. Clement Cornell, b. 5 Sept., 1851; d. 1873.

3. Walter Livingston Cochran, b. 21 Aug., 1853; m. 1881, Pauline Davis, d. Dr. Robert Carter, U. S. A., but d. s. p.

IV. THOMAS BIDDLE, eldest son of James Cornell and Sarah, b. 2 January, 1827. He married, 7 November, 1861, Sarah Fredrica, daughter of William White, Esq., and had:

1. Caldwell Keppele, b. at Rio Janeiro 3 Jan., 1863.

2. Harrison White, b. at Washington, D. C., 16 May, 1864.

3. Sarah White, b. Germantown, 9 Jan., 1867.

4. James Cornell, b. 3 July, 1868.

5. Elizabeth Caldwell, b. at St. Augustine, 28 Jan., 1870.

IV. CALDWELL KEPPELE BIDDLE, second son of James Cornell and Sarah, born 22 January, 1829; married 28 April, 1857, Elizabeth Ricketts, widow of Robert Meade, and had:

Maria Palmer, b. 1858; d. infant.

IV. JAMES CORNELL BIDDLE, third son of James Cornell and Sarah, born 3 October, 1835; married, 27 December, 1862, Gertrude Gouverneur, daughter of Hon. William Morris Meredith, and had:

Catherine Meredith.
Sarah Caldwell.

V. GABRIELLA CHAPMAN, first daughter of John Biddle Chapman, married, November, 1853, Luis de Potesdad, Marquis de Potesdad Fornari, and had:

1. Luis Emilio.
2. Emily Mildred.
3. Emanuel Henry.
4. John Henry.
5. Robert Lee.
6. Maria Gabriella.
7. Julie Francoise Eugenie.

DESCENDANTS OF HANNAH JONES, DAUGHTER OF OWEN AND SUSANNAH JONES, OF MERION, AND AMOS FOULKE.

I. HANNAH JONES, daughter of Owen and Susanna, of Merion, married Amos Foulke[1], born 11th month 5th, 1740; died 1793. He died in Philadelphia. They had three children:

FOULKE ARMS.

1. Susan[2], born 10th month 11th, 1781; died, 2nd month 1st, 1842; unmarried.
2. Edward, born 11th month 17th, 1784; died 7th month 17th, 1851.
3. George, born 7th month 23d, 1786; died 7th month, 1848; unmarried[3].

II. EDWARD FOULKE, of Gwynedd Township, Montgomery County, Pa., son of Amos and Hannah. Born 11th month 17th, 1784, in Market Street, Philadelphia; died at his home, Penllyn, 7th month 17th, 1851. He married 12 month 11th, 1810, Tacy Jones, daughter of Isaac and Gainor, of Montgomery County, Pa.

III. ANN J., born 9 mo. 15, 1811; died 6 mo. 25, 1888; married 12 mo. 26, 1832, Dr. Hiram Corson (born 10 mo. 8, 1804), son of Joseph and Hannah, of Plymouth, Penna., graduate 1828, of the medical department University of Pennsylvania, and has issue, surname *CORSON*, as follows:

---

[1] I am indebted to Robert R. Corson, of Philadelphia, for this data.
[2] He was son of William, son of Thomas, son of Edward Foulke, of Gwynedd.
[3] The remains of Amos and Hannah Foulke's children, Susan, George and Edward (with infant son of Edward), were disinterred from Friends' burying ground, Penllyn, Montgomery Co., Penna., and deposited in lot of Robert R. Corson, at North Laurel Hill, Philadelphia, Penna., October 18th, 1887.

1. Edward F., born 10 mo. 14, 1834; died 6 mo. 22, 1864. Graduate Medical Department of the University of Penna. Assistant Surgeon U. S. Navy previous to and during war of the Rebellion. 2. Joseph K., born 11 mo. 22, 1836. Graduate of Pharmacy and of Medicine, Assistant Surgeon U. S. Vol. and Surgeon U. S. Army; married 11 mo. 2, 1874, Mary Ada, daughter of Judge Wm. Alexander Carter, of Wyoming Territory. (Issue *two* children: Mary Carter, b. 1 mo. 4, 1876; died 6 mo. 30, 1890. Edward b. 11 mo. 30, 1883.) 3. Caroline, born 4 mo. 2, 1839; d. 7, 20, 1865, unm. 4. Tacy F., born 1 mo. 26, 1841; m. 2 mo. 8, 1865, Wm. L. Cresson. (Issue *four* children: Caroline C., b. 2 mo. 7, 1866. James, b. 5 mo. 12, 1869. Mary C., b. 9 mo. 12, 1872. Nancy L. C., b. 12, 3, 1873.) 5. Charles Follen, born 11 mo. 22, 1842; died 5, 30, 1889. Graduate University of Pennsylvania; m. 12, 14, 1876, Mary S. Lukens, daughter of Lewis A. Lukens; she died 9, 7, 1877. Married second time 2, 18, 1889, Margaret Slemmer, of Norristown, Pa. 6. Susan F., born 8 mo. 9, 1845; m. 11 mo. 26, 1868, Jawood Lukens, of Conshohocken, Penna. 7. Bertha, born 12 mo. 17, 1847, m. 6 mo. 17, 1868, James Yocom, Jr., of Philadelphia, Pa. (Issue *seven* children: Fannie C., b. 5 mo. 19, 1869. Thomas C., b. 12 mo. 10, 1870. Bertha E. C., b. 12 mo. 23, 1872. Georgia C., b. 2 mo. 25, 1876. Hiram C., b. 11 mo. 30, 1878. Dorothea C., b. 1 mo. 29, 1881. James C., b. 10 mo. 21, 1887.) 8. Frances C., born 10 mo. 25, 1849; m. 11 mo. 12, 1874, Richard H. Day, of Philadelphia, Pa. (Issue *three* children: Bertha C., b. 8 mo. 20, 1875. Charles, b. 5 mo. 15, 1879. Richard, b. 8 mo. 22, 1891.) 9. Mary, born 11 mo. 26, 1852; unmarried[1].

III. JESSE, born 6, 23, 1813; d. 2, 15, 1892, unmarried.

III. CHARLES, born 12, 14, 1815; d. 12, 30, 1871. Graduate Medical Department University of Penna.; m. 3, 14, 1843, Harriet M. Corson, daughter of Dr. Richard D. Corson, New Hope, Pa. Issue *three* children: 1. Richard C., b. 11

---

[1] The above named are the children and grand children of Dr. Hiram Corson, who is living (February, 1894), in his 90th year.

mo. 2, 1843. Graduate of M. D. University of Penna.; m. 6 mo. 5, 1872, Louisa M. Vansant. (Issue *three* children: Charles, b. 4, 13, 1873. Clarabel V., b. 4, 26, 1875. Rebecca C., b. 8, 18, 1878; d. 3, 15, 1882.) 2. Edward, of Washington, D. C., b. 3, 23, 1847; m. 4, 19, 1876, Lida Van Horn, daughter of Joseph A. Van Horn, Yardley, Penna. (Issue *two* children: Helen, b. 11, 17, 1884; d. 11, 27, 1884. Van Horn, 12, 16, 1886.) 3. Thomas J. C., b. 3, 16, 1851; d. 9, 15, 1883, unmarried.

    III. SUSAN, born 7, 18, 1818; d. 11, 2, 1886, unmarried.

    III. OWEN, born 8, 8, 1820; d. in infancy.

    III. PRISCILLA, born 10, 10, 1821; d. 12, 28, 1882; m. 4, 22, 1849, Thomas Wistar, son of Thomas. Issue *four* children: 1. Edward M., b. 1, 3, 1852; m. 11, 16, 1876, Margaret C. Collins. (Issue *three* children: Thomas, b. 10, 18, 1877. Casper, b. 11, 18, 1880. Elizabeth, b. 10, 10, 1884.) 2. Susan W., b. 5, 12, 1850; m. 5, 27, 1872, Howard Comfort. (Issue *one* child: William W., b. 5, 27, 1874.) 3. Elizabeth B. W., b. 5, 7, 1855; m. 9, 18, 1879, George Warner. 4. Annie M., b. 2, 9, 1862; m. 12, 13, 1888, Henry Ecroyd Haines.

    III. JONATHAN, born 1, 10, 1825; d. in infancy.

    III. LYDIA S., born 2, 18, 1827; d. 8, 27, 1861; m. 6, 3, 1852, Charles W. Bacon, son of John. (Issue *one* child: Anna F., b. 4, 14, 1853; m. 9, 27, 1883, Robert K. Neff, Jr.)

    III. REBECCA J., born 5, 18, 1829; m. 10, 8, 1857, Robert R. Corson, son of Dr. Richard D. Corson, of New Hope, Penna.

    III. HANNAH J., born 9, 18, 1831; m. 5, 20, 1862, Francis Bacon, son of John. Issue *three* children: 1. Lydia F. b. 12, 27, 1863; d. 11, 18, 1890; m. 4, 7, 1890, Thomas H. Miles. 2. Francis L., b. 3, 16, 1868. 3. Albert Edward, b. 9, 27, 1869.

    III. EMILY, born 12, 2, 1834; d. 8, 23, 1892; m. 12, 16, 1858, Charles L. Bacon, who died 2, 26, 1861.

    III. OWEN, born 3, 6, 1838; d. 8, 23, 1838.

ARMS OF IESTYN AP GWRGAN.
Gules, three chevronells, argent.

THE BEVAN FAMILY, OF TREVERIGG, GLAMORGANSHIRE, AND MERION, PENNSYLVANIA.

From the south side of Lancaster Avenue, directly opposite Wynnewood Station, on the main line of the Pennsylvania Railroad, in Lower Merion, a fine Telford street leads directly to the old Haverford Road, the southern border of the original township. The new avenue, one of the most picturesque drives in this section, is bounded for a little distance on the west by the property of Isaac H. Clothier, Esq., and on the east by what was formerly Remington's Park. Passing down this street towards Haverford, we come to a picturesque farm, now, or late, belonging to the Henry Morris estate, and extending to the township line. This land, until a few years since, was the property of the Bevan family, and a part of the original purchase of John Bevan (otherwise called John ap Evan, ab Evan or B'evan), who came here from his paternal estate of Treverigg, in Glamorganshire, in the year 1683. A very old Colonial mansion is yet standing upon the summit of a gentle slope of hill-side, to the west of, and overlooking the way, and if it does not include a part of the first stone house built by the family, it is nevertheless, doubtless, on the site of the home of the first owner of the broad tract, of which this little farm of some 78 acres was all that remained a few years since, when it was sold by Henry C. Bevan, a direct male descendant of John, the first settler. The lands of John Bevan, the original patentee, extended into Haverford Township, and it was at this place that he settled the little company of colonists that he brought out from his Welsh home. The Haverford lands were surveyed to those persons who had contributed towards the purchase money for the 2000 acres patented, whilst the Merion lands were retained by John Bevan for his own use.

The family of Treverigg was one of the most ancient in Glamorganshire, and possessed considerable wealth for that day. The Bevans descended in the direct male line from the ancient Princes or Lords of Glamorgan, whose lineage is traceable for many generations back to the old Cymric Kings of the Island of Britain. The following is the ancestry of John Bevan (beginning in more modern times), compiled from authentic documents and records remaining in Glamorganshire. A brief account of the direct male descendants in Pennsylvania is also added, whilst the descendants in the female lines are given in the last part of this article. As it is understood that the male line in Glamorganshire has failed, and that the earlier male lines from Iestyn ap Gwrgan have died out, it would appear that members of the American branch are not only the sole male representatives of the Treverigg family, but are representatives, as heirs male, according to their respective order, of the ancient Princes of Glamorgan.

The pedigree is as follows:

I. IESTYN AP GWRGAN[1]. He became Prince of the territory now called Glamorganshire, Wales, upon the death of his father, in the year 1030, but owing to his violent and headstrong disposition and his arrogance, he was at first rejected as a ruler, and his uncle, Howell, a mild and wise Lord, was

---

[1] Royal Tribes of Wales, Yorke, Ed. by Richard Williams, 1887, Lond. 4to.

elected instead. It was not, therefore, until the latter's death, which occurred in 1043, that Iestyn succeeded to the Sovereignty which his ancestors had held for so many generations. Some time after this, in 1088, Iestyn, then over seventy years of age, became involved in a war with Rhys ap Tewdwr, Prince of South Wales, by whom he was defeated in battle. In order to win back from Rhys the castles taken by him, Iestyn invited the Normans to assist him, promising them a part of his territory. Having, however, once obtained a foothold in the country, the Normans were not easily satisfied, but finally succeeded in seizing all of Iestyn's territory, and, in conjunction with some dissatisfied subjects, driving him from the country into exile. He fled first to Glastonbury, thence to Bath, and ultimately to the monastery of Llangenys, in Monmouthshire, where he died, in obscurity and forgotten, at the great age, it is said, of 129 years.

Fitzhamon, the leader of the Norman invaders, appropriated Glamorgan, which he divided into nineteen parts. As some of Iestyn's sons were popular with the people, and had not opposed Fitzhamon, four shares of their father's land were set aside for them and one share was given to Einion ap Collwyn, Iestyn's son-in-law, and one to Robert ap Seisyllt.

Iestyn ap[1] Gwrgan married several times. According to the best accounts extant he married first, Denis[2], sister to Bleddyn ap Cynfyn, Prince of Powys; secondly Angharad[3], daughter of Elystan Gloddrudd, Lord of Fferllwg; thirdly[4] Gwenvyn, daughter of Cynfyn ap Gweristan[5].

By his first wife he had issue:
1. Rhydderch.

---

[1] It is presumed that the reader is now familiar with the "modo Wallico," or Welsh system of surnames. The child always took the Christian or given name of his father as his surname, thus John, the son of Thomas, would be called John ap (or ab) Thomas, ap or ab meaning *son of*, or simply John Thomas. If the word ap, wherever it occurs, is simply read *son of*, the difficulty often experienced in fully understanding a Welsh genealogy is greatly lessened.

[2] Limbus Patrum Morganiæ et Glamorganiæ. Dwnn, Yorke.
[3] Iolo MSS., 393.
[4] Limb. Pat. Morg. et Glam.
[5] Powys Fadog IV, p. 175.

2. Meredith.
3. Cadwgan.
4. Griffith.
5. Rhiwallon.
6. Morgan.
7. Elen.

By his second wife he had issue:

1. Caradog, Lord of Avan or Aberaven, vulgo Aberavon, which he purchased[1].
2. Madog, of whom presently.
3. Rhys.
4. Nest, m. Einion ap Collwyn.
5—dau[1].

II. MADOG AP IESTYN, the third son of Iestyn ap Gwrgan, by his second wife, had, probably according to the division made by Fitzhamon, for his share of his father's territory, the Lordship of Ruthyn, and the lands between the Rivers Taff and Ely. He married Janet, daughter of Sytsyll, Lord of Upper Gwent, by whom he had issue a son:

III. HOWELL AP MADOG, who married a daughter of Griffith ap Ivor Bach [or, a lion rampant, argent, debruised by a bend gobonny argent and gules], and had issue:

1. Cynfrig, of whom presently.
2. Jevan.
3. Joan.

IV. CYNFRIG AP HOWELL, eldest son, Lord of Llantrithyd and Radyr. He married Angharad, daughter and co-heiress of Lewis ap Rhys ap Rosser. Cynfrig probably died prior to 6 Edward I., 1280. He had issue:

---

[1]Of the children of his third and possibly a fourth wife there are conflicting accounts, and as they were of the younger lines it is scarcely worth while to consider them. It is claimed that Iestyn had an only daughter by a wife not named here, and an heiress, who was called Asar, or Sara, and who married Paine Tuberville, by whom he got Coity Castle. This story is referred to elsewhere in these pages; but whether she was the daughter of Iestyn, or of his son Morgan, or whether she was actually heiress of the place, or it was only bestowed upon her by her father, does not appear to be clearly determined.

1. Llewelyn[1], of Llantrithyd, of whom presently.
2. Howell, of Radyr.
3. David.
4. Jevan, living 11th year of Edward II., 1318-19[2].
5. Berten, m. Catherine Wlaidd.
6. Thomas Ddu.
7. Yorath Mawr, of Treoda, m. d. Llewelyn|Lleia.
8. Jevan[3].

V. LLEWELYN AP CYNFRIG, eldest son; he was possessed of the lands of Llantrithyd, and was alive in the 6th year of Edward I., 1280, and probably as late as 1317. He married a daughter of Sir Ralph Maylog, and had issue:
1. Evan (Ievan).
2. Llewelyn Ychan.
3. Aeddan.
4. Jevan Mady, of whom presently.
5. David Rhydlavar.
6. Jenet, m. Sir Thomas ap Aaron.
7. Gwardhin.

VI. JEVAN MADY, fourth son of Llewelyn, had the lands of Bwlch Gwyn, whose wife is not mentioned. He had issue:
1. Llewelyn, of whom presently.
2. dau.—m. Griffith Ychan, of Ystradyvodwg.
3. dau.—m. Thomas ap Jenkin ap Rees.
4. dau.—m. Llewelyn Lleia.

VII. LLEWELYN AP JEVAN MADY, only son and heir; is called of Abergorky. He married, first, a daughter of Morgan, of Llantwit; secondly, a daughter of Llewelyn ap Ivorhir; and thirdly, a daughter of Llewelyn Lleia[4]. By his second wife he had issue:

---
[1]Limbus Patrum Morganiæ et Glamorganiæ.
[2]Ibid.
[3]The name Jevan, as used here, is precisely the same as Ievan or Evan, or Ivan, occurring elsewhere in this book. In Glamorganshire genealogies, however, the former mode of spelling is principally followed. It was usual to give several children the same names.
[4]The daughter of Llewelyn Lleia was probably by another wife, or else Llewelyn ap Jevan married his own niece.

Bevan Family.

1. Philip.
2. Howel.
3. William Tew.
4. Thomas Ddu, of whom presently.
5. Jevan.
6. Llewelyn.
7. dau.—m. William Morgan, of Llantrithyd.
8. dau.—m. David ap Ievan.
9. Ellen, m. Thomas Jenkin ap Rees.

VIII. THOMAS DDU (or Thomas with black hair), fourth son of Lewelyn of Abergorky, married Crisly, daughter of Howel ap Philip hir, and had by her:
1. Howel.
2. Jenkin, of whom presently.
3. Richard, d. s. p.

IX. JENKIN AP THOMAS DDU, second son, had, by a daughter of David Llwyd ap Madoc, a son:

X. RALPH AP JENKIN, who married a daughter and heiress of Philip Vawr, and had issue by her:
1. Dio Coch, m. dau. Mathew Tuberville.
2. Jenkin, of whom presently.
3. Richard, m. Wenllian, d. Thomas Rosser.
4. Phillip, m. d. Llewelyn Morgan.
5. Catherine, m. Robert Mathew, of Rhiw-y-Saeson.

XI. JENKIN AP RALPH, second son, living circa 1520; he married first, Wenllian (Gwenllian), daughter of Hen—., and secondly, Margaret, daughter of Richard ap Jevan. By his first wife he had issue:
1. John, of whom presently.
2. Jennet, m. Morgan John, of Treos.

By his second wife he had issue:
1. Richard, m. Mary, d. John Llewelyn, of Caerwigga.
2. Morgan.
3. Wenllian, m. Richard ap Evan.
4. Catherine, m. Robert ap Morgan Williams.

XII. JOHN AP JENKIN, eldest son and heir, living circa 1550; married Wenllian, daughter of Jevan Morgan, descended from Bach ap Grono, and had issue by her:
1. Jevan (Evan), of whom presently.
2. David.
3. Richard.
4. Morgan.
5. Catherine, m. Evan ap Howel.
6. dau. ———

XIII. JEVAN (EVAN) AP JOHN, eldest son, died prior 7 Nov. 5th, Charles I.; married Wenllian, daughter of David ap Llewelyn ap Howel, and had issue by her:
1. John, of Treverigg in Llantrisant[1], of whom presently.

---

[1] Treverigg, spelled also in various other ways, any one of which seems to be correct, is an estate in the parish of Llantrisent, or Llantrisant, a few miles from Cardiff, Glamorganshire. It formed, originally, a part of the possessions of the sons of Iestyn ap Gwrgan, but whether it descended to John Bevan's grandfather, John ap Evan, from Llewelyn ap Cynfrig, who held large tracts of land in the adjoining parish with some detached estates in Llantrisent, or through an alliance with an heiress also descended from Iestyn, cannot at present be satisfactorily explained. The evidence, however, seems to show that this property came to the Bevans through the direct male line. The fact that a natural son—namely, Ralph ap Jenkin—would occur in the chain of title, does not interfere with this supposition, for in Glamorganshire, until a recent date, natural sons inherited and were equal in law to those born in wedlock. The name means the Tref or Hamlet of Meurig. What Meurig gave his name to the place is not certain, but he may have been identical with a certain Meurig who was ancestor to Iestyn, as the name is very ancient. If there was formerly any considerable hamlet here, it has disappeared long since, unless the three farms, called in the will of John Bevan's grandfather "My three Principals," might be so called; but they are a considerable distance from each other. The estate of Treverigg is about two miles long and perhaps a mile wide, and is now, as we have said, divided into three farms, each having its house or hendre. According to the best opinion, the house in which John Bevan was accustomed to reside is that nearest to the little Quaker meeting which he erected upon his own domain. This dwelling, which is said to be a substantial building, is now used as a farm-house. It has every appearance of having been erected in the sixteenth century, and is pleasantly situated near a stream of water, and was, doubtless, near the mill which formerly belonged to the Lords of Treverigg. This mill was standing and in operation in John Bevan's time. The rooms of the house, which are very large, are timbered in heavy oak, and the floors are paved with stone, as usual in Wales at that period. The statement that this particular house, of the three residences belonging to him, was the home of John Bevan, is confirmed by the traditions current in the neighborhood and the statement of his descendants residing at Llantrisant. The near location to the meeting-house and mill, with its then probably existing hamlet of tenements, is also taken into consideration. The other houses are distant, one of them about a mile and a half, and the other about the same distance in another direction. One of these has lately been altered into a fine country seat, and is the residence of the

MEETING-HOUSE ERECTED BY JOHN BEVAN, ON HIS ESTATE OF TREVERIGG, GLAMORGANSHIRE. FROM A SKETCH BY MISS BELL.

Bevan Family.

2. Morgan, m. the widow of ——— Gamage.
3. David, m. Catherine Williams.
4. Richard[1], m. Gwenny, d. Howel ap David Powell, liv. 1630.
5. Wenllian, m. Morris Matthew.
6. Mary, m. David ap Edmond Hughes[2], liv. 1630, 29 July.

XIV. JOHN AP JEVAN (Evan), of Treverigg, in the parish of Llantrisant, born probably circa 1585, died prior to 29 July, 1630, and was buried in Llantrisant Church, where his tomb is said to remain.

He married Elizabeth, daughter of Thomas Richards[3]. She was alive 1630, and her father was living subsequent to 29 July, 1630[4].

The will of John ap Evan remains at Llandaf Registry, Glamorganshire. It has been abstracted (1895) as follows:

Abstract of the will of John ap Evan, grandfather of John Bevan:

John ap Evan of Llantrisant in the county of Glamorgan and Diocese of Llandaf, 27 June, 1630.
To Llandaf cathedral 5s.
To Llantrisant church 5s.
To daughter Wenllian John   100li.
"   "   Chateryn John   50li.

---

present owner of the estate, Mr. Samuel Evans, who purchased it, but is not a descendant. Two descendants of John Bevan now reside in the neighborhood. One of them is Mr. John Bevan, a gentleman of independent means, and advanced in years; and the other in the female line, Mr. William John, of the town of Llantrisent, who comes from Barbara, said to have been the daughter of John Bevan, Jr., of Treverigg, who came from Pennsylvania in 1726-7 to inherit the property after the death of his grandfather. This Barbara married one ——— Davies, who had Rees Davies, from whom Mr. John comes. Treverigg is reached from the town of Llantrisant, in a roundabout way, by an old and now unused lane; but a highway, leading in another direction, runs through the estate. The meeting-house which John Bevan erected upon his land is still standing, and is at present used as a tenement house. A view of it, from a sketch made by Miss Bell, a descendant of John Bevan, whilst on a visit to Wales during the past summer, is given.

[1]Richard ap Evan; he was executor to his brother's will, and living in 1630, on the 29th July.
[2]Edmond Hughes, as well as his son, David, was living 1630.
[3]Limbus Patrum Morganiæ et Glamorganiæ. See also will, here given.
[4]Will of John ap Evan.

To daughter Elizabeth John 40li.
"   "   Barbara John   30li.

"Son Evan John a moiety of my household stuff "together with my three principalles." [Three principal tenements or estates.]

To niece Sisill John, daughter of John Thomas, 4li. "To my nurse Wenllian Evan 20s." Legacies to Evan John and Richard John children of John Richard ap Evan Morgan. "To my servants, Thomas Howell, Morgan Thomas, Edward Thomas and Joan Griffith. To the poor of Llantrisant parish 20s.

"My wedded wife Elizabeth Thomas, to occupy for her life my tenements called Kae Banall [Cae Banal] and Kystille [Cestyll]."

"Item I doe appointe that my executors shall paye unto Dauid Edmond and Marye his wife the sume of twentie two pounds and ffive shillings of lawfull English monie w'ch were heertofour by me tendred uppon the viijth daye of January last past acordinge and in p'susance of an order from the Kings ma^{ts} councell in . . . . . of Wales Beringe date the seaventh daye of November in the ffifth yeare of his mat's Raigne, that nowe is, yffe [if] Edmond hughe ffather . . . . . . Sayd Dauid to geather wth the sayde Dauid Edmond doe p'form & accomplishe . . . . . Order wch are of yeire p'tes [their parts] to be p'formed."

Executors, Thomas Richards, Morice Williams, gent, and my brother Richard ap Evan and my cozen John Dauid.

"Debita petenda.

Of Richard locher, gent xj li.
Of Morgan Mathewe, gent, iiij li.
Of Thomas Edward, xs.
Of Evan Morgan of mynachdy, gent, iij li. iiijs.
Of Morgan g'lym, miller xxs.
Of Thomas dauid xxs.

"Testes": Moris Williams, Dauid John Jenkin, John Richard, Richard Evans, and of Mr. Edmond Treherne, wth others."

"Probatu apud Landaff xix^{o} July Anno dni 1630. Coram, Thomas Gwyn legu. doctor. etc."

John ap Evan had issue[1] by Elizabeth; his wife:

---

[1] It will be observed that they are all mentioned in his will; they may also be found in pedigree in Limb. Pat. Morg. et Glam.

1. Evan (Jevan), of Treverigg, of whom presently.
2. Wenllian, m. Rees ap Hopkin Thomas; she was liv. 1630.
3. Catharine, m. George Mathew, of Flepton; she was liv. 27 June, 1630.
4. Elizabeth m. David ap Morgan. She was liv. 27 June, 1630.
5. Barbara, m. Jevan ap Griffith; she was liv. 27 June, 1630.

XV. EVAN AP JOHN, only son and heir of John ap Evan, of Treverigg, in the parish of Llantrisant, was probably under age at the time of his father's death in 1630, and appears to have died before 1665. He married about the year 1664, Jane, daughter of Richard ap Evan, of Collenna, an estate in the Llantrissant parish. Richard ap Evan's wife was Catherine, daughter of Thomas Basset, of Miscin, by Mary, daughter of David Evans, whose wife was great-great-granddaughter of Henry Somerset, 2nd Earl of Worcester, son of Charles d. 15 April, 1526, son of Henry (Plantagenet) Beaufort, beheaded 1463, great-grandson of Edward III., King of England. (See Chart pedigree.) Evan ap John, of Treverigg, had issue, four sons, who assumed the surname of Bevan, an abbreviation of " Ab Evan" (or ap Evan), i. e., son of Evan. They are named as follows:

1. John Bevan (or ap Evan), of Treverigg, settled in Penna., 1682, of whom presently.
2. Charles Bevan, of Llantwitvardre, Deputy Sheriff of Glamorganshire under William Aubrey of Pencoed.
3. Evan Bevan.
4—Son (Richard ?).
5—dau—d. unm.

XVI. JOHN BEVAN, the eldest son of Evan ap John, of Treverigg, in the parish of Llantrisant, Glamorganshire. In some deeds for Pennsylvania he is described as John ap Evan, of Treverigg, in others as John Bevan. As trustee for a company of Cymric Quaker Adventurers he purchased 2000 acres of land in the Province of Pennsylvania, a part of which was surveyed in Haverford and about 300 acres in Merion, in the Welsh Tract. He removed to Pennsylvania 1683; became a member of the Provincial Assembly, and was a very prominent colonist. (See sketch of his life in following pages). After remaining in Pennsylvania some years he returned to Wales, leaving his married children in the Province. He died upon his ancestral estate of Treverigg, which had been in the possession of his ancestors many hundred years, 1726. His will is dated March, 1724–25, and was proved 21 October, 1726[1], at Llandaf, Glamorganshire. (See sketch of his life.) John Bevan had by Barbara, his wife, the following children:

1. Evan Bevan[2], of whom presently.
2. Jane, m. John Wood (for descendants see future page).
3. Ann, m. Owen Roberts (for descendants see Hugh Roberts, of Merion).
4. Elizabeth. m. Joseph Richardson (for descendants see future page).
5. Barbara, d. in Wales, 1705.

XVII. EVAN BEVAN, eldest son and heir of John, by Barbara, his wife, born in Wales circa 1666–1668; died in Merion, in the Welsh Tract, in the Province of Pennsylvania, prior 13 August, 1720; Letters of Administration were granted upon his estate to Eleanor Bevan, his widow, the above date. He married 11th month 9th, 1693, at Darby Meeting, Pennsylvania, Eleanor, sister of John Wood, of Darby. She died in Merion 28th of 11th month, 1744.

A biographical sketch of her says: "This minister of the gospel was long a member of Haverford Meeting. It appears that many trials had been metered out to her by her heavenly Father, and that she had borne the proving dispensations with patient resignation, under which his presence had been as an arm of strength. For more than forty years she had lived in unity with her friends in Haverford, when in the early part of

---

[1]See infra.
[2]Mentioned in deeds and power of attorney from his father, and in his will.

1737, she removed to the city of Philadelphia, being then an aged woman.

The certificate she brought with her styles her "our ancient friend, Eleanor Bevan," and then certifies "she lived in fellowship with us upwards of forty years, her life circumspect, and her conversation inoffensive, well suiting the tender and seasonable exhortations she sometimes has been concerned to drop publicly amongst us." She returned to Merion and died as above stated. Under the will of John Bevan, of Treverigg, she held a life interest in one-half part of the Merion plantation.

Evan Bevan and Eleanor, his wife, had issue.

1. John Bevan, b. 1694; he was heir to Treverigg in Glamorganshire, to which place he removed, and there died, leaving descendants. He had issue, living 1725.
2. Barbara, b. 1696.
3. Evan Bevan, b. 1698, of whom presently.
4. Aubrey, for whose issue see a future page.
5. Charles.
6. Ann.
7. Catherine.
8. Jane, b. 1707–8.

XVIII. EVAN BEVAN, second son of Evan and Eleanor, born in Merion, 12mo. 14th, 1698; died in Philadelphia 1746. Letters of Administration were granted on his estate 20 August, 1746, to Mary Bevan, his widow. Under his grandfather's will he inherited 300 acres of land in Merion, half at time of death of John, his grandfather, and half after the decease of Eleanor, his mother, to him and the heirs of his body forever, in tail male. It is probable that Evan Bevan was twice married. The name of the last, if not the first wife, was Mary. The names of all his children have not been ascertained, but it is certain that he had:

1. Charles, eldest son and heir.
2. Evan, died in Philadelphia, 1787.

XIX. CHARLES BEVAN, of Philadelphia and Lower Merion, eldest son and heir of Evan, of same places. He appears to have been engaged in business in the city, and did not reside continuously upon his plantation. He died prior to 28 January, 1800[1], at which time letters of administration were granted upon his estate to Tyrringham Palmer and Thomas Stewart, of the city of Philadelphia; the sureties being Joseph Johnson and Anthony Cuthbert, and the amount of bonds required, £1000. His wife's name has not been ascertained, but she was dead before 10 February, 1800, as is evident from the petition[2] of Charles Bevan, apparently an orphan, setting forth that his father, Charles Bevan, died some time ago intestate, leaving an estate to which the petitioner is entitled, that he is above the age of 14 years, and under the age of 21 years—and praying for a guardian—making choice of Hugh Knox and Joseph Price, who are appointed. Nor is any widow of Charles Bevan mentioned in administration to his estate as above. Charles Bevan had, in 1798, alienated 78 acres of his estate to his daughter, Ann Shriver[3], with reversion to the next heirs of the Bevan line, in case of failure in the Shriver[4] line. Charles Bevan had issue (as far as ascertained):

1. Ann, m. Philip Shriver.
2. Charles, of whom presently.

XX. CHARLES BEVAN, of Lower Merion, son and heir of Charles. He was under age 10 February, 1800 (see supra). He married about 1801 or 1802, being probably still a minor, Mary Lippincott[5], of New Jersey, daughter of Henry (see Lippincott Family Tree), and died before 14 August, 1809, as appears by the petition[6] of Mary Bevan (widow of the said

---

[1] Administration Book K, page 34, Philadelphia.

[2] Orphans' Court Docket, for February, 1800, Norristown, Montgomery Co., Penna.

[3] Deed recorded at Philadelphia.

[4] She married Philip Shriver 1 July 1790; First Baptist Church, Philadelphia.

[5] She married 2ndly Osman Henvis, of Lower Merion, vide petition to Orphans' Court, 1831, January Term, Norristown.

[6] Orphans' Court Docket, Norristown, Montgomery Co., Pa.

Charles), David Roberts and Joseph Price, administrators of the estate of Charles Bevan, late of Lower Merion, deceased, setting forth that the deceased intestate left surviving him a widow and two children, who are minors under the age of 14 years; and praying the court to permit the sale of a part of the messuage or tenement of about 200 acres, situate in Lower Merion, of which the said Charles Bevan died seized of; and also letters of administration[1] granted on the estate of said Charles Bevan, 3 February, 1809.

There is also of record the petition[2] of Mary Bevan, widow of Charles, presented 14 August, 1809, setting forth that the said Charles Bevan, deceased, left issue, two children, to wit: John and Henry, minors, under the age of 14 years, and praying the court to appoint Allen Lippincott and Jacob Bailer as guardians, who were accordingly appointed.

The said Charles and Mary Bevan had issue:

1. John L., under age of 21 years in May, 1820[3].
2. Henry Clay.

XXI. HENRY CLAY BEVAN, second son of Charles and Mary Bevan, born in Lower Merion, 1808.

He married, in the Lower Merion Baptist Church, Bryn Mawr, Penna., 9 January, 1834, Emily Horn[4]. He and his

---

[1] Reg. Wills office, Norristown, Montgomery Co., Pa.,
[2] Orphans' Court Docket, Norristown.
[3] Ibid.
[4] The Horn family resided north of Bryn Mawr, Penna., and had intermarried with the Lloyds and other Merion families. This record of marriage can be found in the Collections of the Genealogical Society of Pennsylvania.

The following members of the Horn family are buried in the Lutheran burial ground, southeast of Ardmore, near the Bevan tract:

George Horn, died 15 March, 1778, aged 67 years.
Andrew Horn, died 21 April, 1778, aged 55 years.
George Horn, died 20 July, 1813, aged 75 years, 4 months and 19 days. His tomb has this inscription:

"*This Man Was honest Faithful
Just and True. His Life To
Copy Ought to Be Our View,
But Death has Conquer'd
After Extreme pain And Our
Deep Loss is his eternal Gain.*"

John Horn, died 1 September, 1827, aged 57 years.
Elizabeth Horn, died 11 April, 1844, aged 70 years.
George Horn, died 18 March, 1836, aged 33 years.

brother, John L., appear to have made partition of their lands between them, thus ignoring the entail imposed by the will of John Bevan, of Treverigg, in 1724–5.

Henry C. Bevan had by Emily H., his wife:
1. John Horn.
2. Thomas Jefferson.
3. Henry Clay.
4. Elmira.
5. Emma Elizabeth.
6. Allen Lippincott.
7. Andrew Jackson.
8. William Colflesh.
9. Lewis Kensil.
10. Walter[1], of Rosemont, Penna. (1895).
11. Catherine Colflesh.
12. Charles.

EDWARD III[2]
b. at Windsor 13 Nov. 1312.
Crowned, 1 Feb., 1328;
m. 24 Jan., 1329, Philippa, dau of William, Count of Holland and Hainault, d. at Shene (now Richmond), in Surrey, 21 June, 1377.

JOHN of Gaunt;
b. 24 June 1340;
d. 3 Feb. 1399.
by his 3rd wife, Katharine Swynford, he had:

JOHN DE BEAUFORT, = MARGARET dr. of
Earl of Somerset, Thomas Holland
d. 1 Sep 1440. Earl of Kent.

A

Elizabeth, daughter George and Jane Horn, died 21 Sept., 1844, aged 13 years.
Margaret Horn, sister of Elizabeth, died 20 April, 1835, aged 7 months.
William I. Horn, died 24 May, 1833, aged 56 years.
Rebecca, wife of William Horn, died 6 August, 1828, aged 44 years.
Elizabeth Horn, died 19 April, 1869; born 28 August, 1804.

Near these graves are two stones, one of Charles Schreiber, died 18 August, 1794, aged 3 years, 2 months and 5 days, and the other of Hannah Schreiber, who died 25 August, 1794, aged 9 months, 3 weeks and 4 days. Whether or not the name *Schreiber* in early times was ever written *Shriver*, or whether the children were those of Ann Bevan and Philip Shriver, has not been definitely ascertained.

[1] Twenty-first in descent from Iestyn, Prince of Glamorgan, and 14th in descent from Henry (Plantagenet) Somerset, Earl of Worcester, 1526.

[2] Names in capitals denote lines of descent from Plantagenet blood.

Bevan Family.

EDMUND BEAUFORT, = ELINOR BEAUCHAMP
Fell at St. Albans | dr & Co h, of Richard,
1455 | Earl of Warwick.

HENRY BEAUFORT
beheaded after the
battle of Hexham 1463.
He had a natural Son:
CHARLES SOMERSET = Elizabeth
Assumed the title Lord Herbert; | only dau & h.
Created Earl of Worcester 1514; | of William
d. 15 April 1526. | Herbert Earl
| of Huntingdon.

HENRY SOMERSET
=2nd Earl of Worcester

ELEANOR = SIR ROGER VAUGHAN
of Porthaml in
Talgarth, knighted
about 1550 his
2nd wife Jane dr
of Robert ap Sir Robert
Whitney by
Constance Touchet a
descendant of Edward
III.

WATKIN VAUGHAN = Joan dr. of Evan ap
of Talgarth. | Gwilim Ychan of
| Peytyn Gwyn.

SIR WILLIAM VAUGHAN = Catherine dr. of Jenkin
of Porthaml | Havard of Tredomen.
died 1564.

CATHERINE = David Evans of Neath
Sheriff of Glamorganshire
1563.

MARY (her 1st husband
Edward Turberville
of Sutton). = Thomas Basset of Miscin.

CATHERINE = Richard ap Evan
of Collenna.

Evan or Jevan ap John = JANE
of Treverig.

JOHN BEVAN;
died 1726.

JOHN BEVAN AND HIS FAMILY.[1]

Of John Bevan and his ancestry considerable is known. He was the eldest of the four sons of Evan or Jevan ap John ap Evan, of Treverigg, in the parish of Llantrisant, Glamorganshire; and Jane, one of the daughters of Richard ap Evan, of Collenna, in the same parish. He was born about the year 1646. "His parents died when he was very young, leaving five children, of whom he was the eldest. . . . . His father had left him a considerable estate, but the rest of the children were unprovided for; he, therefore, when he came of age (his sister being dead before), portioned all his brothers, and gave them a helpful subsistence in the world. Some years after, he was convinced of the blessed truth as it is in Jesus[2], ..." The mother of his children was named Barbara. He married her in 1665. According to tradition, and the statements of some of her descendants, she was the daughter of William Awbrey, of Pencoed. In one pedigree she is called "*Barbara* of —— *Wenvoe*"; in another genealogy *Catherine*, the daughter of William Awbrey, of Pencoed, is given as the wife of John Bevan, Senior, of Treverigg[3]. There can be no question of the fact that John Bevan *did* marry a daughter of William Awbrey, of Pencoed (see his will), and if he was not married twice, then the name *Catherine* is a misprint or clerical error for *Barbara*, or else she was baptized *Barbara Catherine*. (See Appendix.)

Barbara was religiously inclined in "her young years, and zealously concerned to observe the ceremonies of the Church of England. . . . . But at one time when she was at worship the Priest pronounced his excommunication against

---

[1] Prepared by Howard Williams Lloyd, Esq., who also supplied a large amount of the data for the preceding pages, including the will of John ap Evan.

[2] A Collection of Memorials, etc., 1787.

[3] He was called *Senior*, to distinguish him from his grandson, John Bevan, who inherited the estate in 1726.

her husband. This so affected her, coming without any previous notice, she became more willing to search closely into the weighty work of the salvation of her immortal soul." Shortly afterward she became convinced, and with her husband became a zealous Quaker.

In 1683 John Bevan, with his wife and children, removed to Pennsylvania. Their certificate of removal is dated Treverigg, Glamorganshire, 10th of 7th mo., 1683. It has the following names signed to it: Watkin Thomas, John David, James Thomas, William Thomas, Thomas Prichard, Jenkin Howell, William Lewis, Howell Thomas, Thomas Howell and others.

—— Ralph Lewis, with his wife Mary and their children, came with John Bevan from the parish of Eglwysilan. This is close to Llantrisant. Their certificate of removal bears the same date. John Bevan was a large purchaser of land in the new colony; not only for himself but as attorney or trustee for others. These transactions are of record at Philadelphia and West Chester. One of these was for land purchased for his cousins, Catherine and Elizabeth Prichard, of Tylcha. They were the daughters of Thomas Prichard or ap Richard ap Evan, of Collenna[1]. Thomas Prichard had married the heiress of Tylcha. He was a brother to Jane, mother of John Bevan. Tylcha is an estate in the parish of Llantrisant. Elizabeth Prichard died without issue. Katherine, in 1697, resold to John Bevan.

Another was for land purchased for Charles Bevan, brother to John. He had married his cousin, Florence, daughter of Morgan ap Evan, of Gelligaled, by Mary, eldest daughter of Richard ap Evan, of Collenna. He resided in the parish of Llantwit Vardre. He also resold to his brother, John, in 1698. Charles' son, Evan Bevan, "alias Jevan," as he sometimes signed himself, was born about the year 1678. "His father having determined to give him a liberal education, sent him to the university of Oxford[2], where he made considerable

---

[1] Limbus Patrum Morg. et Glamorg.
[2] Joseph Foster's "Alumni Oxonienses" Jevans, Evan, son of "Chas. Jefferies"? [Charles Jevanies], of Llantwitvairde Co.,: Glamorgan, gent., Christ Church, matric. 11 Feb., 1695-6, aged 18.

progress in various parts of literature. He subsequently applied himself to the study and practice of the law in Glamorganshire, and served the office of deputy sheriff of that county with reputation. But after a time he was visited in an extraordinary manner with the convictions of the Holy Spirit. . . . He was brought into deep sorrow and anguish. . . . . The Lord was pleased to bind up the bruised reed, . . . and was made a chosen vessel, fit for the great Master's use. He died at Pont y Moil in Monmouthshire the 17th of the second month, 1746[1]. He was one of the overseers to John Bevan's will, as well as one of the witnesses.

Ralph Lewis, as has already been stated, came with John Bevan and was a purchaser of two hundred and fifty acres from him.

John Bevan[2] was an active worker in the religious society of which he was a member. He was a minister, and his name appears often on committees appointed by the Meeting. In the words of the Memorial already referred to: "He was endued with a good understanding in things spiritual and temporal, discreet and prudent in his ways, of an unspotted life and conversation, grave and solid in his deportment and careful to keep concord and unity among friends, constant and unmoveable against that which would divide and rend, yet laboring to restore those that were beguiled thereby."

Although owning land that was laid out to him in different parts of the counties of Philad[a] and Chester, he settled on his plantation, located south of what is now Wynnewood Station, near to the present Philadelphia County and Haverford Township lines (see supra), upon the plantation which descended in the direct male line to Charles Bevan, who died 1809.

He was elected a member of the Assembly as a representative from Philadelphia County for the years 1687, 1695,

---

[1] "Memoir of Evan Bevan," in "The Friends' Library," Vol. XIII.

[2] In deed for 125 acres, dated Aug., 1682, to Matthew Jones, of Carmarthen, Mercer, he is called John ab Evan, of the Parish of Llantrisant, Co. Glamorgan, yeoman. In the one to Elizabeth and Katherine Prichard, called therein of "Telcha" [Tylcha], 8th May, 1682, John ab Evan, of Treverigg.

Bevan Family. 173

1699 and 1700; a Justice of the Peace for Chester County on Nov. 2d, 1689, and for Philadelphia County Nov. 6, 1685.

He made several religious visits to his native country, one of them in the year 1694. His return is noted in a letter written " Ye 29 day of ye 2d Mo., 1695," by Rees Thomas to his father-in-law in Wales. Among other things, he writes: " My unkle John Bevan came over very well and a good voyage he had, he told me he had seen thee twise," etc.

His visit in 1698 is mentioned by Hugh Roberts in the latter's journal. He traveled through New England in 1701. In an account written by himself of his experience in the New World and of his final return to Wales, he says: "We staid there many years, and had four of our children married with our consent, and they had several children, and the aim intended by my wife, was in a good measure answered. When a weighty concern came upon my mind to return to my native country, and that chiefly on truth's account, I laid it before my wife, and she could not be easy to stay behind me and we came over in the year 1704; and through the Lord's great mercy we were preserved in that tedious voyage, north about Scotland through many difficulties and from the cruelties also of the privateers, of which there were many then on that coast, as we were afterwards informed. This wonderful preservation deserves to be remembered with thanksgiving; having lost the fleet, we were only four ships coming together from Virginia, and one of them belonging to Bristol, we thought to remove to that ship, because Bristol was nearer to our habitation in Wales than London, whither our vessel was bound; we agreed with the master for our passage, and next morning we were to go on board, but that night I was under a weighty exercise about our removal, but in the morning it happened to be so stormy that he could not take us in, so he parted from us, and bore his course towards Bristol; then the weight I was under was removed, and I was very easy in my spirit; and I was afterward informed, that ship was taken near Lundy Island: This deliverance and preservation of us, I ascribe to the Lord's great favour and mercy towards us, thanks, honour and praises be rendered and ascribed to him for the same and all other mercies for ever.

In this voyage, our youngest daughter Barbara Bevan accompanied us, and she was of good service on truth's account, the short time she remained in the body; her innocency and sweet behaviour preached truth wherever she came. It is my comfort and great satisfaction, that she left a good Savour and has finished her course in peace with her maker, and is gone to her eternal rest in the mansions of bliss and joy, to laud and magnify him forever.

We landed at last at Shields in Northumberland, and staid over the meeting on first day, where we were comforted with friends; next day we set forward toward our habitation in Wales, having near three hundred miles to travel. We had several good meetings in our way, and about the beginning of the eighth month, 1704, we came to our home at Treveyricke; and from that time forward my dear wife was given up as before, to be serviceable on truth's account, and so continued during her pilgrimage here, being six years and upwards. Her house and heart since her convincement, were open to receive the Lord's messengers, both here and in America, and she was very careful and open hearted to help the poor and weak, both amongst us and others. In her last sickness, she was sensible she was not like to recover out of it, and she was satisfied and contented therein to submit to the Lord's will; speaking to me, she said, 'I take it as a great mercy, that I am to go before thee, we are upwards of forty-five years married, and our love is rather more now towards one another than at the beginning, yet I am willing to part with all, for the Lord is better than all.' She quietly departed this life the 26th of the eleventh month, 1710; aged seventy-three years, and about four months; and tho my loss thereby is great, yet it is her eternal gain."

He passed away at the ripe age of eighty years. His will, of which an abstract is here given, is remarkable for its length. The clerk in sending the particulars of it, writes:

Bevan Family. 175

"The will of John Bevan is a very long one, drawn up with every regard to due legal form. Some seventy or eighty folio. What makes it of such length is that the operative part of it is spun out with every conceivable legal common form, ringing the changes in the manner dear to the draftman's heart in the days when he was paid by the folio. The few religious phrases which commence the document are merely those which headed every will made at that period. There is nothing about them distinctive of the Society of Friends."

Short Particulars of the Will of
JOHN BEVAN, *of Trefeurig, in the parish of Llantrisant, in the County of Glamorgan, made in the first month (March), 1724-5, and proved 21 October, 1726.*

The Testator devised unto his grandson, John Bevan, the capital messuage called Treveyrig and the mill on the lands thereto adjoining.

To the children of his said grandson, John Bevan, namely: John, Richard, Thomas and Barbara, he bequeathed £25 apiece, "and for the better assuring, settling and sure making of all that Plantation or Tenem[t] of Land with all its Rights, Members & Appurtenances scituate, lyeing & being in the Township of Haverford in the County of Chester in the Province of Pennsylvania containing by Estimac'on ninety acres more or less, And all that Plantation or Tenem[t] of Land with all its Rights Members & Appurtenances scituate lyeing and being in the Township of Merion in the County of Philadelphia in the Province afores[d] containing by Estimac'on three hundred acres more or less which two Plantations I gave my son Evan Bevan[1] some time before his decease."

The Plantation at Haverford to be enjoyed by Rowland Powell according to my sons conveyance.

---

[1] In 1707 Evan Bevan paid a visit to his parents in Wales. On his return he presented to the Monthly Meeting here a certificate dated 5th mo. 10th, 1707. It is for Evan Bevan (son of John, of Treveyryg) "who lately come to visit his ancient parents, &c." The names signed to it are David John, Alice Pugh, Lewis Richard, Evan Anthony, John How, John Bevan, Evan Jevans, Barbara Bevan, Florence Jevans, Mary Prichard, Anne John, Alice Anthony, Margaret Pugh and Mary Griffith.

As to the Plantation at Merion: Half to my daughter in Law Eleanor Bevan[1] for the term of her life, with remainder to her Son Evan in fee (or in default of issue of his body, to my grandchildren, Aubrey Bevan or Charles Bevan, or to Barbara, Ann, Catherine and Jane, their sisters). The remaining half to my grandson Evan Bevan in fee[2] or in default of issue of his body, to Aubrey, Charles, &c.

£30 of Pennsylvania money to Aubrey and Charles.

"Executor and Residuary Legatee, my grandson John Bevan."

Overseers, brother-in Law William Aubrey of Pencoed, nephew Evan Bevan of Pont-y-moyle and sons in law John Wood and Owen Roberts.

Witnesses, Evan Prichard, David Morgan, Morgan David, Evan Bevan alias Jevans.

Extracted from the Archives of the District Probate Registry at Llandaff in the County of Glamorgan.

The children of John and Barbara Bevan were:

  Barbara, b. 7 mo. 5th, 1696, married William Musgrove.

1. Evan Bevan married, 11 mo. 9, 1693, at Darby Meeting, Eleanor Wood, of Darby. Children:

  John, b. 11 mo. 23, 1694; heir of Treverigg.
  Evan, b. 12 mo. 14, 1698. (See supra.)
  Aubrey, of Chester.
  Charles, of whom we have no record.
  Anne.
  Catherine.
  Jane, b. 1 mo. 29, 1707–8.

2. Jane Bevan married 10 mo. 1st, 1687, at House of Wm. Howell, in Haverford, John Wood, of Darby. Children:

  Ann, b. 9 11, 1688.

---

[1] Letters of Administration granted to Eleanor Bevan 13 Aug., 1720, at Philadelphia, on estate of her husband, Evan Bevan.

[2] There appears to be some legal term omitted here, in the abstract. The property was not devised in *fee simple*, but in tail male, making it an indefeasible estate of inheritance, and it so remained, there being no proceedings of record for barring the entail.

Bevan Family.

George, b. 1 12, 1690.
William, b. 11 17, 1691.
John, b. 12 14, 1693.
Barbara, b. 3 11, 1696.
Aubrey, b. 9 22, 1698.
Abraham, b. 1 2, 1702. (See Henry and Jordan branch.)

3. Anne Bevan married 1st mo. 23, 1696–7, at Merion Meeting, Owen Roberts, of Merion. Children:

Hugh, b. 5 30, 1699.
John, b. 8 12, 1701.
Jane, b. 4 2, 1703.
Aubrey, b. 4 24, 1705.
Owen, ob. inf.
Owen, b. 8 23, 1711.

4. Elizabeth Bevan married 4th mo. 30th, 1696, at Merion Meeting, Joseph Richardson. Children:

Samuel.	Richard.
Ellinor.	William.
Aubrey.	Barbara.
Edward.	Elizabeth.

5. Barbara Bevan, died unmarried in Wales.

JOHN BEVAN, son of Evan and Eleanor; had children as follows: John Richard, Thomas and Barbara; they removed to Wales[1].

Aubrey Bevan, third child of Evan and Eleanor, b. 1705; d. 1761. [Wills at West Chester, Aubrey Bevan, Feb. 20, 1761, Book D, 309]. Married, 1732, Ann Davis, of Darby. They had:

Mary, b. 1733, at Chester; d. 1817; married Nathaniel Forbes.
Katharine, b. at Chester; d. there, aged one year.
Tacy, b. 1736; married Thomas Pryor, of Philad^a.

---

[1] There is a tomb to one Richard Bevan in Llantrisant Church, middle of 18th century. Barbara is said to have married one Davies, and to have had Catherine, and Rees Davies, the latter ancestor to Mr. William John, now of the town of Llantrisant, Glamorganshire.

Davis, b. 1738, at Chester; d. 1818; married 6 mo.
(a) 12, 1760, Agnes Cowpland.

Jane, b. 1741; d. 1742.

Alice, b. 1743; d. same year.

(a) Children of Davis and Agnes Bevan:

Ann, b. 1761; d. 1835; married Capt. Matthew Lawlor (Mayor of Philad^a, 1801).

David, b. 1763; d. 1812; married at Chester Meeting, 6 1, 1803, Jane Shaw, widow of James Shaw, of Chester, and daughter of Thomas and Martha Sharpless.

Aubrey, b. 1765.

Isabella, b. 1767; d. 1822.

Tacey Anna, b. 1774; d. 1831; married George Stacey.

Matthew Lawlor, b. 1779; married Deborah ———.

THE RICHARDSON, PENNYPACKER AND HARMER[1] BRANCHES OF THE BEVAN FAMILY.

JOSEPH RICHARDSON, son of Samuel, the Provincial Councillor, married Elizabeth, daughter of John and Barbara Bevan. She was born 1678; died 1739 (circa). He died January, 1752. They had:

EDWARD RICHARDSON, died 1751, who married Ann Jones, and had:

SARAH RICHARDSON, died 8 July, 1818, aged 89 years; married Edward Lane, living 1754, and had:

MARY LANE, born 22 May, 1762; died 27 August, 1847; married Isaac Anderson (born 23 November, 1760; died 27 October, 1838), son of Captain Patrick Anderson. Isaac Anderson was member of Congress 1803–1807. They had besides other issue:

SARAH ANDERSON, born 10 February, 1784; died 13 September, 1853; married Mathias Pennypacker, born 15 August, 1786; died 4 April, 1852, and had:

ISAAC ANDERSON PENNYPACKER, born 9 July, 1812, died 13 February, 1856; married Anna Maria Whitaker, and had:

1. HON. SAMUEL WHITAKER PENNYPACKER, now (1895) a Judge of the Court of Common Pleas, Philadelphia (direct descendant of SAMUEL RICHARDSON, one of the first Justices of the same Court).
2. HENRY CLAY PENNYPACKER.
3. ISAAC RUSLING PENNYPACKER.
4. JAMES LANE PENNYPACKER.

---

[1]For an account of the Pennypacker Family, one of the oldest and most distinguished of the families of German descent in Pennsylvania, see recent work by Hon. Samuel W. Pennypacker.

THE HARMER BRANCH.

SAMUEL RICHARDSON, an early settler in Philadelphia, was a member of the Provincial Council and also a member of the Assembly for several years; was one of the early Justices of the county and purchaser of the Bowman Tract of 5000 acres. He died June 10, 1719.

His son, JOSEPH RICHARDSON, married 1696, ELIZABETH BEVAN, daughter of John and Barbara Bevan.

Their daughter, ELEANOR RICHARDSON, married WILLIAM HARMER.

Their daughter, RUTH HARMER, married JAMES INGLES, or Ingalls, of Chester County.

Their daughter, ELEANOR INGLES, married, 1764, JOSEPH GOVETT, of Philadelphia.

Their son, WILLIAM GOVETT, married, 1795, ELIZABETH ANNESLEY, daughter of Joseph Annesley, of Mt. Melick, Ireland.

Their son, ROBERT ANNESLEY GOVETT, married, 1831, ELIZA BUTLER, of Mt. Holly, New Jersey.

Their son, ANNESLEY RICHARDSON GOVETT, married ELIZABETH GRAY JONES, daughter of William and Martha Lloyd Jones, of Darby, Pa[1].

---

[1] Deed Tripartite made 29th of 4th month, now called June, A. D. 1696, in the eighth year of the reign of William the 3d over England and are between Samuel Richardson, of the County of Philadelphia, merchant, and Joseph Richardson, son and heir apparent, of the said Samuel Richardson, of the first part, John Bevan, of Haverford, in the Welsh Tract, Gentleman, and Elizabeth Bevan, one of the said John Bevan's daughters—of the 2d part—and William Hudson, of Philadelphia, in the said County Currier, and John Wood, of Darby, in the County of Chester, Yeoman, of the 3d part—witness that whereas there is a marriage intended to be had between the said Jos. Richardson and the said Elizabeth Bevan; and whereas, the said Samuel Richardson, is seized in this demesne as of fee in a certain capital messuage or tenement and plantation where he now dwells, situate in Bristol Township, in the said County of Philadelphia, together with 500 acres of land thereunto belonging. Now to the end that the said messuage of land and plantation aforesaid with the appurtenances may be settled upon the said Joseph Richardson and Elizabeth and their posterity as hereinafter mentioned, the said Samuel Richardson in consideration of the said marriage and of £200 to be paid by the said John Bevan as the marriage portion of the said Elizabeth and for the mutual love and affection which the said Samuel beareth unto his said son Joseph and for provision and maintenance of the said Joseph and Elizabeth in case the said marriage takes effect the said Samuel Richardson doth for himself, his heirs, executors, administrators, covenants and grants to and with the said Jos. Richardson, William Hudson and John Wood and every of them their heirs, executors, administrators and assigns, by the presents in manner and form following——
—— 200 acres of the 500 acres aforesaid tract of land, etc., in trust for Joseph and

Bevan Family–Richardson-Pennypacker-Harmer Branches   181

Elizabeth during their lives with remainder for the use of the first son after their death and first son's heirs; and for the want of such issue to use and behoof all and every son and sons of the said Jos. and Elizabeth successively, one after the other as they shall be in Seniority of age and privity of birth, and the several and heirs of their bodies. The elder and his heirs to be always preferred before the younger of them and his heirs, and for default of such male issue then to the use and behoof of all the daughters of the said Jos. and Elizabeth, and if no issue in that event to the heirs of Samuel Richardson. The remaining 300 acres of the 500 acre tract to be vested in the other children after the death of their parents and grandparents subject to limitations and appointments of the said Joseph.

Acknowledged in open Court at Philadelphia August 4th, 1696. Recorded May 10th, 1697.

1696. 29 April. Deed of settlement. Samuel Richardson to Jos. Richardson. Recorded at Philadelphia in Exempt. Record Book No. 7, page 26.

LOWRY JONES (daughter of Rees John, who emigrated from Wales in 1684), married, 1698, Robert Lloyd, also a native of Wales; their son, Richard Lloyd, married, 1736, Hannah Sellers, daughter of Samuel and Sarah Smith Sellers, of Darby, Chester County, Pa.; their son, Isaac Lloyd, married, 1765, Ann Gibbons, daughter of Joseph and Hannah Marshall Gibbons, of Westtown, Chester County; their son, Richard Lloyd, married, 1790, Mary Diehl, daughter of Nicholas and Mary Diehl, of Tinicum, Pa.; their daughter, *Martha Lloyd*, married, 1817, William, son of Robert Erwin and Ann Garrett Jones, of Philadelphia; their daughter, Elizabeth Gray Jones, married Annesley Richardson Govett (Elizabeth Jones Govett, Mrs. Annesley Richardson Govett). (See Rees John William, another page.)

WILLIAM GARRETT, son of John Garat, married Ann Kirke, 1668, in England, and emigrated with several children in 1684, and settled in Darby, Chester County, buying a large tract of land; their son, William Garratt, married, 1709, Mary Smith, daughter of John and Eleanor Dolby Smith, who emigrated in 1684; their son, William Garrett, married, 1751, Ann Oborn, daughter of William and Elizabeth Knowles Oborn, of Oxford, Philadelphia County; their daughter Ann Garrett, married, 1794, Robert Erwin Jones, son of William and Elizabeth Gray Jones, of Philadelphia, Pa.; their son, William Jones, married, 1817, Martha Lloyd, daughter of Richard and Mary Diehl Lloyd, of Darby, Pa.; their daughter, Elizabeth Gray Jones, married Annesley Richardson Govett, of Philadelphia. (Elizabeth Jones Govett, Mrs. Annesley Richardson Govett.)

RICHARD COOK was an early settler in Radnor Township. His daughter, Hannah Cook, married, 1698, Henry Oborn, son of William Oborn, an early settler in Chester County; their son, William Oborn, married Elizabeth Knowles, daughter of John and Ann Paul Knowles; their daughter, Ann Oborn, married, 1751, William Garrett (3d), son of John and Mary Smith Garrett; their daughter, Ann Garrett, married, 1794, Robert Erwin Jones, son of William and Elizabeth Gray Jones, of Philadelphia; their son, William Jones, married, 1817, Martha Lloyd, daughter of Richard and Mary Diehl Lloyd, of Darby; their daughter, Elizabeth Gray Jones, married Annesley Richardson Govett. (Elizabeth Jones Govett Mrs. Annesley Richardson Govett.)

GEORGE PEARCE emigrated from England in 1684. He married Ann Gainor, of Thornbury, County of Gloucestershire, 1679. He was one of the earliest and most influential settlers in the township of Thornbury, Chester County, naming the township after the place of his wife's nativity; their daughter, Ann Pearce, married, 1708, James Gibbons, son of John Gibbons, an early settler in Chester County, 1681; their son, Joseph Gibbons, married, 1734, Hannah Marshall, daughter of Abraham and Mary Hunt Marshall, of Chester County; their daughter, Ann Gibbons, married, 1765, Isaac Lloyd, son of Richard and Hannah Sellers Lloyd, of Merion; their son, Richard Lloyd, married, 1790, Mary Diehl, daughter of Nicholas and Mary Diehl; their daughter, Martha Lloyd, married, 1817, William Jones, son of Robert Erwin and Ann Garrett Jones, of Philadelphia; their daughter, Elizabeth Gray Jones, married Annesley Richardson Govett. (Elizabeth Jones Govett, Mrs. Annesley Richardson Govett).

THE HENRY-JORDAN BRANCH OF THE BEVAN FAMILY[1].

I. JANE, daughter of John and Barbara Bevan, d. 10 mo. 12, 1703; married 10 mo. 1, 1687, at house of Wm. Howell, Haverford, Pa. John, son of George Wood, of Darby, Chester County, Pa., Justice of the Peace, 1724, 1726; member of Assembly, 1704, 1710, 1712, 1717.

Issue.

George, b. 1 12, 1690.
William, b. 11 17, 1691.
John, b. 12 14, 1693.
Barbara, b. 3 11, 1696.
Aubrey, b. 9 22, 1698.
Abraham, b. 1 2, 1702; d. 1733.

II. ABRAHAM, son of John and Jane Wood, born 1. 2. 1702, at Darby, Pa.; died Sept., 1733, Makefield Township, Bucks County, Pa.; married Ursula, daughter of Philip and Julian Taylor, of Oxford Township, Philadelphia County; born 1701; died Lancaster, Pa., 1778 (as widow of Joseph Rose, Esq., her second husband).

Issue.

Abraham.
Elizabeth.
Anne, b. Jan. 24, 1734; d. March 8, 1799.

III. ANNE, daughter of Abraham and Ursula Wood, born January 24, 1734; died Lancaster, Pa., March 8, 1799; married William, son of John and Elizabeth (DeVinney) Henry, born in Chester County, Pa., May 19, 1729; died at Lancaster, Pa., December 15, 1786.

---

[1] The author is indebted to John Woolf Jordan, Esq., of the Historical Society of Pennsylvania, for data concerning this branch of the Bevan Family.

His grandparents, Robert and Mary A. Henry, natives of Scotland, with their three sons, emigrated to Pennsylvania in 1722, and took up a tract of land in West Caln Township, Chester County. Shortly after the death of his father, William Henry removed to Lancaster, where he engaged in the manufacture of fire-arms, and furnished supplies to Indian traders. As armorer of the troops of Generals Braddock and Forbes, he accompanied the expeditions against Fort Duquesne. He was commissioned Justice of the Peace, 1758, 1770 and 1777; Associate Justice of the Courts of Common Pleas and Quarter Sessions, 1780; and in 1776, was elected a member of the Assembly; and in 1777, of the Council of Safety. As Treasurer of Lancaster County he served from 1777 to his death in 1786; was Armorer of the State, 1778, and Assistant Commissary General 1778; and from 1784 to 1785, a member of the old Congress. In 1767 he was elected a member of the American Philosophical Society; was one of the first members of the Society for Promoting Agriculture; and a founder of the Juliana Library of Lancaster. As an ingenious inventor he enjoyed a high reputation, particularly in his applications of steam for motive power; in 1771 he invented the screw auger. In 1756, William Henry made the acquaintance of Benjamin West, and became his patron. The first figure picture, which he painted from live models, the "Death of Socrates," with several landscapes and numerous portraits, are in the possession of his descendants. During the occupation of Philadelphia by the British troops, Mr. Henry entertained as his guests at Lancaster, David Rittenhouse, John Hart and Thomas Paine, and the latter wrote his Fifth Crisis during this visit.

Issue.

William, b. March 12, 1757; d. April 21, 1821; m. Sabina Schropp.

John Joseph, b. Nov. 4, 1758; d. April 22, 1811; md. Jane Chambers.

George, d. æt. six months.

Abraham, b. Nov. 10, 1762; d. Sept. 25, 1766.

Elizabeth, b. April 8, 1764; d. Oct., 1764.

Elizabeth, b. March 27, 1765; d. June 1, 1798; md. Rev. John Molther.

Mary, b. Jan'y 11, 1767; d. Aug. 22, 1768.

Abraham, b. March 14, 1768; d. Aug. 12, 1811; md. Elizabeth Martin.

Andrew, b. Dec. 8, 1769; d. March 9, 1772.

James, b. March 13, 1771; d. Jan'y 1, 1813.

Matthew, b. Jan'y 6, 1773; d. March 28, 1804.

Nathaniel, b. April 23, 1775; d. Jan'y 9, 1776.

Benjamin West, b. Jan'y 18, 1777; d. Dec. 26, 1806; md. Catherine Huffnagle.

IV. WILLIAM, son of William and Anne Henry, born March 12, 1757, at Lancaster, Pa.; died at Philadelphia, April 21, 1821. Associate Justice Northampton County Courts, 1788–1814. Presidential Elector, 1792. Married, Nov. 21, 1781, Sabina, daughter of Matthew and Anna Maria Schropp, b. November 5, 1759, at Nazareth, Pa.; died May 8, 1848, at Bethlehem, Pa.

Issue.

Elizabeth, b. Oct. 15, 1782; d. Dec. 15, 1844; md. John Jordan.

John Joseph, b. June 17, 1784; d. Dec. 2, 1836; md. Mary R. Smith.

Anne, b. Sept. 29, 1786; d. Aug. 22, 1803.

Maria, b. May 6, 1788; d. April 8, 1858; md. Rt. Rev. Andrew Benade.

Matthew S., b. Aug. 10, 1790; d. Jan'y 20, 1862; md. 1, Anne C. Henry; 2d, Esther Berg.

Sabina, b. Aug. 4, 1792; d. March 22, 1859; md. John F. Wolle.

William, b. Aug. 15, 1794; d. May 22, 1878; md. 1st, Mary B. Albright; 2d, Sarah Atherton.

Jane, b. July 5, 1796; d. Jan'y 22, 1797.

Edward, b. July 29, 1799; d. Jan'y 22, 1800.

V. ELIZABETH, daughter of William and Sabina Henry, born October 15, 1782; died December 15, 1844; married Aug. 23, 1804, John, son of Frederick and Catharine Jordan, b. Sept. 1, 1770, in Hunterdon County, New Jersey; died in Philadelphia.

Issue.

William Henry, b. Oct. 5, 1806; d. Dec. 20, 1835; unm.

John, Jr., b. May 18, 1808; d. March 23, 1890; md. Jane Bell.

Edward, b. Sept. 10, 1810; d. Oct. 3, 1842; d. unm.

Antoinette, b. Jan'y 10, 1813; m. John T. Bell.

Francis, b. June 26, 1815; d. August 13, 1885; md. Emily Woolf.

VI. FRANCIS, son of John and Elizabeth Jordan, born June 26, 1815, in Philadelphia; died August 13, 1885, at Ocean Beach, N. J.; married Dec. 10, 1839, Emily, daughter of John L. and Margaret E. Woolf, born in Philadelphia Nov. 12, 1821; died Sept. 4, 1889.

Issue.

John Woolf, b. Sept. 14, 1840.

William Henry, b. Jan'y 27, 1842.

Francis, Jr., b. Aug. 28, 1843.

Emily, b. March 18, 1845; d. June 17, 1847.

Ewing, b. March 18, 1847.

Gilbert, b. August 5, 1848.

Antoinette, b. Oct. 17, 1849.

Walter, b. Oct. 23, 1851.

Ella, b. May 25, 1853; d. Dec. 10, 1893.

Augustus Wolle, b. Dec. 4, 1854.

Laurence Thomson, b. May 28, 1856; d. Dec. 5, 1856.

Maria Louisa, December 28, 1857; d. Jan'y 20, 1861.

Rodman, b. March 28, 1860; d. Dec. 12, 1861.

VIII. JOHN WOOLF, eldest son of Francis and Emily Jordan, born Sept. 14, 1840; married, first, Lillie Moore.

Issue.

Edgar Francis, b. Nov. 4, 1867.

Wilfred, b. April 19, 1872; d. June 23, 1873.

John Woolf Jordan, married secondly, Anne, dau. Alfred and Rebecca Page (born Nov. 12, 1859).

Issue.

Wilfred, b. April 3, 1884.
Helen, b. June 14, 1887.
Bevan Page Yeates, b. Feb'y 5, 1893.

SOCIAL AND DOMESTIC AFFAIRS IN WALES AND IN THE WELSH TRACT IN PENNSYLVANIA.

We have spoken, in the opening chapter of this book, of the superiority of the Welsh Colonists, as a class, in point of birth, education and industry, over early settlers of other nationalities on Pennsylvania soil. In behalf of the Cymric Quakers, and in support of this statement, we have offered in evidence the family documents, genealogies and biographical sketches of some of these British Friends, and it is proposed to give in this paper some information regarding their customs, manner of living, pursuits, and their general appearance and personal peculiarities. Those at all familiar with the social conditions of a very large number of Penn's followers and with emigration to other Colonies at that time, can draw here their own conclusions after a comparison has been made.

Even the very early Cymry were not, in any sense, a barbarous people. Their fondness for music, for which, as a nation, they have long been distinguished, and their taste for letters, especially in a line which the fancy of their poetic nature dictated, as shown in the encouragement of the Bardic system, offset doubtless to a considerable degree whatever of harshness or of brutality may have been acquired through centuries of fighting; and their fondness for home, and recognition of the ties of kinship, to the ninth degree, were ever distinguished traits in the Welsh character; second only, indeed, to their lofty patriotism and fiery chivalry.

The ancient Cymric laws governing social life were marked, and in many respects especially peculiar and frequently primitive in their construction. The Welsh, to a very large extent, have always been a race of farmers, or more properly herders, for the stony and sterile mountainous country of many parts of Wales extended, truly, but slight encouragement to agricultural pursuits. The early Cymric land-holder had always two places of abode. One of these, built high up on the mountain side, was called the "Vottai," or summer residence. The other house was his "Hendre," or "Permanent Home," erected in some spot in the low-lands which was sufficiently sheltered from the winter blasts. The latter places were always substantial stone edifices, with foundations of such great thickness and strength that some of the walls, built, according to the best authorities, as early as the fifth century, are yet standing and often in good condition.

An example of such an old building, yet habitable, and erstwhile a respectable, not to say pretentious abode, is Hendre Mawr, a mansion near Bala, formerly the property of the Vaughans, kinsmen, as we shall see, of John ap Thomas, and of John Cadwalader and Edward Rees, of Merion. This place was formerly reached by an old road or path, now unused, leading into the great Roman way which anciently ran from this neighborhood to Chester. The building is one-and-a-half stories high, of stone, and is long and rambling. The walls are very thick and strong.

It is claimed by many that Hendre Mawr was built in the fifth century, and its general style of architecture is certainly distinctly Roman.

Even the comparative modern houses, such as Fron Gôch, Gwern y Brechdwn, and others, built about 1550 to 1600, were frequently erected upon the sites of much more ancient mansions, the material of which and sometimes parts of the old walls were used in building the new structures. Around and near such houses great blocks of stone, sometimes finely carved, have been found. Near Fron Gôch, the home of Robert Owen, and of Evan Robert Lewis, grandfather to the Evans brothers, of Gwynedd, Pennsylvania, who came here in 1698, are several such large stones, some near the house, where they have, doubtless, been undisturbed for several centuries. Some of the Merionethshire and Denbighshire houses, of the sixteenth century, frequently had scythes fastened in the chimneys to prevent the entrance of the bands of outlawed "gentlemen," abounding in Wales at that period. The Vottai were often but wooden houses, probably of logs, with a stockade in case of a hostile attack. There was also a kind of residence, known as " Havod un Nos"—i. e., a house built in one night, which appears to have been a sort of hunting lodge, or temporary summer house. It is worth noting that the Welsh peasantry have always believed that a house built in a single night gives title to the ground upon which it is erected. It is curious how such a belief could have originated.

In the early spring the wealthy farmer left his Hendre, taking with him his family, servants, his cattle and his sheep. The sheep would be sent to the higher mountains but the cattle would be grazed on the joint pasture lands belonging to the different Hendres. So late as the seventeenth century very elaborate and particular agreements were made respecting pasture lands, which were common property, and the number of cows each individual would send, especially specified, together with the number of Hendres possessed by every person.

In August the farmer would return with his cattle to his Hendre, bringing with him the summer product of cheese and butter, to gather his harvest. Later in the season the sheep would be brought from the hills and secured in comfortable quarters for the winter.

The women oversaw the dairy, the poultry, and the spinning and knitting.

At the time of their removal to Pennsylvania, in 1682, the Cymric Quakers farmed their places in much this manner, as their ancestors had done for many hundreds of years before them.

The Welsh laws and customs governing real and personal property were, in early times, in very many respects, different from those observed in England, and these laws, however antique in principle, varied somewhat at different periods in the history of the Principality.

At first the ancient law or custom of Gavel-kind appears to have been very rigorously observed, and was confirmed by the code of Howel Dda.

Under this system the land of the father was, at his decease, partitioned equally between all of his sons. This system was even applied to the Principality itself, and later to the Districts of North and South Wales, and Powys, with most disastrous results. In time this system, when operated in manors or large farms, led to the holding of very small plots of land by the numerous descendants of the first possessor.

Another custom, practiced in some parts of Wales, was to will to the youngest son the best house and farm, and to divide the goods and the remaining fields equally amongst the other children.

English customs, of course, like English fashions, if not laws, gradually came to be followed in the Principality, so that in the sixteenth and seventeenth centuries it was usual to will the entire estate to the eldest son, and entail it upon his offspring and their heirs. It frequently happened, however, when the property had not been entailed, that the eldest son was either provided for at the time of his marriage, or his interest paid him in gold coin upon his arrival at the age of twenty-one years.

It often occurred that all of the sons, if their father was rich, were provided for at their marriage by the transfer of land to trustees, with revisions in case of failure in the line of entail.

In these cases the wills either do not mention the sons so portioned at all, or show only a bequest to such children of very trifling sums, which should never be taken as an indication of the wealth of the testator, but only as a suggestion that such a child had previously been amply endowed.

Before, however, the English system of inheritance had been generally introduced, the old custom of Gavel-kind had done its work very effectually, with the manifest result that large tracts of country, which, as we have observed, were originally the property of one person, were held by a number of individuals, his descendants, some of whom, perhaps, owned very large and productive farms, whilst others were forced to be content with little plots and tenements or stony and barren hill fields.

The latter class of freeholders often leased additional land from their more favored kinsmen, by the help of which they made shift to support their families in comfort, if not in luxury.

Leases were often held, in Wales, for many generations, and were considered valuable property. If the ground leased lay within a barony or manor, the ancient service was payable in the shape of rent to the Lord thereof. When the tenant's eldest son became of age, or married, the tenant appeared before the Steward of the manor and renounced his title in favor of his heir; but such a procedure did not deprive him of his right to sell or mortgage the property. The lease appears to have carried a perpetual title, so long as the Lord's dues were promptly remitted. The dues in such cases had anciently been military service, or domestic duties. Such rents were subsequently changed to payments in money, in lieu of these services. This custom of holding lands was very similar to the quit-rent system pursued by William Penn, and it seems remarkable that there should even have arisen any question but that the titles given by Penn to settlers were, and were intended to be, feudal in their nature.

That the poorer gentlemen of Wales clung to their barren and worthless hill farms which had descended to them as a part of their lordly ancestor's possessions, with a singular and stubborn tenacity, is not at all remarkable when we understand the position which they occupied. The small farmer or grazier was really one of the heirs of his more fortunate kinsman, and some day might, perchance, become the Lord of the neighboring country. The freehold which he inherited, a part of the original domain of his ancestor, was really a proof of his heirship, and this was one of the causes which induced the Welsh to prepare and to preserve so carefully a record of their descent, which was especially important, because, with few exceptions, they had no fixed surname. But if these small herders or farmers were not so rich, or so extensive land-holders as their more lucky kinsmen, they were still their equals in blood, in intelligence, in social standing, and in education. They were equally proud of the noble stock from whence they sprang, and were careful to designate themselves as "gentlemen" in documents of that day, a term which, with them, had a very different significance than is usually understood by it at the present time.

The Welsh held that a well-born man might follow any honorable trade or calling, and yet remain a gentleman; but that a person who could not show at least nine descents in every line to gentle blood, could not properly be so designated, no matter what his wealth, and the base-born son of gentle birth was esteemed of higher rank than the son of an unknown man who had recently acquired riches.

The amusements of the Welsh were few and simple. Games, some of them very ancient and curious, and athletic sports occupied the young, whilst the old amused themselves with their books or with fishing and hunting. Often, especially on Sunday evenings, the Welsh were accustomed to gather at each other's houses to sing and play upon their national instrument, the harp, and they then, as now, held periodical musical festivals. In the morning, it is said, the maidens would go up to the hills to tend the flocks, returning in the evening singing, and playing on their small harps. And it is believed that this old custom is still followed in some parts of the Principality. The introduction of the Quaker faith into Wales seems to have suppressed, to a great extent, the musical tendencies of our Cymric forefathers. That occasionally, however, in their new home beyond the seas, their old ballads were remembered, is yet a tradition in Merion, and more than one Welsh Friend, it is said, was privately admonished that his tuneful inclinations must cease forthwith. It is pleasant, though, whilst looking backward to the first settlement, to think that often through the wild woodland of Colonial Merion there has echoed the burthen of some ancient British war song, chanted ages ago in battle against the legions of Imperial Rome.

Upon leaving their old homes those Cymric Friends who were freeholders often disposed of their holdings to some of their kinsmen, but sometimes they returned to Wales in after years for that purpose.

Their household goods were usually shipped to Pennsylvania. Dr. Edward Jones, writing to John ap Thomas, recommends that such goods be packed in cases, where possible, to prevent mould and damage. The furniture of their houses was simple but massive, and some of it exceedingly old. The earliest inventories of Welsh estates in Pennsylvania show a comfortable if not luxurious manner of living. Napkins and tablecloths, then so rare, are of a common occurrence. Old John Humphrey, who was a widower for many years, and lived between Haverford and Bryn Mawr, on the north side of where the Pennsylvania Railroad now is, and who died in 1700, had a fine linen napkin for each day in the week—seven, and two linen table-cloths for each week.

Everything, then, was of the finest linen, and very valuable it was too, often an heir-loom to be handed down to posterity. Speaking of heir-looms, it was not uncommon for a Merion planter to leave one of his daughters " my best copper pot," as a token of affection. Such a bequest in these days of extravagance and elegance seems on first sight truly absurd, but when we look into these inventories and find that even as late as 1720, in Merion, a large copper pot or kettle was worth as much as a negro slave, namely £30, or $150, say nearly $500 of our money, the gift appears in an altogether different light.

The furniture at that day used in Merion was frequently of oak, probably antique pieces. Some articles of black walnut have also been found. Mention is often made of arm-chairs, rocking-chairs and rush-bottomed parlor chairs. Mahogany dressing or shaving cases, mahogany and oak dining-tables, kitchen or servants' tables, and " best beds," and feather beds, are continually named.

Silverware is rare. John Roberts, of Pencoyd, who died in Revolutionary times, seems to have possessed a large amount of plate, as did some others then; but in early days pewter-ware is largely in evidence. In only one or two instances, in the many inventories examined in the preparation of this work, is any mention made of any provision for lights. The exceptions noted were mentions of silver and iron candlesticks for the wall.

Some of the Welsh were very gay in their tastes.

Edward Williams, who lived where "Overbrook Farms" now are, speaks in his will of a side saddle of blue plush and bridle belonging to his white mare. One can well imagine that Mistress Williams cut quite a figure when attending the Merion Meeting in such style, hardly excusable in a Friend of that day, it might be supposed. Pictures are never found, but gilt-framed mirrors are often mentioned in appraisements as much prized luxuries.

There being no banks in the Province in those early days, we find considerable amounts of cash kept in the various houses, and, from the old inventories, we can frequently form a pretty fair estimate of the credit of the late deceased planter. When Edward Rees, or Price, of Merion, died, he had $1,500 in hard cash in his house. Other Welshmen had amounts ranging from £20 upwards; and all appear to have had goodly sums due them, and often money out at interest, usually secured by bonds.

There were few Welshmen, especially in Merion, who could not boast of a library. Their books were mostly either religious or historical in character, with many Bibles, and some few works in Latin, and now and then something in Welsh. Edward Rees possessed several Bibles in Welsh and English, and also a "Concordance." The Merion Meeting, in conjunction with those of Radnor and Haverford, early took in hand the formation of a circulating library, but of the books issued to members nearly all were upon theology. In 1699 John Humphrey left a sum of money to print the "Twelve Patriarchs," in Welsh, "if convenience be had" in these parts, but that this was never done appears from a subsequent memorandum in the minutes concerning the bequest. A very old and valuable work, formerly a part of the library of John

Social and Domestic Affairs. 195

Humphrey, and afterwards bequeathed by him to Rowland Ellis, is now in the possession of the Friends' Library on Sixteenth Street, Philadelphia. It is a large folio edition of Percy Endibie's History of the Ancient Britains, and has written in it the names of Rowland Ellis, Rowland Ellis, Jr., Herbert Rees, Eleanor Ellis and others. Most of the Welsh colonists, as we have observed, wrote excellent hands at a time when most people were satisfied to make their mark.

If the Cymry erected substantial buildings in their native country, they certainly were careful to do so in Merion. We have seen that their first shelter was in caves dug in the banks of streams, or temporary log huts. Such makeshifts were soon abandoned for more substantial log houses, which were later supplanted by stone structures.

The dwellings of John Roberts, of Pencoyd, commenced in 1684; of Rowland Ellis, at Bryn Mawr (Harriton); that built by Edward Rees, 1693; by Robert Owen, 1695; the houses of John Roberts (Wayne Mill) and Rees Thomas (now Rosemont), and the mansion erected by Jonathan Wynne in 1700 or 1701 (now near the Merion line), are still standing, and mentioned elsewhere in these pages.

Ploughs were very early in use in Merion, and "iron dogs" were used to pull out stumps. Pennsylvania axes were esteemed better than those forged in England, so early as 1682.

It has been asserted that at first all building materials, especially bricks, were hauled to Merion from the river in panniers placed upon the backs of horses or mules, and it is therefore contended that the Schuylkill River was, so late as the commencement of the eighteenth century, navigable for barges or flat-boats, so high up as where Manayunk now stands. It is argued that there being no carts in use, the boats were used to transport bricks and other building materials, and that the same was afterwards carried in panniers, as above, to the houses in course of erection. Without going into an extended argument upon the subject, or submitting in this brief sketch the historical documents extant which show clearly that the Schuylkill was never continuously navigated further than below the Falls by any vessel of greater draught than a birch-bark canoe, it may be authoritatively stated that there remains of record certain proposals for facilitating the navigation of the river, made by an engineer during Penn's government of the Province, and also sundry petitions regarding the Schuylkill fisheries, all of which show that a series of steep rapids and shallows existed, at that time, between the present Manayunk and a point not far above where the Fairmount water-works are now situate.

During the past summer the writer made an accurate survey of the Schuylkill River from a point about a mile above Pencoyd to Race Street, Philadelphia, taking note of the various elevations, and the formation and fall of the river bed. From these notes it is very evident that, even presuming, in 1682, an average depth of ten feet of water over the present flow, which, allowing for all shrinkage on account of depletion of forests and underbrush, etc., is quite improbable—allowing this, we say—no vessel or boat other than a light canoe or skiff could possibly have proceeded downward over the rapids or old Falls, without being dashed to atoms on the rocks, nor could a large vessel be towed up the stream on account of the force of the current. That all building material imported was hauled in ox-carts from Philadelphia cannot be questioned; but it is remarkable that there was but very little brick used in Merion in Colonial days, and what little was consumed was principally of domestic manufacture. The building stone used in the construction of those specimens of Colonial architecture still standing is shown to have been quarried in the immediate neighborhood of the dwellings to be erected. The timber used was from the primeval woodland on the builder's plantation.

We have spoken of log houses as the temporary homes of the colonists. Some of these are yet standing, and others were torn down within the recollection of persons yet living. One of these relics, in a good state of preservation, is yet to be seen at "Harriton," formerly Bryn Mawr, the plantation of Rowland Ellis. It stands a few hundred feet back from the last house erected, and was afterwards used by the Harrisons for their slave quarters. This may have been the first house erected here by Thomas Owen, who acted as an advance agent of Ellis in the matter of taking up and clearing the land.

The log house erected by Katherine Robert, widow of John Thomas, of Llaithgwm, of whom we shall have occasion to speak at length, stood, until recently, upon land still held by her descendants, the Jones family, a short distance above Bala, on the Schuylkill Valley Division of the Pennsylvania Railroad. The second house erected by her, a small stone building, is still extant. Just a little north of Harriton there stood until very lately a log building said to have been erected by Robert Lloyd, and two others occur to the writer as yet existing. One of these is near the old Llewelyn property, not far from Merion Square, and the other on land formerly belonging to John Roberts, of Wayne Mill, on the Mill Creek Road, north of Ardmore. The latter house was lately weatherboarded by the Croft estate, to whom it now belongs.

The Cymric Friends brought many servants with them from Wales. These so-called "servants" were not in all cases menials, but were often experienced husbandmen and farm laborers. The inducements tendered to them of a free passage for themselves and families, together with the farms which they were entitled to under the acts of Concession of Penn, led many poor but worthy persons to sell their services to prospective planters for a term of years. Occasionally these persons were related to their masters, and often on intimate terms with them.

As their term of servitude expired this class of settlers became planters upon their own account, and many of their descendants became in after time distinguished citizens. They did not always settle upon the head lands due to them, but frequently disposed of the same at a good price, and purchased property elsewhere. As the time of such servants expired the planters were forced to look elsewhere for help, and thus negro slavery was early introduced into Merion. A prime negro boy brought £30 in 1725, but a handy workman commanded a little better figure. Good cooks, then as now, were expensive, and few could be bought at the public block for less than £50, but a lusty field laborer was not worth over £20. Dusky wenches as maid servants were in constant demand, and towards the middle of the eighteenth century brought £60 and upwards, in the open market. Friends at this time do not appear to have regarded the holding of slaves as a thing opposed to divine laws, but they were merciful and just in their treatment of their human chattels. The writer has heard it related that many Indians were held in bondage by the settlers, especially in the extreme boundaries of Radnor and Haverford, and it is said that these Indians were members of the great Lenape Tribe, that famous nation of warriors who once, here, were lords of the soil. How far this tale is true, or, if true, how such a state of affairs happened, cannot now be determined.

The Welsh had three meals a day, and their dinner hour was at noon. They were fond of such dishes as mutton, or kid, seethed in milk, boiled venison, barley cakes, broth, and bread made of pounded Indian corn. Milk was a necessity to them, and cheese a national delicacy. Two tables were usually set, among the better classes, one in the living room for the family, the other in the kitchen or, during the summer, out of doors, for the farm help. We have mentioned that table linen and napkins were considered essential, and forks, but lately introduced into England, were in common use in the Welsh Tract. In personal appearance the Welsh settlers of Merion and adjacent townships were usually of medium inches, rather thick-set than otherwise, but withal of light bones and slender frame, a conformation which gave them small hands, finely arched and therefore elastic feet; producing an easy and graceful carriage of the body. They were mostly, it is said, of a ruddy or sanguine complexion, having light or auburn hair and sharp or well defined and finely chiseled features, made more prominent, doubtless, by their clean-shaven faces and closely trimmed hair. Few amongst them, we are told, were very dark. It has been remarked that their eyes were frequently dark hazel or deep blue in color, and that they engaged you with a frank, kindly and gentle expression from under their half-closed lids, but that in moments of great excitement, when the hot Cymric fighting blood overcame, for a moment, the placid Quaker, they flashed in a way that made beholders wink. The women were extremely handsome, a birthright derived from their British ancestresses, of whom it is related by the Bards that they were " more beautiful to behold than the bright sun after a summer shower." Judging from their fair descendants of the present generation, we should accept this statement without further question.

Our Cymric ancestors were not, in appearance, such soberly dressed Friends as are pictured by the painter West or described by many writers. On the contrary, they were inclined to be gay and fashionably attired. We find, from books of account of Philadelphia tradesmen, that they purchased all of their wearing apparel from the leading dealers in Philadelphia, in order that they might be sure of obtaining the very latest styles from London. One of the largest and most enterprising of Philadelphia merchants of that day was Thomas Coates, who appears to have been a great favorite with the Welsh. His account books, which his descendant, Henry T. Coates, Esq., of Philadelphia, has kindly placed at the disposal of the author, show numerous charges for various kinds of merchandise, against the inhabitants of the Barony. Among these articles, and those enumerated in other accounts, are fine beaver hats, silk gowns, silk gloves, Irish linens, silver-mounted canes and riding whips, guns, ginghams of divers hues, silk hose and handkerchiefs, bonnets and shawls, embroidered waistcoats, heavy riding coats and clothes with silver buttons. Such was the apparel worn by Merion Friends. The writer has been asked if the early Welsh were temperate. It may be said that as a race they were, but that they did not advocate prohibition is very evident. Turning again to these old account books we find that the Welsh people consumed large amounts of brandy, gin, wines and spirits. They drank more brandy than any other liquor.

The amounts of powder and shot bought in Philadelphia by the Welsh suggests that they must have been indeed "mighty hunters before the Lord." The purchase of much writing paper would indicate a considerable correspondence, whilst buckskin breeches and plush coats of violent tints would show that on meeting days the meeting-house must have presented a very gay picture. Quantities of cambric and great silk handkerchiefs, mirrors, fine bonnets and hair-pins, with now and then a new silk dress and a pair or so of gloves, impress us with the fact that our great-great-grandmothers did not permit themselves to be forgotten upon market days.

There seems but little else of importance to relate regarding the life of the first Welsh settlers in the Province of Pennsylvania. With but little change, as the years rolled on, they continued to live and to die as their fathers had done before them, and as they prayed their children might also do, until the tidal wave of the Revolution rolled to their doors. Concerning this period of the history of Merion we are for the present silent, for of those gallant troops who went forth from Merion as volunteers in Washington's army, some of whom became food for powder, or of the stirring scenes enacted during the war for Independence, within the limits of the Great Welsh Tract, this book has naught to do.

You can imagine for yourselves how the various household and social duties were regularly performed in the very early days of which we have spoken.

You can see the milkmaids going to and returning from the pasture lands in the morning and evening, the butter-churning, the cheese-making, and the industrious weaving and spinning. It is not difficult either to bring to mind the merry wedding feasts after the return of the newly wedded couple from the meeting-house, or the boisterous frolic that invariably followed upon such an occasion. Nor is it difficult to picture, of a winter's eve, the staid Welsh Friend, with spectacles perched on nose, reading aloud to his family from the Welsh Bible, brought out from dear old Cymru, whilst the great hickory logs sputter merrily in the open fire-place, and the homely tallow dips flicker a doubtful and unsteady light from their shining sockets. Without, the whirling snow is falling, silently but steadily, wrapping all of Merion in a silver brightness, whilst the howl of the gray wolf echoes dismally through the timber. Soon the book will be laid aside and the spectacles wiped and put by. The candles will be extinguished and the fires covered up. Slumber will descend on this Colonial Cymric household, and their sleep will be the sleep of the just and fearless.

The Welsh rested not with loaded match-lock and drawn rapier within easy grasp. No shivering sentry with muffled tramp across the snow, kept watch beyond a loop-holed door. No fear had they of a dread awakening; of a midnight fight against painted demons by the flare of their fired barns. In a country but thinly settled, with a great unbroken wilderness stretching to the west and to northward, the hunting grounds of roving tribes whose trade was death, the Welsh settlers remained undisturbed. Why were they so secure? Because the Province of Pennsylvania was builded upon a rock, and that rock was the policy of truth and justice, a policy preached by the ancient British Druids and cherished by our Cymric ancestors! Because the Quaker, be he Welsh, English or German, could keep his word, even with a naked Indian, and the savage knew it.

A writer has recently stated that the Colonial history of Pennsylvania was devoid of stirring events, and that it lacked the interest and activity which the Indian wars give to the story of early New England. This is true, and we should be ever thankful that it is so, and that the foundations of our state were not raised upon slaughter and cemented in blood. It is singularly pleasing to reflect that the beautiful country included in the Welsh Barony was never in Colonial days the theatre of strife; that the Indians never raised their war-whoop here; that no settler's hand was ever raised, in the Welsh Tract, against a brother's life.

As an addendum to this sketch and as an illustration of the very considerable education possessed by the early Welsh, we insert here the exhortation of Edward Foulke, Senior, to his children. Although a Gwynedd settler, he was closely related by blood to the Merion planters:

My dear Children, there has been for a considerable time something on my mind to say to you by way of advice before I return to Dust and resign my Soul to Him who gave it, though I found some difficulty in delivering my thoughts in writing, my first admonition to you is that you fear the Lord and depart from evil all the days of your life. Secondly as your Brothers and Sisters I beseech you to love one another and your neibours too, if any of your neibours injure you in word or deed bear it with patience and humility. It is more pleasing in the sight of God and good Men to forgive injuries than it is to revenge them, Rather praying for them than wish them any Evil, Least that the text in Scripture which requires an Eye for Eye and a tooth for a tooth come in your minds when you leave this world and you be found wanting; without doubt he that is thoughtless and negligent all his days about the welfare of his Soul will some day or another in the midst of his extremity Call on the rocks and Mountains to secure him from the Vengeance of an Offended God. My dear Children accustom not yourselves to loose vain talking which the Scriptures declare against. It has been hurtful to me in my youth and Stopt me in Virtue. The Temptations of the world are very powerful as Job said by experience: Be watchful over your Evening conversation, Let pious thoughts possess your Souls the moment before you close your Eyes to sleep. And if you do that it will be easier for you to find yourselves in the morning in a meek humble posture before God who preserves you from evil which will create peace and Calmness of mind with a Blessing on your outward affairs as we read of Isaac whose pious Meditation in the field was rewarded with Outward and an inward Blessing. I Desire you not to reject the least appearance of good which may Arise in your minds as if it was what could be Obtained at pleasure give speedy obedience to God who begot that divine emotion in your hearts, for a man's abode in this world is very doubtful, it often happens that Death comes without Warning yet we must go wheather ready or not, where the tree falls there it must lie—I know a man in the Land of my Nativity that went to Bed with his Wife at Night and died before morning unknown to her, Such things are designed I believe as a warning to us that we arm ourselves against the terrors of such a Day, and as of such as Die after that manner, We have little to say save they died and were buried. Placing the rest amongst the Mysteries of the Almighty hence let us view our own weakness and Judge one another with Charity—.

My dear Children that you knew the sorrow I feel now in my Old age for want of being more careful and circumspect in my youth, Altho: I did nothing that brought shame on myself or grief on my Parents yet there was among the loose and inconsiderate youth too many things which they called Innocent without considering all the while that they were building on the sand, And I was often drawn to vain mirth with them: there is a vast difference between the two sentences delivered to those who builded on the Rock and they who built on the sand. Our Saviour said of the latter their fall should be great: Let me intreat of you Dear Children assume not the appearance of Religion without a real possession of it in your hearts, Our dear Saviour compared such to a Sepulchre whited without but within full of dead Mens Bones. Yet I have better hopes of you: I mention this, I have known at times something pressing me to read good books or to go in private to Pray which I neglected and taked my Liberty in other ways, then Indifference and hardness would prevail which deprived me for a considerable time of those good Inclinations, I have also to tell you of my own Experience concerning attending week day meetings whenever I suffered triffling Occasions of my outward affairs & business, if not urgent and interrupt my going. A cool reflection and serious view made me look upon it as a loss or an Injury done to the better part of myself, and generally the business done that day did not answer my expectations of it in the morning. One thing more comes into my mind by searching of myself which is that it had been better for me if I had been more careful in my sitting with my Family at meals with a sober Countenance because Children and Servants have their Eyes and observation on those who have the command and Government of them. It has been a mighty influence on the life and manners of Youth, So my Dear Children Perhaps some of you may get some advantage by this, If you consider with attention this innocent Simplicity of Life and manners I have been speaking of you need not fear but God will protect you in safety from the Snares of the Devil and the Storms of this Inconstant World, By diligence also you shall Obtain victory over the deceitfulness of Riches. I fear there are too many of this age who suffer themselves to be carried away with the torrent of

Corruption, And not only Such as content themselves as it were in the outward Porch, but also such as made greater pretences than those, even they who were looked upon as pillers in the work have, I fear, turned their backs upon it: I lay these things close to you that you may be careful and diligent whilst you have time left, least by degrees Indifference creep upon you under the disguise of an easy mind, and forget it, as he only that holds out to the end shall be saved.

And as for your Father and Mother, Our time is almost come to a period, we have lived together above fifty years and now in Our old Age the Lord is as good and Gracious as ever he was, he gives us a Comfortable living now in the close of our Days. We have fresh Occasion to acknowledge his Benevolence and abounding goodness to us. Now I think I can with peace of mind Conclude with hopes that your prayers for us in the most needful time Especially on a Dying Pillow and our time in this World come to an end that we may have a gentle passage to Eternal rest.

I conclude in the words of the prophet Jermiah the 31st. and 21st. set thee up way marks make thee high hopes. Set thine heart toward the high way Even the way thou wouldst Turn again, Oh Virgin of Israel.

Edward Foulke Sr. was born in Wales 1651—died in Gwynedd, 1741. His pedigree appears on another page.

The above Exhortation was written in British and translated by his grandson, Samuel Foulke, in 1702.

BRYN MAWR AND ROWLAND ELLIS.

> "The peasant finds in thee a home,
> The rustic shed beside thee stands;
> Thy ancient dwellers, like the foam
> That sinks beneath the ocean sands,
> Have perished, and have left no trace
> Of what they would have been, or were;
> Forgotten in their natal place
> Their virtues, and their lineage fair."

It is generally supposed that "Bryn Mawr," so well known as the name of a station on the main line of the Pennsylvania Railroad, was chosen at haphazard, because it had a pleasing sound, and, above all, was Welsh. *Rowland Ellis* No place in Pennsylvania, however, could be more appropriately designated. It was selected because it had been the name originally given by Rowland Ellis to his plantation of some six hundred acres, afterward called "Harriton," in this immediate vicinity, and so called by him after his Welsh home. Along the rolling side of a steep ascent, less than a mile out on the winding road leading southward from the old market town of Dôlgelly, in Merionethshire, basks on the sunlit, craggy hills that ancient messuage, tenement and field, called since the days of Cadwgan, the renowned Britain, and Heaven only knows for how many hundreds of years before, "Tythyn Bryn Mawr." The sleepy little pointed-stone house, perched on the site of the hendre of an early Welsh Prince, amid its deserted garden, broken down stone walls and dilapidated outbuildings, now the abode of a poor mountaineer, was the birthplace of Rowland Ellis, and was built by his grandfather, Rees Lewis. The property seems to have been lately repaired; a new roof has been put on and the quaint old diamond-pane windows replaced by modern sashes. There was also formerly, it is thought, a portico over the doorway. The walls remain untouched, and the interior is unchanged.

A Pennsylvanian who visited Bryn Mawr a few years since says that it is "a comfortable stone house; the floors are of stone; and it was built by Rees Lewis, grandfather of Rowland Ellis, A. D. 1617, as an inscription on one of the rafters tells. To the right of the house are the remains of an ancient garden which has seen better days. Its walls are gone, but there are traces of old paths, while ancient box and venerable yew-trees tell of what has been." The title papers to this property are now in possession of Edward Griffith, Esq., of Springfield, near Dôlgelly, a descendant of Ann, eldest daughter of Rowland Ellis by his first wife. Amongst these old documents is the original marriage contract and settlement made upon the marriage of Ellis Price and Ann Humphrey, the parents of Rowland Ellis, in 1649. The parties to this settlement were: Humphrey (Humffrey) ap Hugh, of Llwyngwril, gentleman, father of Anne Humphrey, Rees Lewis ap John Griffith, of Dyffrydan, gentleman, father of Ellis Price, who was his second son, and Richard Nanney, of Llwyngwril, and David Ellis, of Gwanas, gentlemen, who were to act as trustees. Richard Nanney was cousin to Ann, his father, the Rector of Llangelynin, having married one of the daughters of Hugh Gwyn, of Peniarth. David Ellis was brother-in-law to Rees Lewis, the latter having married his sister Catherine.

Mr. Griffith very kindly permitted me to photograph this ancient document, which is on parchment and exceedingly difficult to decipher. What is here given of it was made out only by the use of a very powerful glass, and at the expense of a very severe strain upon the writer's eyes. The time occupied in making the copy was, altogether, about forty-eight hours. It has been thought best to give at first here an account of the various papers extant concerning Rowland Ellis and his ancestry, because they are parts of the proofs of descent of the allied Pennsylvania families of Ellis, Evans, Humphrey, Owen (through Rebecca, wife of Robert Owen), and others. The marriage settlement in question is as follows, the lines omitted being legal repetitions or indecipherable words:

BRYN MAWR,
Near Dólgelly. Built by Rees Lewis. The Birthplace of Rowland Ellis, 1650.

𝕿𝖍𝖎𝖘 𝕴𝖓𝖉𝖊𝖓𝖙𝖚𝖗𝖊, made the furst day of January in the yeare of Our Lord God, according to the computation of the Church of England, One thousand, Sixe hundreth, forty and nien. 𝕭𝖊𝖙𝖜𝖊𝖊𝖓 Rees Lewis ap John Gruffith, of Dyffrydan in the County of Merionethshire, gentleman, of the first Pty., Humffrey ap Hugh, of Llwyngwril in the sayd Com. of Merioneth, gentleman, of the second Pty., and Richard Nanney, of Llwyngwril in the Sayd County, gentleman, and David Ellis, of Gwanas in the Sayd County of Merioneth, gentleman, of the third Pty., 𝖂𝖎𝖙𝖓𝖊𝖘𝖘𝖊𝖙𝖍—That yt is covenanted granted and fully agreed upon by and between the Sayd Partys to these Presents—And first the Sayd Rees Lewis for himself his heyrs, Executors and Administrators and for any of them doth covenant promise and agree to and with the sayd Humffrey ap Hugh, his heyres, Executors and Administrators ——— and any of them doth covenant promise and agree that Ellis Rees, the Second Sonne of the sayd Rees Lewis, Shall and will before or one this side the feast day of the purification of our blessed Virgin Mary next ensuing, the date hereof, espouse, mary and take to wife, Anne Humffrey, one of the daughters of the sayd Humffrey ap Hugh, if the sayd Anne doth thereunto consent and agree, and the laws of God and the Holy Trinity doe Permit and suffer the same and Likewise the sayd Humffrey ap Hugh for himself his hyres, executors and administrators, or any of them doeth covenant promise and agree with the sayd Rees Lewis his heyres, Executors & Administrators, and with each of them by these presents That the Sayd Anne Humffrey shall and will on this side of the sayd feast of the Purification, espouse, mary and take to Husband the sayd Ellis Price yf the Sayd Ellis doeth thereunto consent and agree and the Laws of God and the Holy Trinity doe Permit and Suffer the same.

Yn Consideration of wch marriage for to be hadd and Solemnized and performed—The Sayd Rees Lewis doeth for himself his heyres executors and administrators, Covenant promise and agree, with the Sayd Humffrey ap Hugh, his executors and Administrators and wth any of them by these Presents—that they the Sayd Rees Lewis and Ellis Price shall and will from tyme to tyme and att all tymes hereafter when and as often as either of them shall reasonably and lawfully be required by the sayd Humphrey ap Hugh, his heyres Executors and Administrators, att the proper costs and charges of the law of the sayd Humffrey ap Hugh, his heyres Executors and Administrators or some of them, Do make Sale and deliver execute and acknowledge, permitt, suffer to be done and acknowledged and executed unto the sayd Richard Nanney or David Ellis, or to such other Person or persons as the sayd Humffrey ap Hugh, his heyres, executors, or administrators, or any of them, shall in that behalf [Select] . . . . [in trust] All those severale messuage, land Tenement hereditment of the sayd Rees Lewis, commonly called and known bo the several and special name and names of Tythyn y Bryn Mawr and Llwyn y Cai Dy, with their rights— and appurtenances, situate lyeing and being in the sayd Township of Dyffrydan and Comt. of Merioneth aforesaid. . . . And yt is fully and absolutely covenanted determined and agreed . . . . That all and singular . . . . . Tythyn Bryn Mawr and Llwyn y Cai Dy, whereupon the bawne called [Yfyndom?] . . . . . the same now are or lately were in the tenure occupation and possession of the Sayd Rees Lewis . . . . . to the use and behoof of the Sayd Ellis Price, for and during the tearme of his natural life . . . . and from and after his decease, then to the use and behoof of the sayd Anne Humffrey for and during the tearme of her natural life, for and in the name of the Said Anne for and during the tearme of her n'rall life for and in the name [Then reserving certain uses to Rees Lewis, to the eldest of the Sayd Ellis Price, and to his eldest son, in tail male, or in default of said issue, then to the Second Son of the Said Ellis Price, by the Said Anne, and so on, until upon exhaustion of the male line, or if there is no male issue of the Said Ellis Price and Ann Humffrey, then to the first daughter, and to her eldest Son, and So on in regular Succession] and in default of such yssue Thyn to the use and behoof of one Rowland Price, thryd sonne of the Sayd Rees Lewis and the hyers of hys body Lawfully yssuing, and in default of such yssue, thyn to the use and behyoff of Griffith ap Rees the fowrth Sonne of the Sayd Rees Lewis and of the hyres of hys body lawefully yssuing and in default of such issue Then to the use and behyoffe of the right heyres of the Sayd Rees Lewis aforesd. [It is further provided] That yf it happin the Sayd Anne Humffrey to dye or [depte] out of thys world before the furst day of May wch Shall in the yeare of our Lord God according to the Said computation one thousand Sixe hundreth fieftie and fower without any yssue of her body by the body of the Sayd Ellis Price lawefully begotten, then Living, or yt the Sayd Anne Shall happen to dye or Depte out of this world before the Sayd furst Day of May wch Shall be the Sayd yeare of our Lord God according to the Sayd computation One thousand Six hundred fieftie and ——— without lawful issue (or if such issue die before then) (then) the sayd moety or one half of the Sayd Severall messuage lande and tenement Tythyn y bryn Mawr and Llwyn y Cae Dy ——— [Shall by the deed of the said Richard Nanney and David Ellis, Trustees, go to the] use and behoof of the Sayd Humffrey ap Hugh, his executor administrators and Assigns, untill and unles the Sayd Rees Lewis or Ellis Price their heyres or assigns doe well and truly pay or cause to be payd unto the Sayd Humffrey ap Hugh hys executors, Administrators or Assigns the full and lawful Sumn of one hundreth pounds of good and Lawefull money of England in one whole Sume and entyier paymt in all or upon the furst day of May next ensuinge such Decease of the Sayd Anne Humphrey, without ysue living as aforesayd or the Decease of such ysue, as aforesayd, att or within [the] Church poarch of the P'ish Church of Llanglynin betweene the houeres of Nien of the clocke in the mornige and Three of the clocke in the afternoone of any of the Sayd Dayes [The final clause contains agreement of revision to Rees Lewis' heirs].

The witnesses to this document were: John ap William ap Humffrey, David John Hugh, Griffith ap Rees Lewis, Edward Vaughan and John ap Hugh. Rowland Ellis, born in 1650, was the only child of Ellis Price (alias ap Rees) and Ann Humphrey, and therefore inherited Bryn Mawr under this settlement, and continued to live there until his permanent removal to Pennsylvania in 1696; when he sold the place to Lewis Owen, of Tyddyn y Garreg, his kinsman, to whom he was indebted.

The deed made by Rowland Ellis at this time for the property is in the possession of Mr. Griffith, who also has the marriage settlement made by Rowland Ellis in 1696 on the marriage of his daughter, Ann, to Rev. Richard Johnston, an Episcopal Clergyman, of whom we shall have occasion to speak more particularly further on.

The descendants of Rowland Ellis in Pennsylvania possess several original papers which are of very considerable interest. One of these, now in the hands of Rowland Evans, Esquire, of Haverford, Lower Merion, who is descended in the direct male line from Eleanor Ellis, daughter of Rowland, and the wife of John Evans, of Gwynedd, is the original manuscript pedigree of Rowland Ellis in his (Rowland Ellis's) own handwriting. This was certainly compiled prior to 1697, because the name of his daughter Catherine, born in that year, is not, apparently, in his hand, but has been added by another person. It is therefore fair to presume that the pedigree was made in Wales just prior to his last voyage to Pennsylvania. A facsimile of the old document is given as an illustration to this article, and also, as the genealogy is in the form of a chart, so much of it as is necessary for explanation is, for convenience, printed here much after the style of the old Welsh Heralds[1]:

Rowland (Ellis) [of Bryn Mawr in Merionethshire, Wales, born 1650.] He was Son of Ellis ap Rees ap Lewis ap Sion[2] ap Gruffydd ap Howell. The mother of Rowland Ellis was Ann verch Humphry ap Hugh ap David ap Howell ap Gronw. The mother of Anne verch Humphry was Elizabeth verch John. The mother of Elizabeth verch John, was Sibil verch Hugh Gwyn of Penarth. The mother of Sibill verch Hugh was Jane verch Sir Hugh Owen.[3] The mother of Humphry ap Hugh was Catherine verch Sion, ap Rhydderch Abergynolwyn. The mother of Hugh ap David, ap Howell, was Mary verch Hugh Sion Bedo. The mother of Ellis ap Rees, ap Lewis, was Catherine verch Elissa, ap Davidd ap Owen ap Thomas ap Howell ap Mrhedydd ap Gruffydd Derwas. The mother of Catherine verch Elissa ap Davidd was Mary verch Sion, ap David ap Gruffydd. The mother of Rees ap Lewis was Ellin verch Howell Gruffydd. The mother of Lewis ap John Gruffydd was Elsbeth verch Dd Llwydd. Rowland Ellis married first Margaret daughter of Ellis Morris, descended from Gruffydd Derwas, and had issue: Anne, and Jane. He married secondly his cousin, Margaret, daughter of Robert ap Owen ap Lewis ap Sion ap Gruffydd ap Howell.

---

[1]All of the lines given by Rowland Ellis are not here run out. The spelling follows the original. See original MS.

[2]Sion is the Welsh way of writing *John*. Rowland Ellis used both forms indifferently. As stated before, these Welsh names were anciently, and are now, spelled in many different ways, any of which are frequently correct.

[3]Should be sister of Sir Hugh Owen and verch Owen ap Hugh.

The mother of Margaret verch Robert ap Owen, was Margaret verch Sion, ap Lewis ap Tyddur ap Ednyved ap Howell ap Mrhedydd ap Gruffydd Derwas. The mother of Margaret verch Sion ap Lewis, was Agnes verch Owen, ap Thomas ap Owen ap Thomas ap Howell ap Mrheydd ap Gruffydd Derwas. The mother of Agnes verch Owen, ap Thomas, was Mary verch Ellisa (Byrin?). The mother of Robert ap Owen, ap Lewis, was Mary, verch Tudwr Vaughan, ap David Llwydd ap Tyddwr Vaughan ap Gruffydd ap Howell [ap Gr. Derwas]. The mother of Mary verch Tudwr Vaughan, was Agnes verch Lewis ap Mrheydd. [The mother of Agnes, was Elin verch Robert ap Howell ap David ap Mevrig]. The mother of Owen ap Lewis, was Elin verch Howell Gruffydd. The mother of Lewis ap Sion Gruffydd, was Elsbeth verch David Lloyd.

The children of Rowland Ellis by his second wife are given as: Elizabeth, Rowland, Robert, Ellin (m. John Evans), (Catherine).

Other records referred to in the compilation of this article were, deed to him for his land in Pennsylvania, he being described therein as " of Brin Mawr, in the County of Merioneth, gentleman"; assignment, in trust, dated after 1717, he being then of Plymouth, Pennsylvania, gentleman, reciting transactions with Humphrey Owen, of Llwyndu (in Llwyngrill), and Lewis Owen, of Tyddyn y Garreg, concerning certain loans on bonds.

There are also several testimonials of him by Friends who knew him both in his native country and in Pennsylvania. Some of these are embodied in the sketch of his life which we reprint in this article. The old pedigree above described having been found to agree in the essential points with the Herald's visitations made out 1585–1601, and with parish registers and other documents remaining in Wales, it is a comparatively easy task for one versed in Welsh genealogy to give a detailed account of the ancestry of Rowland Ellis, who, as we have seen, was the son of Ellis Price, son of Rees ap Lewis ap John Griffith, of Nannau.

Tythyn Bryn Mawr, in Merionethshire, appears to have anciently formed a part of the Nannau Estate, which was the early possessions of Rowland Ellis's ancestors, many of whom lie buried in Dôlgelly Church.

The family from whence Rowland Ellis sprang was of princely lineage, descending in the direct male line from Bleddyn, the son of Cynfyn, who was Prince of Powys, and was so imprudent as to get himself murdered by the amiable "gentlemen of Ystrad Tywy," in the year 1072. This Prince, in defiance to the advice of his countrymen, married Isabel, daughter of Picot de Say, a Norman Knight, and had by her a son called Cadwgan, "the renowned Briton," who, besides being Lord of Ystrad Tywy in Cardigan, was also Lord of Nannau, in Merionethshire.

Cadwgan also fell by the dagger of the assassin, and was succeeded, as Lord of Nannau, by a long line of notable descendants.

As we will give particulars concerning each generation in the chart pedigree on another page of this article, it is only necessary here to mention a few of the most prominent members of this old family.

One of these early Lords of Nannau was Meuric ap Ynyr Vychan, who was living in the 21st year of Edw. III (1347–8). In the Parish Church of Dôlgelly is the tomb of this Lord. It is a sepulchral effigy in mail and plate armor, having a shield on his breast, on which is carved a lion, and the stone bears this inscription: "Hic Jacet Meuric Filius Ynyr Vachan." The effigy formerly stood in the aisle, but was afterward set in the wall under a memorial window of more recent date. Meuric[1] was succeeded by his son Meuric Lloyd, who was father to Howell, of Nannau, commonly called Howell Sele.

---

[1] The father of this Meuric (Ynyr Vychan), appears to have been a very violent man even for the age in which he lived. In the Parliament of 15 and 16 Edward II, (1322–3) he and others were charged with attacking, on the next Wednesday after the feast of St. Gregory, in the 15th of that king, the Castle of John de Grey, of Ruthen, setting fire to the town and killing two men.

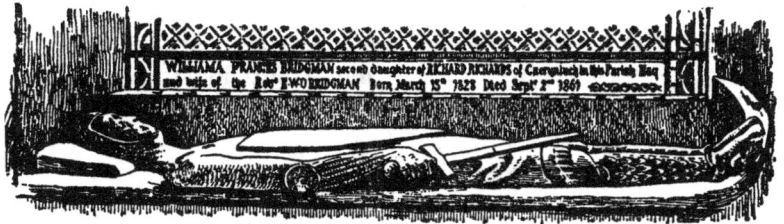

"**Hic Jacet Meuric filius Ynyr Vachan.**"

EFFIGY OF MEURIC, OF NANNAU (ANCESTOR OF ROWLAND ELLIS OF BRYN MAWR), FOURTEENTH CENTURY, IN DÔLGELLY CHURCH, NEAR BRYN MAWR, MERIONETHSHIRE, NORTH WALES.

When Owen Glendower instituted his famous rebellion, the Lancaster Howell Sele (his cousin) refused to join, which enraged Owen to so great an extent that meeting him one day whilst hunting alone in Nannau Park, Owen having one attendant, Madog, they fell upon Howell and slew him, throwing his body into a great oak, hollow through age. This Nannau oak was for centuries an object of superstitious dread to the peasantry of Merionethshire, and fell down on the 13th of July, 1813. Throughout Merionethshire it was known as the Spirit's Blasted Tree—" Conbren Yr Ellyll." The vassals of Nannau, and Howell Sele's family were filled with alarm at his disappearance, but inquiries and searches gave no information of his whereabouts.

After Glendower's death, however, on a dark evening in November, an armed horseman was observed riding furiously up the hill which leads from Dôlgelly to Nannau; it was Madog, who after the death of Glendower, hastened to fulfill his master's last command and unravel the horrid mystery. He told his story and referred to the oak for confirmation.

The tree was cut into and Howell's body discovered, grasping with his right hand his rusty sword. The remains were removed to the neighboring monastery of Cymmer, where they were interred. After the oak fell the wood was made into a variety of utensils, and many engravings of the tree, framed with its wood, are to be found in Dôlgelly.

The story has been woven into a very fine ballad by Mr. Warrington, printed in the notes to *Marmion*, by Scott. It is partly as follows:

> "Led by the ardor of the chace,
>   Far distant from his own domain,
> From where Garthmaelen spreads her shade,
>   The Glyndwr sought the opening plain.
>
> "With head aloft and antlers wide,
>   A red-buck rous'd, then cross'd his view;
> Stung with the sight, and wild with rage,
>   Swift from the wood fierce Howell flew.
>
> * * * * * *
>
> "They fought, and doubtful long the fray,
>   The Glyndwr gave the fatal wound.
> Still mournful must my tale proceed,
>   And its last act all dreadful sound.
>
> "I marked a broad and blasted oak
>   Scorch'd by the lightning's livid glare,
> Hollow its stem from branch to root,
>   And all its shrivell'd arms were bare.
>
> "Be this, I cried, his proper grave!
>   (The thought in me was deadly sin);
> Aloft we rais'd the hapless chief,
>   And dropped his bleeding corpse within.
>
> * * * * * *
>
> "He led them near the blasted oak,
>   Then conscious, from the scene withdrew;
> The peasants work with trembling haste,
>   And lay the whitened bones to view.
>
> "Back they recoil'd: the right hand still
>   Contracted, grasp'd a rusty sword,
> Which erst in many a battle gleamed,
>   And proudly deck'd their slaughtered lord.
>
> "Pale lights on Caday's rocks were seen,
>   And midnight voices heard to moan;
> Twas even said the blasted oak
>   Convulsive heav'd a hollow groan.

DÔLGELLY CHURCH, NEAR BRYN MAWR, Merionethshire, Wales.

> "And to this day the peasant still
> With cautious fear avoids the ground;
> In each wild branch a spectre sees,
> And trembles at each rising sound."

The brave but unfortunate Howell had married Mali, daughter of Einion ap Griffith, of Cors y Gedol, and had a son Meuric Vychan, of Nannau, who, together with his uncle, Griffith Derwas, is named among the heirs of a "Wele," of free land, in the township of Nannau, in an extent of Merionethshire taken 7 Henry V. 1419–20, and the "farm," of the mill of Llan Vachreth was granted to both at Michaelmas, 35 Henry VI. for four years. Meuric, of Nannau, was foreman of the jury at Caernarvon, 1444, and was living, a very aged man, 2 Henry VII., 1486. He married Angharad, daughter of David ap Cadwgan, descended from Elystan Glodrydd, and had a son, called David ap Meuric Vychan, of Nannau, who having married Ellen, daughter of Howell ap Rhys ap David, descended from Owen Brogyntyn, had a son, Howell ap David, of Nannau, whose name appears in a roll of accounts for Merionethshire ending at Michaelmas, 2 Henry VIII. (1510), as surety for William ap Jenkin ap Iorwerth, "farmer" of the mills of Llanvachreth and Llanegryn. Howell married Ellin, daughter unto Robert Salisbury, of Llanrwst, son of Thomas Salisbury, descended from Sir Henry, a Knight of the Holy Sepulchre, and had issue: Griffith ap Howell, of Nannau, who was living 33 Henry VIII., 1541–2. He married Jane, daughter of Humphrey ap Howell, ap Ievan, of Yns-y-maen-gwyn; her mother being Anne, daughter of Sir Richard Herbert, Knight, of Colebrook. Griffith had two sons: Hugh, who was living 1588, and John ap Griffith, who married Elizabeth, daughter of David Lloyd, of Trawvynydd, and had three children: Ellen, Jane and Lewis. Lewis was father to Rees, who had Ellis ap Rees (alias Ellis Price), who married Ann, daughter of Humphrey ap Hugh, of Llwyngwrill, and was father to Rowland Ellis.

ARMS OF THE NANNAU FAMILY.
Or, a lion rampant, azure.

PEDIGREE OF ROWLAND ELLIS, OF BRYN MAWR, BORN ANNO 1650.

I. BLEDDYN AP CYNFYN, Prince of Powys; murdered, 1072. He married 2ndly, Isabel, daughter of Picot de Say, a Norman Baron, and had:

II. CADWGAN AP BLEDDYN, Lord of Yestradtywy, Cardigan, and of Nannau in Merionethshire, murdered about 1109, who married Gwenllian, daughter of Gruffydd ap Cynan, Prince of Gwynedd. She was subsequently the wife of Gruffydd, Prince of South Wales, and is stated to have been killed in battle in 1135. By her he had:

III. MADOC AP CADWGAN, Lord of Nannau, who married Eva, daughter and heiress of Philip ap Uchtryd ap Edwin, Lord of Tegeingle, ap Gronwy ap Einion ap Owen ap Howell Dda, King of all Wales, and had issue:

IV. MEURIC AP MADOC, Lord of Nannau, who espoused Gwenllian, daughter and heiress of Ierwerth ap Predyr ap Gronwy ap Adda ap David Gôch, from Ednowain ap Bradwin, Head of the 15th Noble Tribe of Wales, and a lineal descendant of the kings of Britain. By her he had:

V. YNYR AP MEURIC, Lord of Nannau, whose wife was Gwyrvyl, daughter and heiress of Madog ap Llowarch Vycnan ap Llowarch Gôch, ap Llowarch Holbwrch, Treasurer of Gruffydd, P. of W. They had:

EINION AP YNYR; he was consecrated Bishop of St. Andrews, 21 October, 1268, and:

VI. YNYR AP YNYR, alias Ynyr Vychan, Lord of Nannau, who married Gwenhwyvar, daughter of Gruffydd ap Gwen ap Gronwy ap Einion ap Seissyllt, Lord of Mathafon. He presented a petition to Edward, Prince of Wales, at Kensington, 33 Edw. I. (1304–5), for the office of Raglor of the Comôt of Talybont, stating that the King had given it to him for taking Madoc ap Llewelyn, who, in the last war, had made himself Prince of Wales. The petition, however, was not granted, as no charter could be shown. In the Parliament of 15 and 16 Edw. II. (1322–23), he and others were charged with attacking, on the next Wednesday after the feast of St. Gregory, in the 15th of Edw. II., the Castle of John Grey, at Ruthen, setting fire to the town, and killing two men. (Rec. Caern. 220; Rolls of Parlt. Vol. I, p. 397.) He had issue by Gwenhwyvar, his wife:

VII. MEURIC AP YNYR VYCHAN[1], Lord of Nannau, living 21 Edw. III. (1347–8). He married Angharad, dau. Gruffydd ap Owen ap Bleddyn ap Owen Brogyntyn, Lord of Dinmael and Ediernion, ap Madog ap Meredith, ap Bleddyn, Prince of Powys. He lies buried in Dôlgelly church, and a tomb to his memory is still extant there. It is a sepulchral effigy, in stone, of Meuric, in plate and mail, having his shield charged with the arms which he assumed, a lion passant guardant, with this inscription: "HIC JACET MEURIC FILIUS YNYR VACHAN." She had issue, by Angharad, his wife:

VIII. MEURIC LLOYD AP MEURIC, Lord of Nannau; died before 1400. He married Mallt, dau. Howell Pickhill, ap David ap Gronwy ap Ierworth ap Howell ap Meredith ap Sandde Hardde, Lord of Morton in Denbighshire, and had:

GRUFFYDD DERWAS, liv. 1416; he was Esquire of the Body to Henry VI. From him are descended many of the lines hereafter mentioned (vide Powys Fadog, Vol. V, p. 112), and:

IX. HOWELL SELE, Lord of Nannau; he was slain by Owen Glendower, in Nannau Park about, 1401. He married Mali, dau. Einion ap Gruffydd ap Llewelyn ap Cynric ap Osborn, of Cors y Gedol, Merionethshire, and had:

X. MEURIC VYCHAN, Lord of Nannau; he, with his uncle, Gruffydd Derwas, are named among the heirs of a "Wele" of free land, in the township of Nannau, in an extent of Merionethshire, taken 7 Henry V. (1419–20), and the "farm" of the mill of Llanvachreth was granted to both at Michaelmas 35

---

[1] Powys Fadog, Vol. V, p. 55, etc.; Dwnn II, Nannau.

Henry VI. (1456) for four years. In 1444 Meuric was foreman of the Jury at Caernarvon. He was living 2 Henry VII. (1486), at which time he was probably aged over ninety years. He married Angharad, dau. David ap Cadwgan ap Philip Dorddu ap Howell ap Madoc ap Howell ap Griffith ap Gronwy ap Gwrgenen ap Holdlien gôch ap Cadwgan ap Elystan Glodrydd, Prince of Fferlys, and had:

XI. DAVID AP MEURIC VAUGHAN, of Nannau, who married Ellen, dau. Howell ap Rhys ap David ap Howell ap Gruffydd ap Owen ap Bleddyn, Lord of Dinmael ap Owain Brogyntyn, descended from the Princes of Powysland, and had:

XII. HOWELL AP DAVID, of Nannau. He appears in a roll of accounts for Merionethshire, ending Michaelmas, 2nd Henry VIII. (1510), as surety for one William ap Jenkin ap Ierworth, "farmer," of the mills of Llanvachreth and Llanegryn. He married Ellen, dau. of Robert Salsbury, of Llan-Rwst, ap Thomas Salsbury hên (liv. 1451), ap Sir Henry Salsbury, Knight of the Holy Sepulchre (died about 1399), ap Rawling Salsbury ap William Salsbury, M. P. 1322, and had:

XIII. GRIFFITH AP HOWELL, of Nannau, and Lord thereof; living 33d Henry VIII. (1541–2). Hugh Nannau, the eldest son, signed the pedigree as head of the family, 24 July, 1588. (Dwnn II, p. 226.) He married Jane, dau. Humphrey ap Howell ap Ievan, of Yns y Maen Gwyn. Her mother was Anne, dau. Sir Richard Herbert, Knight of Coldbrook. [Jane was a lineal descendant of Henry IV., King of England,] and had:

HUGH, Lord of Nannau, m. Annest, dau. Rhys Vaughan, of Cors y Gedol, living 1588.	JOHN Nannau, alias John ap Griffith, of Nannau. He held certain lands in the township of Dyffrydan in Dôlgelly Parish, and elsewhere.	=	ELIZABETH, dau. David Lloyd, of Trawsfynedd.	MARGARET m. William ap Tudor, ap Gruffyd ap Ednyfed of Egryn Abbey.	ELIZABETH —— Anne.
	LEWIS AP JOHN GRIFFITH, of Dyffrydan, etc. He was living 28 Augt., 1654, being then described as holding the lands of Dewisbren and Debafeder.	=	ELLEN, dau. Howell ap Griffith.	ELLEN born prior 1588.	JANE born prior 1588.
	A			B	

Bryn Mawr and Rowland Ellis.

A		B
Rees Lewis ap John Griffith, of the township of Dyffrydan, in Co. Merioneth, built Bryn Mawr, 1617; living 1649; called also Rees Lewis, of Dyffrydan, gentleman.	= CATHERINE, dau. Elisha ap David (his son David Ellis was liv. 1649) ap Owen ap Thomas ap Howell ap Meredith ap Griffith Derwas; descended from Bleddyn, P. of Powys. (See supra.)	Owen ap Lewis; he married Mary, daughter of Tudor Vaughan, of Caer y Nwch, in Co. Merioneth, lineally descended from Griffith Derwas, and had Robert, who had Margaret, 2nd wife of Rowland Ellis.

LEWIS AP REES	ELLIS AP REES = ANN HUMPHREY	GRIFFITH Price	ROWLAND Rees
m. Elizabeth, dau. and heiress of ———, and had Elizabeth, only child, who m. Robert ap Owen, whose child Lewis Owen d. s. p. circa 1695; his lands descended to Rowland Ellis, as next heir. (Ellis MS.) Lewis ap Rees was of Maes y helme in 1654.	ELLIS AP REES (alias Ellis Price), of Bryn Mawr, in the township of Dyffrydan, "gentleman"; his marriage settlement is dated 1649, by which his father transferred to him Tythyn Bryn Mawr. He was living 11th of 1st month (March), 1678–9, but died before 1696. = ANN HUMPHREY, daughter of Humphrey ap Hugh, of Llwyn Gwrill, gentleman, 1649. He was son of Hugh ap David ap Howell ap Gronwy ap Einion.	liv. 1649.	liv. 1649.

MARGARET = ROWLAND ELLIS, of = MARGARET, daughter of Robert ap
dau. and heiress | Bryn Mawr, in the | Owen ap Lewis ap John Gruffydd,
of Ellis Morris, | township of Dyffry- | of Dyffryddan. (See supra.) She
of Dolgun, his | dan, Merionethshire, | was his cousin. She died about
kinswoman. She | "gentleman"; born | 1730.
was married | 1650 at Bryn Mawr;
about 1672; | died at Gwynedd,
died soon after. | Pennsylvania, in the
| 7th month, 1731.
| (See MS. pedigree in
| his own handwriting
| herewith.)

ANN	JANE	ELIZABETH	ROWLAND	ROBERT	ELLIN	CATHERINE
m. Rev. Richard Johnston, Curate of Dôlgelly. He was at one time minister of St. Illtyd,		d. unm.	ELLIS, JR.	ELLIS.	m. John Evans, of Gwynedd, son of Cadwalader Evans,	d. unm.

near Dôlgelly. The present representative of this line is Edward Griffith, Esq., now (1895) of Springfield, Dôlgelly.

son of Evan ap Evan Robert Lewis, of Fron Gôch, Merionethshire. The present representatives of this line are Rowland and Allen Evans, Esqs., of Haverford, Penna. (1895.) (See infra.)

Many years ago there appeared in the *Friend* such an excellent account of Rowland Ellis, that we have thought well to reprint it here, making some slight corrections.

"Rowland Ellis was born near Dôlgelly, in Merionethshire, North Wales, in the year 1650. His place of abode was on his paternal estate, called Brin-Mawr. Soon after he was of age he married a young woman of some wealth and distinction near by, who was soon taken from him, leaving him a child, Ann, who, by her mother's death, became heiress to considerable estate. About the twenty-second year of his age he was convinced of the Truth as held by the people called Quakers, and receiving it in the love of it, he walked with faithfulness therein. He now married again. His second wife appears to have been Margaret . . . . . by whom he had several children. She was of a family who had already become members amongst Friends. He was soon called to suffer in support of his principles. In the year 1676 he was imprisoned with others on the charge of not resorting to the 'parish church,' so called, and on the 6th of the Sixth-month, the prisoners were brought before the judges at Baala. These did not proceed to try them on the indictment, but tendered them the oaths of allegiance and supremacy. These they could not take for conscience sake, seeing that he whom they

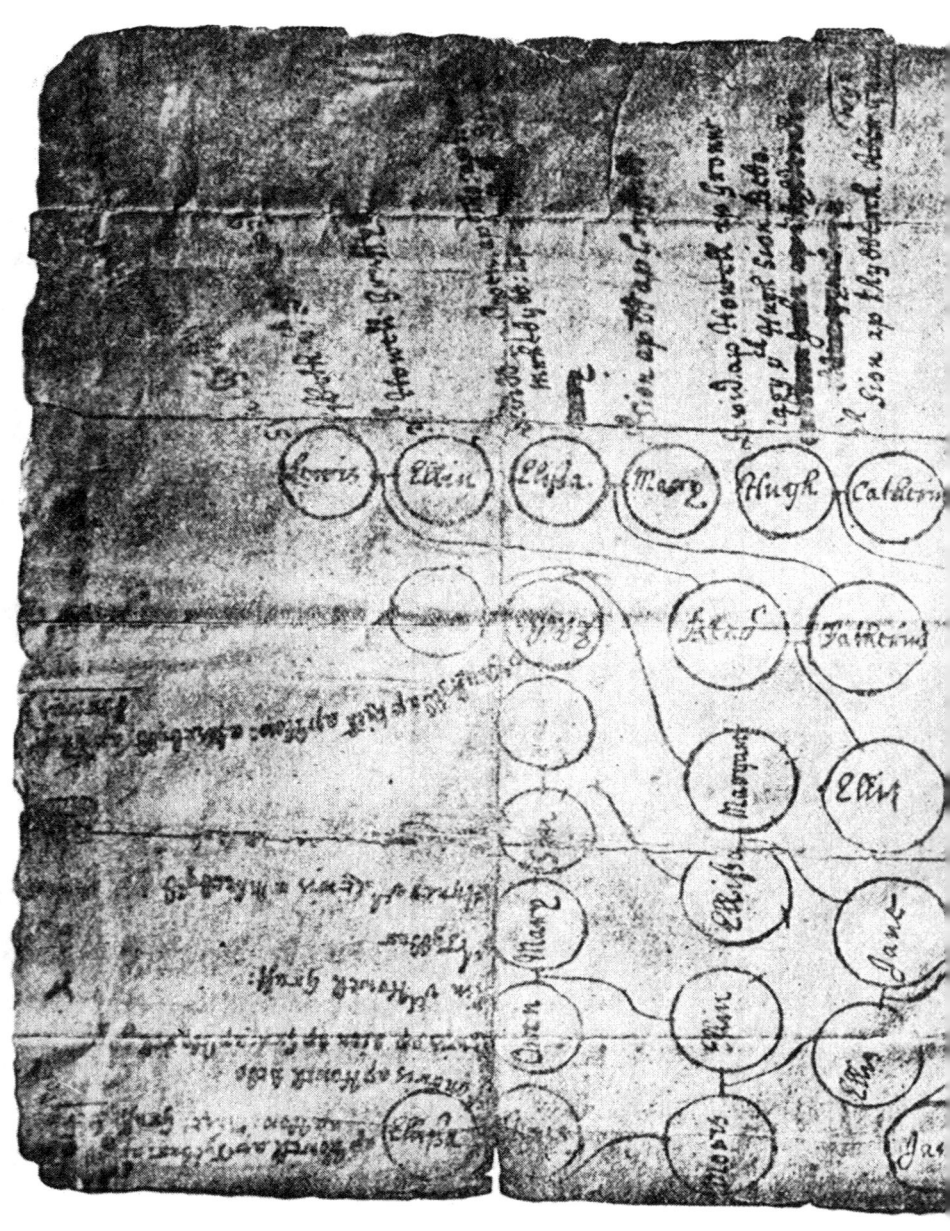

PEDIGREE IN THE HANDWRITING OF ROWLAND ELLIS. THE
AND THE LATTER

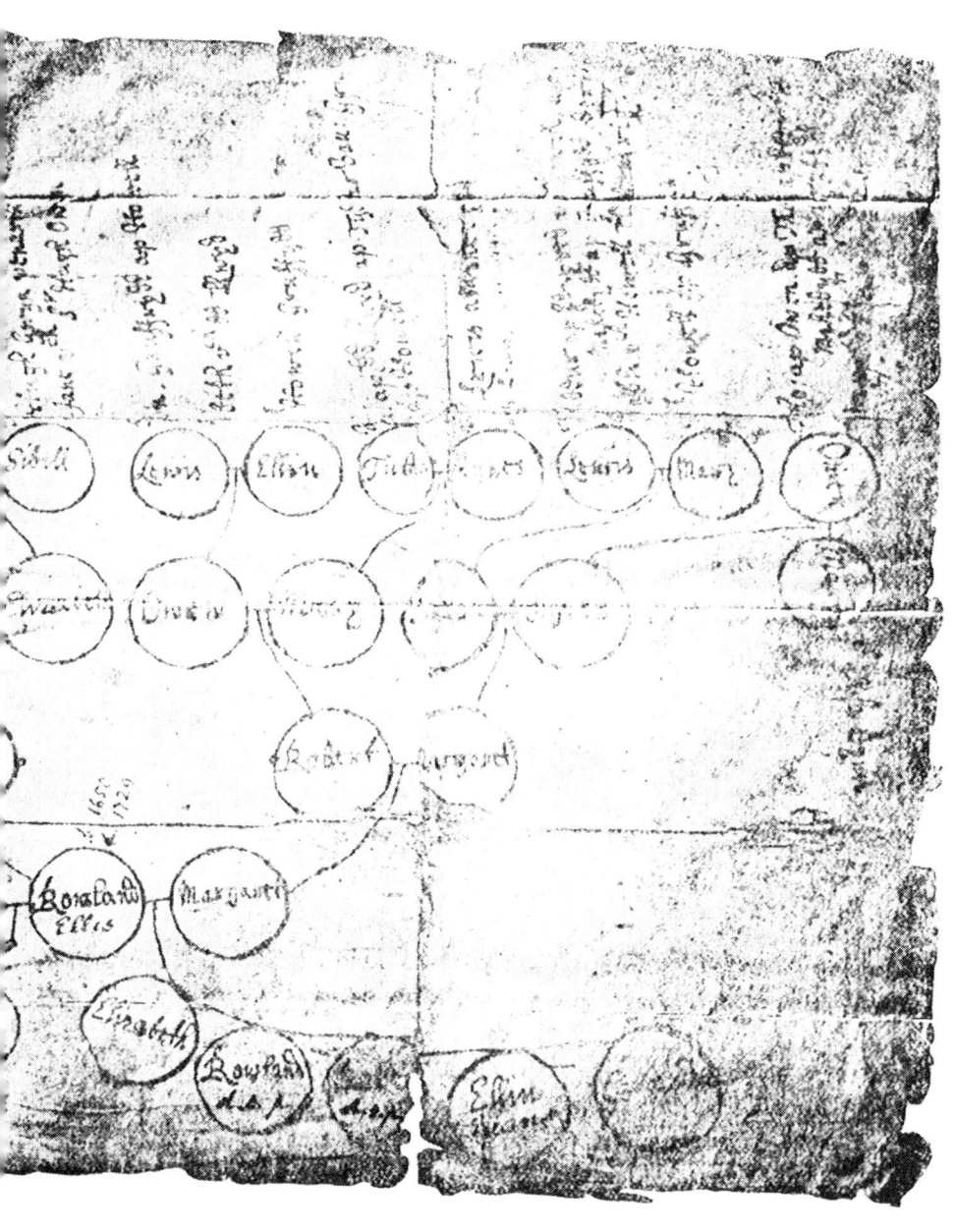

OF HIS BIRTH, AND DEATH (1729) HAVE BEEN ADDED RECENTLY,
ARS TO BE ERRONEOUS.

were bound above all to obey, had charged his flock 'swear not at all.' On declining to take them, one of the judges irritated out of all decency at the Christian firmness of the prisoners, declared that 'if they did refuse the oath a second time they should be proceeded against as traitors, the men to be hanged and quartered, and the women burned.' On the 1st of the Seventh-month they were brought again before the justices and the oaths again tendered them. The prisoners made a solemn declaration of their allegiance to the King and abhorrence of Popery; but they declined to violate their consciences, and were remanded to close imprisonment, to be kept as felons and traitors. Winter came on, and during the severe frost they were not allowed the benefit of a fire or fire-place. The goaler would probably have treated them more kindly, but he was in awe of the parson of Dôlgelly, in which place the Friends were confined, who would have complained to the judges[1] of any favor shown the prisoners. Edward Rice, one of them, a man above sixty years of age, unable to bear such suffering as fell to their lot during the severity of the cold, perished under it, dying during the extremity of the frost.

How long the rest of the Friends were imprisoned we do not know. Rowland, after his enlargement, continued faithful to his inward guide, and growing in grace and religious experience, a dispensation of gospel ministry was committed to him. When Pennsylvania was conveyed to Penn he felt drawn to the new country, and sent thither Thomas Owen and family to make a settlement[2]. His own way to remove was not clear, his master having further service for him in Wales. Friends being constant in suffering in support of their principles, their honest neighbors taking note of their innocent courage and steadfastness, began to feel kindly towards them, and under the powerful influence of popular feeling, even the cruel intentions of persecutors began to relax. [In 1685, the Yearly Meeting of Wales addressed a letter to the yearly meeting in London, showing that such was the case at that time.]

---
[1] See Besse's Sufferings of Friends.
[2] This was the 1100 acres which he purchased.

Rowland Ellis was a man of note in the neighborhood in which he resided, and had a competent estate. In the year 1686 the subject of a removal to Pennsylvania pressing on his mind he concluded to visit the Province, and make such arrangements as might be best for the accommodation of his family, when the time should fully come for transporting them there. On the 16th of the Eighth-month, 1686, he took passage at Milford Haven in a Bristol ship bound for Pennsylvania, by the southern route, then a favorite one. He took his eldest son, Rowland, with him, and about one hundred of his neighbors accompanied them. The passage was a very long one, in which many of the passengers died from hunger, and others, soon after their arrival, from the effects of the privations they had endured. Some who long survived never recovered their usual strength. The amount of suffering and death would doubtless have been even greater if the vessel had not touched at Barbadoes, where it remained nearly six weeks. Here the kind entertainment of Friends and some others did much to recruit such as were not too much exhausted. They were twenty-four weeks in reaching their port, and arrived about the beginning of Second-month, 1687. On reaching Philadelphia all who were able hastened to their respective settlements, and Rowland Ellis among them. He stayed about nine months, " in which time," it is said, " he had laid a foundation towards such improvements as were necessary to accommodate the family he intended to bring over." Leaving his son with his maternal uncle, John Humphrey, a valuable Friend, he, in the spring of 1688, returned to his own country. From what took place after his return, it is evident that he made a purchase of part of the Plymouth tract[1], the original settlers of which being chiefly tradesmen, and not able profitably to farm had left it, and removed into Philadelphia.

He found that some of his property had been seized for distraints during his absence, but this being no new feature

---

[1] If he purchased any land in Plymouth at this time it was in connection with others. He was afterwards quite a speculator in land, losing all of his fortune in schemes to get rich quickly.

of suffering, was not difficult to bear. His way was not yet clear to remove to his newly obtained possessions, and he awaited the time with patience and hope. A gift of the ministry of the gospel had been bestowed upon him, and although his labors in that line were not as frequent as some, yet being sound and lively, they were to the edification of the churches. A great trial awaited him. One of his daughters, doubtless, Ann, the heiress, married the priest of the parish at Dôlgelly. We know not what circumstances had occurred to bring about an acquaintanceship between them, but we must suppose the young woman had never submitted to the restraining influence of true religion, when she thus openly contemned the principles and admonitions of her godly parents. The troubles and trials she brought upon those parents, whom she must have both loved and reverenced, although little thought of when in the enjoyment of gratified affection, would doubtless be present to her mind, bringing deep bitterness in seasons of sorrow and sickness.[1]

In the year 1696 Hugh Roberts visited Wales from Pennsylvania on religious service. He, during his visit there, doubtless, at the desire of his valuable friend, her father, called twice to see this strayed, rebellious child and her husband. In the year 1697 Rowland Ellis came to Pennsylvania with his remaining family, and settled at Plymouth[2]. Soon after his arrival William Ellis, a minister from England, paid a religious visit in America. With this Friend Rowland Ellis had had deep religious fellowship, and after his return to his native country, Rowland wrote him the following letter. It shows the anxious desire of a father panting for the well-being of a disobedient yet still well-beloved child:

---

[1] It is not likely that Rowland Ellis was so greatly troubled regarding his daughter's marriage as the writer of this memorial seems to think. Further on we will give a letter from Rowland Ellis to his son-in-law. Doubtless he was very desirous of having her return to the Quaker Faith, as appears by the efforts he made to induce her to come back, but he appears to have regarded Mr. Johnston with respect.

[2] This is a mistake for Bryn Mawr. He did not go to Plymouth until after he sold the Merion Plantation.

THE 28TH OF THE FIRST-MONTH, 1699.
My Much Esteemed Friend, William Ellis:

If these lines come to thy hands, thou mayst understand what often hath been in my mind to tell thee, that if ever it come before thee to visit Friends in Wales, I desire this kindness of thee, partly for thy name's Sake, but rather upon Truth's account, when at Dólgelly meeting, in Merionethshire, in North Wales, to inquire for my daughter, if she be then alive, and for her husband, who is a priest. If thou findest thyself free, and anything inclined thereto, knock at his door, and see whether she is quite dead, or Slumbering among the dead. I do believe a living invitation may call home a strayed sheep, though gone far into the wilderness, and there, it may be, fast entangled in briars, and bound up in strong chains. If there is any breath left in her, she may answer, though in a land of darkness, and under the shadow of death. The good Shepherd takes great pains to unloose the lost sheep from their bonds and entanglements, and David-like, killing the lion, and delivering the lamb out of his mouth, to bring the same to their right mind, to know the Shepherd's tents. Well, my friend! I believe some have done things of this nature; and who can tell, if it come before thee, but thou mayst, through the power of God, be instrumental to open their eyes; they both are very kind to Friends. Our friend, Hugh Roberts, hath twice visited them, they being sick; her husband took it very kindly. So, with my dear love unto thee,

I remain thy friend

ROWLAND ELLIS.

Being a man of good natural ability, a sufficient education, and comfortable estate, his neighbors soon brought him into public life. In 1700 he was elected to represent Philadelphia county in the Assemby of the Province, a service for which he was well qualified. ————. His public labors were not allowed to interfere with his domestic duties. He was earnestly concerned for the proper education of his children, and sought by timely instruction, and righteous restraint, to inculcate the principles of Truth, and to repress the practice of error. He was often concerned to have religious opportunities in his family, in which he hoped and prayed that his children might be drawn to wait upon God for themselves, and become acquainted with the teachings and leadings of the

Holy Spirit. To some of his children, if not all, his labors were blessed, and they long survived him, bright, shining examples of true Christian virtue, of strong minds, bowing under the Cross of Christ.

His friends testify that he was of 'a sound judgment, ready and willing to assist his neighbors and Friends,' when his aid and advice was desired. "He was zealous for supporting our Christian discipline, and exemplary in conducting himself agreeable therewith, sometimes saying, 'If the hedge of discipline was not kept up, the labour of the husbandman would be laid waste.' Thus he lived in love and usefulness till he had entered his eightieth year. His children were married; his beloved wife, Margaret, had been just removed from him by death, and, doubtless, he had experienced many other strippings, but he was green and cheerful in spirit, getting out to his religious meetings. He was, and it probably was his last visit to Philadelphia, at the Quarterly Meeting held there in Fifth-month 31st, and Sixth-month 2d, 1731. In the Sixth-month he attended his own monthly meeting, held at Gwynedd, and whilst in it was taken unwell. Being conveyed to the house of John Evans, the husband of his beloved daughter, Ellen, he said to several friends, who had gathered round him, 'I am glad I was here to-day, for I had a lively meeting, and though I now feel much weakness, and the infirmities attending my advancing age, yet I can say, Truth is as dear and as sweet as ever.'

Another remark he made was, 'Satan sometimes lies in wait like a roaring lion to devour me, but I find he is chained by a secret hand, which limits his power, so that he cannot harm me.'

He died at the house of his son-in-law, about the beginning of the Seventh-month, 1731, and his body was interred in Friends' burying ground at Plymouth."

Rowland Ellis settled first at Bryn Mawr, now Lower Merion, on the six hundred acres of his eleven hundred acre tract, surveyed there. His plantation is now known as "Harriton," and the larger home which he built was afterwards the residence of Charles Thomson, Secretary of the Continental Congress. The place adjoins the Taylor College, of Bryn Mawr, on the north, and is now well known as the Morris property.

The following letter was written by Rowland Ellis to his son-in-law, Rev. Richard Johnston, in 1698[1]. The plantation described is the " Harriton" place, at Bryn Mawr :

As for ye account of our passage I think I have been something large in my last wch I hope came to thy hands, least it came not, we have had a good passage in six weeks time from land to land, none died in ye ship but one old woman, one other woman was brought to bed; she & her child did very well, so we kept our numbers through the mercy of God. We had our health very well only sea sickness and as for ye country I like it very well; we had a very cold winter, such another people here cannot remember, hard frost, & deep snow, which continued untill ye beginning of this month; we bore it I think as well as most; we had an indifferent good house; very good & large chimney; we made fire night & day. Our house lies under ye Cold N. W. wind & just to the South Sun, in a very warm bottom near a stream of very good water. We have cleared about this run ab^t 10 or 12 Acres for meadow land, very good soil, black mould moist over. I do think for ye most part, if not all ye river will soon overflow it, which runs through it, it being set thick of [thorn] bryars, & small scrubs; a man upon a horse could not ride through it. We hope to mow ye next harvest store of hay; we have as much more such ground for meadow, when we may have to enclose it. Few or none among our countrymen have the like conveniency of Meadow land. We have above 6 acres of wheat sown in good order, & an *accer* & half of ye last summer fallow for Barley. We now begin to clear in order for to sow Oats, if ye Lord gives us life & health, if we can between this & the beginning of May, & about 6 accers, & for Indian Corn as much as we can. We are about to enclose with rail fence by ye latter end of spring above 40 acres. Our Accer^s of land is 40 Perch in length & 4 in breadth. Our Perch is 16 ft & half, *an accre* of land containing about 76 Roods at least. Ye Rood wh^{ch} is ye common measure of land with you near Dôlgelley is 6 yards square, by this thee mayest compute

---
[1] This letter is now in the possession of Mr. Elias, of Denbighshire, Wales. See Pennsylvania Magazine of History and Biography, 1894.

measures together. We have a good soil under a very rough coat; many things sown bring good increase. Ye country grass is very rough & Course in hand as most things by nature, but as it be naturalized, we hope it will prove better; yt wh is good for Winter fodder. Our land generally is dry, and some places strong; some places very level, but ours hereaway, little rising grounds, few hills, fine springs, & running streams of as good water as any I saw; good stately Oaks several sorts of Poplars & great many kinds of trees, also black & white Wallnut, Cipresse, Pine, & Cedar in some places grow plentifully. They begin now to build the houses with Stone, & many with brick, wh^{ch} may be made in any place here. There is Limestone within, 3 little miles to my house. English hay does very kindly, especially white honey suckle (Dutch Clover?), where yt take root it mightily increases, & kills all wild roots (as they say) where it so takes. Ye red clover does well. There are but few of the natives now. Not 1 to 10 as was formerly. As many as there is, are very quiet a new comer may supply himself with horses, cows or sheep, as many as he wants; good horse £4. with you, may cost £8. more or less, Good Cow here £5 or £6., beef ye last fall 2½ per pound, pork 3^d, cheese 7^d butter 10^d to 1^s per pound mutton 5^d also, wheat 8^s Rye 6^s Malt 6^s ye bushell. All other things are very dear, accordingly all things, whether foreign or country commodities will fall. We hear of ye peace concluded between England and France. It has been very sickly season here ye last fall & winter; severall died of our Countrymen; the Lord hath preserved us hitherto. Since I began to write this letter my wife had ye distemper, now she is recovered very well, blessed be God. If I live to receive a few lines from thee when opportunity p'sents, I hope if all things be well to return to the a few other acct^s how we do. Also of any other things if worth sending and I desire y^t none may take occasion by any word yt discovers, nor suppose if I do nor did repent of my coming, for be it far from me from encouraging any to venture y^{m}selves, & what they have, furtherly they live comfortable in their native country to ye danger of ye seas and many more inconvenience yt may happen & on ye other hand discourage any yt hath any real inclinations to transport themselves into ye hands of providence. Some came here might have better staid in their own country, & it is my thought yt great many more would have done better here yt ever they are like to do in their own country.

In an article styled "Settlers in Merion—Harriton Plantation," in the *Pennsylvania Magazine of History and Biography*, George Vaux thus refers to the place:

"Richard Harrison's second wife, Hannah Norris, was the second daughter of Isaac Norris, and granddaughter of Deputy Governor Thomas Lloyd. She was a most affectionate and pious woman, and a minister in the Society of Friends.

Richard Harrison and Hannah Norris were married in Philadelphia in 1717, and soon after he returned with his bride to his residence at Herring Creek. He had, however, promised Hannah Norris prior to the marriage, that if, after residing in Maryland one year, she did not like it for a home, he would dispose of his property at Herring Creek and remove to Pennsylvania. The year's trial did not prove satisfactory to Hannah Harrison, and, in accordance with his promise, her husband made preparations to remove to the vicinity of Philadelphia. In 1719 he purchased, of Rowland Ellis, an estate of seven hundred acres in Merion, about ten miles from Philadelphia, situated on what was in those early times one of the main roads leading out of the city, now known as the Old Gulf Road. This road passes diagonally through the southern part of the tract, and bounds it on the southwest side throughout most of its length. The ancient eleven- and twelve-mile-stone, marking the distance from the old Court-House at Second and Market Streets, yet remain on the premises. The mansion-house, still standing, was erected by the former owner, Rowland Ellis[1], in

---

[1] Harriton is particularly well known as the home of Charles Thomson, and on account of the quaint old cemetery on the grounds. "Harriton Family Cemetery is about eighty-five feet long and forty-six feet wide. The entrance is by a flight of stone steps ascending the wall on one side, and a similar flight descending on the other. A grass walk extends across the breadth of the enclosure. Immediately on the left-hand side of this walk are two rows of family graves, in which were interred several generations of the Harrison family. Still farther to the left, and entirely apart from these interments, are a number of stones marking the graves of strangers to the family blood, buried here by permission between 1795 and 1828. On the right of the grass walk are several other rows of graves, many of which are those of slaves employed in the Harrison family. The house servants alone were buried here, the slaves generally being interred in a selected spot in one of the fields. A block of soapstone is built in the front wall of the cemetery, showing inscriptions on both sides. On the exterior side are the words "Harriton Family Cemetery Anno 1719." On the interior side is the following inscription: "This stone is opposite the division between two rows of family graves, wherein were interred Richard Harrison (died March 2, 1747), and a number of his descendants. Also Charles Thomson, Secretary of Continental Congress (died Aug. 16, 1824), and Hannah Thomson wife of Chas: Thomson, daughter of Richard Harrison, grand-daughter of Isaac Norris, & great-grand-

HARRITON—(BRYN MAWR.)
Built by Rowland Ellis, afterward the Residence of Charles Thomson, Secretary of the Continental Congress.

1704.[1] It is said that all the stone, sand, and other similar materials used in its construction were carried on panniers.

This house, afterwards the residence of Richard Harrison's son-in-law Charles Thomson, is built of pointed stone, two stories high, with dormer windows above. The main doorway opens into the principal room on the first floor, used as a dining-room in early times, and occupied by Charles Thomson as his study. It was here that the principal part of the work was done on his translation of the Bible from the Septuagint. Until within a few years there was a date-stone in the southwest gable of the house marked 1704 (1714?).

To this plantation Richard Harrison and his wife removed. He called it Harriton, after his own name, changing only the letter *s* into *t*.

The following is an account of the descendants of Rowland Ellis, in Pennsylvania, so far as ascertained, and the author desires to express here his obligation to Mr. Howard M. Jenkins, from whose *Historical Collections of Gwynedd* considerable data concerning the descendants of John Evans was taken.[2]

It is claimed by some that Rowland Ellis, Jr., died s. p., and also his brother, Robert, and that Elizabeth and Catherine remained unmarried. In the appendix will be found all the information that the writer could gather upon this point.

---

daughter of Governor Thomas Lloyd (died Sept. 6, 1807)." In Charles Thomson's time the burial-ground was in full view from the windows of the mansion-house, through a vista cut in the woodland which surrounds it.

[1] It is doubtful whether the date was 1704 or 1714. See Appendix.

[2] It will be observed that the arms given on the next page and the beginning of the Owen genealogy, whilst those of Trahairn Gôch, the common ancestor of the two families, are yet different from the arms used by the Evans branch of the family. This is explained by the fact that Trahairn Gôch assumed the arms of his paternal grandmother, which were the *three dolphins and chevron*, instead of using the arms of his grandfather, Rhys Glôf. Some of his descendants also used the dolphins; some the *Lion within a bordure*, of Rhys Glôf; whilst others, more correctly, quartered the two shields.

DESCENDANTS OF ROWLAND ELLIS IN PENNSYLVANIA.

JOHN EVANS[1], of Gwynedd, eldest son of Cadwalader, descended from Trahairn Gôch, of Llyn, born in Denbighshire, Wales, 1689, died at Gwynedd, 9th mo. 23, 1756, married ELEANOR, daughter of ROWLAND ELLIS, of Merion, at Merion Meeting-house, 4th mo. 8, 1715. ELEANOR, born at Bryn Mawr, Merionethshire, Wales, 1685, died 4th mo. 29, 1765. JOHN was a celebrated preacher among Friends. His will,

---

[1] John Evans was the son of Cadwalader Evans, of Gwynedd, son of Evan ap Evan, of Fron Gôch, one of the four brothers who settled at Gwynedd in 1698. For their genealogy in the direct male line, see Owen Family, another page. Cadwalader Evans, who died at Gwynedd, where he lived, near his brothers, Robert and Owen Evans, married in Wales, Ellen, daughter of John Morris, of Bryn Gwyn [White Hill], in Denbighshire. Of the ancestry of her father, John Morris, we know but little, but from an old MS. pedigree of the Owen and Evan families, in the handwriting of Cadwalader Evans, third, we ascertain that her mother was Eleanor, daughter of Ellis ap William, of Cai Fadog. Her descent was as follows: Cadwgan, Lord of Nannau, had Madog, who had Einion, of Ciltalgarth (Azure, a bow and arrow, point downward, argent), who had Madog Hyddgam, of Ciltalgarth (Kiltalgarth), who Cadwgan, who had Madog, of Ciltalgarth, who had Ievan, surnamed "y Cott," who had Ievan Fychan, of Ciltalgarth, who had Madog, who had David, who had Thomas ap David, who had Hugh ap Thomas, of Ciltalgarth, who had William ap Hugh, of Ciltalgarth, who had Ellis Williams, of Cai Fadog, who had two daughters: Eleanor, who married John Morris, of Bryn Gwyn, and had Ellen, who married Cadwalader Evan; and Gwen, who married Hugh ap Cadwalader, and had Eleanor, who became the wife of Edward Foulke, of Gwynedd.

dated 9th mo. 16, 1756, was proved June 22, 1757. He leaves to his daughter, Jane Hubbs, a life interest with remainder to her children, in a lot of 2½ acres, "part of the tract of 100 acres which I hold, to be laid out for her the west side of Montgomery road, adjoining George Maris's field." He gives his daughters, Margaret, Ellen, and Elizabeth, 50 acres, "to be divided off the upper end, next Owen Evans's land." He mentions his sons Rowland and John, and appoints them with his son Cadwalader executors.

Children of John and Eleanor:

1. Cadwalader, b. 1716, d. 1773, m. Jane Owen.
2. Rowland, b. 1717–18, d. 1789, m. Susanna Foulke.
3. Margaret, b. 5th mo. 26, 1719, m. Anthony Williams; but left no issue.
4. Jane, b. 1st mo. 30, 1721, m. John Hubbs. "She left two sons, John and Charles, and three daughters, Rachel, Ellen, and Mary.

Ellen m., 1781, Amos Lewis, of Upper Dublin [son of Ellis Lewis, 2d, and his first wife Mary], and Rachel also m., 1785, Amos Lewis.

5. Ellen, b. 11th mo. 21, 1722, m., at Gwynedd m. h., 12th mo. 18, 1764, Ellis Lewis, 2d [widower], of Upper Dublin. *Ellis* d. 1783; *Ellen* survived him.
6. John, b. 1724, d. 1727.
7. Elizabeth, b. 6th mo. 26, 1726, d. 3d mo. 6, 1805, unm. She is mentioned as living with her bro. John, and giving information embodied by her nephew in the Evans Record.
8. John, b. 1730, d. 1807, m. Margaret Foulke.

JOHN EVANS, of Gwynedd, youngest son of John and Eleanor, born 12th mo. (February), 1730, died 9th mo. (September) 1807, married Nov. 19, 1734, MARGARET FOULKE, daughter of Evan and Ellen, of Gwynedd[1]. (MARGARET was born 4th mo. 19, 1726, and died 3d mo. 6, 1798.) It was this JOHN who furnished Cadwalader, his nephew (son of Rowland), with the family data which form the basis of the 1797 Record. He was known in Gwynedd as "John Evans, the elder" (though his own father's name was John), in order to distinguish him from his son John. He was a prominent and active member of Gwynedd meeting. He lived all his life at the old home of his father and grandfather, in Gwynedd (now

---

[1] See genealogy of Edward Foulke under pedigree of Edward Price.

the Bellows place). His will, which proves that he was quite a rich man, was probated November 6, 1807. He gives his son John the "plantation, consisting of three tracts, where he now dwells, in Gwynedd, about 192 acres; directs his son Cadwalader to release any supposed claim he may have on the fee or title, in consideration of bequests now made him; leaves two tracts (homestead) to his son Cadwalader, one 245 acres, the other 36, he to pay £500 to his [the testator's] grandsons John and Robert; bequeaths to his friends Levi Foulke, Jesse Foulke, and John Jones, Jr., son of Evan, or their survivors, £20 in trust to keep up the burial ground enclosure at Gwynedd meeting, the fund to be used in the discretion of Gwynedd preparative meeting; gives his son Cadwalader two undivided thirds in 50 acres of land adjoining the homestead, "late estate of brother Cadwalader;" gives son Cadwalader the half residue of estate, the other half to grandson Robert; gives £200 to son John; gives £200 to grandsons Rowland and Evan in equal shares; appoints son Cadwalader and grandson Robert executors.

Children of John and Margaret:

1. Evan, d. 1757, aged 9 mos.
2. John, b. Sep. 7, 1759, d. 1814, m. Gaynor Iredell, Eleanor Ely.
3. Cadwalader, b. 1762, d. 1841, m. Harriet V. Musser.
4. Rowland, b. 1762 [twin brother to Cadwalader], "a merchant in Philadelphia," d. 10th mo. 10, 1793, of yellow fever, unmarried.

CADWALADER EVANS, 3d son of John and Margaret, of Gwynedd, born at Gwynedd, Dec. 25, 1762, died Oct. 26, 1841, married HARRIET VERENA MUSSER, daughter of John, of Lancaster, Pa.

Children of Cadwalader and Harriet:

1. Juliana Doddridge, d. 1866, unm.
2. Margaret Eleanor, unm.
3. John Glendour, d. 1827, unm.
4. Rowland Edanis, d. 1866, unm.
5. Edmund Cadwalader, b. 1812, d. 1881, m. Mary Louisa Allen.
6. William Elbert, b. 1816, d. 1869, m. Anna Smith, Emma Fotterall.
7. Cadwalader, d. 1861, unm.
8. Manlius Glendower, b. 1821, d. 1879, m. Ellen Kuhn.

9. Harriet Verena, m. Gouverneur Morris Ogden, Esq., of New York (d. July, 1884), and had issue: Cadwalader E., David B., Gouverneur Morris.

EDMUND CADWALADER EVANS, M. D., son of Cadwalader and Harriet V., born at Gwynedd, August 12, 1812. He graduated at the University of Pennsylvania, studied medicine, took his degree of M. D., and for several years practiced his profession near Paoli, in Tredyffrin, Chester County. Later, he resided near West Chester, but in 1865 removed to Lower Merion, near the first Pennsylvania home of his ancestor Rowland Ellis. He died May 20, 1881. He married April 17, 1844, MARY LOUISA ALLEN, daughter of Rev. Benjamin Allen, of Hyde Park, N. Y. She died 1861. (Four children died in infancy; the survivors are here given.)

Children of Edmund C. and Mary Louisa:

1. Rowland, b. July 12, 1847, in Tredyffrin; now a member of the Philadelphia bar, residing in Lower Merion; he m., 1878, Mary Binney Montgomery, dau. of Richard R. Montgomery, Esq., of Bryn Mawr, and has issue:

2. Allen, b. Dec. 8, 1849, in Tredyffrin; an architect in Philadelphia; resides in Lower Merion. He married, 1876, Rebecca Lewis, daughter of John T. Lewis, Esq., of Philadelphia, and has issue:

WILLIAM ELBERT EVANS, son of Cadwalader and Harriet V., born in Philadelphia, 1816, where he resided all his life. He married 1st, ANNA SMITH, daughter of Jacob Smith, Esq., of Philadelphia, and 2nd, EMMA FOTTERALL, daughter of William Fotterall, Esq., who survives, without issue. WILLIAM E. died 1869. His children, besides others who died in infancy, were two in number.

Children of William E. and Anna:

1. Emily, m. John Henry Livingston, of Dutchess co., N. Y.

2. Glendower, graduated with distinction at Harvard University; a member of the bar in Boston, Mass.; m. Bessy, dau. of Edward Gardiner, Esq., of Boston.

MANLIUS GLENDOWER EVANS, son of Cadwalader and Harriet V., born in Philadelphia, and resided there until when he removed to New York in 1870 and thence to Europe in 1875 where he continued to live until his death in 1879. He left by his wife Ellen, daughter of Hartman Kuhn, four children, but had others who died young. His wife survived him.

Children of Manlius G. and Ellen:

1. Cadwalader, b. 1847, in Philadelphia, d. in New York, 1880, m. Angelina B., dau. of Israel Corse, Esq., of New York, and had issue: Lena, and Edith Wharton.

2. Ellen Lyle, m. Alfred T. Mahan, Commander U. S. N., and has issue: Helen Evans, Ellen Kuhn, Lyle Evans.

3. Rosalie, unm., resides with her mother, in N. Y.

4. Hartman Kuhn, b. in Philada., 1860, unm. Returning to the United States, after the death of his father, he engaged in sheep ranching in Wyoming Territory.

Or, a Lion rampt., Azure.

ELLIS LEWIS AND HIS DESCENDANTS.

[The facts regarding Ellis Lewis, his ancestry and descendants here given, are derived from a very exhaustive and carefully compiled genealogy of this family[1] of Lewis, prepared by Philip Syng Physick Conner, Esq., of Philadelphia, and Octorara, Maryland. This genealogy, which is now before me, is based, so far as the ancestry is concerned, upon a bequest in the will of Ellis Lewis, which will is dated 25th of 12th month (February), 1747-8; proved at New Castle, Delaware, 29 October, 1750, and now remaining in the office of Register of Wills at Wilmington, Delaware (Will Book G, Vol. I, page 430, etc.). This bequest of Ellis Lewis is to his "*loving couzens, Elizabeth and Catherine Ellis*, who, Mr. Conner assures us, he has identified as *Elizabeth and Catherine, daughters of Rowland Ellis*, who were, he says, *both* unmarried, and alive about 1747. The line claimed is through John ap Griffith, of Nannau, a direct male descendant of the ancient native Princes of Powys. (See Pedigree of Rowland Ellis, elsewhere in this volume.) This person had Lewis John ap Griffith, who had (besides Rees Lewis, grandfather of Rowland Ellis) Owen Lewis, who, by Mary, daughter of Tudor Vaughan, had Robert ap Owen, who married Margaret, daughter of John ap Lewis (Rowland Ellis Papers) and had (according to the authorities cited in the Lewis pedigree) a son, Lewis ap Robert, who, by Mary ——, (afterwards wife to one Owen Roberts) had ELLIS LEWIS, the ancestor of the family in this country.]

ELLIS LEWIS was born in Wales in or about the year 1680, his father dying while he was quite young. His mother

---

[1] Lewis Pedigree, drawn up by P. S. P. Conner, 1894.

remarried, as stated above. In or about the year 1698 the family were prepared to embark for America but were prevented by illness, their household goods, however, going on; and this explains Ellis Lewis's declaration, in his Certificate, that he had "substance" in Pennsylvania as well as "relations" (Rowland Ellis's family, for instance). Later they went to Ireland, and thence to Pennsylvania, Ellis Lewis's Certificate of Removal being dated at Mount Mellick, Ireland, the 25th of the 5th month, 1708. Upon his arrival in Pennsylvania, Ellis Lewis went first to Haverford, in the neighborhood of his cousins, the Ellises, Rowland and his family not yet having removed into Gwynedd. Subsequently, he (E. L.) settled in Kennett Township, Chester County, said Province, where he was highly esteemed, being "a man of good understanding," and long an Elder of Friends. He was twice married; first, in 1713, at Concord Meeting, in said County, to Elizabeth Newlin, the mother of his children, as stated below; secondly, to Mary Baldwin, a widow (at Falls Meeting, Bucks County, 11 1 mo., 1723), who survived him. He died at Wilmington, Delaware, on the 31st of the 6th month, 1750, and was buried at Kennett. In his will, made on the 25th of the 12th month (February), 1744-8, and proved on the 29th of October, 1750, and now (1893) of record at Wilmington, he mentions his "loving couzins Elizabeth and Catherine Ellis" and leaves them a legacy. To return to his first wife: She was Elizabeth (born 3 1st mo., 1687-8), the daughter of Nathaniel Newlin, the owner and settler of Newlin Township, in the said County of Chester, member of the Provincial Assembly in 1698 *et seqq.*, in 1700 one of the Committee on the Revision of the Laws and Government of Pennsylvania, subsequently, a Justice of the County Courts (1703 *et seqq.*) and one of the Proprietary's Commissioners of Property. From 1722 until his death in 1729, one of the Trustees of the General Loan Office of the Province. His first wife, and the mother of the said Elizabeth, was Mary Mendenhall or Mildenhall, of Mildenhall, County Wilts, England, whom he married April the 17th, 1685; his second, Mary Fincher, survived him a short

Ellis Lewis and His Descendants. 237

time, dying childless. His father, Nicholas Newlin, an Englishman by birth, came from Mt. Mellick, Queen's County, Ireland, to Pennsylvania in 1683, settling in Concord Township, Chester County. In 1684 he was commissioned, by Governor Penn, one of the Justices of the Courts of the said County, while, in the following year, he was called to the Council of the said Governor and Proprietary, William Penn, the founder of Pennsylvania. Nicholas Newlin died in May, 1699, his wife (Elizabeth Paggot) in 1717.

To return to Ellis Lewis: He had by his wife, the said Elizabeth Newlin, four children: namely, Robert, b. 21 1-mo., 1714, of whose line we now treat; Nathaniel, b. 11 10-mo., 1717, d. 1 7-mo., 1751, without issue; Ellis, b. 22 3-mo.,1719 (had Eli, who had Ellis Lewis, Chief Justice of Pennsylvania); and Mary, b. 6 1-mo., 1716, d. 22 8-mo., 1760, m. at Kennett, Joshua Pusey, 29 8-mo., 1734 (issue). The eldest son:

Robert Lewis, member of the Assemby from the County of Chester (1745–46), b. 21 1-mo., 1714; m. at Concord, 23 3-mo., 1733, Mary Pyle; he d. in the 77th year of his age, and was buried 13 4-mo., 1790, will proved at Philadelphia September 18, said year. She was b. in 1714; d. 26 6-mo., 1782. Mr. Lewis established his family in Philadelphia, where he long lived, using his inherited fortune in mercantile pursuits. His wife, the aforesaid Mary, was the daughter of William Pyle, of Thornbury, Chester County, a member of the Assembly and a Justice of the Courts. Mr. Lewis had issue by his said wife, five children, viz.: Ellis, Nathaniel, Robert, William and Phoebe, with seven others[1]. Of these twelve the eldest son:

---

[1] Of these five, Ellis, the eldest, married and left issue as already stated; Nathaniel m. Lucy Lawrence and had issue; Robert m. Frances Swift and has issue as shown in Note B, p. 10 a; William m. Rachel Wharton (issue); Phœbe m. 1st, Samuel Morton, and 2ndly, James Pemberton. Beside these five children, Mr. and Mrs. Robert Lewis had seven others; viz.: Eli, b. 6 m. 3, 1735; Elizabeth, b. 10-mo. 7, 1736; Mary, b. 5-mo. 24, 1739, d. 3-mo. 4, 1794; William (1st), b. 11-mo. 26, 1742-3; Lydia, b. 12-month 5, 1745-6; Joshua, b. 10-mo. 29, 1749; Ann, b. 12-mo. 26, 1753.

Ellis Lewis (b. July 15, 1734; d. Philadelphia 24 7-mo., 1776) m. 1st, Hannah Miller (issue, a dau.[1]), and 2ndly, Mary, dau. of David Deshler, of Philadelphia. This last marriage took place on the 16th of June, 1763, and by it he had the four following children: David, Robert, Phoebe and Esther. Besides a country place, or "plantation," Mr. Lewis possessed as his town residence, the noted "Great House" or "Governors' House," as it was called, it having been the abode of several rulers of the Province, including William Penn. It was built in 1693, by Mayor Shippen. Of the four[2] children, above mentioned, the eldest son was:

David Lewis, of Springbrook, and of Philadelphia (b. July 9, 1776; d. August 28, 1840). He married on May 22, 1794 (Bishop White officiating), Mary, dau. of Colonel Thomas Darch[3], of Pine Hill, near Sunbury, Pennsylvania, but formerly of Netherclay House[4], County Somerset, England. By this marriage Mr. Lewis's family was restored to the Anglican Church, after a separation of more than a century. An active and public-spirited man, Mr. Lewis early became a member of the well known mercantile firm of Wharton & Lewis, President of the Phœnix Insurance Company, and, as a commissioned officer, he served in the suppression of the Western Insurrection of 1794, making the march of seven hundred miles, to and from Pittsburg.

---

[1]Issue by Ellis Lewis's first marriage with Hannah Miller; to wit: a daughter, named Mary, who m. William Green.

[2]Of the four children mentioned of Ellis Lewis by his second wife, Mary Deshler, David m. as stated; Robert m. Sarah Fish; Phœbe m. Robert Waln, member of Congress from Philadelphia City, in 1798; Hester, or Esther, m. George Eddy.

[3]Colonel Darch bore: Gules, three arches argent; impaling, per chevron embattled or and azure, three eagles displayed counter-changed (Manley, his wife being Joan, a daughter of that family). Crest: A dove, holding an olive branch in its beak, proper. Motto: Ubi libertas, ibi patria. Of Col. Darch's two sons, Edmund died a prisoner in France; the other, Thomas, Private Secretary to the Lords of the Admiralty, left a son, Henry Darch, Esq., Collector of Launceton, Van Diemen's Land.

[1]Netherclay House, in the parish of Bishop's Hull, near Taunton. According to the "List of Principal Seats in Somersetshire," given in Kelly's Directory of the county, Netherclay was, in 1889, the residence of Major-General John Thomas Leishman, R. A.

Upon the threatened war with France, in 1798, he sought and received the appointment of Lieutenant in a company of infantry accepted for service by President Adams, as the first had been by Washington. The commission from Mr. Adams now rests, very peaceably, along with one from that President's old enemy, Lord North, appointing Mr. Lewis's father-in-law, Thomas Darch, Lieutenant-Colonel of the Earl of Cork's regiment of Somerset Militia, in 1787. By his wife, who died June 9th, 1819, in her forty-eighth year, Mr. Lewis had ten children, as follows: George, died without issue; Ellis, whose male line is now extinct; David, by whom the line is continued, as shown below; Thomas, Edmund and Mary died unmarried; Sarah, Phœbe, Elizabeth and Anne Wharton.

David Lewis, of Philadelphia, now the sole surviving child of the above mentioned David Lewis[1], by his wife, Mary, was born at his father's country place of Springbrook, on the Delaware, September 4th, in the year 18 . As before stated, he is the head of the family by right of seniority in male descent, being, as shown, the oldest surviving son of the oldest surviving male line. Mr. Lewis has long retired to private life, but, in past years, he was an active man of affairs, serving on the boards of several corporations and being the secretary of the Mutual Assurance Company, a Director in the Philadelphia Library, and one of the Trustees of the University of Pennsylvania. On May 5th, 1825, he was married (by the Rev. Dr. DeLancey, Rector of Christ Church and St. Peter's)

---

[1] Of the ten children of David and Mary Lewis, George, Thomas, Edmund and Mary died unmarried; Elizabeth married William Redwood Fisher, but left no issue; Ellis (of the Bar of Philadelphia) m. Hester, dau. of Samuel Powel Griffitts, M. D., of the said city, and had a son (David) who died, unmarried and without issue, in his father's lifetime, and two daughters, viz.: Mary and Camilla now living (1893), and another (Emma) who died unmarried. The remaining four, viz.: Sarah, m. John Wocherer but left no issue, his daughter Ellen Glen being the child of his first wife, Frances, the dau. of James Glen, M. D., of Savannah, Georgia, by the latter's wife, Mary, dau. of Robert, son of Robert, son of Ellis Lewis and Elizabeth Newlin, of this pedigree; Phœbe, m. the Rev. John Clemson, D. D. (issue): Anne Wharton, m. Edward Jones Glen, M. D., and left issue, with others, Frances, the wife of Edwin Rowland Warrington, of Philadelphia: David the head of the family in line male, whose pedigree is here traced. As Mrs. Warrington's father was the son of the Dr. James Glen, of Savannah, mentioned above, it is evident that she has two lines of descent from the Lewis family.

to Camilla, daughter of William Phillips, of Riversdale, Esq[1]., and also of Philadelphia. By this lady, who died at the latter place on July the 21st, 1887, in her 34th year, he had the following five children, who now (1893) survive (one other, Frank, having died in infancy): William Phillips, Edmund Darch, Clifford, Anna Phillips and Mary Darch.

NOTE.—Joseph E. Gillingham, Esq., of Villa Nova, Pennsylvania, is a lineal descendant of Ellis Lewis. Owing to his continued absence in Europe, the author was unable to obtain accurate particulars regarding his branch of the family. If the same are obtained in time, they will be found in the Appendix.

---

[1] Of the five surviving children of David and Camilla Lewis, mentioned on page 11, William Phillips Lewis, D. D., m. Sarah, dau. of Samuel L. Shober, by his wife, Mary: Edmund Darch Lewis, unm.: Clifford Lewis, m. Ella Eugenia, dau. of William Burr Nash Cozens, by his wife, Henrietta, and has David Lewis, Clifford Lewis, William Burr Nash Lewis, and one daughter, Eleanor Lewis; Anna Phillips Lewis, m. 1st Samuel Emlen Randolph, and 2ndly Samuel Welsh; issue (by first marriage only), Philip Syng Physick Randolph, m. to Hannah, dau. of Ferdinand L. Fetherston, by his wife, Emily: Mary Darch Lewis, m. Philip Syng Physick Conner, the tracer of this pedigree, and has Camilla Conner, the wife of Arthur Hale, eldest son of the Rev. Edward Everett Hale, D. D., of Boston; and Edward Conner, married to Frances Marie, dau. of the said Mr. and Mrs. Fetherston. With the exception of Dr. Hale, all of the above mentioned persons are, or were, of Philadelphia. Riversdale, Mr. Phillips's country-seat, was situated on the Delaware, some miles above Philadelphia; his town-house was at the southeast corner of Spruce and Eleventh streets, in the said city. He bore: Azure, on a chevron engrailed or three falcons' heads erased of the field. Crest: A demi-lion rampant, proper.

THE HUMPHREYS FAMILY.

There were few Cymric families of Pennsylvania descended from better stock than the Humphreys. In Colonial times the name was frequently written both *Humphrey* and *Humphreys*, and in Wales the spelling *Humffrey* was commonly, but not always, used.

There were several branches of this family in the Welsh Tract. The family long settled on the site of the central part of what is now Bryn Mawr, formerly Humphreysville, and whose house, a fine old Colonial dwelling, is still standing near the College Grounds, was descended from Benjamin Humphrey, son of Samuel Humphrey[1], of Wales, whilst the Humphreys, of Haverford, come from Daniel Humphrey, the elder brother of Benjamin. At the time of the first settlement a very large part of Merion was held by the representatives of this family. John Humphreys, who died childless, and after him his nephew, Benjamin, certainly held a large part of the present Bryn Mawr, whilst Benjamin, after the death of his kinsman, Thomas John Thomas, inherited a large tract of land to the east, lying to the northward of the present Montgomery avenue at Haverford station, several hundred acres in all. Directly northwest of the Humphrey tract was old Bryn Mawr, now " Harriton," six hundred acres, belonging to Rowland Ellis, nephew to John Humphrey. Living alongside John Humphreys was his nephew, Joshua Owen[2], son of Owen Humphrey, of Llwyn-du, whilst between the present Ardmore and Wynnewood stations, to the northwest and southeast of Montgomery avenue, was the four hundred and fifty acre plantation of Robert Owen, son-in-law to Owen Humphrey, and north of and adjoining his land was the property of John

---
[1] The children of Samuel Humphrey at first called themselves " *Samuel*," according to the " modo wallico," or Cymric system of surnames. After 1678 they assumed the surname of *Humphreys*.

[2] His brother John lived near by.

Roberts, called "Wayn Mill," now Mill creek, at the conjunction of Mill Creek road and the old Gulph road, being about five hundred acres in all. So that the Humphrey family and its branches held some 1,900 acres of land in the upper part of Merion (but not Upper Merion), comprising the present towns of Bryn Mawr, North Haverford, North Ardmore, Mill Creek, and the land north of Wynnwood.

The earlier lineage of this family is given in the ancient pedigree by Rowland Ellis, reproduced on another page[1]. The line is there given in the direct male descent from one *Gronwy*, who must have been born circa 1480, to Humphrey ap Hugh (of Llwyn-du), who was father to Owen Humphrey, John Humphrey and Samuel Humphrey, and also Anne, who married, in 1649, Ellis Price, and had Rowland Ellis.

Referring to the visitations of Wales made by Lewis Dwnn[2], who gives this male line of the Humphreys in the Tal y Lyn pedigree[3], we find another generation, namely *Einion*, who Dwnn gives as the father of *Gronwy*, above mentioned, and who we may consider to have been born about the year 1450[4].

From the title papers to the old Quaker grave-yard at Llwyngwrill, we find that the estate called Llwyn-du was "an indefeasible estate of inheritance," and had, therefore, in all probability descended from this Gronwy ap Einion or his son Howell to Humphrey ap Hugh, who held it so late as 1662[5]. Therefore, it is very evident that to find the ancestors of *Gronwy ap Einion* it is necessary to ascertain the owners of the "ancient capital messuage[6]" called Llwyn-du, in the township of Llwyn-

---
[1]See article on Rowland Ellis.
[2]He was Deputy Herald, by Patent under seal of Clarenceux and Norroy Kings at Arms.
[3]Dwnn, II., p. 252, 1603; we give the pedigree on another page of this article.
[4]In making this estimation 30 years was allowed as an average generation. This, however, cannot be absolutely relied upon in all cases, as there are many exceptions to this rule.
[5]Diary of Richard Davies.
[6]Article on Quaker Burial Ground, Merionethshire, Montgomeryshire Collections. In this article a clerical error makes Owen Humphrey the possessor of Llwyn-du in *1646*, instead of *1664*, which is the date the graveyard was donated.

gwrill and parish of Llangelynin, in the Comôt of Talybont, Merionethshire, about and prior to the year 1500, *Einion* having been born, according to estimation, circa 1450, as we have seen. Unfortunately early Welsh titles are exceedingly difficult to trace, but from another pedigree by Dwnn[1] we learn that about the time mentioned one *Gronwy ap Einion ap Howell* held a large part of Llwyngwrill and neighborhood. He was descended from Ednowain ap Bradwen, and would seem at first sight to have been the same person as the *Gronwy ap Einion*, of Llwyngwrill, mentioned in the pedigree of Rowland Ellis and in the visitation by Dwnn.

Let us, however, examine into the title of the Llwyn-du property so far as the imperfect records will permit. The first person mentioned in the title is Ednowen ap Bradwen. Of him a good account is given in manuscript of the middle of the 17th century[2]. This paper, probably a copy of Vaughan of Hengwrt's work, says: " Ednowen ap Bradwen is by many writers called Lord of Merionydd, but I apprehend erroneously, as the Princes and their issue were always Lords of Merionydd. . . . . Yet certain it is that he and his issue were possessed of all Talybont . . . . . save Nanney and the Princes' demesnes. He is presumed to have been alive 1137[3], though some question if he lived quite so early, without I think any ground for their assertion, for this date is in accordance with facts." That the possessions of Ednowen included, therefore, Llwyn-du, in Llwyngwrill, in which the Princes and their issue do not appear to have had any demesne, cannot be questioned, nor can it be doubted that the property descended, being as we have seen an indefeasible estate of inheritance, directly from Ednowain to Humphrey ap Hugh. The only question now is, *How* did it descend[4]?

---

[1] Dwnn, II., 278, Powys Fadog, Peniarth.
[2] Dwnn, Powys Fadog, Cambrian Register.
[3] He bore, Gales, 3 snakes, nowed, argent.
[4] The editor wrote several times, during the past ten years to the present owners of Llwyn-du, asking for information from their title papers, there being no provision in England for the recording of deeds. If these letters ever reached their destination no notice was taken of them. It is hoped that some information may yet be received from this source.

We find that Ednowain's possessions[1], particularly in Llwyngwrill and neighborhood, came to his descendant, Llewelyn ap Tudor, who died prior to the 7th year of Henry V. In that year a part of Llwyngwrill was held by the grandsons of Llewelyn, to wit: "Eig'n" (alias Ednyfed) ap Aaron, and Gruffydd ap Aaron[2]. It appears of record that this Eignion or Ednyfed (who are held by some to have been the same person, and by others to have been brothers, because the extent sets forth that there were other children of Aaron heirs to Llwyngwrill[3]) had two sons, Gruffydd, who was Raglor of Talybont in 1452[4], and Howell, living circa 1450, who seems to have held a part of Llwyngwrill. He had issue Einion, born circa 1450[5], who had *Gronwy ap Einion*[6], born circa 1480, who, as we have said, might be considered on very good grounds to have been identical with *Gronwy ap Einion of the same township*[7], whose issue held Llwyn-du, which had unquestionably been the property of the former's ancestor, Aaron ap Ednyfed[8], of the line of Ednowain, the owner of all of Talybont in the 12th century[9].

Unfortunately for this line of argument, however, it has been definitely ascertained that the Llwyn-du property descended to Humphrey ap Hugh (1662) from Ednowain ap

---

[1] Cambrian Register, 1796.

[2] Records of Caernarvon, which include the extent of the County of Merioneth, taken in the 7th year of Henry V., and which mention a "wele," called "wele" "Nyrion Llywelyn ap Tudor," the domicile of the grandchildren of Llewelyn ap Tudor, and that the freeholders of the said "wele" were; Eig'n (alias Ednyfed) ap Aron, Gruff ap Aron, and others. A wele, says Wotton, "seems to have been an estate, descending to child, or children, of the same common stock."

[3] Records of Caernarvon. Extent of Merioneth.

[4] Powys Fodog, Peniarth.

[5] Dwnn, II., 278, etc. Powys Fadog.

[6] Ibid.

[7] MS. Rowland Ellis; Dwnn, II., 252.

[8] Records of Caernarvon. Extent of Merioneth. Vill Llwyn Gwrill.

[9] It is worthy of note that almost all of the lands of Llangelynin and Llanergrin continued in the possession of the descendants of Aaron, except a part which the antiquary Vaughan of Hengwrt claims was sold to Cadwgan ap Ievan, a gentleman of South Wales, who had married a daughter of David ap Ievan, of Gwyddelvynnydd, Merionethshire, a descendant of this person, one *Einion*, of Talybont, temp. of Henry VI., was confused by some with Einion ap Howell, but the investigation of the late Sir S. Rush Meyrick seems to have settled this question.

Bradwen through an *heiress*, and that Gronwy ap Einion, with whom our pedigree begins, was descended in the male line from Callwyn ap Tagno, Lord of Llyn, one of those descendants, married an heiress descended from Ednowen ap Bradwen, thus bringing the Llwyn-du property into the possession of the ancestors of Humphrey ap Hugh.

Which of the generations given, formed this alliance cannot now be determined, but that it was prior to the marriage of David ap Howell (born circa 1540) with Mary, daughter of Hugh ap John, of Tal y Llwyn, seems clear.

The above information was brought to light by the discovery of a seal used by John Humphreys (or Humphrey), brother to Owen Humphrey, of Llwyn-du. This seal, used before 1691, bears the arms of Collwyn ap Tangno, of Llyn (a chevron inter 3 fleur-de-lys), in the first and fourth quarter, and the arms of Ednowain ap Bradwen (the three snakes nowed), in the second and fourth quarter. This seal is attached to a document signed by a number of settlers in the Welsh Tract, but written, directed and sealed by John Humphreys. The ownership of these arms was further confirmed by the examination of other documents.

Leaving the earlier portion of this pedigree, however, entirely out of the question, we commence the Humphrey genealogy with:

EINION was probably born circa 1450. He had a son:

GRONWY AP EINION, who had:

HOWELL, who had:

DAVID AP HOWELL, of Llwyngwrill, Talybont, born circa 1540, who married Mary, daughter of Hugh ap John, of Tal y Llyn[1], a parish in the Union of Dôlgelly, in the cômot of of Estimaner, Merionethshire, eight miles southwest of Dôlgelly Town. Hugh ap John was the son of John ap Meredith ap David ap Ievan ap Llewelyn ap Einion, of Llwydiarth, in Montgomeryshire (mentioned in grant of 7 Henry V., but it is perhaps doubtful if he was alive in that year), ap Einion

---

[1]MS. of Rowland Ellis, 1696.

ap Celynin (living 14 Edward III., 1340) ap Celynin ap Ririd ap Cynddelw ap Ierworth ap Gwrgeney ap Uchdryd ap Aleth, Prince of Dyfed. Arms: "Arvan rhain yw'r bwch gwyn dans ei defians of molet." [Dwnn II., p. 252.] Hugh ap Hugh, brother of Mary, was living 1603. The family of Tal y Llyn, descended by its various alliances, from Griffith Derwas, of Nannau, of the line of Meuric ap Ynyr Vychan, whose tomb in Dôlgelly Church has been described; from Iorwerth ap Adda, of Dolgôch, from the Princes of Powys and many other noble families of Wales. David ap Howell had[1] by Mary (Mali), his wife:

HUGH AP DAVID, of Llwyngwrill, who married Catherine, daughter of John (Sion) ap Rhydderch, of Abergynolwyn. According to some characters preserved by descendants in Wales, this family of Abergynolwyn appears to be traceable to about 1400, or earlier. (See *Pvgh* of *Cwmllow*, Montg. Colls.)

This couple had issue:

Humphrey ap Hugh, of whom presently.

John ap Hugh, living 1 January, 1649, at which time he was witness to marriage contract. He had David John ap Hugh, of age at that time (1649).

David ap Hugh Gôch, living, 1636[2].

HUMPHREY AP HUGH, of Llwyngrill; he signed the marriage settlement of his daughter, Anne, who espoused Ellis Price (father of Rowland Ellis), 1 January, 1649, and was living at Llwyn-du in 1662. He died there circa 1664, having married circa 1625, Elizabeth, daughter of John Powel (alias John ap Howell), of Llanwddyn, Montgomeryshire. John Powell, alias John ap Howell Gôch, of Gadfa, was buried in the Church of Llanwddyn, 24 July, 1636. His wife was Sibill, daughter of Hugh Gwyn, of Penarth, High Sheriff of Caer-

---

[1] John William, thought to have been identical with John William ap Humphrey is believed to have been of this family.

[2] See Subsidy Roll, Merionethshire, being the 3d Subsidy of 1636, Cambrian Magazine, Vol. III. He is thought to have died s. p. before 1649, and may have been the eldest son, in which case the property would have gone to Humphrey ap Hugh.

The Humphreys Family. 247

naronshire, 1600, descended from Sir William Griffith, of Penrhyn, the Herberts of Raglan, and from Edward I. and Edward III., Kings of England. The wife of Hugh Gwyn was Jane, daughter of Owen ap Hugh, of Bodeon, in Anglesey, High Sheriff of Anglesey, 1579–80, who died 1613; descended from Merick ap Llewelyn ap Halkin, of Bodeon, 8th in descent from Hava, son of Kundhelw, Lord of Cwmwd Lhivon, living 1150.

Humphrey ap Hugh had by Elizabeth, his wife:

1. Owen Humphrey.
2. John Humphrey, m. Jane, sister of Richard Humphrey[1].
3. Samuel Humphrey, m. Elizabeth Rees.
4. Ann Humphrey, m. Ellis Price, of Bryn Mawr, 1649, and had other daughters.

Rowland Ellis, of Bryn Mawr, born 1650.

---

[1]John Humphreys, son of Humphrey ap Hugh, of Llwyn-du, married his cousin, Jane, daughter of Humphrey ———, and sister to Richard Humphrey, of the same parish (i. e. Llangelyrin, Merionethshire). As this Richard Humphrey had brothers, John and Owen Humphrey, and was also cousin to the Humphreys of Llwyn-du, the genealogical tangle resulting is exceedingly confusing. The following facts may assist to elucidate it. Richard Humphrey, of the parish of Llangelynin, Merionethshire, was grantee in a deed dated 30 July, 1682, for 156 acres of land in the Province of Pennsylvania, which were subsequently surveyed to him in Radnor Township. He came to the Province in 1683; his certificate of removal being dated 5th mo. 27, 1683. His will is dated 12th month 2, 1691, and proved at Philadelphia 18th of 12th month, 1692-3. He bequeathes his plantation to "my brother in law John Humphreys." "Item I give and bequeath Four pounds to be sent to the Land of my nativity to be disposed as followeth, viz.: one pound of English money to my brother *John Humphrey*, & one pound to my brother Owen Humphrey, & one pound to my cousin John Owen, & one pound to my sister Katherine or her children." "Item I give and bequeath to Lydia Ellis Two pounds, to Ann Humphrey Two pounds, to Daniel Humphrey two pounds, to Benjamin Humphrey two pounds, to Joseph Humphrey two pounds. Bequests to cousin Alika Humphrey. John Humphrey, his brother-in-law, Executor. The witnesses are: Theodore Roberts, Benjamin Humphrey and Rowland Ellis. John Humphrey, the Executor, and to whom the plantation was devised, sold the land soon after." (See former records of land titles of Richard Davies Company.) It may be mentioned that John Humphrey in this narrative of his and others sufferings mentions that his wife, Jane, before she was married, resided in the same parish, or very near him, and near Llwyn du, in Llangelyn. This was before John Humphrey removed to Llanwddyn Parish, in Montgomeryshire, near to his maternal cousins, Thomas John ap Thomas and John Howell and others. (See Historical Collections of Gwynedd, by Howard M. Jenkins.) This is a good example of the confusion arising from the Welsh system of surnames.

OWEN HUMPHREY, eldest son and heir of Humphrey ap Hugh, of Llwyn-du, was born circa 1625, and died prior to 1699.[1] He was, it is stated, an officer under Oliver Cromwell, and he served as a Justice of the Peace for Merionethshire under the Protectorate. He was amongst the first in Wales to join the Quakers, and his name is of very frequent occurrence in Besse's "*Sufferings of Friends.*" In 1662, having with his brother Samuel "refused to pay a demand for tithes," he was prosecuted in the Sheriff's Court, and execution was awarded against him, by which his cattle were seized."

After his father's decease, in 1664–1665, he became seized in the "ancient demesne lands of Llwyn-du," and deeded thereupon a lot of ground for a burial place for the Cymric Friends, as did Lewis Owen, his kinsman, of Tyddyn y Garreg, a part of his estate, the lands adjoining.

Llwyn-du had, as we have seen, been the ancestral estate for many generations. The title papers relating to the gift of the burial lot recites that: "Owen Humphrey, of Llwyn-du, in Llwyn Gwrill, in the said county [Merionethshire], Esquire, now long since deceased, was in his life time (that is to say), in the year 1646 [should be 1664], seized in his demesne of a good and indefeasible estate of inheritance of and in that ancient capital Messuage, Tenement and Lands called Llwyn-du." In 1678[2] he signed the marriage certificate, and also the marriage settlement of his daughter, Rebecca, and Robert Owen, of Fron Gôch (Vron Gôch), and he signed numerous certificates of removal for persons coming from Wales to Pennsylvania, between the years 1683–1690.[3] He is mentioned in the will of his brother, John Humphrey,[4] who died in Penn-

---

[1]Will of John Humphreys, Will Book B., p. 65. Reg. Wills, Phila.
[2]Original Document produced. See copy, and fac simile Owen article.
[3]Friends Records—Certificates of Removal, Merion, Radnor and Haverford, Mtg.
[4]Will John Humphreys, dated 22, 7mo., 1699. Proved 31 Aug., 1700.

The Humphreys Family.

sylvania 1701, as then deceased. Of the children of Owen Humphrey, John, Joshua, Elizabeth and Rebecca (then wife of Robert Owen), removed to Pennsylvania. His eldest son Humphrey Owen Humphrey, inherited the estate.

Owen Humphrey, having been very frequently heavily fined (on one occasion to the amount of £20 for praying at a meeting), it is believed that he left little personal estate, in fact what little money he had remaining he lent freely to Friends going to Pennsylvania, as appears of record, much of which he doubtless never recovered. He married, it is thought, twice. All of his children were by his first wife, and were:

1. Humphrey Owen Humphrey, of Llwyn-du [vide Deed in re. Tyddyn-y-Garreg Burial Ground, Montg. Colls.]

2. John Owen; removed to Pennsylvania 1683[1].

3. Rowland Owen; his name appears attached as a witness to the marriage certificate of 1678, and to other documents.

4. Joshua Owen; he removed to Pennsylvania in 1683, bringing with him a certificate of removal from meeting held at Tyddyn y Garreg, describing him as "late of Llwyn-du." He signs with near relatives of the Owens in marriage certificates in Pennsylvania. He married Martha Shinn, and went to live in Burlington county, New Jersey, where he was living in 1739 with Rowland and Robert Ellis.

5. Owen Owen, mentioned as of Llwyn-du in minutes of Montgomeryshire Meeting.[2]

---

[1] John Owen is mentioned in Certificate of Removal as "ye 2nd son of Owen Humphrey of Llwyn-du."

[2] A memorandum that I, Mary Davies, of Llandloes, received of Caleb Iurchee a sum of money at the yearly meeting, in Builth, in Radnorshire, to convey for Owen Owen, of Llwyn-du, in Merionethshire, and Humphrey Humphreys, of Lloydyarthfach in Montgomeryshire, to pay for repairing the meeting house and graveyard at Caiye Bychen, in Llanwthin (Llanwddyn), and Humphrey Humphreys gave the door-frame, door and hinges, at his own expense, at the time that I, Mary Davies, did live with Humphrey Humphreys, at Lloydyarthfach.

The mark of
MARY (M.) DAVIES.

Witness—DAVID OWEN.
Record 10th Monthly Mtg.
Dolobran, Montgomeryshire, 1713. Montgomery Collections, XI., p. 123.

6. Rebecca Owen, m. 1678, Robert Owen, of Fron Gôch, Merionethshire, "gentleman," and is mentioned in the marriage certificate as " eldest daughter of Owen Humphrey, of Llwyn-du."

7. Elizabeth Owen; removed to Pennsylvania, with her brother, John Owen, and m. in Pennsylvania, John Roberts, of Pen y Chwd, Denbighshire.

Children of Samuel Humphrey and Elizabeth Rees:

1. Daniel, m. 1695, Hannah Wynne, daughter of Thomas Wynne.
2. Joseph.
3. Anne, m. Edward Roberts, son of Hugh Roberts, 1699.
4. Benjamin, m. 1694, Mary Llewelyn, dau. Morris Llewelyn, 1694.
5. Lydia, m. Ellis Ellis, son of Thomas Ells, who d. 1706.
6. Gobitha, d. 1687.
7. Rebecca, m. 1713, Edward Rees, of Merion (his 2nd wife, see Price).
8. Elizabeth, m., 1693, Thomas Abel.

Children of Daniel Humphrey and Hannah Wynne:

1. Samuel, b. 6-mo. 3, 1696.
2. Thomas, b. 4-mo. 20, 1697.
3. Jonathan, b. 7-mo. 9, 1698; m. Sarah ———.
4. Hannah, b. 11-mo. 7, 1699.
5. Benjamin, b. 11-mo. 7, 1701–2.
6. Elizabeth, b. 8-mo. 16, 1703.
7. Mary, b. 12-mo. 10, 1704–5.
8. Solomon, b. 10-mo. 16, 1706.
9. Joshua, b. 1-mo. 10, 1707–8.
10. Edward, b. 12-mo. 28, 1709.
11. Martha, b. 9-mo. 9, 1711.
12. Charles, b. 7-mo. 19, 1714.
13. Rebecca, b. 10-mo. 2, 1716.

The Humphreys Family.

Children of Benjamin Humphrey and Mary Llewelyn:
1. John, b. 7-mo. 8, 1695.
2. Joseph, b. 11-mo. 11, 1697.
3. David, b. 2-mo. 6, 1703.
4. Ann, b. 5-mo. 24, 1708; m. Gerrad Jones, son of Robert, of Merion, 10-mo. 23, 1742.
5. Owen, b. 11-mo. 27, 1713; Sarah Hughes, widow of John, of Haverford, 7-mo. 29, 1738.
6. Elizabeth, m. John Scarlet, s. John, of Robeson township, Lancaster County, 1741.

The descendants of Benjamin Humphrey continued to reside at the present Bryn Mawr, Merion, and at the present time their descendants live in the neighborhood. There are also many descendants of Daniel Humphrey, but limited space prevents us from extending this genealogy. It may be mentioned that Joshua Humphreys, called the "Father of the American Navy," and General Humphreys were descendants of this family.

THE ARMS OF JOHN CADWALADER, 1697.[1]
Gules, a lion rampant argent, armed and langued Azure.

CADWALADER, OF MERION, AND AFTERWARDS OF PHILADELPHIA, PENNSYLVANIA.

[The main facts in this genealogy are drawn from an ancient MS. pedigree on parchment, made out under the supervision of John ap Thomas, uncle to John Cadwalader, in the year 1682; from the Visitations of North Wales, taken 1585–1603, by Lewis Dwnn, Deputy Herald; from wills in the District Registry of the St. Asaph Court of Probate, Wales, and at Philadelphia, Pennsylvania; and from family papers and documents. For details regarding the old MS. pedigree *see Pennsylvania Magazine,* Vol. IV.]

MARCHWEITHIAN, Lord of Is-Aled ; he = had his castle at Llyweni. His arms

A

---

[1] The arms given here are from a seal used by the family in 1682; from a MS. pedigree of that date, and from the Herald's Visitations of Wales, wherein these arms are recorded as those of this family. They were very generally borne by the descendants of Marchweithian, Lord of Is-Aled (Isaled), in Merionethshire. The coat lately blazoned as that of the Cadwalader family, of Philadelphia, and now used by some of the descendants of John Cadwalader, are totally without authority for their use. They are the arms fancifully attributed to an early British Prince by name of Cadwalader, who lived some centuries before Heraldry was known as an exact science, and they were, doubtless, appropriated by the Cadwalader family at the suggestion of some person totally ignorant of Heraldry, and unacquainted with the genealogy of the family. In spite of a protest and explanation made by the author in the Philadelphia Press, the arms have been reproduced in several works on American Heraldry. The name of Cadwalader, or Cadwallader, is a Cymric Christian name, and a very common one in Wales, and, as will appear in the following pedigree, was first assumed as a surname by this family, by *John Cadwalader,* son of *Cadwalader Thomas, ap Hugh* of Wern Fawr, Merionethshshire, gentleman. One of the seals above mentioned was attached to the will of John Thomas, of Llaithgwn, 1682, but has lately been lost.

Cadwalader, of Merion.

were: Gules, a lion rampant, argent, armed and langued Azure.

A

MARCHWYSTLE, Lord of Is-Aled. =

YSTRWYTH AP MARCHWYSTLE. =

TANGO AP YSTRWYTH; his house = was on the top of Fron Fawr.

TYFYD FARFSYCH, 2nd son; was of = Carwedd Fynydd.

HELIN GLÔFF, of Carwedd Fynydd. = NEST, dau. of Cadwgan ap
(i. e. Helin the lame.) Lowarch ap Bran, Lord of Cwmwd Menai.

LLYWARCH AP HEILIN, of Carwedd = GWENLLIAN, dau. of Madog
Fynydd. ap Rhirid Flaidd, Lord of Penllyn. (See another page.)

CYNWRIG AP LLYWARCH, of Carwedd = DYDDGU, dau. of Cadwgan
Fynydd. ap Ednyfed, of Llys Llywarch.

EINION AP CYNWRIG, 2nd son of = Cerrig y Drudion, in the County of Denbigh, North Wales.

DAVID AP EINION, of Caer y = Drudion (called also Kerrig and Cerrig y Drudion).

IEVAN DDU (Evan the black-haired), of = Cerrig y Drudion.

IEVAN GÔCH (Evan the red-haired) of = GWENHWYFER, dau. of Thomas, ap
Cwm Pen Aner, in the parish of Cerrig David Gam (having one eye). Sir
y Drudion, in the County of Denbigh. David Gam was slain at Agincourt,
("Of Bryammer in the Parish of Ker- Knighted by Henry V., in 1415, as
rig y Drudion, and County Denbigh" his last breath was escaping, on the
MS. pedigree by Jno ap Thomas.) field of battle.

RHYS AP IEVAN GÔCH. = = GRIFFITH AP IEVAN GÔCH.

TUDOR AP RHYS. = = ROBERT AP GRIFFITH.

RHYS GÔCH AP TUDOR. = CATHERINE, who m. Thomas Lloyd, of Gwern y Brechtwn, and had

A

Merion in the Welsh Tract.

IEVAN AP RHYS GÔCH. = A. — Mary Lloyd, who m. Richard, of Tyddyn Tyfod, ancestor of Edward Rees, alias Price, of Merion, Penna., 1682.

HUGH AP IEVAN AP RHYS GÔCH. =

THOMAS AP HUGH, of Wern Fawr, in the parish of Llandderfel, in the Cômot of Penllyn, Merionethshire, "gentleman"; died prior 1682. Will proved at District Registry of the Court of Probate, at St. Asaph, North Wales.
[The undernamed John ap Thomas is the person who made out the old parchment pedigree, above mentioned, in 1682. His sons brought it with them to Merion, Pennsylvania, and a branch of the family have since held it.]

= OWEN AP HUGH, of Penllyn. He had besides other issue: Ellin, Elizabeth, m. Thomas Andrews, of Philadelphia, 1698; and Mably, who m. Edward Rees, alias Price, of Merion, Penna. (See that family.)

Daughter m. Robert, and had Thomas and Elizabeth Roberts.

CADWALADER THOMAS, of Penllyn, Mer., "gentleman"; died at Wern Fawr, in the parish of Llandderfel, prior to 9 Feb., 1682; he m. Ellen, 2nd daughter of Owen ap Evan, of Fron Gôch, and had issue: 1. Thomas Cadwalader. 2. JOHN CADWALADER. 3. Jane. 4. Katherine. John Cadwalader, the 2nd son, removed to Pennsylvania in 1697, and settled in Merion Township.

JOHN AP THOMAS, of Llaethgwm, Penllyn, Mer., "gentleman," d. 1682, in Wales. Will proved at Philadelphia, 1688; he m. Katherine Robert, and left issue: Thomas, Robert, Cadwalader, Evan, Katherine, Mary, Sidney. The family removed to Penna. and settled in Merion. See Jones family, of Merion, the sons of John ap Thomas having assumed that surname.

HUGH.

CATHERINE m. Gaven Vaughan, of Hendre Mawr, and had Robert Vaughan.

ELIZABETH m. Maurice Edward, of Cae Mor in Hafod Gynfor, and had Edward Morris, of Parc Eyton, Denbighshire.

THOMAS AP HUGH, of Wern Fawr (see above pedigree), in the parish of Llandderfel, in the Cômot of Penllyn, Merionethshire, "gentleman," was born near Bala, probably at Wern Fawr, circa 1605–1610, and died some time prior to 1682, at that place. His will is on file at the District Probate Registry of St. Asaph, North Wales. His wife appears to have died before him, as she is not named.

He mentions " my son Hugh Thomas," " my son John Thomas," " my son Cadwalader Thomas," " my brother Owen ap Hugh," " my granddaughter Sydney," " my son-in-law Garsen (Garven or Gawen) Vaughan, and my daughter Catherine, his wife." " My daughter Elizabeth and grandchild, Edward Maurice," " my nephew Thomas ap Robert, and niece, Elizabeth vch Robert." He appoints his son, Cadwalader Thomas, sole executor, and names as " overseers " of his will "sons John Thomas and Hugh Thomas, and Maurice Edward and Garven Vaughan," the latter his sons-in-law.

The places named in the will are : Cefn y fedw, Bettws, Tydyn y Berth, and Penmaen.

Considerable information can be gathered from this will. Garven Vaughan, who had married Catherine, one of the daughters of Thomas ap Hugh, was the father of Robert Vaughan, whose letters to his " aunt Katherine Robert," are referred to elsewhere. Elizabeth, the other daughter, had married Maurice ap Edward, of Cae Mor in Havod Gynfor [vide Hist. Powys Fadog, I. Y. W. Lloyd, Vol. IV., pp. 107, 108]. Their son, Edward Maurice, writing under date of 3 September, 1692, from Eyton Park, Denbighshire, to Katherine Robert, widow of John ap Thomas, in Pennsylvania (Merion), calls himself " your loving nephew."

Thomas ap Hugh[1] had issue :

---

[1] The issue of Thomas ap Hugh's brother, Owen ap Hugh, of Penllyn, have been noted briefly in chart, and given elsewhere (see Price). It may, however, be stated here that Elizabeth, daughter of Owen ap Hugh, came to Pennsylvania, and married at Philadelphia meeting, 8mo. 25th, 1689, Thomas Andrews, of Philadelphia, widower. He had a son by his first wife named Simon Andrews. The will of Thomas Andrews is recorded at Philadelphia, Book A. p. 397. It is dated 1mo 29, 1698; proved 20 April, 1698. His wife, Elizabeth Owen, outlived him until 1718, when she died, leaving a will dated 4 October, 1718; proved at Philadelphia 7 January, 1718-19. Will Book D, p. 112. She leaves bequests to the two daughters of " sister Ellin Owen, to be deposited in trust in the hands of cousin Robert Vaughan, of Hendre Mawr, near Bala, Merionethshire." " To cousin Robert, son of my sister Gwen [i. e., her sister-in-law], to his brothers Hugh and Thomas, and his sisters Elizabeth and Grace." " To cousin Robert, son of my brother Hugh (i. e., brother-in-law) and his sisters." " To Edward Rees [Price], son of my nephew Rees, my sister Mably's son." " To Elizabeth, daughter of cousin Thomas Jones, of Merion—Ann, daughter of his brother, Robert Jones "—" Thomas Cadwalader, son of cousin John Cadwalader—Mary and Rebecca, daughters of said cousin John (Cadwalader). Martha, daughter of Rebecca Cadwalader." Executors : " Nephew Rees Prees " [Price], and " Cousins

1. Cadwalader Thomas, of Penllyn; m. Ellin Owen; of whom presently.

2. John ap Thomas (alias John Thomas, of Llaithgwm, Penllyn, "gentleman") died in Wales 1682; will dated 9 February, 1682; proved at Philadelphia, Penna., 1688. He m. Katherine Robert and had issue several children, who all, except the wife of Rees Evan, removed with their mother to Pennsylvania and settled in Merion, where they continued to reside, having assumed, according to the *modo wallico*, the name of Jones, by which surname their descendants continue to be known to the present time. For an account of them see John ap Thomas.

3. Hugh Thomas, of Penllyn; living circa 1680.

4. Catherine, m. "Garsen" (alias Gaven or Gawen) Vaughan, and had Robert Vaughan, of Hendre Mawr, near Bala, living 1718; trustee of Elizabeth Andrews, of Philadelphia, Thomas Vaughan, and possibly other issue.

5. Elizabeth, m. Maurice ap Edward, of Cae Mor, and had Edward Maurice, of Parc Eyton, Denbighshire.

CADWALADER THOMAS, eldest son of Thomas ap Hugh, of Wern Fawr, is usually designated as of the township of Kiltalgarth, in Penllyn. Before his father's death he leased a large farm here, and was forced to relinquish his lease because he permitted Friends' meetings to be held at his home, although his landlord was his kinsman. He was a very considerable sufferer from the persecution of the Quakers, and his death was caused by exposure to cold on such an occasion.

His descendant, Charles E. Cadwalader, M. D., of Philadelphia, says of him: "His determined resistance and refusal to yield the dictates of his own conscience under a severe

---

Robert Jones and John Cadwalader, Trustees." The author is indebted for the above data and for other particulars concerning this line to Howard Williams Lloyd, Esq., and for many valuable manuscripts and information regarding the family in Pennsylvania to Charles E. Cadwalader, M. D.

persecution, would appear to have cost him his life. As in the cases of Charles Lloyd, Thomas Lloyd, Robert Vaughan, Hugh Roberts, Robert Owen and other members of the principal families of North Wales, he was made an example of a special prosecution by the Government." After repeated confiscations of his property and imprisonments, he was again arraigned, and refusing to take the oaths, the Judges of the Circuit Court, by whom the commitment was made, had come to the extraordinary determination that the prosecution should be conducted under the statutes for High Treason and the writ De Haeretico Comlurendo, the penalties under the latter process not having been exercised since Queen Mary's time. They declared in open court that the sentence for a second refusal to take the prescribed oaths would be hanging and quartering as traitors for the men, and burning for the women.

After a short interval Cadwalader Thomas was again brought into court and the oaths tendered him, and being again refused, though he made a "solemn declaration of his allegiance to the King, and abhorrence of Popery," he was remanded to close imprisonment and strictly kept as a " felon or traitor, and during a very great frost was not allowed the benefit of a fireplace." It is said that a cold contracted at this time hastened his death. He died before February, 1682, having married, some years before, Ellen (or Ellin), daughter of Owen ap Evan, of Fron Gôch, near Bala, descended from Trahairn Gôch, of Llyn (see Owen

ARMS OF TRAHAIRN GÔCH. Family), by whom he had issue[1] :

1. Thomas Cadwalader.[2]

---

[1] In the *Owen Genealogy* it will be noted that his daughters are given, from one authority, as *Elizabeth*, and Jane. The names here given are correct, and the daughter *Elizabeth*, is probably an error for Katherine, unless there was another daughter who died in infancy before 1682, at which date the above children, only, were living.

[2] Thomas Cadwalader, who inherited the family estate, remained in Wales. "He appears to have been an active and leading man from the frequency with which his name appears in the Welsh Records and Memorials. Robert Vaughan,

2. John Cadwalader, who removed to Pennsylvania in 1697; of whom presently.
3. Jane.
4. Katherine.

JOHN CADWALADER,[1] the eldest son of Cadwalader Thomas, of Kiltalgarth (afterwards of Wern Fawr), and Ellen Owen, his

wife, daughter of Owen ap Evan, of Fron Gôch, was born in Penllyn, Merionethshire, circa 1677-8, and was sent to school in Pembrokeshire, from which place he had a certificate of removal to Pennsylvania in 1697. His friends say of him: "We have known him since the age of thirteen, he hath the reputation of an apt scholar, and hath attained to as good a degree of learning as any at the school. His demeanour has been sober and innocent." He was cordially welcomed by his kinsmen in Merion, where he at first settled, having decided

---

in one of his letters, written in 1703, speaks of his cousin, Thomas Cadwalader, being on a visit to Dolobran, the homestead of Charles Lloyd, elder brother of Thomas Lloyd, Deputy Governor of Pennsylvania, and as being occupied there in the translation of an English work into Welsh, which would seem to indicate that he was of a literary turn of mind. Vaughan refers to him, in the same letter, as engaged in the administration of the family estate." Charles E. Cadwalader, M. D., of Philadelphia, informs the author that he has a number of letters of Thomas Cadwalader and Robert Vaughan to John Cadwalader. It is to be regretted that Dr. Cadwalader, up to the present writing, has been so much engaged as to prevent an examination of these letters, which, doubtless, throw considerable light upon the early Welsh.

[1] "A preacher among Friends, of the same name, very eminent in the early religious history of the Province, died at Tortola, in the West Indies, while on a religious visit to that place, A. D. 1742. A short memorial respecting him by Abington Meeting, of which he was a member, may be found in 'Collections of Memorials of Deceased Ministers' (Philad. 1786). A more extended notice of him, and of his wife Margaret Cadwalader, is given in 'Memoirs of Friends, eminent for piety and virtue, of the Yearly Meeting of Philadelphia, from the settlement of the Colony to the present time (1770)' by John Smith, of Burlington, New Jersey."

to open a school there. The writer has heard it stated that whilst in Merion, he resided for a time in the Owen home, during the minority of his cousin, Evan Owen. He was married at Merion Meeting, 10-mo. 26, 1699, to Martha, daughter of Dr. Edward Jones, of Merion, and granddaughter of Dr. Thomas Wynne. John Cadwalader removed to Philadelphia, and in July, 1705,[1] was admitted as a freeman of the city. In 1718 he was elected a member of the Common Council, and in 1729, a member of the Provincial Assembly, which offices he continued to hold until his death, in 1733. He held many other important positions, and was a useful and prominent citizen. Unfortunately the scope of this work does not permit of a more lengthy account of his services.

As several accounts of the descendants of John Cadwalader have already appeared in print, particularly in Mr. Keith's *Provincial Councillors of Pennsylvania*, and as extended biographical notices of the distinguished careers of the several members of the family appeared lately in *Contemporary Biography*, it is not considered necessary here to give a detailed account of the various branches of the family, even if it could be properly accomplished in the space allotted to this article. John Cadwalader had, besides several children who died in infancy, a son, Dr. Thomas Cadwalader, whose distinguished professional career, and services in the Provincial Council, and subsequently, during the Revolution, are well known. His sons, Gen. John and Col. Lambert Cadwalader, served with especial distinction in the Revolutionary War, and their descendants have continued to hold high positions in military and civil life. Of John Cadwalader's daughters, Mary

---

[1] I should be inclined to doubt that he was admitted to the freedom of the city so early as the date given were it not for the statement to that effect by Mr. Charles P. Keith in his *Provincial Councillors of Pennsylvania*. Dr. Cadwalader states that at the time of his removal to the city a fortune was left him by a relative, which enabled him to embark in mercantile pursuits. This must have been from estates in Wales.

married, in 1731, Judge Samuel Dickinson, and became mother of John Dickinson, who with his brother, Philemon, are well known for their devotion to the cause of Independence.

Hannah, another daughter, married Samuel Morris, and her sister, Rebecca, married William Morris, but died s. p. Frances, daughter of General Cadwalader, married Lord Erskine, and from her are descended the present Duke of Portland, and the wife of Lord Archibald Campbell.

WYNNEWOOD AND THE WYNNES[1].

To the right hand, as we ride westward in the fast express trains of the Pennsylvania Railroad, the name "Wynnewood" flashes on our vision. How did this name originate? It has an inviting sound, as of a cool retreat, as well as an aristocratic ring. A roomy mansion, semi-colonial in style, occupies a commanding position near the station. This is owned by the wife of the late Colonel Owen Jones, who was a lineal descendant of Dr. Edward Jones (see infra), whose wife was Mary, a daughter of Dr. Thomas Wynne, the friend, associate and physician of William Penn. The estate was named in remembrance of Dr. Wynne, and the station, Wynnewood, from its location on the estate[2].

Dr. Thomas Wynne was an interesting character. He was born about the year 1630, in one of the northern counties of Wales. The exact date and place of his birth are, however, unknown. About the year 1655-7, in the time of the Commonwealth and during the Protectorate of Cromwell, he married his first wife, Martha Buttall. At this period religous feeling was intense. George Fox had started his movement calling on the people "to give sincere and earnest heed to the *inner light—the light of Christ*—which God had placed in every human heart." There was also great independence in religious thought, and the Buttalls were no exception to the many minor families of England in affiliating themselves with the Independents. They were identified with the town of Wrexham. It was here that Noncomformity was preached as

---

[1] Prepared by Howard Williams Lloyd, Esq.

[2] It must not, however, be supposed that this property ever belonged to Dr. Thomas Wynne or to Dr. Edward Jones, his son-in-law. It was originally the plantation of Robert Owen, and was sold by Evan Owen, son and heir of Robert, to his brother-in-law, Jonathan, son of Dr. Edward Jones, from whom it descended to the late Colonel Jones (see Jones). The family at a later date called the place Wynnewood as explained by Mr. Lloyd. The northern half of this farm has been long known as "St. Marys." T. A. G.

early as 1634. Walter Cradock, whose stay in Wrexham lasted from October, 1634, to September, 1635, was the first to expound the doctrines of Puritanism in that town. It was in an atmosphere of this kind that Martha Buttall passed her young days. In 1653 Morgan Lloyd, of Cynfael, then in charge of the church at Wrexham, sent two of his members to England to learn more about the Quakers. George Fox says in his Journal: "When these triers came down among us the power of the Lord overcame them and they were, both of them, convinced of the truth. So they stayed some time with us and then returned into Wales, where afterwards one of them departed from his convincement, but the other, whose name was John ap John, abode in the truth, and received a gift in the ministry to which he continued faithful." It was this John ap John who was afterwards associated with Dr. Wynne in the purchase of large tracts of land in Pennsylvania. No doubt, it was through his preaching and influence that Martha and her husband became Quakers. Mention is made in "*Besse's Sufferings*" of one Nathaniel Buttall, with Bryan Sixsmith, Thomas Gwin [Wynne?] and others "being met together in their own hired house at Wrexham, taken to the Common Goal at Writhen."[1] This was in December, 1661.

Some members of the Buttall family settled in or near London. One of these was Jonathan Buttall, of Battersea, in the County of Surrey. He was a successful sugar baker or manufacturer. In his will, dated 26th day of August, 1695, proved at London, 19th of September, 1695, he left legacies as follows: "To nurse Gunning £20." "To Mr. William Collins £20," Mr. Edward Harrison, £10. "To my sister Rebecca, £50." "To the poor of the congregation to which "I belong, £20, to sister Abigail £50. To my son Jonathan "Buttall £1000, my daughter Ann Buttall £1000, my wife "Sarah Buttall £1600. To my son Samuel Buttall £400, my "wife to have the education of my said son and to put out the

---

[1] "*A Collection of the Sufferings of the People Called Quakers,*" &c. Joseph Besse.

"said legacy at interest for his use. If the said Samuel die
"then my said wife shall have half the said legacy and the
"said Jonathan and Ann the other half. In case all my said
"children die, I give their said legacies amongst my relations
"as follows: amongst the children of my sister *Martha Wynn*,
"of my brother *Samuel Buttall*, of my sister Rebecca Keeting
"and of my sister Abigail Owen."

"Also to Joshua Buttall and James Buttall, sons of my
"uncle Richard Buttall, £10. All the rest of my goods I
"give to my wife Sarah Buttall, whom I make sole executrix.
"I appoint my brother Samuel Buttall and my friends Mr.
"Allyn Smith of Battersea and Mr. Edward Lewis of London,
"Overseers of this my will. To my cousins John Herbert,
"and Daniel Hailes £10 each. To my honoured Aunt Mrs.
"Anne Smith £20 to buy her a ring." Witnesses Hannah
Hodgson, Mary Smalbon, John Bouth.

P. C. C. Sept., —65, Irby.[1]

From this will is gathered the information that Jonathan
and Samuel Buttall were brothers-in-law of Dr. Wynne. This
is further confirmed by the will of the latter, referred to later
on. About the year 1670 Martha Wynne died. It might be
well to state that a diligent endeavor (covering a period of
several years) has been made to find the exact dates of birth,
marriage, etc., of Thomas and Martha Wynne. Owing to the
disturbed condition of the country at that time there were practically no records of nonconformist congregations kept. None
belonging to the Society of Friends of North Wales are now
known to be in existence. Nearly all of the Church of England
Registers, with few exceptions, contain gaps, and many wills
were not probated owing to the fact that an order was issued
requiring them to be deposited in the Prerogative Court of Canterbury. In those times an expensive trip. Martha is believed
to have been the mother of all of Thomas Wynne's children.
A few years after her death he married a widow named Row-

---

[1] For more information of the Buttalls, one of whom was Gainsborough's
"Blue Boy," see Alfred Neobard Palmer's, "*A History of the Older Nonconformity
of Wrexham and Its Neighborhood*," and other works by the same writer.

den. By her former husband she had a daughter named Elizabeth, who came to Pennsylvania and married John Brock (see future page)[1].

Elizabeth Wynne died prior to the summer of 1676, when the doctor made a third matrimonial venture. This time also to a widow. A copy of the entry in the book belonging to the Religious Society of Friends, recording this event, is here given. From the extracts at Devonshire House and from the original book at Somerset House, Lancashire MeetingRecords, Monthly Meeting of Hardshaw East:

Thomas Wynne, of Carwis, in the County of Flint, in Wales, Chirurgeon and Elizabeth Maud, of Rainhill, in Lancashire, were joyned together in marriage ye 20th day of ye 5th month 1676 at John Chorley's house in the presence of

Alexander Chorley	ffaith Chorley
John Chorley	Alice Southworth
John Barnes	Ester Sixmith
Bruen Sixmith	Sarah Gandy
Sam: Dunbabin	Bridget Wilson
John Southworth	Alice Dunbabin
William Crowdson	Margaret Dunbabin
James Wright	Mary Southworth
William Sixmith	Alice Barnes.

Carwis is intended for Caerwys, which was the place of residence of Thomas Wynne at the time of this marriage. It is very doubtful whether any of the witnesses were related to him. They may have been to Elizabeth Maud. Alexander Chorley and John Chorley were brothers. The latter married Ellen, daughter of John Barnes, of Warrington. Bruen or Bryan Sixmith [Sixsmith?] has already been mentioned. He was at one time a draper in Wrexham. He had a shop in High Street, next the Golden Lion. At the time of his death in 1692 he was a resident of Great Sankey. His brother, William, who died in 1698, was living in Ashton, both places near Rainhill, southern part of Lancashire, east of Liverpool. He may have been a connection of the Buttalls, as certain given names are used in both families.

---

[1] This Elizabeth Rowden is one of the witnesses to the will of Richard Thomas, late of Whitford Garne, County of Flint.

Joshua Maud, of Wakefield, Yorkshire, believed to have been a son of John Maud, of Alverthorpe, was the first husband of Elizabeth, whose maiden name was Parr. By him she had a son named Joshua, who remained in Wakefield; a daughter Jane, who removed to Pennsylvania and was married to a man by the name of Willbank,[1] but died without issue, and a daughter Margery. The latter married at Lewistown [Lewes], Delaware, Thomas Fisher, son of John Fisher, from Clithero, Lancashire, and Margaret [Hindle?], his wife. They were the progenitors of the present Fisher family of Philadelphia and Lewes.

Thomas Wynne was a man of parts. He took great interest in the religious society of which he was an early convinced member. He became an able minister of the Gospel of Christ, and appears to have visited various places in his native country giving forth his religious views. In 1677 he wrote a pamphlet on: "*The Antiquity of the Quakers, proved out of the Scriptures of Truth. Published in Love to the Papists, Protestants, Presbyterians, Independents and Anabaptists. With a Salutation of Pure Love to all the Tender-hearted Welshmen. But more especially to Flintshire, Denbighshire, Caernarvonshire and Anglesea. By their Countryman and Friend, Thomas Wynne.*" *Printed in the year 1677.*

Besides the English part, this address contains two pages of Welsh. He signs himself your real friend, Thomas Wynne. These words are added: "*Y Llythyr i anner chfy an wy l wladwyr y Cymru.*"

Carwys y 4 mis yr ail dydd 1677.

In reply to this pamphlet a Welshman named William Jones wrote: "*Work for a Cooper.*" *Being an Answer to a Libel Written by Thomas Wynne, the Cooper, the Ale-Man, the Quack and the Speaking Quaker. With a brief Account, how that Dissembling People differ at this day from what at first they were. By one who abundantly pities their Ignorance and*

---

[1] Is this an error for Wiltbank. Helminus Wiltbank, a Swede, was a very early settler near Lewis. His descendants are numerous. T. A. G.

Folly. [*Anon.*] London. Printed by J. C. for S. C., at the Prince of Wales Arms near the Royal Exchange MDCLXXIX.

In the front of this pamphlet there is a curious, finely etched portrait of Thomas Wynne tempted by the Devil[1].

In this answer it criticises some of Thomas Wynne's remarks, and says there were certain things:

"'Tis well he did not say at Holy-well or Caerwys." . . . "No, he's much fitter to plant Tobacco, &c. . . . to mind his Ax and saw, the Joynter and the Adz (alias Nedde), the Crisle and the Head knife, the Spoak & the Round Shreve, the Dowling and the Taper Bitts, the Tap & Bungbore. . . . I believe he is ignorant in his very trade of Quack—Chyrurgery."

A postscript in Welsh is headed: "*Atteb i'r Cowper o'Gaerwys o'i Lythyr anraflon at y Cymru.*"

These few extracts are given merely to show the occupations of Thomas Wynne. The book throughout is scurrilous.[2]

In 1679 Thomas Wynne had printed: *An Anti-Christian Conspiracy Detected and Satan's Champion Defeated. Being a Reply to an Envious & Scurrilous Libel, without any Name to it, called Work for a Cooper. Being also a vindication of my Book entitled The Antiquity of the Quakers. From the Base Insinuations, False Doctrine and False Charge therein contained against me, my Book and against God's People, called Quakers in general. By me Thomas Wynne.* To this there is a postscript by William Gibson.

It would seem from the above that among his various callings Thomas Wynne was a Cooper. He may have been also a Maltster and Brewer. He was also a successful Chirurgeon and "Practitioner in Physics," the latter being what he styles himself in his will. He is said to have practiced in London. His name does not appear in Sidney Young's "*Annals of the Barber-Surgeons of London,*" nor on the roll of the Royal College of Surgeons or Royal College of Phy-

---

[1] The editor is assured that this is probably not a real portrait of Dr. Wynne. Mr. Charles Roberts, of Philadelphia, who has a large collection of Anti-Quaker tracts, says that the same plate was used to represent other persons also.

[2] Joseph Smith's *Catalogue of Friends' Books*. Joseph Smith's *Catalogue of Books Anti-Quakeriana*. Charles Roberts, Esq., of Philadelphia, who possesses these pamphlets, kindly allowed the writer to make extracts from them.

sicians. If a graduate of either Oxford or Cambridge it would be difficult to state which he could claim as his Alma Mater. In *Graduati Cantabrigiensis* there is one of his name, an A. B. 1667. In a list of *Graduates of Oxford* there is also a Thomas Wynne, Christ Church, B. A., Feb. 23, 1670.

As early as the 32nd of Edward I., 1305-6, there was a guild of Barber-Chirurgeons at Shrewsbury. A company of Fletchers, Coopers and Bowyers also, from the 27th of Henry VI., 1449. It is possible that Thomas Wynne was a member of one of these companies, Shrewsbury being close to the Welsh border. Chester, on the very edge of Flintshire, also had its guilds and trading companies. Thomas Wynne was well versed in the law. He held several responsible positions that required a knowledge of this kind. These will be referred to in their proper place, after the account of his arrival in the Province of Pennsylvania.

Richard Davies, in his very interesting autobiography, writing of one of his visits to North Wales in 1681, says: " I acquainted my friend William Penn and some Friends that I intended to give Bishop Lloyd a visit." [This was Dr. William Lloyd, who had been in charge of St. Martin's in London, afterwards bishop of St. Asaph.] " I went to my friend Thomas Wynne's, who lived in Caerwys, in Flintshire, not far from the bishop's palace, and he went with me. When we came there the bishop's secretary came to the gate. I asked him whether the bishop was within; he said he was. . . . . The Bishop sent for us, in there were several clergymen with him, among the rest the dean of Bangor. . . . . We went soon to dispute about water-baptism. I told them, there was one Lord, one faith and one baptism. . . . . . So this and such like discourse, held us till it was late at night, and then I went to my friend's house."

In the early part of the year 1682 there was a committee appointed to visit Whitehall to try to induce Lord Hyde, Sir Lionel Jenkins, Secretary of State, and others in authority, to influence the king to relieve the sufferings of the Friends of

Bristol. The three Friends on the committee from the country were Charles Lloyd, Thomas Wynne and Richard Davies. At this time Thomas Wynne was a resident of Bronvadog, and was one of the overseers of the will of John ap Thomas, which was dated 9th February, 1682, being styled "Thomas Wynne, late of Bronvadog, near Caerwys, in the county of fflynt churyrgeon." Isceiviog, the parish in which this place is located, is four miles southwest of Holywell, on the road from Nannerch to Whitford.

William Penn having obtained his charter for the Province of Pennsylvania was desirous of selling off portions of the land to intending settlers.

Thomas Wynne in connection with John ap John (who has already been referred to), for themselves, as well as trustees for others, purchased from Penn 5,000 acres, to be laid out in the Welsh Tract. The Proprietor, having completed his arrangements for sailing, departed from England in the Sixth month, 1682, on the ship Welcome. Robert Proud, in his *History of Pennsylvania*, writes as follows: " The number of passengers in this ship was about one hundred, mostly Quakers, the major part of them from Sussex, the Proprietary's place of residence. In their passage many of them were taken sick of the small-pox, and about thirty of their number died."

In about six weeks they sighted the American coast at about Egg Harbor, New Jersey. On the 24th of October the Proprietary landed at New Castle, and at Upland, now Chester, on the fourth day of the Tenth month (December). Dr. Wynne was a passenger, and doubtless practised his profession, administering medicine and relieving the sufferings of those overtaken by the above mentioned disease. He acted as adviser to those who finding themselves about to die desired to dispose of their possessions by will. One of these was Thomas Heriott. He made his nuncupative will, and in it he is styled late of Hurst pre poynt [Hurst Pierreepoint] Sussex Co., England, yeoman. Made on board the ship Welcome, Robert Greenway, commander, bound for Pennsylvania, &c. The date is September 19th, 1682. Thomas Wynne, chirurgeon, one of the witnesses. Proved at Philad*, Book A 4. No. 3 of 1683.

At the preliminary Legislative Assembly held at Chester the 4th day of the 10th-month, 1682, Nicholas Moore presided. Thomas Holmes, Surveyor General; Thomas Wynne, William Clark and Edward Southbrin, were appointed a committee to desire the Governor to transmit a "Constitute" [Constitution]. The session lasted three days. It will thus be seen that the doctor at once took an interest in the welfare of the infant Colony. He was present at the first monthly meeting of the Religious Society of Friends, held in Philadelphia 11th-month 9th, 1682. He was one of those appointed to select a site for a meeting-house, and to consider the manner and form of the building. At the first regular Assembly, held in the same town, the 12th day of the 1st-month [March], 1682-3, he was chosen Speaker. He was one of the representatives from Philadelphia County, the body being composed of nine members from each of the counties of Philadelphia, Chester, Bucks, New Castle, Kent and Sussex.

Among the various accounts which have been written of our city, one states the fact that among the first brick houses built was that of Thomas Wynne. It was located on Front Street, west side, above Chestnut Street, the latter being for a short time called Wynne Street. As many of the earlier Colonists had to be content with log houses, and indeed even with caves, dug out of the bank along the river front, the above fact shows the doctor to have been a man of means and standing among the new-comers. Having some business to attend to in the old country, he laid before his monthly meeting the prospect he had of a visit with his wife to England. Philadelphia Monthly Meeting Minute Book shows the following entry bearing on the case:

"First day of ye 5th month 1684" "John Brock and Elizabeth Rowden appear in the meeting the first time declaring their intentions of marriage, being presented to the meeting by Margaret Lewis and Elizabeth Ible. Thomas Wynne father in-law [i. e. step-father] to Elizabeth Rowden being immediately to depart for England together with his wife moves that the marriage of the above said parties might be accomplished somewhat sooner than usual, that so they might be at the said marriage." Friends therefore agreed that John Brock should bring his certificate of clearness to the 5th day meeting at Philadelphia falling upon the 10th day of this instant and it was also agreed that Henry Lewis and John Moon should make inquiry into the clearness of the above parties and make report there of at the 5th day meeting aforesaid."

The young couple were married on the 6th-month 5, 1684.

John Brock came from near Stockport, Cheshire, "Arrived in the Delaware the 28th of the 7th mo., 1682, in the ship the 'Friends' Adventure.'"

It is supposed that Thomas Wynne accompanied William Penn to England in the ketch "Endeavour." This ship sailed from Philadelphia the 12th of 6th-month, 1684, and made port in about seven weeks. On the 23d of 9th month in London William Gibson was buried. It was he who had written the postscript to the Doctor's last publication. On this occasion a meeting was held in White Hart Court Meeting-House. It is stated that more than a thousand persons were at the burial-place, when it was publicly said of the body "That it had been often beaten and imprisoned for Christ's sake." At another time, while Thomas Wynne and twenty-three others were on their way to the meeting-house at White-Hart-Court they were arrested in Angel Court and sent to prison. On 10th month (December) 8th, they were tried at Guildhall. The charge was, "Being guilty of a riotous assembly, with force and arms, &c." in White-Hart-Court. They all pleaded not guilty. They had not been in White-Hart-Court at all. The evidence produced by the prosecution showed this. This objection was overruled, as it was in the same ward of the city. They stated that their being together in Angel-Court was accidental. They had been stopped while passing through. One of the witnesses testified that while they were assembled in a common thoroughfare a woman spoke he knew not what. Notwithstanding this testimony and the errors in the charge, the prisoners were all sent to Newgate prison and fined.

The length of time that Thomas Wynne remained in England is unknown. On his return he settled on an estate he had purchased at Lewes. He again took part in public affairs, as the "Sussex County Court Records" show. Here are a few entries as taken from that book:

"Att A Court Held by the King's Authority & in the proprietary's name at Lewis, for the County of Sussex, the 3 day of the 3 month, 1687.
Comitioners present,

William Clarke   Thomas Price
John Roades   Robert Clifton
Thomas Wynne   Samuel Gray.

Thomas Wynnes Comition to be one of ye justices in the Roome of Thomas Langhorne was Read viz.:
By the President and Councill of the Province of Pennsylvania and Territorys thereunto belonging.

To oure Loving and trusty ffriend Thomas Winn justice of the yeare for the County of Sussex in the roome of Thomas Langhorne.

Reposing Confidence in thy allegiance to the King and fidellity to the Govern'r and Government now doe by the Kings Authority & in the name of the proprietary and Govern'r appointe thee to be justice of the County of Sussex. Authorizing thee to Act as justice of ye yeare both in Court or any part of that County. Requiring all persons whatsoever to yield thee due obedience accordingly this Comission to stand in force soe long as the Generall Comission for that County shall soe Remain. Dated at Philadelphia the thirteenth day of the second month in the third yeare of ye Reigne of King James the Second and Seventh of ye Proprietarys Government Ano Dom 1687.

Tho Lloyd. Pr'sid't.

"The Declaration that the other justices have signed and sealed for the performing ye trust reposed in them and to Act therein according to Law was read, after which ye sd Tho: Wynn declared his willingness to sign and seale ye same & thereto put his hand."

During the year 1688, while holding the position of Associate Justice of Sussex County he was also a Representative from that county in the Assembly at Philadelphia. This body met on the 10th day of 3rd month. In the same year on the 6th of 5th month Rachel Lloyd, a daughter of Thomas Lloyd, Deputy-Governor of the Province, was married to Samuel Preston, a meeting being held for that purpose at the house of Frances Cornwall, in Sussex. Among the signers to the marriage certificate were Thomas Wynne, his wife and children. In the year 1691 the Doctor was in Philadelphia. He attended the Monthly Meetings held in the 11th month and 12th month. Soon after he was taken sick and died. He was buried on the 17th of 1st month, 1692. He made his will on the "16th day of first month, 1691–2." This was probated 2nd-mo. 20th, 1692, at Philadelphia [Book A, p. 200]. In it he is called "Thomas Wynne, of Philadelphia, in the Province of Pennsylvania, practitioner in Physic." He gives his messuage and plantation, near the town of Lewes, to his wife, Elizabeth Wynne, during her natural life, after her death to his son Jonathan Wynne. He also gives to the latter the plantation of two hundred acres at Cedar Creek, in the county of Sussex. He gives one-half of his personal estate to his children in America, viz.: Jonathan, Mary, Rebecca, Sidney and Hannah. His daughter Tabitha was living in England; he gave her fifty shillings as a last mark of love. "She hath already sufficiently partaken of my fatherly care and tenderness of her." The other half of his personal estate he bequeathed to his beloved wife, Elizabeth, who he makes executrix. He mentions a certain bond for £50 due by him to his brother-in-law, Samuel Buttall, on which twenty-five pounds had been paid. He desires "my dear friends, Thomas Lloyd, Dep. Gov. of this Province, and Griffith Owen, to be overseers." The witnesses were Arthur Cooke, Phineas Pemberton, Richard Thomas, Theo[r] Roberts and Mary Holme.

In the inventory, filed the 19th of 3d-mo., called May, 1692, the plantation and mansion near Lewes was valued at £80. The two hundred acres of land at Cedar Creek, £20. There is mention of one negro man, one negro woman, and a girl about one year and a half old, valued at £60. One servant youth, having about one year and a half to serve, £3. There is a long list of farming and household utensils. A barrel worm, copper still, a hogshead worm, &c. A chest of medicine, &c. The total amout of the inventory is £430, 1s., 3d.

The Children of Thomas and Martha Wynne were:

Mary, born circa 1659; married, in or about the year 1677, Dr. Edward Jones (see future page).

Tabitha, remained in England and was probably married.

Rebecca, born 1662; married first to Solomon Thomas, in 3rd-mo., 1685, at Thirdhaven Meeting, Talbot County, Maryland. He died leaving no issue. Second, to John Dickinson, of Talbot County, planter, at his house, 23rd of 7th month, 1692. He was a son of Walter Dickinson, of Crosia-doré, and an uncle of Samuel Dickinson, who married Mary Cadwalader, daughter of John Cadwalader and Martha Jones. The latter a daughter of Dr. Edward Jones and Mary Wynne.

Sidney, married 10th-mo. 20th, 1690, at the house of William Richardson, in Anne Arundel County, Maryland, William Chew, son of Samuel and Ann Chew, of that place.

Hannah, married at Merion Meeting 8th-mo. 25th, 1695, Daniel Humphrey, son of Samuel and Elizabeth Humphrey.

Jonathan, only son and heir, and believed to have been the youngest child. His will, dated January 29th, 1719, was probated at Philadelphia May 17th, 1721. He married, about the year 1694, Sarah [Graves or Greave?]. In the year 1705, on the 18th of 4th month, he applied to Edward Shippen, Griffith Owen and James Logan, Commissioners of Property for a warrant for 400 acres in the Welsh Tract. He alleged that his father's joint purchase with John ap John of 5,000 acres was not fully taken up. His request was granted, and an order issued to David Powel, Surveyor. The latter part of his life he resided in Blockley township, Philadelphia County. He left to his eldest son, Thomas, all the home plantation after the death, or second marriage, of his widow. To his son, John, 250 acres near the Great Valley (Chester Valley). To son Jonathan, 250 acres in the same locality. To each of his two eldest daughters, Hannah and Mary, lot in High street, Philadelphia, 60x300 ft., to be equally divided. To his three younger daughters, Sidney, Martha and Elizabeth, 400 acres near the Great Valley, " or in the great meadows," to be equally divided, with power to sell at 18 or marriage. His trustees were his brothers-in-law Edward Jones and Daniel Humphrey, in case of their decease John Cadwalader and Jonathan Jones. His wife, Sarah, executrix.

Of the ancestry of Dr. Thomas Wynne, nothing is positively known at this time. Owen Jones, Sen., born 1711, died 1793, says of his great-grandfather that " He was descended from a very ancient and honorable family." As is well known, and has been referred to in these pages, some of the early Welsh settlers brought with them pedigrees of their families. These were to be recorded in their Meeting Books. Here is an entry from Merion Minutes: "Preparative Meeting held at Merion Meeting House, the 5th day of the 11th month, 1704."

. . . . . . "An account was brought concerning Thomas Wynne, of Cayrwys, in flintshire, formerly, and his family to this meeting by Edward Jones."

Unfortunately, these records are now missing. If a copy of the Wynne pedigree is in existence among any branches of the family it is unknown to the writer[1].

Some years ago an attempt was made, from circumstantial evidence only, to connect Thomas Wynne with the family of Wynn of the Tower. This building is in the township of Broncoed, and parish of Mold, County Flint. It so happens that the seal attached to Dr. Wynne's will has on it the design of a triple-towered castle. At once the conclusion was reached that this meant he was a descendant of the Tower Wynns. To show how erroneous this is, it need only be stated that the Tower Wynns' armorial bearings are the same as those of Cynwrig Efell, from whom they descend, *gules, on a bend argent, a lion passant, sable.*

The probable solution of the problem of the use of this seal may be found in the statement that the Maudes of Ireland used for their arms: [2]*Gules, a tower, triple-towered, Argent.*

It will be remembered that the last wife of Dr. Wynne, and the one that came with him to Pennsylvania was a widow surnamed Maud. Although she came from Lancashire and her first husband's family were seated in Yorkshire, there may have been some connection with the early branch that went to Ireland.

---

[1] The editor of this work (as well as Mr. Lloyd), although meeting in all cases with the utmost courtesy, and a desire by persons interested to place at his disposal all papers in their possession bearing upon the Welsh settlement, is sorry to repeat here that it is to be much regretted that access was declined by some persons, without any apparent reason, to collections of family documents which might have thrown much light upon the ancestry of Dr. Thomas Wynne and other early Welshmen, and upon the history of Merion.

[2] *"An Alphabetical Dictionary of Coats of Arms belonging to Families in Great Britain and Ireland, &c.,"* by the late John W. Papworth, F. R. I. B. A. Edited by Alfred W. Morant, F. G. L. London, 1874.

Watson in his Annals of Philadelphia says that a brother came with Dr. Wynne in 1682.

This may have been John Wynne, who was on a jury in 1687, in Sussex County. The same man appears as an attorney in a case reported in the Sussex County Court Records, in the same year. There was a John Wynn "chyrurgeon" whose will was probated at Annapolis in 1684. A Thomas Wynn was in Maryland in 1671. He was a "sub-Sheriff" in 1678, and at one time Doorkeeper to the Assembly. His ancestry is known. He was a son of Gruffydd Wynn, of Bryn yr Owen, ap Richard ap John Wynn, of Trefechan, near Wrexham and Ruabon, Denbighshire.

If Dr. Thomas Wynne was born or baptized in Caerwys (which is very much doubted), a copy of the entry can not be had. The parish registers do not begin until 1673. The transcripts at the Bishop's Palace have no Wynne event recorded until 1666. Gwyn or Wynn, means white or fair-haired, and in early times there were hundreds of the name in Wales. [See Appendix.]

HOWARD WILLIAMS LLOYD.

NOTE.—It appears that Jonathan Wynne settled in Blockley Township, which was formerly a part of the Liberty Lands, of Philadelphia Town, at an early date. It is believed that the house which he lived in, and which he called "Wynnestay," was built soon after 1700. Whether this was built upon land purchased by him personally, or upon a part of the Liberty Land belonging to his father's joint purchase with John ap John, is not known. If the latter, it may have been the Liberty Land belonging to the grant in Chester Valley, but previously allowed him, or it may have been a part of the land first allotted to his father. The title to this property has not been searched by the writer, partly on account of the extra amount of labor it would involve without any especial result, and partly because it was never in Merion. T. A. G.

Descendants of Dr. Thomas Wynne. The Wister Branch.[1]

DANIEL WISTER, the oldest son of John and Catharine Wister, was born in Philadelphia on 2nd-mo. 4th, 1738-9, and died 10th-mo. 27th, 1805, æt. 68 years. On the 5th of the 5th month, 1760, he married LOWRY JONES, DAUGHTER OF OWEN JONES AND SUSANNAH, his wife. Owen Jones was son of JONATHAN JONES, eldest son of Dr. EDWARD JONES and MARY, daughter of Dr. THOMAS WYNNE. Daniel Wister was educated at Ephrata, Lancaster county, Pennsylvania. He was a prominent merchant of Philadelphia, and together with his father was a signer of the non-importation act, which was so important a measure, historically. His wife, Lowry Wister, was born 1743, and died 2nd-mo. 15th, 1804, æt. 61 years.

Daniel and Lowry Wister had 9 children, viz.: Sarah (the authoress of "Sally Wister's Journal of the Revolution"), born 7th-mo. 20th, 1761, and died, s. p., 4th-mo. 21st, 1804, æt. 43 years. Elizabeth, born 2nd-mo. 27th, 1764, o. s. p. 1812, æt. 48 years. Hannah, born 11th-mo. 19th, 1767, o. s. p. (*circa*), 1827. Susannah, born 2nd-mo. 24th, 1773, obt. 11th-mo. 27th, 1862, æt. 90 years. John, born 3rd-mo. 20th, 1776, obt. 12th-mo. 12th, 1862, æt. 86 years. Charles Jones, born 4th-mo. 12th, 1782, obt. 7th-mo. 23rd, 1865, æt. 84 years. William Wynne Wister, born 4th-mo. 16th, 1784, obt. 11th-mo. 16th, 1806, æt. 23 years, s. p.

---

[1] Herr Hans Caspar and Anna Katherina Wister, of Hillsbach, near Heidelberg, Germany. The former Hans Caspar was Fürst Jager in the service of the Prince Palatine. The Herr appears on the Church Record prefixed to his name and distinguished him from the Bourgeois. He was born about the middle of the 17th century, say 1650, and had seven children, two of whom came to America, Caspar in 1717, and John, my ancestor, in 1727. Caspar married, in 1726, Katherine Johnson, by Friends' ceremony, and had many descendants in the male line, and in the female e. g., Vauxes, Morrises, Haineses, McMurtries, etc. John Wister married, 2 mo. 9th, 1731, Salome Zimmerman, a German by birth. From these are descended the Chancellors, etc. Salome Wister having died 1736, John Wister married Anna Catherina Rubenkam. They had three children who lived to maternity, Daniel, born, 1738-9; Catherine, born 1742-3, ancestress of Mileses, McKeans, etc., and William, born 1746, o. s. p. My grandfather, Daniel Wister, married Lowery Jones, 5th-mo. 5th, 1760. She was the daughter of Owen Jones, Colonial Treasurer of the state of Penna, and Susannah Evans, and here begins the Welsh connection. Owen Jones was the son of Jonathan and Gainor (Owen) Jones. Gainor Owen was daughter of Robert Owen, and Jonathan Jones was son of Dr. Ed. Jones, who m. the daughter of Dr. Thomas Wynne.

To return to the Wister branch, Marie, daughter of Hans Caspar Wister, born (circa) 1690; married, 1711, Captain David Deshler, Aid-de-Camp to the Prince Palatine, this son, David, came to America and entered the counting-house of his uncle, John Wister. He married and had descendants of his own name, also Lewises (David Lewis, recently obt.), Mortons, Conners, etc. Anna Barbara Wister, daughter of Hans Caspar Wister, married Bauer Councillor of Manheim, Germany.

"WYNNESTAY."
Built by Jonathan Wynne, about 1701.

SUSANNAH WISTER, daughter of the above Daniel and Lowry Wister, married 3rd-mo. 10th, 1796, Colonel John M. Price, son of John and Rebecca Price. The ceremony was performed, although she was a Friend, by the Right Rev. Bishop White—J. M. Price being a member of the Episcopal Church. They had six children who reached maturity, viz.: Lowry, born 9th-mo. 4th, 1797, married Charles Humphreys, of the old Welsh family of that name, Lowry Humphreys, o. s. p., 8th-mo. 15th, 1876, æt. 79 years. Rebecca, daughter of S. and J. M. Price, was born 5th-mo. 10th, 1799. She married Robert Toland and had five children. Susan Wister Price, born 3rd-mo 25th, 1803, o. s. p., 7th-mo. 16th, 1881, æt. 78 years. Glendower and Wister Price both o. s. p. John M. Price obt. 2nd-mo. 2nd, 1828, æt. 57 years.

The children of Robert and Rebecca Price Toland, who came to maturity were: Henry, o. s. p. 4th-mo. 1862. Robert, married Annie Dale, had children: 1. Edward Dale, married, 1st-mo. 29th, 1883, Charlotte Rush, daughter of Col. Richard Rush. 2. Susan, married 4th-mo 26, 1860, Richard Tilghman, had six children. 3. Sarah, married 7th-mo. 9th, 1862, General Isaac J. Wister, o. s. p. 1st-mo. 11th, 1895. 4. George W. Toland, married, 9th-mo. 18, 1862, Angela L. Turner, daughter of Admiral Thomas Turner, U. S. N. They had four children, of whom Helen m. Mr. Moore.

JOHN WISTER, of Vernon, Germantown, son of Daniel and Lowry Wister, was married, 1798, to Elizabeth Harvey, of Bordentown, N. J., and had nine children who came to maturity: 1. Sarah, b. 4th-mo. 4th, 1800, married to John Stevenson, had four children. T. W. Stevenson, obt. 3rd-mo. 9th, 1848, æt. 48 years. 2. William, son of John and Elizabeth Wister, born 2nd-mo. 2nd, 1803, obt. 11th-mo. 19th, 1881, married, 9th-mo. 26th, 1826, Sarah Logan Fisher, had six children who came to maturity: 1. William Rotch, m. 3rd-mo. 4th, 1868, Mary Eustis, of Milton, Mass., had children: (1.) Mary Channing; (2.) Frances Anne; (3.) Ella Eustis. 2. John, son of Wm. and Sarah Wister, m., 1864, Sally Tyler Boas. III. Col. Langhorne Wister, o. s. p. 3rd-mo. 19th, 1891, æt. 56 years. IV. Jones Wister, m. Caroline de Tousard Stocker, obt. Oct. 6, 1868, had four children: Ella Middleton Maxwell, Alice Logan, Ann, Ethel Langhorne. V. Frances Wister, m. 2nd-mo. 1880, Mary Chancellor Tiers. VI. Rodman Wister, m. 4th-mo. 12th, 1872, Betty Black, of Pittsburg, Pa. 3. John Wister, son of John and Elizabeth Wister, of Vernon, o. s. p. 1st-mo. 28, 1883. 4. Charles, o. s. p. 8th-mo. 9th, 1893, æt. 83 years. 5. Ann, o. s. p. 10th-mo. 3, 1888, æt. 80 years. 6. Jones, o. s. p. 11th-mo. 14, 1837, in Paris, France. 6. Mary, o. s. p. 10th-mo. 24, 1886, æt. 73. 7. Susan, m. 4th-mo. 28, 1846, John Dickenson Logan, M. D., of Stenton, had son, Algernon Sydney, m. Mary Wynne Wister, daughter of Wm. Wynne Wister,

11th-mo. 4th, 1873, had son, Robert Logan. 8. Louis Wister, son of John and Elizabeth Wister m. 7th-mo. 3rd, 1850, Elizabeth Randolph, had children: (1) Elsie, m. Charles P. Keith, 12th-mo. 18, 1883; (2) Sara Edythe.

CHARLES JONES WISTER, son of Daniel and Lowry Wister, m. 12th-mo. 15th, 1803, Rebecca Bullock. The ceremony was performed by Rev. James Abercrombie, D. D., rector of St. Peter's Church, Phila. They had children who reached maturity: 1. William Wynne, b. 3rd-mo. 25th, 1807, m. Hannah Lewis Wilson, and had children: Rachael, William Wynne, Alexander Wilson, Hannah Lewis, Mary Wynne, Emily Wynne. Of the above, Rachael m. 11th-mo. 12, 1862, William B. Rogers; Alexander m., 12th-mo. 31st, 1862, Susan Wilson; Mary Wynne m., 11th-mo. 4, 1873, Algernon Sydney Logan; as already recorded under descendants of John Wister. 2. Mary Boynton Wister, m. 10th-mo. 23, 1839, Dr. W. S. W. Ruschenberger, U. S. N., had children: Fanny, o. s. p. 3rd-mo. 3, 1883; Charles Wister Ruschenberger, U. S. N. 3. Emily Wister, b. 12th-mo. 3, 1809, o. s. p. 8th-mo. 1831, æt. 21 years. Rebecca Bullock Wister obt. 9th-mo. 20th, 1812. 12th-mo. 4th, 1817, C. J. Wister m. Sarah, daughter of John and Sarah Whitesides. The ceremony was performed by the Rev. Mr. Depuy, the first rector of St. Luke's Church, Germantown. The children of this union who lived to maturity were: 1. Caspar, born 9th-mo. 15, 1818, obt. 12th-mo. 20th, 1888, æt. 70 years; married, 7th-mo. 20th, 1846, Lydia H. Simmons, had daughter, Lilly, m. Clifford Rossel. They had daughter, Annis Wister Rossel; Lydia having died, 1848; Caspar, m. 6th-mo. 26th, 1854, Annis Lee Furness, had son Caspar, obt. childhood. 2. Susan Wister, born 10th-mo. 21st, 1819, o. s. p. July 23, 1843. 3. Charles J. Wister, born 4th-mo. 6, 1822. 4. Owen Jones, born 10th-mo. 5, 1825; married 10th-mo. 1st, 1859, Sarah, daughter of Pierce Butler, had son, Owen Wister. 5. Sarah Elizabeth, daughter of C. J. and Sarah Wister, b. 11th-mo. 19, 1827, o. s. p. 8th-mo. 28, 1868.[1]

GERMANTOWN, 8-mo. 5th, 1895.

[1]MR. THOMAS ALLEN GLENN:

Dear Sir—In the list of descendants of the Welsh settlers of the "Great Welsh Tract," which I forwarded to you some weeks since, there were omissions which I now beg leave to supply. It may be too late for your proposed volume. If so, however, they may be introduced in some future publication.

John Wister, son of William and Sarah Fisher Wister, of Belfield, married, 1864, Sarah Tyler Boas, and had children who came to maturity: (1) Elizabeth, who married, 10-mo. 20, 1892, Charles Stewart Wurts, Jr.; (2) Sarah Logan; (3) Margaret Wister, II, Rodman Wister, son of Wm. and S. F. Wister, married 4-mo. 12th, 1872.

Betty Mifflin Black, had children, Langhorne Harvey and Rodman Mifflin Wister.

Of the children of William Wynne Wister and Hannah Lewis Wister, who reached maturity (1) Wm. Wynne Wister, (2) Rachael married, 11-mo. 12, 1862, William B. Rogers, had Barton, obt. in infancy; Harry Darwin, and Mabel.

(III) Alexander Wilson Wister married, Dec. 31st, 1862, Susan Wilson and had four sons who came to maturity: (1) Lewis Wynne, married, 2-mo, 16th, 1887, Elizabeth Walcott Henry, and had one son, Lewis Caspar; (2) Alexander Wilson; (3) Charles Jones, married, 6-mo. 5, 1894, Elizabeth E. Morgan; (4) James Wilson. (IV) Hannah Lewis; (V) Mary Wynne, already mentioned; (VI) Emily Wynne Wister.

Respectfully yours, CHARLES J. WISTER.

NOTE.—As the above letter explains, the author is indebted to Charles J. Wister, Esq., for the above complete list of the descendants of Dr. Thomas Wynne, of the Wister branch.

ROBERTS, OF MERION AND BLOCKLEY.

The first of this family of whom we have any account is one William Roberts, who was living in the township of Merion prior to 1697, but who, in that year, purchased land in the township of Blockley, just across the Merion line. "Family tradition is that a Hugh Roberts came from Wales in the ship with William Penn. His only child, William Roberts, then a boy, accompanied him, and on the vessel met Elizabeth Warner, whom he married some years afterwards. This son William, according to tradition, lived to be over 100 years of age. By his first wife he had three children, viz. : Thomas, Mordecai and a daughter. By his second wife he had one son, Joseph. In his old age, while his second wife was still living, he became much reduced in circumstances. The wife of Hugh had been a Presbyterian, and had considerable property in Wales which was forfeited when she became a Quaker. They were all members of Merion Meeting."

This tradition, with some slight variations, exists in all of the branches of the family, but the very careful investigations of Joseph Fornance, Esq., of Norristown, who lately made a very careful examination of the title to the property in Blockley purchased in 1697 by William Roberts, and until recently held by his descendants, has upset this narrative. From Mr. Fornance's researches and from some data gathered by the writer we are able to present the following facts regarding this family of Roberts. It appears that William Roberts, of Merion, is the first generation we can speak of with certainty. There is, indeed, but little clue to his parentage. He may have come direct from Wales, prior to 1697, in which case it is possible he may have been identical with the William Roberts referred to as a tenant of Richard Price, of Tyddin Tyfod, Merionethshire, in a letter written from Wales about 1700 (see article on Rees John William). It is also possible that he may have been an elder son of one Robert William, of Merion, a widower, who married Gwen Cadwalader, of Radnor, spinster, 19th of 4th month, 1691. As to him having been a son of Hugh Roberts, of Merion, it is simply out of the question, if the Provincial Councillor is meant.[1] There was, however, another Hugh Roberts, of Merion, who came with the first settlers, whose son he might have been. Turning from conjecture to actual facts we find that the first recorded purchase of property by him was by Deed Poll, dated September, 1697; recorded at Philadelphia, 789 in Deed Book B. R. D., 20., page 481, &c., from John Tatham, of Burlington County, New Jersey, to William Roberts, "of Merion, in the County of Philadelphia," for 100 acres of land in "the Town Bounds of Philadelphia, beyond the Schuylkill." The tradition above quoted states that he married Elizabeth Warner, whom he met on shipboard with Penn. That this could not be so is evident from the fact that William Warner, whose daughter she is supposed to have been, was settled in Blockley Township many years before Penn ever came into his Province, and the township was named after his native parish in Worcestershire.

Nor does this William Warner in his will mention any daughter as having married a Roberts. His son, William Roberts, is probably the person alluded to in the tradition.

It is, however, very probable that the purchase of the Blockley land was about the time of his marriage. In support of this theory we offer the following abstract from a letter written by Robert Owen, of Merion, to his brother-in-law, Hugh Roberts, then travelling in Wales. It will be remembered that the date of Roberts' Blockley purchase was September (7th month), *1697*. The date is 24th of 2nd month, *1697*: "Richard Hays in the Election of Marriage with B. Lewis, H. Lewis' sister, William, Robert and Richard Walters wives' sister." On the first perusal of this statement it appeared that the writer of the letter intended to mean that

---
[1] Hugh Roberts, the Councillor, had, however, a son, William Roberts, who died in infancy.

B. Lewis (Elizabeth or Bessie), Henry Lewis' sister, was sister to William Robert and Richard Walters' wives, but upon investigation it would appear that it might also mean that *William Robert* was about to marry Richard Walters' wife's sister. A very careful examination of the records might clear this up. The will of this William Roberts, of Blockley, is dated September 8th, 1707, and was proved in Philadelphia 1719 (W. B. D., page 134), devising his 100 acres of land to his eldest son, John, when he comes of age, subject to £20 to be paid to "youngest son, William Roberts," and appoints his wife, Affy Roberts, sole executrix. It appears that John died an infant, and the younger son, William Roberts, inherited the property (see Deed 10 Dec. 1788. Rec. 1789, Phila., D. B. D. 20, page 481) to William Smith for 89½ acres of said land.

The said William Roberts had issue by Affy, his wife:
1. John, died infant.
2. William.

WILLIAM ROBERTS,[1] the second son of William, living 10 December, 1788,[2] inherited, through the early decease of his brother, John, the 100 acres in Blockley, which farm or plantation, as it was then called, was upon the old Haverford road which he afterwards sold, in 1788, to William Smith. He married, first, Elizabeth (Warner?), probably a grandchild of William Warner, of Blockley, a Provincial Councillor of Pennsylvania, who owned the adjoining land. William Roberts married, secondly, Ann ———. By his first wife he had:
1. Thomas, m. Jane (Pyott?).
2. Mordecai, who left descendants.
3. ——— Daughter, m. ——— Evans.

---

[1] There can be but little question that this was the William Roberts mentioned in the family tradition as living to the age of over 100 years, and who married Elizabeth Warner. He died before 1812.

[2] Deed, 10 Dec., 1788, William Roberts and Ann, his wife, to William Smith. Recorded in Philadelphia, 1789, in Deed Book D 20, page 481, for 89½ acres, it being a part of the 100 acres left by William Roberts, of Blockley, to his son, John, and the said son John having departed this life, the said premises descended to William, the second son. See Orphans' Court Book, Philadelphia, No. 24, 78, 89, and 113.

By his second wife William Roberts had:
Joseph.

THOMAS ROBERTS, " of Blockley," eldest son of William, married Jane (Pyott?). (Swedes' Church Records, Philadelphia.) He was living 20 March, 1812, and died before 1846, when the remaining part of the 100 acres, viz.: 11½ acres were sold by his executors to Philip Esray.

Thomas Roberts had issue:

1. Phineas, m. Ellen Ervien and removed to Pike County, Pa., and there died. He had issue: John, Cadwalader, Ellen, Jane, Rebecca Barnes, Catherine, Thomas, Sarah.

2. Elizabeth, 1765–1844; m. John Fornance, and had: John, d. s. p., Rebecca, m. John Carr, but d. s. p., and Joseph Fornance (2nd), who married Anna B. McKnight, and had: Joseph Fornance, Esq. (1895), of Norristown, (3d), John, d. s. p., Elizabeth, m. Edward P. Jones, Mary, Catherine, m. F. H. Edmunds, James, Thomas.

3. John, d. s. p.

4. Rebecca, m. Wm. Keyser, but d. s. p.

5. Deborah, m. Anthony Kite, and had: Rebecca, Kitty, m. — Heafly, Isaac.

6. Thomas, — 1774–1846, m. Susan Rittenhouse, and had: Margaret, 1815–1893, d. single, Rebecca, 1820, m. Jacob S. Kidd, Thos. R., 1824–1874, d. s. p.

7. Sarah, m. Daniel Rittenhouse, and had: Maria, who m. William Umstead and left issue, and five other children, d. s. p.

8. James, m. Hannah ———; moved to Ohio.

9. Janet, m. Dr. George Vanderslice, and had: Edward, Thomas, d. s. p., James, Rebecca, unm.; Emma unm.; Deborah, m. Samuel Hopper, Kate Joseph, William R.; Samuel Hopper's daughter married Hon. William B. Hanna, Judge of the Orphans' Court, of Philadelphia; and a son, Harry S. Hopper, resides at Narberth, Lower Merion, and Philadelphia.

ROBERTS.

"Herewith is some information relating to our family which I trust will be of interest. We have only recently been able to find who the parents of Aaron Roberts (born about 1682) were. This has puzzled us for several years. The difficulty has been that the early Welsh settlers usually named their children after their father's given name (thus, John ap Evan, Owen ap Robert, or John the son of Evan, Owen the son of Robert), and these given names thus became the family names (as in the above cases, John Evans, Owen Roberts). This was very generally done at the time of their coming to this country. In the letter of removal which the father of our ancestor, Aaron Roberts, brought with him to this country in 1690 his name is given Robert Ellis. He afterward signed it Ellis Robert (or else this was his son's signature). He came over at the time that Hugh Roberts, who was a noted minister among the Friends, returned to this country after a religious visit to his old home. Hugh had previously come over about 1683. The letter of removal given to Robert Ellis is a very fine one, and speaks of both himself and his wife, Elin, as having been "Preachers of Righteousness to and amongst their neighbors," and as having been "convinced of the truth about twenty years before" (i. e., before 1690). At the same Quarterly Meeting at Tyddyn y Gareg, a very beautiful letter was given to Hugh Roberts, then returning to this country. As he and Ellis came over together, it seems altogether likely that they were related, and this is supported by the fact that all the children of Robert Ellis took the name of Roberts as their family name.[1] The first son, Abel, married Mary Prince in 1701, and to his marriage certificate, in the family column,

---

[1] There is certainly nothing in this fact to prove any relationship to Hugh Roberts or to any other family of that name. The sons simply took their father's Christian name as their surname. That is all.—T. A. G.

under the name of himself and wife, appear the names of Moses Robert, Ellis Robert, Aaron Robert and Evan Robert, which are the names of four of the children of Robert Ellis, as given in his letter of removal, and undoubtedly these four were his children and the brothers of Abel.

SUMMARY.

WILLIS READ ROBERTS, born Dec. 9th, 1854, is the son of John Roberts (born 11-mo. 8, 1823) and Mary Read, married 11-mo. 1, 1849.

John Roberts was the son of John Roberts (born 9-mo. 8, 1769) and Rachel Shoemaker (married 12-mo. 10, 1801). This John Roberts was the son of Joseph Roberts (born 9-mo. 11, 1729) and Hannah Rees (married 11-mo. 13, 1757). Joseph Roberts was the son of Aaron Roberts (born about 1682) and Sarah Longworthy (married 8-mo. 6, 1727). This Aaron Roberts was the son of Robert Ellis, as his name is given in his letter of removal from the Quarterly Meeting at Tyddyn y Gareg in Merioneth, Wales, dated 5-mo. 28th, 1690, and Elin, his wife. He and his wife and seven children, Abel, Moses, Ellis, Aaron, Evan, Rachel and Jane, came to this country in 1690. They were probably both of middle age (perhaps 45 to 50 years old) when they came over. Aaron, the fourth child, was probably 8 or 10 years old in 1690. He bought land in Norriton (now in and about Norristown) in 1714; married Sarah Longworthy of Radnor, in 1727, and was our great-great-grandfather. Aaron, born 1682; Joseph, 1729; John, 1769; John, 1823; and Willis, 1854.

My father, John Roberts, born Nov. 8th, 1823, married on Nov. 1st, 1849, Mary Adamson Read, born Sep. 14th, 1824. Their children were Elihu R., born December 12th, 1851; Willis Read, born Dec. 9th, 1854; Ellen, Nov. 17th, 1858, died March 11th, 1863; and Joseph, born April 4th, 1864, died Jan. 2, 1865. Elihu R., married September 3, 1891, Isabella Webster, born August 19, 1856, and they have one daughter, Gene, born Nov. 9th, 1893.

Willis Read Roberts, married June 3rd, 1880, Margaret Martin Jamison, born June 4th, 1856. They have three sons, Willis Read, born May 1, 1881 ; Victor Jamison, born Jan. 29, 1883 ; and Paul Greir, born Nov. 15, 1888.

Communicated by WILLIS READ ROBERTS, 6 22, 1895.

NOTES ON THE WALKER AND THOMAS FAMILY, OF RADNOR.[1]

LEWIS WALKER came to America in 1687 from Merioneth in Wales, the vessel having, tradition says, an exceedingly tedious passage. One of the passengers, upon this same ship, was Mary Morris. Lewis Walker and Mary Morris were married 2nd-mo. 22nd, 1693, at Friends' Meeting-house, Chester, now Delaware County. They settled first in Radnor, where Lewis purchased three hundred acres of land, and took up two hundred more on rent; about 1708 he sold this property and purchased one thousand acres in the Great Valley, Tredryffrin Township, Chester County. This was about seven miles from their Radnor home, and it was a great trial to his wife to remove so far into the wilderness—the other side of the Welsh Mountains, as the South Valley Hills were then called. On account of the great spring near which they built their new home he called the place "Rehobath." Much of this land, including "Rehobath," is still owned and occupied by his descendants. A letter to Lewis Walker from his sister, Jane, which is still preserved, is copied because it gives some account of the members of the family remaining in Great Britain. So far as is known Jane Walker never came to this country. The Valley Friends' Meeting was held first at the house of Lewis Walker in the 2nd-mo., 1714, and from that time till 1731 was held alternately at Lewis Walker's and Joseph Richardson's. By his will, which is dated 10th-mo. 14th, 1728, Lewis Walker gave the land now occupied as the Friends' Valley Graveyard "to the people of his persuasion for a graveyard forever." Upon a portion of this land a meeting-house was erected, which was torn down in 1871, and a new house erected on the opposite side of the road.

---

[1] Communicated by Mr. Joseph R. Rhoads, of Overbrook, Pennsylvania, 1895.

Lewis Walker was buried 10th-mo. 23rd, 1728, and his wife, Mary Walker, died 3rd-mo. 19th, 1747, aged 80 years. They were both interred in the ground which he had given to Friends.

Lewis and Mary Walker had eight children:
I. Lewis Walker married Mary Morris.
II. Isaac Walker married Sarah Jerman.
III. Joseph Walker married Sarah Thomas.
IV. Zillah Walker married Abel Thomas.
V. Naomi Thomas married Joseph Rhoads.
VI. James Rhoads married Alice Sellers.
VII. Joseph R. Rhoads, of Overbrook, Pennsylvania, married Amanda Seal.
VIII. Alice S. Rhoads, born 1868, married to Henry W. Marston, 1870.
VIII. Joseph Howard Rhoads.

THE THOMAS FAMILY.

I. DAVID THOMAS married Anna Noble.
II. Abel Thomas married Zillah Walker.
III. Noami Thomas married Joseph Roads.
IV. James Roads married Alice Sellers.
V. Joseph R. Roads, of Overbrook.

DAVID THOMAS, it is believed, came from Wales, but all efforts to trace him, among the numerous "David Thomases" mentioned among the early settlers of Pennsylvania, have failed. An old Bible belonging to his family which is remembered as having many closely written pages of Family Record was lost in the "Great Fire" of 1850, when the house of Isaiah Jeanes was destroyed. This much we find in the records of Abington Monthly Meeting, that David Thomas and Anna Noble (see page 49) were married at a Friends' Meeting held at Abington, Montgomery County, 8th-mo., 1731.

ABEL THOMAS received a certificate from Gwynedd Monthly Meeting to Radnor Monthly Meeting dated 11th-mo. 30th, 1773, "to proceed in marriage with a member of that Meeting." He married Zillah Walker, daughter of Joseph and Sarah Walker, at the Valley Meeting-House, Tredyffrin, Chester County, 12th-mo. 29th, 1773. In 1774 Abel and Zillah Thomas removed from Cwynedd to Radnor. In 1778 twenty-six pounds, twelve shillings and six pence were taken from Abel Thomas as substitute money. About this time he purchased a farm at Abington, but his wife's failing health making her loath to remove so far from her relatives, he sold the place, receiving the price in "Continental" money, which, before he could reinvest, became utterly worthless. Through the dishonesty of his partner in the milling business he lost the remainder of his property. The wife of Abel Thomas died about 1793, and his own death, in 1797, left his children unprovided for. The loss of the family Bible, before referred to, and the loss of some of the Monthly Meeting Records in the time of the Revolutionary War, make it impossible, now, to give many of the dates accurately. It is related that when Mary Thomas, daughter of said Abel Thomas, was a little girl she was spinning on an old wheel which broke the thread very frequently. Governor Mifflin calling to see her father on business noticed the circumstance, and the conduct of the child, which pleased him so much he ordered a new wheel to be sent her with the message, "that it was for the most patient little girl he had ever seen."

NAOMI THOMAS, after the death of her parents, before she was fourteen years of age, resided for a time with her father's sister, Anna Roberts, and afterwards with her uncle, William Thomas, who had married her mother's sister, Naomi, but who, so far as is known, was no relation to her father, Abel Thomas. Notwithstanding the kindness of her uncle and aunt the young orphan felt very lonely in the large family of cousins, among whom she was now thrown. So when her father's brother, Joshua Thomas, offered her a home in his almost childless household, she gladly accepted the offer, and his home was hers until the 16th of 1st-mo., 1806, at which time she married Joseph Rhoads. He brought his bride home to his widowed mother, and she, who had not known a mother's love since a little child, found a kind, loving and motherly heart ready and willing to lighten the burden and teach the inexperienced young housekeeper. And, after thirty-six years of happy married life, her pure spirit passed away to eternal rest on the 9th of the 8th-mo., 1842.

THE PARRY FAMILY, OF RADNOR.

THOMAS PARRY, " the son of Henry Rees, of ye Parish of Henllan in ye Co. of Cardigan," married " Elinor, dau. of John ap Edward, of ye Parish of Lanelwi in ye Co. of Radnor," Wales.

Thomas Parry owned land in Radnor, Pa., and also other land which he sold 14th of 12th-mo., 1702, for £70 to Richard Moore.

The record of Deed recites that Roger Hughes, of Llanvihanglryd, in Co. of Radnor, yeoman, hath sold to Thomas Parry, of Llanelwith, in Co. aforesaid, weaver, the number and quantity of 125 acres of land, in township of Radnor, together with city lot and city liberty in city of Philadelphia, for sum of £6, lawful money of England. Thomas Parry's certificate from the Quarterly Meeting in Radnorshire bears date 5th of ye 5th-mo., 1699. His eldest son, Edward, married, 8th-mo. 6, 1710, Jane Evans, spinster, second daughter of Robert Evans, of County of Philadelphia, and Province of Pennsylvania. Edward died 2nd-mo. 28, 1726.

THOMAS PARRY, JR., son of above Thomas, married Jane Philips, 8th-mo. 27, 1715, a daughter of Philip Philips, one of the early Welsh Quaker settlers of Radnor, who died 12th-mo. 25, 1697, and Phoebe Evans, his wife (md. 4th-mo. 1, 1693), daughter of Stephen Evans and Elizabeth, of ye Parish of Llanbister, Radnorshire. Thomas Parry, Jr.'s, children were : Thomas, Philip, John, Stephen, Edward, David, Mary, Jacob, Isaac and Martha. He owned a grist mill a few years before his death, and was Township Collector at Horsham 1723. He died 5th-mo. 18, 1749.

JOHN PARRY, son of above Thomas Parry, Jr., and Jane Philips, was born 2nd-mo. 25, 1721, died 11th-mo. 10, 1789. He lived about one mile from Willow Grove, at what is now known as Morgan's Corner. The assessment in Horsham for

1776 mentions John Parry as having a grist mill and 106 acres of ground. He married at Horsham Monthly 9th-mo. 21, 1751, Margaret Tyson, a daughter of Derrick Tyson and Ann Hooten, and granddaughter of Rinert Tisen and Margaret, his wife, who were among the first settlers of Germantown. John Parry's children were Thomas, who md. Elizabeth Childs; John md. Elizabeth Roberts; Benjamin md. Jane Paxson; Phebe md. Silas Walton; Stephen died young. David and Daniel, who md. Martha Dilworth, Parryville, Carbon Co., Pa., is named for Daniel Parry, who owned land in Carbon, Wayne and Luzerne Counties.

BENJAMIN PARRY, son of John Parry and Margaret (Tyson), born 3rd-mo. 1, 1757; md. Jane Paxson, the dau. of Oliver and Ruth (Watson) Paxson. Their children were: Oliver, born 12th-mo. 20, 1794, who md. Rachel Randolph, a dau. of Edward Randolph, of Philadelphia; Ruth and Jane, who never married; and Margaret, who md. Charles B. Knowles; Benjamin Parry purchased property at New Hope, Bucks Co., Pa., in 1784, and erected flour and saw mills and afterwards an oil mill for the manufacture of linseed oil, and added another flour mill on the opposite side of the Delaware River, in New Jersey, about 1800, which he called Prime Hope Mills. He was also interested with Timothy Paxson in the flour commission and storage business in Philadelphia. It was mainly due to the exertions of Samuel D. Ingham and Benj. Parry that the act to build the bridge across the Delaware River at New Hope was obtained. He was a man of considerable scientific attainment.

OLIVER PARRY, son of Benjamin Parry and Jane (Paxson), married Rachel Randolph, dau. of Edward Randolph and Julianna (Steele). Their children were: Julianna R., who married John Tatum, of Philadelphia, Pa.; Jane P., md. Caleb Winslow, M. D., of Baltimore, Md.; Elizabeth R. died young; Major Edward R. Parry, U. S. A.,[1] md. Frances E., dau. of

---

[1] Major Edward R. Parry, United States Army, appointed from Minnesota, First Lieutenant Eleventh Infantry, May, 1861; on recruiting duty July to Sep-

Gen. Justin Dimick, U. S. A.; Ruth E. died young; Richard Randolph Parry md. Ellen L. Read, dau. of Rufus Read, of Portland, Me.; Margaret J. died young; George R. Parry, M. D., Ph. G., md. Elizabeth Van Etten; Mary R., md. Professor Joseph Gibbons Richardson, M. D., of Philadelphia; Emma, md. William Jolliffe, C. E., of Boutetourt Co., Va.; Oliver P. died young, and Helen R. md. Thomas Marsh Smith, Jr., of Baltimore, Md.

---

tember, 1861; with regiment to December, 1861; on recruiting duty to April, 1862; Assistant Commissary of Subsistence; Quartermaster and Adjutant, Post of Fort Warren, Boston Harbor, Mass., to September, 1864; rejoined regiment First Brigade, Second Division, Fifth Corps, Army of Potomac, and engaged at the siege of Petersburg, battle of Weldon Railroad, actions of Chapel House, Boynton Plank Road, and battle of Hatcher's Run, Va.; Assistant Adjutant General of the regular Brigade; with the Headquarters Army of the Potomac to the surrender of Gen. R. E. Lee; with regiment at Richmond, Va., to October, 1866; Chief Commissary of Musters Department of the Potomac, Washington, D. C., to January, 1867; Captain Eleventh United States Infantry, October, 1864; transferred to the Twentieth United States Infantry by the reorganization of the army; Brevet Major United States Army for gallant and meritorious services during the war; in the Department of the Gulf and Recorder of the Retiring Board, New York City.

[Military Record of Civilian Appointments in the United States Army. By Guy V. Henry. New York: Carleton, publisher, 1869.]

ARMS OF JOHN THOMAS.
Gules, a lion rampant, argent, armed and langued azure.

JOHN AP THOMAS AND THE JONES FAMILY, OF MERION, DESCENDED FROM HIM.

North of Narberth station, between Montgomery Avenue and the Schuylkill River, beginning just beyond the Price farm, near Merion Meeting-House, and extending westward, formerly as far as the farm known as St. Mary's, a part of the property of the late Colonel Owen Jones, stretched, in Colonial times, the great plantation of the three brothers Thomas, Robert and Cadwalader Jones, and to this very day is mostly owned by their descendants. The writer penetrated this picturesque but little known part of Lower Merion one morning last summer. This region, called by some "The Jones Country," is full of historic interest to any one familiar with the early settlement of Merion. So far as can be ascertained probably six or seven hundred acres are still held, here, by the descendants of John Thomas, the first purchaser. Silas Jones, Esquire, an attorney-at-law in Philadelphia, is one of the present owners and descendants.

Not far from his house is the home of his kinsman, Mr. Walter Jones, a descendant of the first Silas, so he informed me, and the fortunate owner of the original homestead, which he kindly pointed out. It stands but a few hundred yards to the eastward of Mr. Silas Jones' place.

There were until recently three houses here grouped near together. One of these was the original log house built by Katherine Robert, widow of John Thomas, and her eldest son, Thomas Jones. This ancient land-mark, I was informed, was recently taken down, having been first photographed by the family. Another house, yet in good condition, is the stone building which in a few years after the first settlement took the place of the log hut. The third house is a comfortable mansion erected later on in Colonial days, and since altered and modernized. The ancestor of this family was John ap Thomas, "gentleman," as he called himself, of Llaithgwm Township in Penllyn, Merionethshire.

Of this early Cymric Friend, who, with Dr. Edward Jones, was a trustee of the Company of Merioneth Adventurers and therefore one of the founders of old Merion Township, much has been said in the opening chapters of this work. His genealogy, derived partly from the old MS. parchment pedigree made out for him in 1682, in Wales and partly by the comparison thereof with the Herald's Visitations and Welsh Records, is given very fully under the head of the *Cadwalader Family*, who are descended from Cadwalader Thomas ap Hugh, the elder brother of John Thomas. Under these circumstances, as the pedigree can readily be referred to in the pages of this work, only the later generations, in brief form, will be given here:

EINION AP CYNWRIG (a 2nd son of Cynwrig ap Llywarch, of Carwedd Fynydd), is described as of Cerrig y Drudion, in the County of Denbigh, North Wales, and was a direct male descendant of MARCHWEITHIAN, Lord of Is-Aled, who claimed descent from the early Kings of the Island of Britain.

Einion ap Cynwrig was no doubt deceased before 1380 or sooner. He had a son: DAVID AP EINION, who had a son: IEVAN DDU, who had a son: IEVAN GÔCH, of Cwm Pen Aner, in the parish of Cerrig y Drudion (called of Brammer in the parish of Kerrig y Drudion, and County Denbigh, in MS. Pedigree of John ap Thomas, 1682). This Ievan Gôch married Gwenhwyfer, a daughter of Thomas ap David Gam, who was Knighted on the field of Agincourt by Henry V., when dying, 1415. By her Ievan had two sons. One of these was called Griffith ap Ievan Gôch, who had a son by name of Robert ap Griffith, whose daughter Catherine espoused Thomas Lloyd, of Gwern y Brechtwn, and had Mary Lloyd, who married one Richard, of Tyddin Tyfod in Merionethshire, ancestor to Edward Price (alias Rees), of Merion, and Hannah, wife of Rees John William, etc., besides which the above named Thomas Lloyd was direct male ancestor unto Edward Foulke Lloyd, alias Edward Foulke, who settled in Gwynedd, Pennsylvania, in the year 1698; and of divers others among the early colonists in the Province of Pennsylvania.

The other son of Ievan Gôch was RHYS AP IEVAN GÔCH, of Cerrig y Drudion as aforesaid. He had a son called: TUDOR AP RHYS, who had: RHYS GÔCH AP TUDOR, who had: IEVAN AP RHYS GÔCH, who had: HUGH AP IEVAN AP RHYS GÔCH.

They and their issue were always the best men in their county and had many descendants who were counted amongst the most respectable families of Merionethshire and Denbighshire, and likewise of the most thrifty and foremost among those who settled in Penn's Province. This Hugh ap Ievan, who was probably alive circa 1650, had, so far as we are informed, two sons and one daughter. The daughter married one Robert ap ———, and had issue. The younger son, called Owen ap Hugh, was of Penllyn. He married and had issue. One of his daughters married Thomas Andrews, of Philadelphia, in Pennsylvania, and her sister, Mably, married Edward Rees (alias Price), of Merion.

John ap Thomas and the Jones Family.

The eldest son of Hugh ap Ievan was called THOMAS AP HUGH, of Wern Fawr, in the Parish of Llandderfel, in the Comôt of Penllyn, Merionethshire, "gentleman;" died prior to 1682. His will was proved at St. Asaph. He had several children : the eldest son was called Cadwalader Thomas ap Hugh, and was the father of John Cadwalader, of Merion, 1697. (See Cadwalader.) There was a third son, Hugh Thomas, and two daughters, one of whom married Gawen Vaughan, of Hendre Mawr (and had Robert and Thomas Vaughan), and the other one married Maurice Edward, of Cae Mor.

The second son of Thomas ap Hugh was called JOHN AP THOMAS, or as he often wrote it, JOHN THOMAS (1682), who was the associate of Dr. Edward Jones, one of the founders of old Merioneth Town, and the father of the three brothers : Thomas, Robert and Cadwalader, who were therefore *ap John* or *John's sons*, but who assumed the surname of Jones, a name which their descendants have ever since retained. Some years since the late J. J. Levick, M. D., printed in the *Pennsylvania Magazine of History and Biography* (Vol. IV.), a detailed and interesting sketch of John ap Thomas.

As Dr. Levick, although not a descendant, had in his possession the family papers of Thomas Jones, the eldest son, little of interest can be added to that sketch, so that we will draw very freely upon it here. John ap Thomas had never been in robust health, and the exposures which he endured on account of his religious convictions, tended to shorten his life. He died upon the 3d day of the 3d-month, just as he was about embarking for the Province of Pennsylvania to settle his 1000 acres of land, his share in the company.

After the death of John Thomas his widow, called after the Welsh fashion, Katherine Robert, i. e., Katherine, the daughter of Robert, and his children, made immediate preparations to embark for Pennsylvania.

" The certificate of removal, furnished by the religious society of which she was a member, is in these words :

To all whom it may concern:

WHEREAS, Katerine Robert, of Llaithgwm, in ye County of Merioneth, widow, hath declared before us her intention in order to her and her families removal to Pensilvania in America, wee thought it convenient to certify in her and their behalfe yt she is one yt received the truth for these ten years past, and that hath walked since answerable to the truth according to her measure. She is a woman yt never gave occasion to ye the enemies of truth to open their mouths against ye truth which she owned: her children taught and educated in the fear of the Lord from their infancy Answerable to ye duty of parents, both professing and possessing ye truth.

from our mens & womens meetings ye 18 of 5mo. 1683.

ROBERT OWEN	EDWARD GRIFFITH	ELIZABETH WM. BOWEN
RICHARD PRICE	CADD LEWIS	ELIZABETH JOHN
		MARGARET CADWALADER
		& others.

And so, in the 7th-month, 1683, Katherine Thomas, with her sons, daughters and servants, numbering in all twenty persons, in the ship Morning Star, of Chester, Thomas Hayes, Master, set sail for the New World.

It was a long and sad voyage, as these records in their family Bible, made by her son, Thomas Jones, show. 'Our dear sister Sydney departed this Life the 29th day of the 7th month, 1683, as we were a coming from ye said place (Merionethshire) to Pennsylvania, on board the ship Morning Star, Thomas Hayes, Master.' A little later occurs another sad record. 'Our dear sister Mary departed this Life the 18th of ye 8th month, 1683, at sea in the said Journey.'

As has already been said the surviving members of the family arrived here in November, 1683, and at once proceeded to their 'country home called Gelli yr Cochiaid,[1] in the township of Merion in ye county of Philadelphia.'

Stricken and bereaved as she was, Katherine Thomas still had left to her brave, manly sons and loving daughters, who seem to have left nothing undone for her comfort that filial respect and affection could suggest. She lived fourteen years longer, but does not seem to have been much from her home.

---

[1] "Gelli yr Cochiaid"—"the grove of the red partridges."

The marriage of her son Robert Jones, bachelor, to Ellen Jones, spinster, took place at her house 11-mo. 3, 1693. Her death is thus recorded in the family Bible, by her son Thomas Jones. 'Our dear mother, Katherin Thomas, departed this life the 18th day of ye 11 month, 1697, about ye 2d or 3d hour in ye morning (as we thought), & she was buryed next day." One month later her son Evan[1] died, and there were left of her children, Katherine, Robert, Cadwalader, and Thomas ap John, or, as they now wrote the name, Jones.

Katharine married Robert Roberts, son of Hugh Roberts, an eminent minister in the Society of Friends, whose descendants are well known and respected in Philadelphia.

Cadwalader Jones engaged in the shipping trade, made many voyages to Barbadoes and elsewhere, and seems to have prospered largely.

Robert Jones was a useful member of both civil and religious society, was a justice of the peace, a member of the Provincial Assembly, and altogether a very popular man. His marriage with Ellen Jones,[2] spinster, has already been noted.

Thomas Jones married Anne, daughter of Griffith John, and was father of one son and several daughters. He died 8-mo. 6, 1727. In the memorial prepared by his Meeting concerning him it is said, ' his conduct was exemplary, his ministry sound and edifying, inoffensive in life and conversation, and zealously concerned for the promotion of the Truth. He lived in love and unity among Friends, and died 8-mo. 6, 1727.' His will, a copy of which is among these old papers, shows that, in addition to several hundred acres of land owned by him in Merion, adjoining lands of Jonathan Jones (Wynewood) he had also a tract of land in Goshen, Chester County, Pennsylvania. It was by Thomas Jones that these old and original papers, which have been quoted, were preserved, and

---

[1] The minutes of Merion Preparative Meeting show that Evan Jones bequeathed a small legacy to the Meeting for the use of its poor.

[2] Ellen Jones was a sister of David Jones, of Blockley, who, with his wife Katherine, emigrated to Pennsylvania in the year 1699.

by his daughter transmitted to his descendants. As has already been said, everything that is left by him shows him to have been no ordinary man. Beside those already given, among his manuscripts are drafts of the Minutes of the Meetings of Ministers and Elders of Haverford Monthly Meeting (A. D. 1709, *et seq.*), letters to their relatives in Wales respecting fatherless children whose welfare he had kindly looked after, ' testimonies' concerning deceased ministers of his own religious society, and other interesting papers.

Faithful in the discharge of his duties to his fellowmen, active in civil and in religious society, an earnest and yet an humble Christian, he proved of inestimable value to the members of the new colony with whom his lot was cast, and was a worthy descendant of the old and noble race from which he came."

It has been stated that John ap Thomas died 3-mo. 3rd, 1682. His will, remaining at Philadelphia, was proved here 1688, and has been abstracted as follows:

Will of John Thomas.

"Be it known unto all whom it may concern that I John Thomas of Llaethgwm in the Comott of Penllin within the County of Merionyth, Gentleman, being weak in body," etc.

Clause concerning 5000 acres of land purchased of William Penn by himself and Edward Jones, of Bala, as trustees.

Sons, Thomas Jones, Robert John, Evan John, Cadwalader John; Daughters, Katharine, Mary, Sidney and "Elizabeth, now wife of Rees Evan, of the township of Penmaen, in the County of Merionyth."

Wife, Kathrine.

"My nephew John the younger son of my Brother Cadwalader Thomas."

"My nephew Thomas Cadwalader."

"My Brother Cadwalader Thomas Late of Kiltalgarth and now deceased."

"Nieces Katherine and Jane, daughters of Cadwalader Thomas."

"Kathrine my dear wife I doe hereby nominate and appoint to be sole Executrix of this my last will and Testament; and I doe desire my Dear trusty and well beloved Friends John ap John of the parish of Rhiwabon in the County of Denbigh; Thomas Ellis of Cyfanedd in the County of Merionyth; Thomas Wynne late of

John ap Thomas and the Jones Family.

Bronvadog near Caerwys in the County of fflynt; Robert David of Gwernevel in the County of Merionyth; Hugh Roberts of Kiltalgarth in sd County; Edward Jones late of Bala Chirurgion of the same County; Robert Vaughn of Gwernevel aforesaid in the sd County of Merionyth; Edward Moris of Lavodgyfaner in the foresd. County of Denbigh; Robert Owen late of fron goch, and my son in law Rees Evans of fronween, both neer Bala in the foresd. County of Merionyth; to be overseeors of this my last Will." Dated 9th Feb. 1682; proved at Philadelphia, 1688; original No. 41 of that year, Rec. in Will-Book A. pp. 77-82.

In this will, which is quite a lengthy document, he leaves his share of his Pennsylvania land, namely 1000 acres, to be equally divided amongst his sons, with reversions, excepting the dower interests of his wife in the same property. He leaves also to each of his children the sum of £20 in cash, probably equal to $700 or $800 of our money, and mentions his interest in the Society of Free Traders of Pennsylvania. John ap Thomas, or his wife, was in some way related to Dr. Edward Jones, of Merion, probably a first cousin.

Katherine Thomas, alias Katherine Robert, left a will, but this cannot now be found, although it was apparently probated. The children of this couple took the surname of *Jones*.

John ap Thomas left issue by Katherine, his wife:

1. Thomas Jones, m. Anne, dau. Griffith John.
2. Robert Jones, m. Ellen Jones, sister of David Jones.
3. Evan Jones, d. unm., 12-mo., 1697.
4. Cadwalader Jones.
5. Katherine, m. Robert Roberts.
6. Mary, d. 18th of 8th mo., 1683; unm. (at sea).
7. Sidney, d. 29th of 7th mo., 1683; unm. (at sea).
8. Elizabeth, m. Rees Evan, of Fron Ween, Penmaen, Penllyn, Merionethshire. Their son, Evan Rees, removed to Pennsylvania, and his daughter, Sidney, married Robert Roberts, of Pencoyd, ancestor to George B. Roberts, President of the Pennsylvania Railroad. (See that family.)

THOMAS JONES, of Merion, "yeoman," eldest son of John ap Thomas,[1] of Laithgwm, "gentleman," born at Llaithgwm, Merionethshire, Wales; died in Merion Township, Philadelphia County, 8-mo. 6th, 1727. (For particulars see supra.) He married Anne, daughter of Griffith John[2] (alias Griffith Jones), of Merion. He was a son of John ap Evan, of Penllyn, Merionethshire, Wales,[3] son of Evan ap Robert ap Lewis ap Griffith ap Howell ap Einion ap Deikws Ddu ap Madog ap Ievan Gôch ap David Gôch, of Penllech, ap Trahairn Gôch,[4] ap Madoc ap Rhys Glôff, Lord of Cymytmaen. Griffith John was first cousin to Robert Owen, and quite a prominent person. He held a tract of about 187 acres of land to the northwest of where Bala station now is. He had two sons, who assumed the surname of Griffith, viz.: Evan and John. The will of Thomas Jones bears date 6-month 31st, and was proved 5 August, 1728.[5] He mentions his wife, Anne, then living, and his children: Evan, Elizabeth and Robert. He names as trustees, his "cousins, Robert Roberts and Jonathan Jones." The witnesses are: Thomas Moore, Richard George and Robert Jones.

ROBERT JONES, of Merion, "yeoman," 2nd son of John ap Thomas, of Llaithgwm, "gentleman," born at Llaithgwm, Merionethshire, Wales; died in Merion Township, Philadelphia County, 1746. He married Ellin, sister of David Jones, of Blockley Township. Robert Jones was a Justice of the Peace for Merion, a member of the Provincial Assembly, and a very prominent man among Friends. He purchased the plantation called "Mount Arrarat," from David Hugh; was the owner of "Glanrason," containing 189 acres, and of con-

---

[1] See will of John ap Thomas here produced. Thomas Jones was under age 9 February, 1682.
[2] Friends' Records.
[3] MS. pedigree of the Owen and Evans Families.
[4] See Owen Genealogy.
[5] Will Book E, p. 85, Philadelphia.

siderable other land, inherited from his father, including a large tract in Goshen, Chester County. Altogether he was possessed, at the time of his death, of about 1000 acres in Merion, and 426 acres in Goshen and neighborhood. By his will dated 21st of 7-mo. 1746, he devised "Glanrason" and other lands to his son, Gerrad Jones; "Mount Arrarat" and other lands to his daughter Elizabeth Jones, and his other plantations to his son Robert Jones. Robert and Ellin Jones had issue:

1. Elizabeth, b. 9-mo. 6th, 1695.
2. John, b. 10-mo. 29th, 1697; d. infant.
3. John, b. 11-mo. 20th, 1698; d. infant.
4. Katherine, b. 11-mo. 12th, 1700; m. Thomas Evans.
5. Ann, b. 7-mo. 14th, 1702; m. James Jones, of Blockley.
6. Gerrad, b. 12-mo. 28th, 1705–6; m. 1st, Sarah Lloyd; m. 2ndly, Ann Humphrey.
7. Robert, b. 6-mo. 3d, 1709.

GERRAD JONES, of "Glanrason," in Merion, eldest son of Robert and Ellin, born in Merion Township 12-mo. 28th, 1705–6; died there prior to 1782. He married, 1st, Sarah, daughter of Robert Lloyd, of Merion, and Lowry, daughter Rees John William; married, 2ndly, Ann, daughter of Benjamin Humphrey, of Merion.

Gerrad Jones had by his first wife:

1. Priscilla, b. 1730; supposed to have d. unm.
2. Robert, b. 1731.
3. Silas,[1] b. 1733.
4. Ellin; m., 1st, Robert Roberts; 2ndly Isaac Lewis.
5. Paul; m. Phœbe Roberts, of whom presently.
6. Sarah; d. infant.

---

[1] The History of the *Levering Family*, of Pennsylvania, gives the marriage of a Levering with a Silas Jones, of this family. There were numerous descendants of this marriage, but whether this is the Silas mentioned, or a later generation, the absence of information on the subject from the family prevents my determining.

NOTE.—The scope of this work will not permit of any extended genealogy of the descendants of John ap Thomas. The notes here given are only intended to serve as a guide for the investigator.

By his second wife he had:
1. Benjamin.
2. Edward.

PAUL JONES, 3d son of Gerrad Jones, of Merion, married 9th month 24th, 1764, Phebe Roberts, and had:

REES JONES, born in Merion, 1st month 14th, 1772; died in Ohio, 5th month 13th, 1849. He married, first, in 1793, Hannah Powell, and had by her four children, and married, secondly, Catharine Humbert [Von Stadtenfield], and had ten children.

Children of Rees Jones by Hannah Powell:
1. Rebecca Ann, m. Francis Laesher.
2. Hannah, m. Charles Sontag.
3. Benjamin, ob. infant.
4. Rees Roberts, m. Lydia F. Shepperd.

Children of Rees Jones by Catharine, his second wife:
1. Paul, ob. unm.
2. Ellen, m. Rev. John McIlhenny.
3. Catharine, m. William Thorne.
4. David, m. Emeline Jones.
5. Lydia, m. Ralph Means.
6. William Lloyd, m. Mary Laing.
7. Marcus Aurelius, m. Salina Snowdon.
8. Caroline Alden, m. David Aiken, Jr., of Pittsburg, Pennsylvania (1895).
9. George.
10. Mary, m. George W. Morris.

THE HERBERT AND AWBREY FAMILIES OF WALES, AND THEIR DESCENDANTS IN MERION TOWNSHIP IN THE PROVINCE OF PENNSYLVANIA. REES AND MARTHA (AWBREY) THOMAS.

JENKIN AP ADAM, Lord of Kevendyglwydd, who lived in the time of Edward III. and Richard II., kings of England, is the first ancestor of the Herbert family of whom we have any authentic record. He is said by some to have also borne the surname of HERBERT, and to have been the descendant of a Norman family of that name which was famous at the time of the Conquest; but this is questionable. He had: GWILIM (WILLIAM) AP JENKIN, Lord of Kevendyglwydd, who married Wenllian (died 1377), a daughter of Howell Vychan, descended from Ynir "King," or Lord, of Gwent. Gwilim had a fourth son:

THOMAS AP GWILIM, of Perthir, who died 1438; he married Maud, daughter and heiress of Sir John Morley, knight, and had a fifth son:

SIR WILLIAM AP THOMAS; knighted in the year 1426, died 1446. He acquired the castle and demesne lands of Raglan in some way from the Morley family, his mother's people, and married, for his second wife, Gwladis, daughter of Sir David Gam, and widow of Sir Roger Vaughan of Tre'rtwr.

David Gam, says a Welsh historian, deserves more than a passing notice. The name by which he was known at the time he lived was David ap Llewelyn, the dignity of knighthood being only conferred upon him as his last breath was escaping on the stricken field of Agincourt. Of impulsive and violent temper, he was a dangerous man either to a friend or foe. "He lived like a wolf," says his historian, "and died like a lion."

He started in life by slaying a kinsman in the streets of Brecon, and fled to England to escape the consequences. He was a strong partisan, after this, of the English Kings, Henry IV. and Henry V., under the former of which he undertook, in 1402, the assassination of the patriot Owen Glendower, his brother-in-law, who had just traversed Breconshire with fire and sword, at Machynlleth; and for his pains, though on account of his relationship to Glendower, he escaped execution, got several years imprisonment. This was the darkest blot on the stormy life of David Gam, for though the provocation was doubtless great, yet the mode of retaliation was base and atrocious. He was no sooner released than he again devoted himself to the cause of the Henry's. In 1415 Henry V. met the French, at Agincourt, and there, in the crisis of a signal victory, when Henry himself was hemmed in and borne down by the French knights, David Gam, with others of his countrymen, rushed to the rescue of the king and effected his deliverance; but the brave deliverer fell mortally wounded. Henry, on the spot, as the last blood was ebbing, with his shivered sword, dubbed him a knight, conferring the same honor on Gam's son-in-law, Roger Vaughan, who also fell.

The name of this cruel, but brave, Welshman was long remembered, and is made immortal by Shakespeare (in his Play of Henry V.), who makes the Herald, calling out the names of the illustrious dead on the field of Agincourt, read from the muster roll of the King's household troops that of "Davy Gam, Esquire."

Let us then pass over his frailties, which were not perhaps so great as those of many of his companions in arms, and,

> "Say, he died a gallant knight,
> With sword in hand for England's right."

Sir William Thomas, who was also at Agincourt, and is also called William Thomas Herbert, had by his second wife several sons, two of whom were:

1. William Herbert, created Earl of Pembroke.
2. Sir Richard Herbert.

SIR RICHARD HERBERT, second son of Sir William Thomas (Herbert), was of Coldbrook, and was slain at Banbury in 1469. Of him his great-great-grandson, Lord Her-

GATEWAY AT RAGLAN, WALES.

bert, of Cherbury, writes as "that incomparable hero, who (in the history of Hall and Grafton as it appears) twice passed through a great army of northern men alone, with his poleaxe in his hand, and returned without mortal hurt, which is more than is famed of Amardis de Galle, or the Knight of the Sun."

Coldbrook House is about a mile from the town of Abergavenny in Monmouthshire. Sir Richard Herbert, having married Margaret, daughter of Thomas ap Griffith Nicholas, of Dynevor, and sister to the renowned Sir Rhys ap Thomas, who slew Richard III. on Bosworth Field, had among other issue:

1. Sir William Herbert, from whom descended the family of Hugh Gwyn, of Peniarth; the Powells, of Llanwddyn; the Humphreys, of Llwyn-du; the Owen family, of Merion in Pennsylvania, and from them the families of Cadwalader, Biddle, Evans, Wharton, Ogden, Glenn, and many others.

2. Sir Richard Herbert.

SIR RICHARD HERBERT, KNIGHT, the second son, was of Montgomery Castle, called also "of Cwm Ystwith and Pencelly." He was Gentleman Usher to King Henry VIII., and resided in very great luxury at Blackhall.

Of him his great-grandson, Lord Herbert, of Cherbury, relates, among other things, that "he delighted also much in hospitality, as having a very long table twice covered, every meal, with the best that could be gotten. This table, so richly was it set every day, that everything that flies seems to have been brought to it, and it was an ordinary saying in the country at that time, when any fowl was seen to rise, 'Fly where thou wilt thou wilt light at Blackhall.'"

Sir Richard married, as his second wife, Jane, daughter of Gwilim ap Rees Philip, of Llwynhowell, in Carmarthenshire. Their fourth child was:

JANE HERBERT, who married first, THOMAS LLOYD, and secondly, WILLIAM AWBREY, ESQUIRE, OF ABERKYNFRIG, who died 27 June, 1547. This William Awbrey was the son of Hopkin Awbrey, a (by a daughter of John Griffith, of Gwyn,

Esquire) son of Jenkin Awbrey, Esquire (by Gwenlliam, daughter of Owain ap Griffith, Esquire, of Tal y Llyn), son of Morgan Awbrey, Esquire, of Abenkynfrig (by Alice, daughter of Watkin Thomas David Lloyd), son of Gwalter Awbrey (by Juhan, daughter and heiress of Rees Morgan ap Einion, of Carmarthen), son of Richard Awbrey (by Creslie, daughter of Phe ap Eledr), son of Thomas Awbrey Gôch, or the Red-haired (by Nest, daughter of Owain Gethyn, of Glyn Taway), son of Thomas Awbrey, of Aberkynfrig, Constable, and Ranger of the Forest of Brecon (by Johan, daughter of Trahaerne ap Einion, Lord of Comond), son of Thomas Awbrey (by Anne, daughter of John Cayraw, baron of Cayrowe, Carew), son of William Awbrey, of Aberkynfrig (by Julia, daughter of Sir William Gunter, Knight), second son of Sir Rinallt Awbrey (by a daughter of the Earl of Clare and Priany), son of "Stiant Awbrey, a second brother to the Lord Awbrey Earle of Bullen and Earle Marchall, of France, came to England with Wm. ye Conquerer in anno 1066." William Awbrey, of Aberkynfrig (deceased 1547), and Jane Herbert, his wife, had issue:

RICHARD AWBREY, of Aberkynfrig. He was the eldest son by Jane Herbert. He sold Aberkynfrig to Dr. William Awbrey, his kinsman, and died 1580, leaving issue by Margaret, his wife, daughter unto Thomas Gunter, of Gileston:

RICHARD AWBREY, of Llanelyw, who departed out of this life anno 1646, "and was buried under the floor of the chancel of the church of Llanelyw. His grave is covered with a flat tombstone, forming part of the pavement, which has upon it the following inscription:

"*Here lyeth the body of Richard Awbrey of Llanelyw Gent., who married Anne Vaughan daughter to William Vaughan of Llanelyw, who had issue William, Richard, Thomas, John, Theophilius and Elizabeth. Died the 23 day of September, 1646.*"

The arms of the Awbrey and Vaughan families appear upon the tomb, "and the inscription, as far as it precedes the statement of issue, runs around the four sides of the tablet, be-

ginning at the top and terminating at the upper end of the left-hand side." By his wife, Anne, Richard Awbrey had :[1]
1. William.
2. Richard, Vicar of Boughrod in Radnor.
3. Thomas.
4. John.
5. Theophilus.
6. Elizabeth.

THOMAS AWBREY, the third son, who had:

WILLIAM AWBREY, who was married in 1646, being then under age, to Elizabeth Awbrey, daughter of William, eldest son of Richard (who died 1646).

"It is Probable that William Awbrey was a member of the Society of Friends.[2] It is certain that his sons, Richard and William (the latter of whom married Letitia Penn for his second wife), and his daughter, Martha, belonged to that religious denomination. He had ten children by his wife Elizabeth. He died in 1716, aged ninety, and was buried in Llanelyw church-yard, where is still to be seen an altar-tomb erected over his remains, with the following inscription:

'*Here lyeth the Body of William Awbrey of Llanelyw, Son of Thomas Awbrey Gent. Married Elizabeth daughter of William Awbrey. Had issue Ten. Richard, William, 2 Thomas, Theophilus, Anne, Mary 2 Martha & Elizabeth Departed this*

---

[1] "Richard Awbrey (the second) had several children, as above stated, of whom William, the eldest, and Thomas, the third son, as well as their father, were Puritans and Parliamentarians. The second son, Richard (the third), was an adherent of the king, and a clergyman, being vicar of Boughrod in Radnorshire. William had no son, and the Llanelyw estate being entailed, the heir to it was the second brother, Richard. In order to keep the property in the hands of the descendants of Puritan stock, William, finding his death likely to be near, hastily married his only daughter, Elizabeth, to her first cousin, William, the oldest son of his brother Thomas, both of them then being under age. This was in 1646, about a year before his decease, and by his will he sought to place his son-in-law in the position of a son of his own. Richard, the clerical brother and heir in tail, instituted legal proceedings to recover the property, but the matter was finally settled by arbitration."

[2] This abstract is from a contribution of George Vaux to the *Pennsylvania Magazine*, and will be found in Vol. XIII, p. 294, of the same. The author questions that William Awbrey was a Friend; but if so, he rejoined the Anglican Church, wherein he was buried.

life in Hope of a Joyful Resurrection the 16 of December 1716 aged 90.

The figures 2 before the names Thomas and Martha indicate that there were two children of these names. There are tombstone inscriptions at Llanelyw, showing that the first Martha died in 1662, and the first Thomas in 1669."

MARTHA AWBREY, the 9th child of William Awbrey, was born subsequent to 1662; she joined the Society of Friends and became engaged to REES THOMAS, a kinsman of John Bevan, of Treverigg, Glamorganshire. She accompanied Rees Thomas and John and Barbara Bevan to Pennsylvania in 1683, and was married to him 18 June, 1692, at Haverford Meeting, Pennsylvania.

There is considerable doubt as to the ancestry of Rees Thomas, but there is but little question that he came from Glamorganshire. It will be observed in the following letter that he speaks of "My uncle John Bevan." Some have thought that the relationship (uncle in Wales did not always mean the same kinship which we understand by the term) came through his wife, Martha Awbrey, John Bevan's wife, Barbara, being, it is claimed, an Awbrey (see Bevan Genealogy); but it is more likely that the relationship was with John Bevan's family direct. If the latter was the case it was probably through John Bevan's wife. If she *was* an Awbrey, as is claimed, then it might have been through the Thomas family, one of whom was mother to the daughter of William Awbrey, of Pencoyd, who *did* marry John Bevan, but whether as his first or second wife, is not known. In one pedigree Barbara, wife of John Bevan, is said to have been *Barbara, of Wenvoe*. The Thomas family, of Wenvoe, were well known, and it may have been from them that Rees Thomas sprang. He was, we know, cousin to William and David Thomas, of Radnor, and it is therefore evident that he was of a Thomas family which had assumed the surname before their removal to Pennsylvania. (See Appendix.)

Be this, however, as it may, Rees Thomas became a very prominent settler in Merion. He was a Justice of the Peace and a member of the Provincial Assembly.

Rees Thomas purchased from Sarah Eckley, widow of John, three hundred acres of land in " Merion township, in the Welsh tract." The deed was dated 6-mo. 15, 1692, and the land is described as follows: " Beginning at a stake in Ellis Hughes' line and extending thence E. N. E. 102 Perches, thence S. E. 480 Perches, thence S. W. 102 Perches, to the road dividing it and the Radnor township, and thence by said road N. N. W. 480 Perches to place of Beginning." He subsequently bought of Edward Prichard an adjoining tract. In his will, dated 10th September, 1742, Rees Thomas leaves " unto my son William Thomas . . . two hundred acres of land to be laid out of the N. end of tract of land that I bought of Sarah Eckley wid. . . . Unto my son Rees Thomas. . . . my dwelling house and plantation. . . . being 290 acres of land (that is to say) 100 acres that I bought of Sarah Eckley and 170 acres part of the tract of land I bought of Edward Prichard." This will was proved at Philadelphia 12th February, 1742.[1] A part of this property long continued in the possession of descendants. In 1787 Anthony Tunis and Mary his wife, daughter of Rees Thomas 3d, conveyed their share in a parcel of it to William Thomas, eldest son of said Rees Thomas 3d, and brother of Mary. This William Thomas and Naomi his wife sold some of the same to William Colflesh ; it, however, reverted by deed to Thomas in 1805. William Thomas left a will proved in 1840, by which he devised to his daughter Jane W. Cleaver (widow in 1842) a part of same ; who sold it to Thomas Stanley.

---

[1] In this will Rees Thomas refers to a settlement which was intended to have been made at the time of his (Rees Thomas') marriage with Martha Awbrey, by which settlement he says provision was to be made by *John Bevan*, in his favor, to revert to his eldest son, viz., Rees Thomas, Jr. This settlement, Rees Thomas claims, was never consummated, but Rees Thomas, Jr., claimed under it, and provision was made by his father to disinherit him if he ever pushed the claim. The matter was a subject for litigation for a long time.

This property is situate at Rosemont station, Pennsylvania Railroad, and included what is now the town of Rosemont on the south side of the railroad, late the Arthur property, and extending north and west from the railroad, including the old Ashbridge farm. Some claim that the Ashbridge house was originally Rees Thomas' home, whilst others say that it was to the south, near the old houses on the Arthur property, if not on the site of one of them. The property comprised, also, probably a portion of the Curwen place.

"A few years after their marriage, Rees and Martha Thomas[1] wrote jointly to her aged father. The original of this letter is still preserved in the hands of a descendant. It is dated, ' Ye 29th day of ye 2d mo 1695,' and is addressed, ' Most dear & tender Father.' The following extracts will be found interesting, the original spelling being preserved :"

Our dutyfull and harty Respects salute thee hoping these few lines will find thee in good health as I & my wife & two children are all this present time—my son Aubrey was borne ye 30th day of ye 11th month and ye fourth day of ye weeke 1694 his mother and he now very harty praysed be to ye Lord for ye same I doe understand yt thou were not well pleased yt my oldest son [Rees] was not caled an Aubrey. I will assure thee I was not against it, but my neibors wood have him be caled my name, being I bought ye Land and I So beloved amongst them. I doe admite to what thee sayes in thy letter ye an Aubrey was better known then I: though I am hear very well aquainted with most in those parts, he is ye first Aubrey in Pensilvania and a stout boy he is of his age, being now a quarter. My unkle John Bevan came over very well and a good voyage he had, he tould me he had seen thee twise, which we were very glad of thy well keeping in years and also hopeing noe vexation nor trouble will come upon thee upon either hand which will be a great exercise to us to hear of nothing but what will atend to thy goodness: hopeing my brother Richard and his wife will make much of thee in thy ould age, thy dater & I would wish to see thee hear and I hope wood be a nurse to thee in thy ould age —I was now very sorry to hear of ye death our brother William his wife, where in ther was great commendation of her integrity in ye truth by severall hear yt knows her and I will writ to him.

I have been very weake in body ye Last winter having a great fite of sickness, but ye Lord pleased to recover me & bring

---

[1] *This letter was printed in the Pennsylvania Magazine of History and Biography.*

me up agen blessed be ye Lord for his gyodness & tender delings to me both outwordly & inwordly: my wife had her health very well all a Longe since shee came to ye country.

I lost much time in going to faires and markets, William Fishier of Rose formerly [is] now living in Philadelphia.

Thy dater desires thee to aquaint her of her age in ye next letter. My son Rees Remembers his Love to his Granfather and also to his nanty Anne, he doth speake very Liberally but unkle is a hard word for [him], his Love is to Richard, a brave bould boy he is now without a mayd servant for they are very scarce hear, upon noe terms an ordinary man of seven or eight pounds att Lest and cannot have them upon no account.

I had about 16 score bushels of wheat this year. I have 15 heds of cattle, six horses what dyed this winter, for it was a hard winter, they say they never saw ye like of.

Rees Thomas survived his wife a number of years. Martha died in 1726. After her death a small book was published by S. Keimer, entitled "*A collection of Elegiac Poems devoted to the Memory of the late virtuous and excellent Matron and worthy Elder in the Church of Christ of the Society of Friends Martha Thomas, late wife of Rees Thomas of Merion of the County of Philadelphia in the Province of Pennsylvania and Daughter of William Awbrey of Llanelieu in the County of Brecknock in Great Britain who departed this life the 7th of 12th Mo. 1726-7.*"

A modern edition of the same, bearing the above title, was printed by Lydia R. Bailey, Philadelphia, 1837.

Rees and Martha Thomas[1] had issue:

1. Rees, b. 2-mo. 22, 1693; m. Elizabeth, d. Edward Jones.

2. Awbrey, b. 11-mo. 30, 1694; m. Gulielma, only d. Wm. Penn, Jr., and d. s. p.

3. Herbert, b. 9-mo. 3, 1696; m. Mary, d. John Havard; d. s. p.

4. Elizabeth, b. 8-mo. 10, 1698.

5. William, b. 5-mo. 2, 1701.

6. Richard, b. 5-mo. 23, 1703.

---

[1] It will be noted that Martha Awbrey was sister to the William Awbrey who married Laetitia, daughter of William Penn.

As it was found impossible to obtain the data desired concerning the descendants of Rees Thomas, in time to insert here, the reader is referred to the Appendix. Among the Philadelphia families who trace their lineage to Rees and Martha Thomas are those bearing the surnames of Lloyd, Williams, Perot, Egbert, etc.

DR. EDWARD JONES AND HIS DESCENDANTS.

Dr. Edward Jones may be termed one of the principal founders of Lower Merion Township, for it was he and John ap Thomas who organized the little Company of Adventurers that first planted Merioneth Town in the Welsh Tract, and it was Edward Jones who personally led the first Welsh settlers to Pennsylvania in August, 1682, and selected the location of their purchases.

Concerning his parentage, very little can be ascertained with certainty. When the Merion Preparative Meeting, in 1704, desired that Welsh Friends should bring an account of their family and descent to the Meeting to be recorded, we read that Edward Jones brought such an account to the meeting. It has already been stated that these records are now missing, and no copy of the document can be found in any papers accessible to the writer, although it is believed on good grounds that a copy exists. The name of Jones at that time was as common as now, if not more so. It signified simply that the person so called was the son of a man bearing the Christian name of *John*, Jones meaning Johnes, or John's sons. There were, however, a few families by that name in Wales at the period of which we speak that had retained *Jones* as a surname for several generations. Whether Dr. Edward Jones was one of these does not appear. His will bears a seal with a lion rampant, but it might not have been his. According to a letter written some years since by a descendant the arms used in the Jones family for many years were: Or, within a burdure, a lion rampant azure. Crest, a lion rampant azure, having in his sinister paw a harp or. No motto is given. These are the arms of a family of Jones anciently of Merionethshire, and are so given in Burke's *General Armory*, although from the letter in question it would seem apparent that they were used by the family long prior to their appearance in Burke.

The writer, some years since, found in Philadelphia a copy of the same coat of arms, correctly but crudely blazoned, and evidently a copy of the original design. It differed, however, so far as the mantling, etc., went, from a sketch sent with the letter above referred to. Moreover, there was a motto attached, in three languages, and some reference to the family as well as giving the designer's name. This paper has the following:

"*Coat of Arms of Griffin Jones, of Merionethshire, A. D. 1569, and of Flintshire, South Wales, A. D. 1584.*" ARMS: *Or, within a burdure a lion rampant azure.* CREST: *A lion rampant azure holding in his sinister paw a harp or.* MOTTO: "Vulgar, *Foremost yet Steady.*" "Classic, *Progressus Sed Firmus.*" "Barbaric, "*Blaenaf etto yn anhyblygg.*" The paper has this endorsement: "*Done by Henry Salt, Heraldic Engraver, No. 9, Great Turnstile, Lincoln's Inn, London.*" The writer was told that this was presumed to be the coat of arms of the Merion Jones family, but nothing more definite is known regarding them.

The above data is given, of course, as a suggestion relating to the origin of the family, and is not entitled to any particular weight. It is definitely known that Jonathan Jones was a cousin of the sons of John ap Thomas. It has been suggested that the relationship might have come through their mother, Katherine Robert, who *may* have been *Katherine Robert Jones.*

This, however, is all conjecture. What we do know is that Edward Jones was born, probably in Merionethshire, in or about the year 1645.[1] He was "of ancient and honorable family," and connected with the gentry of Wales, and was bred a physician and surgeon. He seems to have followed the latter calling chiefly in his native country, and in 1682 is described as "of Bala in the County of Merionethshire, Chir-

---

[1] He was aged 92 at the time of his decease.

urgion." We have noted his connection with the settlement of Merion in the chapter devoted to that subject. He arrived in Pennsylvania in the fall of 1682, before Penn's coming, and had a part of his land surveyed to him near the Schuylkill, northward of the present Montgomery Avenue, and near the Falls. " His original purchase was 306¼ acres, of which he kept only one half to himself."[1] Dr. Jones became a very prominent man in the township, and, indeed, in the Province. He was a Justice of the Peace and a member of the Provincial Assembly. He died in Merion the 26th of the 12th month, 1737, and was buried in the ground of the Merion Meeting.

Thomas Chalkley in his journal says: "He was one of the first settlers of Pennsylvania, a man much given to hospitality, a lover of good and virtuous people and was beloved by them. I had a concern to be at that meeting before I left my home at Frankford and before I heard of this Friend's death. There were many hundreds at his funeral."[2]

There appears to be some confusion respecting the date of death of Mary, wife of Dr. Jones.

In *The Friend*, Vol. XXIX, p. 76, it states that she died 7th mo. 29th, 1726, and was buried at Merion. This must be a mistake, for Edward Jones, in his will dated "the Twenty Seventh day of the Third month in the year of our Lord one thousand seven hundred & thirty two," appoints " my wife Mary, my son-in-law John Cadwalader and sons Jonathan Edward & Evan afore said my Executors." This will was probated in 1738, and is No. 177 of that year, Register of Wills office, Philadelphia, Book N, 320.

The children of Dr. Edward Jones and Mary, his wife, daughter of Dr. Thomas Wynne, as named in his will, were Martha, Jonathan, Edward, Thomas, Evan, John, Elizabeth, and Mary.

Edward Jones had issue by Mary, his wife, the following children:

---

[1] His original purchase was 312½ acres, but he disposed of the Liberty lands belonging thereto, which makes the difference.
[2] The Philadelphia Friend, Vol. 29, p. 396.

1. Martha, b. Wales; m. 1699, John Cadwalader.
2. Jonathan, b. Wales, 1680; m. Gainor Owen; see infra.
3. Edward, b. Merion; he and his younger brothers got the original land.
4. Thomas, b. Merion; he is believed to have married and had issue.
5. Evan, b. Merion; m. 1st, Mary Stephenson, New York, and 2ndly, dau. of Colonel Mathews, of Fort Albany, N. Y. He is believed to have been the father of Dr. John Jones, who attended General Washington, in Philadelphia.
6. John, b. Merion.
7. Elizabeth, m. Rees Thomas, Jr.
8. Mary.

JONATHAN JONES, eldest son of Edward and Mary (Wynne) Jones, born in Wales in 1680; died in Lower Merion Township, 1770; will dated 19 May, 1768; proved 1 September, 1770.[1]

"Jonathan Jones, son of Edward and Mary Jones, was born in Bala, Merionethshire, North Wales, Great Britain, the third day of the Eleventh-month, 1680, came with his parents to Pennsylvania in the year 1682; was married at Merion the 4th day of the Eighth-month, 1706, to Gainor Owen, daughter of Robert and Rebecca Owen, some time past of Fron Gôch. She was born the 26th of the Eighth-month, 1688. They had eleven children, who lived to years of maturity.

Jonathan Jones died the 30th day of the Seventh-month, 1770, and buried at Merion the 8th of the Eighth-month following. Many hundred people respectfully attending his interment."[2]

WHEREAS, Jonathan Jones, son of Edward Jones, of Merion, in ye Welsh Tract, Chyrgeon, and Gainor Owen, daughter of Robert Owen, late of ye same place, yeoman, deceased. Having declared their intention of marriage with each other before several Monthly Meetings of ye people of God called Quakers, in ye Welsh Tract aforsayd, according to ye good order used among them, whose proceedings therein, after a deliberate consideration

---
[1] Proved at Philadelphia and remains on file in the Register's office there.
[2] Family MS.

thereof, having consent of parents and relations concerned, nothing to obstruct, are approved of. Now these are to certifie all whom it may concern, that for ye full accomplishment of their said intentions this 4th day of ye 8th mo. in ye year 1706, they ye sayd Jonathan Jones & Gainor Owen appeared in the publick meeting of the sayd People, and others met together, at the publick meeting place at Merion aforsayd & ye s'd Jonathan Jones taking ye sayd Gainor Owen by ye hand did in solemn manner openly declare that he took her to be his wife, promising to be unto her a faithful and loving husband until death should seperate them, & then and there in ye sayd assembly ye sayd Gainor Owen did in like manner declare that she took ye sayd Jonathan Jones to be her husband & promising to be unto him a faithful and loving wife until death should seperate them, and morover ye sayd Jonathan Jones and Gainor Owen, She according to ye custom of marriage assuming ye name of her husband as a further confirmation thereof, did then and there to these presents set their hands, and we whose names are hereunto subscribed, being, among others, present at the solemnization of ye sayd marriage, as Witnesses thereunto have also to these presents set our hands ye day & year above written :

Catharine Humphrey	Gainor Roberts	Jonathan Jones
Rebecca Humphrey	Thomas Lloyd	Gainor Jones
Rebecca Roberts	Martha Owen	
Jane Jones	Thomas Evan	Edward Jones
Gainor Lloyd	Robert Evan	Mary Jones
Eliza Lloyd	Owen Bevan	Griffith John
Anne Jones	Cadwallader Evan	Rowland Ellis
Anne Roberts	Robert John	John Roberts
Griffith Owen	Edward Roberts	Edward Jones Jr.
Joshua Salkeld	Robert Ellis	Evan Jones
Rees Thomas	Gainor Jones	Eliza. Jones
Caleb Pusey	John Griffith	Robert Lloyd
David Meredith	Evan Griffith	Evan Owen
Edward Rees	Mary Badcock	Hugh Griffith
Rees ap Ed.	Mary Ormes	Owen Bevan
John Moore	Sarah Owen	Owen Owen
Robert Jones	Martha Thomas	John Owen
John Owen	Ellen Jones	John Jones
John Jones	Jane Price	John Owen
Wm. Edwards	Catharine Jones	Robert Owen
Cadwallader Roberts	Eleanor Bevan	Jonathan Wynne
Edward Roberts	Jane ap Bedward	Joshua Owen
William C———	Sarah Williams	Daniel Humphrey
Rees Price	Mary Badcock	Hannah Humphrey
John Williams	Eliza. Badcock	John Cadwalader
Edward Griffith	Catharine Orme	Martha Cadwalader
Richard Jones	Elizabeth Roberts	Eliza. Owen
Robert Roberts		Jane Roberts

Jonathan Jones, shortly after his marriage, purchased of his wife's brother, Evan Owen, the plantation now called Wynnewood and St. Mary's, which continued in the family to the present time. The title to this tract was as follows: Thomas Lloyd, by deed, dated 5th of 6-mo., 1691, granted to Robert Owen, of Merion, 548 acres (448) in Merion, of Charles Lloyd's and Margaret Davis' Purchase, and the said Robert deceasing, devised it by his last will to his son, Evan Owen, in whose behalf John Roberts, trustee for the said Evan, requested a resurvey 3d of 3d-month, 1703. By one survey it appears to have been 451 acres.

Jonathan Jones left by will as above, 350 acres to his son Owen, and 101 acres[1] to his son Jonathan. He had issue by Gainor, his wife:

1. Mary, m. Benjamin Hayes.

2. Edward, b. 1708; d. unm. He had, as a gift from his father, a farm which the latter had purchased from Amos Roberts.

3. Rebecca, b. 1709; m. John Roberts, of Pencoyd, son of Robert Roberts, and grandson of John Roberts, of Llyn, Caernarvonshire.

4. Owen, b. 1711; m. Susanna Evans. See infra.

5. Ezekiel, believed to have d. s. p. His father did not know if he were living in 1768.

6. Jacob, b. 1713; living 1768. He is believed to have married and left issue.

7. Jonathan, b. 1715; m. ———, and had surviving him two daughters, Gainor and Mary Jones. This Jonathan had by deed from his father 101 acres of land, which by will, 11 of 5-mo., 1747, and proved 2 Nov., 1747, he left to his two daughters as mentioned, who sold the same to their uncle, Owen Jones. This 101-acre tract was probably to the north of the old Owen house, and east of Cherry lane. Jonathan Jones probably erected a stone farm house here.

---

[1] In addition to this 101 acres he left him 20 acres for a "wood lot." Of the wood lot, 17 acres belong to Edward Glenn, a lineal descendant of Robert Owen, and 3 acres and some perches to A. J. Cassatt.

OWEN JONES, second son of Jonathan and Gainor, of Merion, born in Merion 19th of 9-month, 1711; died 9 Oct., 1793. He married 30 May, 1740, Susanna, second daughter of Hugh Evans, of Merion, by his 3d wife, Lowry, widow of Robert Lloyd, of Merion, and daughter of Rees John William of the same place. (See Rees John William.) Owen Jones was Provincial Treasurer of Pennsylvania. His will is dated 11 Oct., 1791; proved at Philadelphia. He left 350 acres of land to son Owen, and the 101 acres[1] which he had purchased from his nieces, to son Jonathan.

Owen and Susanna Jones had issue, the following children:

1. Jane, b. 5th 1-mo., 1740–41; m. Caleb Foulke.
2. Lowry, b. 30th 10-mo., 1742; m. Daniel Wister. See *Wynne.*
3. Owen,[1] b. 15th 1-mo., 1744–5; m. 1st, Mary Wharton; 2ndly, Hannah Smith; no issue survive.
4. Susanna, b. 4th 7-mo., 1747; m. John Nancarro.
5. Hannah, b. 28th 10-mo., 1749; m. Amos Foulke. See *Owen, Foulke Branch.*
6. Ann, b. 13th 3d-mo., 1752; d. unm.
7. Martha, b. 10th 3-mo., 1754; d. unm.
8. Rebecca, b. 3d 7-mo., 1757; m. John Jones, who d. s. p.
9. Sarah, b. 30th 5-mo., 1760; m. Samuel Rutter.
10. Jonathan, b. 15th 7-mo., 1762; m. 1st, Mary Potts; 2ndly, Mary McClenaghan.

JONATHAN JONES, youngest child of Owen and Susanna Jones, born in Lower Merion, 15th of 7th-month, 1762; died there prior 1822. His will was signed 15 March, 1821. He married 1st, Mary Potts, of Plymouth; 2ndly, Mary Mc-

---

[1] Owen Jones, Junior, was born 1745. During the Revolutionary War, when the British were about to occupy Philadelphia, he was arrested in mistake for his father, who sympathized with England, and in order to save his father, suffered himself to be sent under guard to Virginia. He died s. p. in Philadelphia. His will is dated 15 June, 1822; proved 14 May, 1825, by which he leaves one-half part of the 350 acres devised to him by his father, to his nephew, Owen Jones, son of Jonathan, and the other half part he leaves to his nephew, John Wister, and his heirs. Louis Wister now holds this.

Clenaghan, widow, daughter of William Thomas, of Lower Merion.

They had issue as follows:

Colonel Owen Jones, member of Congress, Colonel of the First Pennsylvania Cavalry, War of the Rebellion. He married Mary Roberts, and had J. Awbrey Jones, of Wynnewood, late deceased s. p., and a daughter who died young unm.

HUGH ROBERTS, OF MERION AND CHESTNUT HILL.

Of Hugh Roberts considerable has, at various times, been written, but such matter is principally in the form of memorial and biographical sketches. The writer has made a most exhaustive search during the past few years with a view of discovering Hugh's ancestry, but with small success. It is true that if certain existing records in Wales could be critically examined in person some definite information might be gained, but this would need a visit to the Principality. This much, however, has been definitely ascertained. Hugh Roberts, or Hugh ap Robert (sometimes written Hugh Robert), was born on a large farm called Llyndedwyd, in Penllyn, Merionethshire. This property is near Bala Lake. His father was Robert ap Hugh, alias Robert Pugh, of the above place, and was a farmer or herder by occupation. Both father and son are called "gentlemen," in various documents of their time.[1] As we have explained, this in Wales at that day meant simply that they were descended from one of the ancient noble Tribes, and did not imply great wealth or especial distinction. The writer has investigated the title of the property called Llyndedwyd, with a view of ascertaining a connection between its ancient owners and Robert Pugh. It seems that the premises descended through an heiress from its original owners to the Price Family, of Rhiwlas, by whom it was held after 1600, and from whom Robert Pugh appears to have leased it. That he had no fee in the land seems quite evident. It is, however, pos-

---

[1] A case in point is a Bond, dated 20 December, 1691. John ap John de Ruabon, in the County of Denbigh, yeoman, et Thomas Wynne de ———— Chyrurgeon, to Hugon (Hugh) Roberts de Pensylvania, in America, *gentleman*. Witnessed by: Robert Vaughan, of Hendremawr; Thomas Cadwalader, of Llanerch; David Jones, of Kiltalgarth.

sible that he descended in some line from the same stock as the Price family, and this is still further suggested by the use in the family of Hugh Roberts, of a seal[1] bearing a very curious crest, which may have had some connection with the Price ancestry. Another theory, and probably a more likely one, is that Robert Pugh descended from the ancient owners of Cil Talgarth, who were of the blood of the Lords of Nannau. If this theory is correct, Hugh Roberts would have been a near kinsman to Edward Foulke, of Gwynedd, Pennsylvania, 1698, to Cadwalader Evans, and many other settlers, both of Gwynedd and Merion.[2]

Hugh Roberts' mother was called Elizabeth Williams, and she was the daughter of William Owen, of the parish of Llanfawr, Penllyn. William Owen was a land-holder, and was assessed in the same parish as such in the year 1636. Elizabeth was a very religious woman and careful to bring up her children well. In 1683, she being then, and having for many years been a widow, accompanied her son, Hugh Roberts, to Pennsylvania, and died in Merion Township in the year 1699. Hugh Robert, as he often wrote his name, especially prior to his removal to Pennsylvania, lived for a considerable time in the township of Kiltalgarth, or Ciltalgarth. It is not true, however, as stated by some writers, that his home (i. e., the house in which he resided) was so called. He probably continued to rent and reside upon his father's farm named Llyndedwyd. Hugh Roberts, as we shall call him, early joined the Society of Friends, but is said to have been a Presbyterian, his parents' original faith, before his convincement. His name is of frequent occurrence in connection with the imprisonment of Quakers in Merionethshire. He married first, Jane, the daughter of Owen ap Evan, of Fron Gôch, son of Evan Robert

---

[1] The seal in question was first used, so far as known, by Edward Roberts, son of Hugh, about 1705. It may have been used before this. It is a crest, having over the usual wreath a rose ppr., under a royal crown, being all between two human hearts, emitting flames, ppr. There are no arms or motto.

[2] Since writing the above the attention of the author has been called to a silver cup, in possession of the Vaux family, said to have originally belonged to Hugh Roberts. If the arms thereon were his, it would indicate that he descended from Einion of Llwydiarth. (See Appendix.)

Lewis, descended from Trahairn Gôch, of Llyn. (See Owen genealogy.) She accompanied him to Pennsylvania in 1683, and died in Merion.

He married secondly, 31st of 5th month, 1689, at Llwyn y Braner Meeting, Penllyn, Merionethshire, Elizabeth John. This was during one of his visits to his native country. Hugh Roberts was a member of the Merioneth Company and a first purchaser of land, as we have seen, and he was one of the largest holders. He did not, however, arrive in Pennsylvania until 1683.

The certificate of membership, granted him by his friends at home, is: "From our Monthly Meeting of Penllin, ye 2d of 5 mo. 1683," and speaks of him as " Hugh Roberts, of the Parish of Llanvawr, in the county of Merionethshire, North Wales." It says of him, that " he hath received, declared, and owned the truth for seventeen years, and walked since blameless in conversation, and peaceable in his place upon all accounts; he is of good reputation among his neighbors and acquaintances. His wife is like minded, walking in the truth, and a good example to others in life and conversation; their children educated in the fear of the Lord from their infancy." "Almost immediately after his arrival on these shores Hugh Roberts began an active public life, both in Church and in State. His name occurs very frequently on the minute-books of his meeting as appointed to some service. Before the building of the Merion Meeting-house, religious meetings were often held at his house, and, until the year 1695, nearly all the marriages among Friends were solemnized at the house of Katharine, widow of John ap Thomas, or that of Hugh Roberts, probably because they were large and convenient for the young people."

Hugh Roberts made at least two visits to Wales, one in 1688–9, and another in 1696–7. Of the first visit, taken immediately after his first wife's death, we know but little, save that he brought back a second wife, Elizabeth John, as we have seen.

Of his second visit to his native country we have very full particulars from his journal, now in the possession of Miss Meta Vaux, and printed in the *Pennsylvania Magazine of History and Biography*, from which we abstract the following:

A Brief Journal of Hugh Roberts' Travels from Pennsylvania to England and Wales.

In the year 1697, the 15th of ye 12th-mo. I set out from home to visit Friends in England & Wales; Samuel Carpenter & John Ascue accompanying me to Maryland, viz. to Susquehana & From thence to West River, to Mordecai Moore, to New London & Back again to the said Mordecai Moore. From thence to Samuel Galoway—From thence to Richard Harrisons—From thence to Herring Creek to a Burial where we had a Meeting. From thence to Potuxen to David Rawlins where we had a precious Meeting at their Meeting House[1] Here I parted with my Dear Friend Samuel Carpenter. From thence Friends sent a man and a couple of Horses to set me over Potuxon and so to Potomock, to one Widdow Blackstone who was no Friend where I have been very kindly Entertained for two days and two nights waiting for a Conveniency to pass over that Great River, being six miles broad. After they set me over refusing to take anything for their trouble I laid there The people being very kind, but could not hire me a horse to go to ye next River Rapahanock, so I went thro ye woods alone and came to one Capt. Taylor, who was very kind to me, not only in giving me good meat and Drink, But also setting me over ye river, three miles broad, where I stay'd that night ye people being kind. Next morning ye man in whose house I lodged put me on my way, and Directed me to one that would hire a horse, and so he did and came with me about 14 miles. From thence I went afoot that night about 6 miles To a friend George Wilson, a place where I had been before: and here I had a very open Meeting amongst ye people of ye world. From thence I went to New Kent where there is a meeting of Friends. Next day there was a Monthly Meeting at Curles at James River, to which I went along with Friends. And here I had a good service, afterwards going back again to New Kent I there met dear James Dickinson and with him went back

---

[1] Letter dated "Potuxen the 28th of ye 12th mo. 1696–7."
Dear Children . . .
Sixthly I desire of you to take the advise of them I left Guardians over you (in every thing you do) within and without & that you do nothing without their council who are Robt. Owen, John Roberts, Cadwalader Morgan & Robert Jones, who I know will be ready to give you the best advise, who love the truth, love you and whom I chose of all my friends in whom is my trust . . . Be tender and loving towards your grandmother who hath not been short in takeing care for you and be it that you can do anything for her do it willingly, for it is your duty . . .   HUGH ROBERTS.

to Curles where we had a good meeting and after meeting we returned to New Kent that night. I had one Meeting there before I met them, and one with them. So we parted, they going to Mataponij from whence I came.

And I went to Edward Thomas at James River. Charles Fleming coming along with me. Next day we went from thence to a Quarterly Meeting at Tenbigh where we had a blessed meeting, and after meeting that same day we came to Alexander Llywelyn. We traveled that same day 46 miles besides keeping ye Meeting, and it was not hard for us to do it because of ye Melting love and power of God was set over all. From thence we went to Edward Thomas again, where James Dickinson and J. H's and we appointed a Meeting to meet again which was very good, we appointed another at Alexander Llywelyns which also was a precious Meeting. Here I parted with them they going toward ye ship and I over James River to Walter Bartlets and so to Sevenech, where I had a good meeting at the Meeting house. Thence I went back again to Henry Wiges, to a meeting of William Cooks and back to Henry Wiges, where I had a sweet opportunity amongst them. From thence to Richard Ratliff, where I had a good open meeting, so to Daniel Sanburn and to John Coopland. From thence to ye meeting at Chuckatuck, where I had a good and large meeting, so back again to J. C and R. R. where I had another open good meeting; thence to Chuckatuck again, where there was abundance of Friends and others. Met at their Meeting house, a good and blessed meeting we had. From thence to William Scot at Brance, where I had a great and open good meeting. From thence to Leven Buffstins where I had a precious Meeting at which there were many Friends and many of the World's people. From thence I went to a meeting at Elizabeth Gallowell's which was a good meeting, from thence to John Coopland and to Daniel Sanburn and back again to J. C. where I met James Dickinson and Jacob F. again. From thence we went to a Meeting at Elizabeth Hollowell, a very good meeting. From thence to John Coopland and to Daniel Sanburn, and back again to a Meeting at Eliz: Hollowell where we had a precious Meeting. From thence on board ye ship, which was to ye mouth of James River, where ye Fleet mett, we stayed on board 15 days before we sailed and had several meetings from ship to ship to ye great comfort and Satisfaction of our Souls, and upon ye 7th day of ye 3d month we sailed out of ye Capes of Virginia. Many brave and precious meetings we had aboard.

Upon ye 14th day of the 4th Month we struck ground at 85 fathom watter and on ye 17th Day we saw ye Land old England, in ye 22d of ye said month we arrived at Plymouth; and had there a meeting next day and a precious meeting it was, to ye great comfort of many. From thence we passed to Exiter and from thence to Topsham where we had a meeting; from thence I went to Exiter again and thence to a Quarterly Meeting at Colomton, It being upon the first day where I have had a blessed meeting, and tho' I never had seen any of ye faces that were there, nor they mine, yet were we made very near and dear one to another. That night James and Jacob came to me, so we went on to Turston, and so to John Kancks, where we were received with much love. From thence we passed to Bristol, where we have had a precious meeting the power of ye Lord being over all. Here we met our dear friend William Penn and were not a little glad to see one another. We stayed but one meeting tho' Friends were very unwilling we should go so soon, yet we all parted James went homewards; Jacob towards London, and I passed to Monmouthshire in Wales. The weight of my service drawing me mostly that way. So I passed over to Panlymoyl, where there was a great meeting and I had a good service for ye Lord; From thence I went to Pant where I had a very open meeting, From thence to a Quarterly Meeting at John Meirick's where I had a good service; From thence to Castletown where there was a great tenderness and brokeness amongst Friends and ye World's people and some presbiterians, one of them being convinced. From thence I went to Cardiff within a mile of ye Town, and thence to Trefrug where John Bevan liveth, and glad we were to meet one another. There away I had several good meetings; from thence I passed to Swansey a great town in Wales. Here I had a hard meeting, many of them having made a profession of truth for many years, but did not possess it as they ought. From thence I went to Pembrookshire to Rediston and had a very precious meeting there. From thence I went to Haverford west, where I had several blessed meetings, to ye great comfort and satisfaction of Friends. From thence I went to Naish where I had a meeting; from thence to Rediston again where I had a very good meeting at James Lewis's and from thence to Lackarn where I had a little meeting. From thence I passed to Carmarthin another great town, where I had a good service amongst ye World's people, being but few Friends here. From thence I went to Owen Bowen and from thence to James Preece's to ye meeting at City Boom and back again; here I had a good meeting. From thence to Hwgfan, where I had a good sweet meeting; thus far John Bevan accompanied me, from his own being and so returned home. From thence I went to Radnershire to Lanole, where I had a little meeting, so I passed to Roger Hughes, where I had a good open meeting, so I went to Lanthdu[1] where I met many Friends and abundance of ye World's people. So to Edward Jones where we had a little meeting. From thence to David Powel's where there was a great meeting. From thence I passed to Thomas Goodin's where I had a blessed meeting, from thence I went to Muchunlleh where

---

[1] Probably Llwyn-du is intended.

I had a meeting amongst ye World's people, who at first were very rude, especially ye young ones. But after a while they were like other people, very attentive and modest, and many of them tender and broken so that Truth went over them all. This was in side of North Wales. From this place I returned back to Cardiganshire which is upon ye seaside in South Wales at a town called Aberystreyth. I had a great meeting mostly of World's people. From this place I passed towards North Wales again and came to Meirionethshire to Lwyndu where I had a good meeting, from thence to Lewis Owen near Dollegelley where I had a very good tender meeting. To the great comfort and edification of Friends. From this place I went to Balaa and Penllyn where I was born and bred. It was upon ye 6th day of ye week, so notice was given for a meeting to be at Ciltalgarth ye First day and with all I desired Friends to give notice to as many of my old acquaintance and relations as they could, that I did not intend to stay there but that day and so to go on my way. I knew abundance would be willing to see me and I was more desirous to see them at a meeting than any other place, for I had some secret hope that some of them would be reached, and so it was. Abundance of people came to ye meeting, there had been great meetings formerly, but never so many together before. After this meeting I went away as I said but they thought when they heard of it that I would come no more, but I did not intend it, I did it purposely to get them together that I might clear myself of my service. So I passed to Montgomeryshire to Lanwoddun where I had a good service; so to Dolobran where I received abundance of love from Charles Lloyd, his wife and friends; here I had a precious meeting, went on to Cloddiccochion, where I likewise had a good meeting. Hence I returned to Charles Lloyd, and so to Penllyn again, where I had a meeting at Robert Vaughan's which was bigger than that I had before. There was neither house nor barn that could contain the people, so that we were forced to keep several meetings out of doors. From thence I went to Denbyshire and meeting at Demightown and came back to Penllyn where I had a meeting Lwyn y branez, ye meeting house being too little we went to a great house that was hard by, but this was likewise too little by a great deal. A glorious meeting it was. I left Penllyn and went to Denbyshire and Wrecsam where I had a good meeting, from thence to John Merricks, so to Newtown—here I had a good open meeting and met old Isaac Asten, who accompanied me to Vock Savage, to Peter Prickles house, from thence to Feanly meeting where I had a great meeting. From thence went to Thomas Williamsons at Crawton, from thence to tareploy to Samuel Trafford, from thence to a meeting at Gilbert Woolsons. From thence to Middlewitch and after to Congtergen where I found a good meeting, and lodged at Thomas Welch. From thence to John Melor and so to a meeting at Lecke where I saw my dear and ancient friend John ab John. From thence I passed to Maxfield to John Hughes and thence to the meeting house near Whansley, where I had a good meeting and met Benjamin Banks. So I passed into Manchester where I had a meeting, and so to Warrington and to ye meeting at Lanckey which was very large and precious. From thence I went to Wrecsam and so to Penllyn, where I had another heavenly meeting—it was as large or larger than any before. From thence I went to Dolgelle to a Quarterly meeting where I met many friends from many places, and back again to Penllyn. I passed then to Montgomeryshire to a Quarterly Meeting held at Charles Lloyd's, where I had a good meeting and back again to Penllyn to a meeting at Robert Vaughans. At this meeting I was to take my leave of ye people as I thought of who came there in abundance, so that after we began ye meeting at ye house, which was one of the greatest in ye country, it could not contain one-half of ye people, so we kept it out of doors and a blessed meeting it was—there were people from seven parishes. I appointed another meeting at Cilltalgarth to take leave of friends, and the day following at Robert Vaughans, which I thought then should be ye last meeting in Penllyn. From thence I went to ye monthly meeting at Lewis Owen's, where we had a parting meeting, in which there was great tenderness, and love to truth and one to another.

It was during this last visit of his that his brother-in-law, Robert Owen, who was one of those left to oversee his children, writes to him from Pennsylvania as follows:

Dear Bro. H. R.

In yt Antient Love wherewithin we have Loved eath other, am I drawn forth at this time, to write unto thee, and in ye same is my soul exercised at this moment of time, I deeply affected in a sense of ye same, not forgetting ye many blessed seasons and opportunitys we have had together for mutual comffort and consolation, and certainly I cannot tell where to begin or where or when to end, if I should call to mind ye many Mercy and Loving kindness of ye Lord unto our word, to be sure time would faile me to Rehearse or make mention of it, therefore shall I forbear for scarcely will this opportunity admitt of time, for to give thee a short hint of what I have in my heart for to impart unto thee in Relation to thy own family and other Frds.

Thy daughter in Law K. has been ill all along since thee went and so doe continue as far as I see by her, though it may be supposed by some yt she is something better, yet have I but small hopes of her Recovery, for in my judgment and observation she is in a consuming condition. She bears it with patience and is given up to ye will of god, her husband and mother much afflicted and cast down, upon her account. Thy son Owen is Married and as far as I see Like to doe well. Neddie is much concerned because of thy going away and takes as it were naturally a good share of thy concerns upon him, he is like to prove witty, and to observe well wt thee gave him in charge in all Respects.

My wife is brought to bed, we have a young Rebekah added to our family since the went. Robert Barrow Arrived here, through abundants of hardships and difficultys far beyond what I may Relate, but . . . he was aboard of Jos: Curle coming from Jameaca . . . they were cast away at ye gulffe of florida and fell among barbarous and savage Indians, but they were Meraculously preserved by the speciall hand and providence of God. There was with him one Dickinson and wife and family coming from thence here to live who lost as I am informed 1500 £ by their shipwreck. I suppose thee will have it more at large by some other hand.

Will Howell has bought ye plantation where the students lived.

Wm. Jenkins bought Jo. Barns plantation, they go yt side to live, Evan Harry is to Marry K. Davies; young Rich. Hays in election of Marrage with B. Lewis, H. Lewis' sister Wm. Robt and Rich Walter's wive's sister.

I am at present at Philadelphia where I had ye first opportunity to Speak to Sam Carpenter, this week he returned from Marry Land, he acquainted me with this opportunity to send to thee and with some straitness have 1 gott time to write these lines.

Although I am forced to conclude yt my unfeigned Love doth and shall Remaine to thee, who am thy true and constant fd and Brother   R. O.

24th—2d mo. 1697

My kind Love to James Dickinson and Jacob Hallowfield.

In this letter it is stated that his son, " Ned," that is Edward Roberts, afterwards Mayor of Philadelphia, but then a boy, was engaged in looking after his father's affairs. It may be observed that Hugh Roberts, like other of his fellow-Welshmen, was induced to speculate very considerably in Pennsylvania lands on account of the sharp advance which at first took place; and they not only held large tracts of land on options, by which is meant an agreement to purchase within a certain number of months, but they invested heavily in the various land speculation companies which sprang into existence, besides being large holders of the stock of the Company of Free Traders.

Hugh Roberts, heavily encumbered by such purchases and investments, did not hesitate to leave them all in the hands of his son, Edward, and embark for Wales. It may have been that whilst in his native place he was able to secure certain loans; at any rate his affairs after his return were in a much better condition than when he left. After his return to Pennsylvania he continued in the ministry, but did not long survive. Whilst in Long Island he was taken ill at the house of John Rodman, and returning home, died at Merion the 18th of 6-month, 1702, and upon the 20th was interred at the meeting-ground. His will has been abstracted as follows:

Will of Hugh Roberts, "of near Merion;" dated 25th 5-mo. 1702. Proved 7 Dec., 1702. Will Book B, p. 265.

"To eldest son, Robert, ½ of the meadow which was formerly called *clean John's meadow.*"

"Unto my second son, Owen, what I have in his (my?) hands towards that Legacie which his grandfather left him."[1]

"My daughter Elizabeth."

"To my son, Edward, 200 acres of land, with the plantation, my dwelling house and all buildings, which is called *Chesnut Hill.*"

"Also my two servant lads, Griffith and Morris."

"My grandson, Hugh Roberts, son of Owen."

To Meirion Meeting £5.

"To my old servant Morris Roberts, 50s., and to my old servant John Roberts 50s.

Mentions 1100 acres of land belonging to him in Goshen in the Welsh Tract.

Sons, Robert, Owen and Edward, Executors.

Trustees: John Roberts, Cadwalader Morgan, Griffith John and Griffith Owen.

Witnesses: Sam'l Jennings, Samuel Browne, Griffith (John?).

Hugh Roberts' extensive transactions in real estate in the Province of Pennsylvania have been noted. Some of the details of these purchases are not without interest, as showing the early changes of land in Merion Township in those early

---

[1] This could hardly have been Owen ap Evan, of Fron Gôch, the maternal grandfather of Hugh Roberts' children, because he died apparently before the birth of Owen; yet it is claimed that Robert Pugh, the paternal grandfather, was also deceased before that date, although the latter is a surmise based upon a statement made by Hugh Roberts in his Journal to the effect that his mother had been long a widow. This statement, however, seems not very clear, and capable of a different interpretation. It is also *possible* that Owen ap Evan *was* alive in 1677, the date of Owen's birth. The other explanations are that the bequest was in the nature of a reversion to the children of Hugh or of Jane Owen, by either grandparents, or that the person who left the bequest was William Owen, the great-grandfather. Neither the wills of Owen ap Evan nor of Robert Pugh can be found in the Registries of St. Asaph or Bangor up to this writing.

times. It will be recollected that Hugh Roberts' first purchase was as a member of the Merioneth Adventurers. This was 312½ acres. His next transaction was to buy out in Wales the interest of John Watkins, being 156¼ acres, 1 April, 1682. Thus it appears that the grantor did not come out to Merion as intended. On the 1st of the 4th month, 1688, he had a warrant of survey issued to him for 200 acres "to be taken up in the Welsh Tract, purchased by Hugh of the Commissioners, of which he sold 100 acres to Katherine Thomas (alias Katherine Robert), relict of John Thomas." He had this land confirmed by Patent, 22d 10 br., 1701. At the same last mentioned date he had a Patent for "100 acres of Liberty land upon the Indian Creek and Mill Creek near Adam Rhode's land," said title being in right of the original purchase of Richard Thomas, of Whitford Garne, in the County of Flint, deceased.

In 1701 it is noted that "Hugh Roberts, being seated on some of the Proprietor's Land within the Liberty, on west side of Schuylkill, obtained a survey on 200 acres," but did not get title as he owed yet £60 on the same. These are only a few of the transfers to him. As appears by his will he held nearly, if not quite, 1400 acres of land at the time of his decease, in 1702.

His principal home plantation, probably that called in the will "Chestnut Hill," afterwards became the property of the George family. It is said to have covered the site of the present George's Hill, Fairmount Park.

Hugh Roberts had, by Jane, his first wife, the following children:

1. Robert Roberts, b. 11-mo. 7, 1673, of whom presently.
2. Ellin Roberts, b. 10-mo. 4th, 1675.
3. Owen Roberts, b. 10-mo. 1st, 1677; m. Ann Bevan.
4. Edward Roberts, b. 2-mo. 4th, 1680; of whom presently.
5. William Roberts, b. 3-mo. 26th, 1682; d. 1697.
6. Elizabeth Roberts, b. 12-mo. 24th, 1683.

ROBERT ROBERTS, eldest son of Hugh, born in Wales, 1673, is said to have removed to Maryland (A),[1] and there died, leaving, according to several accounts, a son Richard Roberts, (B) who was father to Robert Roberts, who returned to Philadelphia, and married Catherine, daughter of David Deshler, of Philadelphia, and became a prominent merchant of that city. (See Appendix.)

Robert Roberts married 1st, Catherine Jones; 2ndly, Priscilla Johns.

OWEN ROBERTS, 2nd son of Hugh and Jane Roberts, born in Township of Kiltalgarth, Merionethshire, 10-month 1st, 1677; died in Philadelphia, Penna., 10-month, 1723; will dated 31 1-month, 1706; proved 1723. He married 1-mo. 23d, 1696-7, Ann Bevan, daughter of John Bevan (see Bevan). Removed from Merion to Philadelphia, described as "merchant;" he was High Sheriff of Philadelphia County and City 1716–23. Having been Treasurer of Philadelphia from 22 July, 1712, to 1716. Member of Common Council 1711. Member of Provincial Assembly 1711. Appointed Collector of Imposts 1716–23. His wife was living 1723.

Children of Owen Roberts and Ann, his wife:
1. Hugh Roberts, b. 5-mo. 30, 1699.
2. John Roberts, b. 8-mo. 12, 1701; m. Mary Jones.
3. Jane Roberts, b. 4-mo. 2, 1703; d. 4-mo. 2, 1703.
4. Awbrey Roberts, b. 4 24, 1705.
5. Owen Roberts, b. 7-mo. 18, 1708; d. infant.
6. Owen Roberts, b. 8-mo. 23, 1711.

---

[1]The above is inserted on the authority of C. Morton Smith, Esq. (as to A), and Edmund H. McCullough, Esq. (as to B). It appears, from the writer's investigations, that Richard Roberts, brother of John Roberts, of Pencoyd, also probably removed to Maryland, and the Christian name of Richard suggests a possibility that Richard Roberts, father of Robert Roberts, deceased 1792, might have been son of this first Richard, instead of Robert Roberts, son of Hugh. The whole matter, however, is inserted in a suggestive way, for further investigation.

EDWARD ROBERTS, "ESQUIRE," third son of Hugh Roberts and Jane, his 1st wife, born in Township of Ciltalgarth, County Merioneth, 2-mo. 4, 1680; died in Philadelphia, Pennsylvania, 1741. Will proved 6 May, 1741. He was Mayor of Philadelphia from Oct. 2nd, 1739; having been a member of Common Council 1717. He was Alderman and Justice of the Peace from 12 May, 1725, to 1741; Associate Justice City Court prior 3 Oct., 1727; Justice Orphans' Court from 10 June, 1724. He married first, Susanna Painter, daughter of George Painter; secondly, Martha Hoskins, and thirdly, Martha Cox.

Children of Edward Roberts:

1. Hugh Roberts.
2. Jane Roberts, m. William Fishbourn, Mayor of Philadelphia.
3. Mary Roberts.
4. Elizabeth Roberts, m. ——— Bond.

NOTE.—It is not the intention of this work to give, in every case, complete lists of descendants of the Merion settlers. Such an undertaking would necessitate several volumes of the size of the present publication. It may be briefly noted here that among the descendants of this line are the families of Vaux, Parrish, Bond and many others. Among the descendants is Charles Morton Smith, Esq., of Philadelphia, who has in MS. a detailed account of most of Hugh Roberts' descendants. Owing to his absence from the city during the continuation of this work, it was thought best to omit further notes.

LLOYD OF DOLOBRAN.

LLOYD OF DOLOBRAN. THE PEDIGREE OF THE FAMILY AND AN ACCOUNT OF SOME OF THE AMERICAN DESCENDANTS.

There is no house within the parish of Meifod, in Montgomeryshire, Wales, to which, or to the family once belonging to it, a more singular or interesting history is attached than to Dolobran. This ancient family was seated at Dolobran for many generations (from 1476 to 1780), and trace their lineage up to a remote period of genealogy; and after some reverses, its male descendants are widely spread, and have held and still occupy most important positions, both in England and Pennsylvania[1]. Thomas Lloyd, Penn's Deputy Governor, was a very considerable owner of land in Merion Township, a part of which had been one-half part of the purchase of his brother, Charles Lloyd, and Margaret Davies, widow. (See a former page.) A part of this land lay north of Haverford station, Lower Merion, and part northeast of Ardmore station. The

---

[1] Collections of the Powysland Club.

former is owned in part by Thomas Lloyd's descendant, Clement A. Griscom, whose country place, called " Dolobran," is on Grey's Lane, just beyond the Merion Cricket Club's House.

Dolobran Hall, which is prettily situated, overlooking the Vyrnwy, is now merely used as a farm-house, and the old meeting house which stands close by, built by Charles Lloyd, the Quaker, about 1660, has of late years been gradually dismantled of its carved oak gallery and panellings. There is strong reason for believing that William Penn worshipped and not improbably preached in this old Quaker chapel, and Hugh Roberts, of Merion, Robert Owen, and other Cymric Friends, were accustomed to address their countrymen within its walls. The Lloyds had a common origin with the distinguished family of the Vaughans, of Llwydiarth, now extinct in the male line.

CELYNIN, of Llwydiarth, the first of this race who settled in Montgomeryshire, fled there after having slain, in single combat, the Mayor of Carmarthen. His lineage from ALETH, "King," or Prince of Dyfed, is as follows: ALETH had UCHDRYD, who by Mared, daughter of Cadiver Vawr, Lord of Blaen Cych, had GWRGENEY, who by Ales, daughter of Goronwy ap Einion, had IERWERTH, who by Eva, daughter of Sir Aron ap Rees, had CYNDDELW, who by Jane, daughter of Gorwareth, of Kemmes, had RIRID, who by Gwladus[1], daughter of Richard, Lord of Dinas Certhin, had the above CELYNIN.

It has been suggested that Celynin is probably identical with "*Celine filio Cheugret*" (i. e. Ririd, who appears as one of the lay witnesses to the foundation charter of the Abbey of Ystrad Marchell, and although the charter itself was of a much

---

[1](Lewis Dwnn, vol. ii., p. 277.) But this is not accordant with the Llwydiarth pedigree in Dwnn, vol. i., p. 294. There " Gwenllian, the daughter of Meredith ap Rhyddarch ap Tewdwr Mawr," is stated to be the wife of Celynin, and "Gwladys," to be his mother. It is said, however, in the Salisbury MSS. at Wynnstay that Gwladys. the daughter of Ririd ap Cynwrig Efell, was the mother of Celynin, and not the wife. This would account for the possession of Llwydiarth.

earlier date, yet the time of execution of the testing clause, to which the name is appended, would correspond with Celynin's date.

How Celynin acquired Llwydiarth, from his mother or by marriage, is still a mooted question. The authority of the express statement of Lewis Dwnn that Celynin married " Gwladus v. aeres Ririd ap Cynwig Evell ag a ga vas Llwydiarth Ymhowys" (and obtained Llwydiarth in Powys), can, we think, be safely relied upon; and to reconcile it with the statement elsewhere, made by the same Herald, that Celynin married " Gwenllian v' Meredith ap Rhydderch ap Tewdwr Mawr," it may be assumed that he married twice: (1) Gwenllian and (2) Gwladys. Celynin, after his flight to Montgomeryshire, became Steward to Charleton, Lord Powys. His eldest son and heir was:

EINION AP CELYNIN, of Llwydiarth. John de Charleton, Lord of Powys, granted unto this Einion, by the designation of " Anian ap Kelynnin," on the Thursday after the Decolation of St. John the Baptist, 14 Edward III. [1340], Weston in the Ville of Pennayrth, in Glas Meynoc. He married the daughter of Adda ap Meyric, Rector of Meifod, a descendant of Brochwel Ysgythrog, and by her had a son who succeeded him, by name:

LLEWELYN AP EINION, of Llwydiarth. He is mentioned in a grant dated 7 May, 7 Henry V., whereby Edward de Charleton, Lord Powys, pardoned his (Llewelyn's) grandson, Gryffith ap Jenkin ap Llewelyn for complicity in the rebellion of Owen Glendower. He married " Lleuca, the daughter of Griffith ap Eden " (Edneved), Lloid, styled " *relicte dicti Llewelyn*" in the above grant. They had three sons:

1. Jenkin ap Llewelyn, styled in same above mentioned grant " *Jenkin ap Llewelyn, filii predicti Llewelyn et Leuca Patris Griffini*," ancestor of the Vaughans, of Llwydiarth.

2. Ievan ap Llewelyn[1], ancestor of the Vaughans, of Powys, and of the Tal y Lyn branch, Merionethshire.

---

[1] IEVAN AP LLEWELYN AP EINION, of Llwydiarth, married Gwenevor, daughter of Ievan Gethin ap Madog Cyfin, and had: DAVID AP IEVAN, who married

3. David ap Llewelyn, of Dolobran, of whom presently.
Llewelyn divided his estates amongst his sons and to his youngest son, David, he gave Dolobran and Coedcowrid.

DAVID AP LLEWELYN married twice; by his first wife, Mary, the daughter of Griffith Gôch, Esq., he had a son, OWEN, who was ancestor of the *Vaughans*, of *Glascoed*, and whose second son was probably DAVID AP OWEN, Abbot, of Ystrad Marchell, and afterwards Bishop of St. Asaph, who died about 1512, and whose monument was in the Cathedral of St. Asaph. David ap Llewelyn married for his second wife, Medisis, daughter of Griffith Deuddwr, Esq., of the Tribe of Brochwel Ysgythrog. He was succeeded by his eldest son:

IEVAN TEG (or the Handsome), of Dolobran. He married Maud, daughter of Evan Blayney, of Castle Blayney in Ireland, and had a son:

OWEN, OF DOLOBRAN, who was the first of the family who took the surname of *Lloyd*, probably from Llwydiarth, the estate of his ancestor, Celynin. He married Katherine, the daughter of Raynalt, son of Sir Griffith Vaughan, Knight Banneret, of Agincourt, and had two sons and one daughter. They were:

1. Evan, of Dolobran, of whom presently.
2. David, of Rhosvawr.
3. Ellen, m. John Grey.

EVAN LLOYD, of Dolobran, the eldest son, married Gwenhwyvar, daughter of Meredith Lloyd, of Meifod, by whom he had:

Janet, daughter of Ievan Gôch ap Ievan Vaughan ap Ievan ap Iorwerth ap Adda, of Dolgôch, and had: MEREDITH AP DAVID, who married Maud, daughter of Meredith ap Griffith Derwas, of Nannau (see pedigree of Rowland Ellis), and had: JOHN AP MEREDITH, who married Gwenllian, daughter of Ednyvet ap David ap Howell ap Einion (possibly of the line of Ednowain ap Bradwen) and had: HUGH AP JOHN, of Tal y Lyn (a parish in the hundred—or Comôt—of Estimaner, Merionethshire, about eight miles southwest of Dôlgelly) and had: MARY VERCH HUGH, who married DAVID AP HOWELL, of Llwyngwrill, Merionethshire. Her mother was Catherine, daughter of Rhys ap David ap Ievan ap Jackws ap David ap Ievan. David ap Howell had: HUGH AP DAVID, who, by Catherine, of Abergynolwyn, had: HUMPHREY AP HUGH, of Llwyn-du, who, by Elizabeth, daughter of John Powel, of Llanwddyn, had: OWEN HUMPHREY, of Llwyn-du, ancestor to the Humphreys, Owen, Ellis and other families of Pennsylvania.

1. David, of Dolobran, of whom presently.
2. John Wyn, of Dyffryn.

DAVID LLOYD, of Dolobran (born 1523), the eldest son, appears under the name of "*DD. Lloid ap Ieu'n (Evan) ap Owen, Gentleman,*" on Grand Juries, in the County of Montgomery, 34 Henry VIII. [A. D. 1542]. He married, first, Eva, daughter of Edward Price, of Eglusig, by whom he had no issue ; and secondly, Eva, daughter of Evan David Gôch, son of Jenkin Vaughan, of Bodfach, by whom he had :

DAVID LLOYD, of Dolobran (born 1549). He appears in county Grand Juries in 8th, 19th, 20th, 23d and 25th of Elizabeth, and as "*David ap DD. Lloyd, of Dolobran, Gentleman,*" in the 34th of Elizabeth. He married Ales, daughter of David Lloyd, of Llanarmon Mynydd Mawr, Esq., descended from Ririd Flaidd, Lord of Penllyn, and had a son :

JOHN LLOYD, of Dolobran (born 1575), who married his cousin Katherine, the daughter and coheiress of Humphrey Wynn, of Dyffryn, son of the above named John Wynn, of Dyffryn, by his wife, Margaret, daughter of Sir Roger Kynaston. " He kept his abode at Coedcowryd, and wainscoted the parlour thereof and lived there in great state, having twenty-four men with halberts to attend him to Meivod Church, and placed them in his great pew under the pulpit. He also bought Owen John Humphrey's estate in Meivod." He appears as "*Johes Lloyd, gen.,*" on the county Grand Jury, 8 James I., and as "*Johes Lloyd de Dolobran, gen.,*" 20 James I., and as "*Johes Lloyd, of Dolobran, Ar.,*" as a grand juror or magistrate in 2nd, 4th and 9th Charles I. He disappears from the list of Justice's of the Peace 14 Charles I. He was succeeded by his son :

CHARLES LLOYD (I.), of Dolobran (born 1613). He married Elizabeth Stanley, daughter of Thomas Stanley, of Knockin, in the County of Salop (son of Sir Edward Stanley, son of Sir Foulk Stanley, son of Sir Piers Stanley, son of Sir Rowland Stanley, brother of Lord Stanley, of Knockin). " He lived at Dolobran Hall, and enlarged the same by adding to it the timber buildings on the north side thereof, making the said hall's platform to resemble the figure of a capital L."

There was previous to the year 1780 an oak panel over the fire-place of the old hall at Dolobran, upon which was emblazoned the shield of Charles Lloyd of fifteen quarterings, impaling the Stanley arms with six quarterings in right of his wife, Elizabeth Stanley. This panel was removed by James Lloyd before he sold Dolobran Hall, and presented to his relative Charles Lloyd, from whom it came to the grandson of the latter, James Farmer Lloyd, of London, who now owns it. Charles Lloyd was esteemed one of the most eminent genealogists and antiquarians of his time. He died in 1657, and his burial is thus entered in Meivod Register:

" BURIALS, } *Charles Lloyd, Esq., of Dolobran, was buried*
1657. } *17 day August.*"

His will was dated 17 June, 1651. He had three sons:

1. Charles, b. 9 Dec., 1637, of Dolobran; the Quaker, grad. Oxford, M. D^r.

2. John, of Jesus College, Oxford, grad. M. D.; clerk in chancery.

3. Thomas, Dep. Gov. Penna., of whom presently.

THOMAS LLOYD, of Dolobran, third son of Charles, was born 17 Feb., 1640, and died in Pennsylvania 10 September, 1694. " He graduated from Jesus College, Oxford,"[2] and is stated to have also been a doctor of medicine. His record as a minister among Friends, both in Wales and America, is well known, and, as well as his political career, is referred to elsewhere. He was Deputy Governor and President of Provincial Council 1684–93. An account of his purchases in Merion has also been given, and suffice it to say here that his lands were partly in the immediate neighborhood of Haverford Station, where several of his descendants now reside at " Dolobran."

---

[1] Charles Lloyd (II.), of Dolobran, the celebrated Quaker, married first, Elizabeth, daughter of Sampson Lort, and left issue. The author has not verified the statement that Charles and his brother Thomas Lloyd were graduates of Oxford. The statement is made upon the word of others. A further investigation is suggested.

[2] See supra.

He married first, 9 September, 1665, Mary, daughter of Roger Jones, of Welshpool, Montgomeryshire, Wales, and secondly, Patience Gardiner, widow unto Robert Story and, by his first wife, who died in 1680, he had ten children, viz. :

1. Hannah, b. 1666; m. John Delaval; m., 2ndly, Richard Hill; for issue see *Lloyd-Carpenter Family*.
2. Rachel, b. 1667-8; m. Samuel Preston.
3. Mordicai, b. 1669; d. s. p. at Sea, in 1694.
4. John, b. 1671; d. s. p. at Jamaica, 1692.
5. Mary, b. 1674; m. Isaac Norris.
6. Thomas, b. 1675; m. Sarah Young.
7. Elizabeth, b. 1677; d. 1704; m., 1700, Daniel Zachary, and had Dr. Lloyd Zachary, of Philadelphia.
8. Margaret, b. 1685; d. 1693.
9. Deborah, b. 1682; m. Dr. Mordecai Moore.
10. Samuel, b. 1684; d. infant.

THOMAS LLOYD, of Goodmansfields, in London, son of Governor Thomas Lloyd, b. 1675; d. ante 1718; m. Sarah Young, and had:

THOMAS LLOYD, of Philadelphia, d. 1754; m. Susannah, d. 1740, daughter of Philip Kearney, of Philadelphia, and widow of Dr. Edward Owen, and had:

SARAH LLOYD, d. 1788, who m. William Moore, of Philadelphia, President of the Supreme Executive Council of Pennsylvania in 1781, who d. 1793, and had: ELIZABETH MOORE, who m. 1784, Francois Barbé, Marquis de Marbois, Chargé d'Affaires of France in the United States, and had issue, and:

MAJOR THOMAS LLOYD MOORE, of Philadelphia, b. 1759; d. 1813; m. Sarah, daughter of Joseph Stamper, and had:

ELIZA MOORE, b. 1786; d. 1823; who m. Richard Willing, of Philadelphia, b. 1775; d. 1858; and had:

    I. THOMAS MOORE WILLING, of Philadelphia, d. 1850, who m., 1831, Matilda Lee, daughter of Bernard Moore Carter, of Virginia, and had children: I. WILLIAM BINGHAM; II. MILDRED THERESA; III. MATILDA L.; IV. ARTHUR LEE.

2. MARY WILLING, d. s. p., 1860; m. John M. Dale, of Philadelphia, son of Richard Dale, Commodore of the United States Navy.
3. HENRY WILLING.
4. ELLEN WILLING, m. Comte Blondeel van Cuelebroeck, of Belgium.
5. CAROLINE WILLING, d. 1860, who m. Dr. E. Peace, and had issue, who assumed the name of *Willing:*
> I. ELLA MOORE WILLING, m. Oswold Jackson, of New York, a descendant of Chief Justice Chew, of Pennsylvania, and had:
>> 1. LAURA CARROLL; 2. OSWALD.
>
> II. RICHARD LLOYD WILLING, m. Elizabeth Kent, daughter of William Henry Ashhurst, and had:
>> 1. CHARLES; 2. WILLIAM HENRY ASHHURST; 3. LIONEL; 4. JAMES KENT.

6. ELIZABETH WILLING, m. John Jacob Ridgway, of Philadelphia, and had:
> I. EMILY RIDGWAY, m. Etienne, Comte de Ganay. Issue.
>
> II. CHARLES HENRY RIDGWAY.

7. EDWARD SHIPPEN WILLING, of Philadelphia, m. Alice C., daughter of Dr. John Rhea Barton, of Philadelphia, and had:
> I. JOHN RHEA BARTON WILLING.
>
> II. SUSAN R. WILLING, of Philadelphia.
>
> III. AVA LOWLE WILLING, who m. 17 February, 1891, John Jacob Astor, of New York City.

The Carpenter Branch.

RACHEL LLOYD, daughter of Thomas Lloyd, married Samuel Preston, of Pennsylvania, and had:

HANNAH PRESTON, who married Samuel Carpenter, Jr., and had:

PRESTON CARPENTER, of Salem, N. J., d. 1785, who had by his first wife, Hannah Smith, HANNAH, and:

I. WILLIAM CARPENTER, of Salem, 1754–1837, m., first, 1782, Elizabeth, daughter of Bartholomew Wyatt, of Salem, issue; m., secondly, Mary, daughter of John Redman, and had:

1. SAMUEL PRESTON CARPENTER, of Salem, who m., first, 1837, Hannah, daughter of Benjamin Acton, of Salem, and had:

    I. JOHN REDMAN CARPENTER, of Salem, who m. Mary C., daughter of Joseph B. Thompson, and had:

    1. PRESTON; 2. ELIZABETH; 3. MAURICE.

    II. SAMUEL PRESTON CARPENTER, of Salem, m. Rebecca Bassett, and had:

    1. BENJAMIN A.; 2. WILLIAM.

    III. SARAH W., m. Richard H. Reeve, of Camden, N. J. Issue.

    IV. MARY R., m. Benjamin C. Reeve, of Camden, N. J. Issue.

    V. WILLIAM CARPENTER, of Salem, N. J.

2. MARY WYATT, wife of James Hunt. Issue.
3. WILLIAM CARPENTER, m., first, Hannah Scull; m., secondly, Phebe Warren.
4. JOHN REDMAN CARPENTER, d. s. p., 1833.
5. RACHEL R., wife of Charles Sheppard. Issue.

II. THOMAS CARPENTER, of Carpenter's Landing, Gloucester Co., N. J., 1752–1847; m. Mary Tonkins, and had:

EDWARD CARPENTER, of Glassboro', N. J., 1777–1813; m., 1799, Sarah, daughter of Dr. James Stratton, of Swedesboro', N. J., and had:

I. THOMAS PRESTON CARPENTER, of Camden, N. J., 1804–76; m. Rebecca, daughter of Dr. Samuel Hopkins, of Philadelphia, had: JAMES H.

II. DR. JAMES STRATTON CARPENTER, of Pottsville, Pa., 1807–72; m. Camilla J., daughter of John Sanderson, and had:

1. DR. JOHN T. CARPENTER, of Pottsville. Issue.

2. SARAH S., m. Rev. Daniel Washburne. Issue.

3. PRESTON CARPENTER, of Pottsville. Issue.

III. EDWARD CARPENTER, of Philadelphia, m. Anna Maria, daughter of Benjamin M. Howey, of Gloucester County, N. J., and had:

1. MAJOR JAMES EDWARD CARPENTER, of Philadelphia, who m., 17 October, 1867, Harriet Odin, daughter of Rev. Benjamin Dorr, D. D. Issue:

I. EDWARD; II. HELEN; III. GRACE, d. young; IV. WILLIAM DORR; V. LLOYD PRESTON.

2. THOMAS P. CARPENTER, of Buffalo, N. Y., unm.

3. CHARLES C. S. CARPENTER, d. 1881.

4. COLONEL LOUIS HENRY CARPENTER, U. S. Army, unm.

5. SARAH CAROLINE CARPENTER, m. Andrew Wheeler, of Philadelphia and Bryn Mawr. Issue:

I. ANDREW WHEELER, JR., of Philadelphia, m. Mary Wilcox, daughter of Rev. Edward Shippen Watson, and had:

1. SOPHIA WILCOX; 2. ELEANOR LEDLIE.

II. ANNA, d. young; III. JAMES MAY, d. young; IV. SAMUEL BOWMAN; V. ARTHUR LEDLIE; VI. WALTER STRATTON; VII. HERBERT.

6. MARY HOWELL CARPENTER, unm.

IV. MARY TONKINS CARPENTER, who m. Richard W. Howell, of Camden, N. J., and had:

1. DR. SAMUEL B. HOWELL, of Philadelphia, m. Maria E., daughter of Rev. William Neill, D. D. Issue.

2. ANNA, m. Malcolm Lloyd, of Philadelphia. Issue.
3. CHARLES STRATTON HOWELL.
4. JOSHUA LADD HOWELL, m. Mary E., daughter of William L. Savage, of Philadelphia. Issue: EVELYN VIRGINIA.
5. THOMAS JAMES HOWELL, k. in battle, 1862.

FRANCIS LEE HOWELL, d. s. p., 1872.

V. REV. SAMUEL T. CARPENTER, m., first, Frances Champlain, of Derby, Conn.; m., secondly, Emily D. Thompson, of Wilmington, Del. Issue.

III. ELIZABETH CARPENTER, m., 1767, Ezra Firth, of Salem County, N. J., and had:

1. PRESTON C., issue; 2. JOHN, issue; 3. THOMAS; 4. SAMUEL, issue.
5. HANNAH FIRTH, m. Isaac C. Jones, of Philadelphia, and had:
I. SAMUEL TONKINS JONES, of New York, m., first, Sarah M. Thomas; secondly, Martha M. Thomas.

The Morris Branch.

RACHEL LLOYD, who m., 1688, Samuel Preston, Mayor of Philadelphia, and had:

HANNAH PRESTON, who m. Samuel Carpenter, Jr., of Philadelphia, and had:

HANNAH CARPENTER, d. 1766, who m., 1746, as his first wife, Samuel Shoemaker, Mayor of Philadelphia, son of Samuel Shoemaker, Mayor of Philadelphia, and had:

BENJAMIN SHOEMAKER, of Philadelphia, b. 1746, who m., 1773, Elizabeth, daughter of Edward and Anna Warner, and had:

ANNA SHOEMAKER, b. 1777; d. 1865, who m., first, 1796, Robert Morris, Jr., of Philadelphia, son of Robert Morris, and had by him:

I. ELIZABETH ANNA MORRIS, d. 1870; m., first, Sylvester Malsan, and had:
1. JOHN FRANCIS MALSAN, m. Sarah Bennet Browñ, of Blandford, England.
2. HENRY MORRIS MALSAN, m. Sarah E. White, of Whitesboro', N. Y.

ELIZABETH ANNA MORRIS, m., secondly, John Cosgrove, of Albany, N. Y., and had by him:
MARY ELIZABETH, m. Joseph J. Manifold.

II. MARY WHITE MORRIS, d. 1838; m., 1827, Dr. Paul Hamilton Wilkins, of Georgia.

III. DR. ROBERT MORRIS, of Philadelphia, who m., first, 27 May, 1836, Caroline, daughter of Henry and Maria (Morris) Nixon, and m., secondly, 1 June, 1854, Lucy P., daughter of Robert Morris Marshall, of Fauquier County, Va., son of Judge James Markham and Hetty (Morris) Marshall, of Virginia; Dr. Morris had by his first wife:

ROBERT MORRIS, of Philadelphia, Major, U. S. Volunteers, d. in Libby Prison, 1863; m., 19 January, 1860, Ellen M., daughter of George M. Wharton, and had:
I. CAROLINE NIXON MORRIS.
II. MARION WHARTON MORRIS, who m., 20 April, 1882, Richard Norris Williams.

DR. ROBERT MORRIS had by his second wife:
1. DR. HENRY MORRIS, of Philadelphia, who m., 12 October, 1880, Bessie T. Elliott.
2. JAMES MARKHAM, d. 1864; 3. ANNA; 4. SUSAN MARSHALL; 5. LUCY MARSHALL.

RACHEL LLOYD, who m., 6 July, 1688, Samuel Preston, Mayor of Philadelphia, 1711; Treasurer of the Province of Pennsylvania, 1714–43, and member of the Governor's Council; d. 1743, and had:

HANNAH PRESTON, b. 1693; d. 1772; m., 1711, Samuel Carpenter, of Philadelphia, son of Samuel Carpenter, Treasurer of the Province of Pennsylvania, and had:

JUDGE PRESTON CARPENTER, of Salem, N. J., b. 1721; d. 1785; m., first, 1742, Hannah, daughter of Samuel Smith, of Salem County, N. J., and had by her:

HANNAH CARPENTER, b. 1743; d. 1820; m., first, 1768, Charles Ellet, of Salem, N. J. (his second wife), and m., secondly, Jedediah Allen, of Salem, N. J., by whom she had:

HANNAH ALLEN, who m. James Smith, of Salem, N. J., and had:

SARAH ANN SMITH, who m. Dr. David M. Davis, of Woodstown, N. J. Issue.

HANNAH CARPENTER had by her first husband:

I. JOHN ELLET, of Salem County, N. J., b. 1769; d. 1824; m., first, 1792, Mary, daughter of William Smith, of Salem, N. J., and m., secondly, Sarah English, and had by his first wife:

HANNAH CARPENTER ELLET, b. 1793; d. 1862; who m., first, 1813, George Wishart Smith, of Princess Anne County, Va., m., secondly, Joseph E. Brown, of Salem, N. J., and had by him, who d. in 1844:

I. WILLIAM HENRY BROWN, of Salem, N. J. Issue.

II. JOSEPH FRANCIS BROWN, U. S. Army.

By her first husband, who d. in Philadelphia, in 1821, she had:

I. CHARLES PERRIN SMITH, of Trenton, N. J., b. 1819; d. 1883; m., 1843, Hester A., daughter of Colonel Matthew Driver, of Caroline County, Md., and had:

1. ELLEN WISHART; 2. CHARLES PERRIN; 3. ELIZABETH ALFORD; 4. FLORENCE BURMAN.

II. MARY ELLET SMITH, who m. General Richard Thomas, of Queen Anne County, Md. Issue.

III. GEORGIANA WISHART SMITH, who m. Samuel C. Harbert, of Philadelphia, Colonel U. S. Volunteers, and had:
1. MARY V. HARBERT.
2. ELLA M., wife of Howard Hamilton, of Philadelphia. Issue.

JOHN ELLET had by his second wife:
JUDGE HENRY T. ELLET, of Memphis, Tenn., M. C., who m., first, Rebecca Champneys, daughter of Elias P. Seeley, Governor of New Jersey, and m., secondly, Kate S., daughter of John B. Coleman, of Mississippi. Issue:
I. JANE S., m. Dr. Richard B. Maury. Issue.
II. JOSEPH R. ELLET, m. Laura Brantley. Issue.
III. KATE C., m. Evan Shelby Jeffries. Issue.
IV. HENRY T.; V. JOHN E.; VI. EDWARD C.; VII. SARAH E.; VIII. RICHARD MAURY.

II. CHARLES ELLET, of Salem, N. J., b. 1777; d. 1847; m., 1801, Mary, daughter of Israel Israel, Sheriff of Philadelphia County, Pa., and had:
I. JOHN ISRAEL ELLET, of Atchison, Kas., m., first, Laura Scarritt, and m., secondly, Mary Skillman. By his first wife he had:
COLONEL JOHN A. ELLET, of Boulder, Col., who m. Elizabeth K. Church, and had:
1. LAURA; 2. CHARLES LIPPINCOTT.

JOHN I. ELLET had by his second wife:
I. CHARLES; II. HENRY; III. WINTHROP C.; IV. ANNE.
V. RICHARD S. ELLET, m. Bettie Cullen. Issue: ALFRED.
VI. ARTHUR; VII. ALFRED.

2. ALFRED W. ELLET, of Eldorado, Kas., Brigadier-General, U. S. Volunteers, who had by his first wife, Sarah J. Robarts, of Philadelphia, who d. 1875:
    I. DR. EDWARD C. ELLET, of Bunker Hill, Ill., m. Fannie Van Dorn. Issue.
    II. WILLIAM H. ELLET. Issue.
    III. ELVIRA A., wife of Charles J. Kendall. Issue.

3. CHARLES ELLET, b. 1810; d. from wound received in battle at Memphis, 1862; m. Elvira A., daughter of Judge William Daniels, of Lynchburg, Va., and had:
    I. DR. CHARLES RIVERS ELLET, Lieutenant-Colonel, U. S. Volunteers, d. s. p., 1863.
    II. MARY V., m. William Cabell, of Virginia. Issue.
    III. CORNELIA E., d. unm.; IV. WILLIAM D.

4. HANNAH ELLET, d. 1847, who m. George C. Hale, and had:
    MARY ANN, m. Cleaveland M. Crandell.

5. MARY, d. s. p., 1834, wife of James Bailey.

6. ELIZA ELLET, who m. George S. Bryan, and had:
    MARY E., d. s. p., 1869, wife of Robert Albree, of Pittsburg, Pa.

7. DR. EDWARD C. ELLET, of Alton, Ill. Issue:

III. RACHEL C. ELLET, b. 1780, d. 1855; m. James Wainwright, of Maryland, and had:
    1. THOMAS B. WAINWRIGHT, of Pittsburg, Pa., m. Emily Watson, and had:
        I. JOHN WATSON, d. s. p.; II. RACHEL, d. unm.; III. SARAH E., d. unm.
        IV. CAROLINE, m. Hiram Kimball.
        V. ALICE, m. Arthur Miller, of Philadelphia, and had:

Lloyd of Dolobran. 351

    1. WILLIAM HARTSHORNE; 2. ARTHUR; 3. LLEWELLYN W.
  2. WILLIAM J. WAINWRIGHT, of Philadelphia, d. 1869; m. Sarah Church, and had:
    I. ALICE; II. SALLIE E.
  3. JAMES E. WAINWRIGHT, of San Francisco, d. 1869; m. Mary Delaney, of Delaware, and had:
    I. MARY; II. CHARLES L.
IV. SARAH, d. s. p., wife of Joseph Reeve, of Salem, N. J.
V. WILLIAM ELLET, of New York, d. 1836, m. Elizabeth Taggert, of New Jersey, and had:
  1. SARAH ANN ELLET, d. unm.
  2. PROFESSOR WILLIAM H. ELLET, M. D., d. 1859; m. Elizabeth Fries, daughter of Dr. William N. Lummis, of New York.
  3. CHARLES ELLET, of New York, k. 1868.

DEBORAH LLOYD, daughter of Thomas Lloyd, married, 1704, Dr. Mordecai Moore, of Anne Arundel County, Maryland, as his 2nd wife, and had:

DEBORAH MOORE, b. 1705; d. 1751; m., 1720, Dr. Richard Hill, of Hill's Point, Md., b. 1698; d., Funchal, 1762, and had:

MARGARET HILL, b. 1737; d. 1816; m., 1758, William Morris, of Philadelphia, d. 1766, and had:

  1. GULIELMA MARIA MORRIS, b. 1766; d. 1826; m., 1784, John Smith, of "Green Hill," Philadelphia, b. 1761; d. 1803.

  2. RICHARD HILL MORRIS, of Philadelphia, d. 1841; m., second, 1798, Mary, d. 1848, daughter of Richard S. Smith, of Burlington, N. J., and had:

    I. WILLIAM HENRY MORRIS, of Philadelphia, b. 1799; d. 1846; m. Margaret Edwards Maris, ot Bucks County, Pa., and had:

      1. MARTHA MOORE MORRIS, d. 1870, who m. William Gummeré, of Burlington, N. J., and had:

  I. RICHARD MORRIS GUMMERE, Bethlehem, Pa., m. Elizabeth Hunt, and had: REBECCA H. and WILLIAM.
  II. MARGARET MORRIS GUMMERE, unm.
  III. FRANCES MARSH GUMMERE, who m. James Craig Perrine, of Trenton, d. 1879, and had: MARTHA G.
  IV. WILLIAM HENRY GUMMERE, of Burlington, N. J.
 2. ELIZABETH MARIS MORRIS, who m. Dillwyn Smith, of Burlington, N. J.
 3. JANE M. MORRIS, who m., 1865, Francis William Milnor, of Burlington, N. J. Issue: THOMAS W.

II. EDMUND MORRIS, of Burlington, b. 1804; d. 1874; m., 1827, Mary P., d. 1876, daughter of William Jenks, and had:
 1. ANNA MARGRETTA MORRIS, d. 1876, who m., 1849, Rev. Marcus F. Hyde, D. D., of Burlington, N. J.; d. 1880, and had:
  PROFESSOR EDMUND MORRIS HYDE, of Chester, Pa.
 2. ELLEN A., m. George Dugdale. Issue: HORACE C.
 3. MARY ANN MORRIS, m., 5 November, 1863, Alexander Fergusson, of Philadelphia, and had:
  I. EDMUND M.; II. AGNES M.; III. HENRY A.; IV. MARY M.; V. ALEXANDER C.; VI. HELEN.
 4. HENRY BURLING MORRIS, of Ithaca, N. Y., m., first, 1867, Anne B. Knapp; m., second, 1879, Florence A. Dowe. Issue:
  I. EDMUND; II. SAMUEL TRACY KNAPP; III. HAROLD B.

III. CHARLES MOORE MORRIS, of Philadelphia, b. 1810; m., 1831, Anna, daughter of William Jenks, of Bucks County, Pa., and had:

1. WILLIAM JENKS MORRIS, m., 1858, Anna M., daughter of Sterne Humphreys. Issue:
2. MARY ANNA, wife of Sanderson R. Martin. Issue.

3. DR. JOHN MORRIS, of Philadelphia, b. 1759; d. 1793; m., 1783, Abigail Dorsey; d. 1793, and had:
    I. MARTHA MILCAH MORRIS, d. 1826, who m., 1809, first, Thomas Lawrie, and m., secondly, 1821, Jacob B. Clark.

The Woodnutt-Griscom Branch.

MARGARET CARPENTER, dau. Preston Carpenter, m., 1776, James Mason Woodnutt, of Salem, N. J., and had:
1. HANNAH WOODNUTT, m. Clement Acton, of Salem, N. J., and had:
    I. CLEMENT J. ACTON, of Cincinnati, m. Mary, daughter of Colonel John Noble, of Columbus, Ohio, and had:
        1. MARGARET W., m. Augustus W. Durkee, of New York.
        2. LILLIE, m. Frank K. Hickok, of New York. Issue.
    II. MARGARET W. ACTON, m. Dr. John D. Griscom, of Philadelphia, and had:
        1. CLEMENT ACTON GRISCOM, of Philadelphia and Dolobran, Pa., m. Frances Canby Biddle[1]. Issue:
            I. HELEN B.; II. CLEMENT A.; III. RODMAN E.; IV. LLOYD C.; V. FRANCES C.
        2. HANNAH W., m. Frank L. Neall, of Philadelphia. Issue:
        3. WILLIAM WOODNUTT GRISCOM, of Philadelphia, m. Dora Ingham Hale.
2. MARGARET WOODNUTT, m. Judge William J. Shinn, of Salem, N. J., and had:

---

[1] Mrs. Griscom is descended from Owen Biddle, son of John, by a daughter of Owen Owen, Esq., son of Robert Owen, of Merion.

  I. MARY, m. Dr. Thomas Reed, of Philadelphia. Issue.
  II. MARTHA, m. Dr. Isaiah D. Clawson, M. C., of New Jersey. Issue.
3. MARTHA, m. Joshua Reeves, of Salem. Issue.
4. MARY, m. Benjamin Newlin, of Pennsylvania.
5. JONATHAN WOODNUTT, m., first, Mary Goodwin; m., secondly, Sarah Dennis. Issue:
  I. RICHARD WOODNUTT, m. Lydia Hall. Issue.
  II. WILLIAM WOODNUTT, m. Elizabeth Bassett. Issue.
  III. THOMAS WOODNUTT, m. Hannah Morgan. Issue.
  IV. MARY, wife of Edward A. Acton. Issue.
6. PRESTON WOODNUTT, m. Rachel Goodwin, and had:
  I. ELIZABETH, m. Annesly Newlin. Issue.
  II. JAMES M. WOODNUTT, m. Elizabeth Denn. Issue.
  III. EDWARD; IV. PRESTON C.
  V. HANNAH ANN, m. Nathan Baker. Issue.
7. ELIZABETH, m. Morris Hall, of Salem, N. J. Issue.

NOTE.—The above notes of the descendants of the Lloyds of Dolobran are from the *Lloyd-Carpenter Genealogy*, by Smith; from C. P. Keith's *Provincial Councillors of Pennsylvania;* and from data furnished by descendants. The lines are incomplete, and are only intended to show the ramification of some branches. The author assumes no responsibility beyond accuracy in transcribing.

BROOKE AND MORGAN FAMILIES.

In Colonial days Gulph Mills was the terminus of the main highway leading from Philadelphia through Merion Township, but prior to the Revolutionary period, the Gulph itself produced but little now of interest, even to the local historian. It marked, indeed, in very primitive times, the boundary between well cared for plantations and a hilly wilderness.

The mills early established here were not the first in the Great Welsh Tract, for we know that those erected by John Roberts in the picturesque valley of the Mill Creek, a mile or so north of Ardmore, and called by him "Wayn Mills," and that built by Rowland Powell upon Darby Creek, in Haverford, antedate them many years. One Joseph Williams, a Welshman, appears as overseer and operator of the early Gulph mills. As years rolled by the superior location and fine water supply tempted others to locate here, and among these was Benjamin Brooke.

It had been the privilege of this man to serve in General Washington's army. After the termination of the struggle for Independence he established an extensive forge at the Gulph, where he, "by improved machinery, greatly increased the value of the screw auger and cheapened its price. With equal vigor and success he took hold of the scythe, sickle, spade and shovel making, and the forging round iron by water-power, with other branches of smithing and cutlery ——. Previously the supply had been almost wholly from England."

This is but another illustration of the effect of Welsh blood and Welsh brains, for many of Benjamin Brooke's ancestors were of Cymric lineage, although the direct ancestry was English.

The first of the family in America was one JOHN BROOKE, who came from Yorkshire and settled in the County of Gloucester, in the Province of West New Jersey, where he died at the house of William Cooper, in 1699. Will dated 25th of 8th month, 1699, proved 1st of March, 1699–1700. According to this will he had issue : Jonathan, James, Mathew, Abigail, who married Robert Todd, and Elizabeth, who married Joshua Sirbey.

The eldest son Jonathan (who had George), and the two daughters were living in England in 1699. His will shows him to have been quite a wealthy man for his day.

He mentions " seven hundred and fifty acres of land which I bought of William Penn, lying and being in ye Province of Pensilvenia, between Sasquehanna & Delaware, which I bought jointly with Thomas Musgrove." His personal estate amounted to the respectable sum of £200, 15s., 02d., equal to several thousand dollars of our money. The will is witnessed by *John Kay, executor*, William Cooper, Hannah Cooper and Sarah Canthrog. The inventory was made 6th of 12th month, 1699, by John Dale and Thomas Sharp. His wife's name is said to have been Frances.

JAMES BROOKE, the son of John, died in 1720. The family had now removed to Limerick, and JONATHAN BROOKE, son of James, married Elizabeth Reece, a Welsh woman, and died in 1751 (will proved 8, 11, 1751), leaving a son named JAMES BROOKE, born 1723 ; died 6th month, 1787, having married Mary Evans, also of Cymric lineage. His son was Benjamin Brooke, who established the Forge at the Gulph. BENJAMIN BROOKE was born in Limerick, 9th month 24th, 1753, and died at his residence at the Gulph Mills, Upper Merion, 7th month 22, 1834. He married, 25th of 4th month, 1776, Anna Davis (she was of Welsh descent and was born 11th month 29th, 1754; died 9th month 7th, 1823). Benjamin Brooke was a man of very considerable energy and force of character and an uncompromising patriot. Upon the breaking out of the Revolutionary War he volunteered his services in the field, which were accepted, and in March, 1776, we find that Benjamin Brooke, gentleman, was commissioned a Lieutenant of a company of foot in the Third Battalion of Associators in the County of Philadelphia, by the Assembly, John

RESIDENCE OF BENJAMIN BROOKE, AT GULPH MILLS.

Morton, speaker. From this time until the close of the war, years later, his sword was never sheathed. " On the eve of the Revolution he had just commenced life as the head of a family. He embarked in his country's camp with all the energy of his character. Through every stage of the struggle he stood faithful to his principles and his duty to his country. In '76 he left a promising business to lead a company of his fellow citizens to Amboy. Among the sacrifices and sufferings of that trying period was the loss of his previously acquired property."

Thus did this brave man risk his life and fortune for the cause of Liberty and his sacred honor. On the 12th of May, 1777, he was commissioned Captain of a company of foot in the Sixth Battalion of Militia, in the County of Philadelphia; " In the name and by the authority of the Freemen of the Commonwealth of Pennsylvania."

Benjamin Brooke had a son, NATHAN BROOKE, of Lower Merion, born 2, 8, 1778; died 2, 5, 1815, who married 10, 11, 1804, Mary, daughter of Hugh Jones, and had, HUGH JONES BROOKE, of Radnor, born 12, 27, 1805; died 12, 19, 1876; married 4, 16, 1829, Jemima Elizabeth Longmire, of Nottingham, England, and had, FRANCIS MARK BROOKE, born 7, 4, 1836; married 7, 19, 1862, Adelaide Hunter Vogdes (born 2, 11, 1840; died 11, 25, 1888). She was a lineal descendant of Anthony Wayne, grandfather of General Wayne.[1]

Hugh Jones, above mentioned, was born in Merion 3, 12, 1748, and died in Maple 12, 29, 1796. He married 2, 11, 1777, Mary Hunter, of Radnor (born 11, 12, 1757; died 8, 20, 1820), daughter of James Hunter, of Radnor, and Hannah Morgan, his wife, of whom presently.

Hugh Jones was the son of Hugh Jones, of Merion, born 1705; died 8, 8, 1790, and Mary, his wife. This Hugh Jones was the owner of the property known as " Brookfield," north of Bryn Mawr, and now owned by Wayne MacVeagh, Esq.

---

[1]The author is under obligation to Francis Mark Brooke, Esq., of Philadelphia, for some of the above and other information, some of which unfortunately, on account of want of space, it was impossible to use.

He had originally purchased a part of the Lloyd plantation and subsequently increased his holdings until they included nearly seven hundred acres. He was the son of another Hugh Jones, born say circa 1675, doubtless the same person who bought land in this spot in 1700, and possibly brother to Robert Jones. This family, however, is not to be confused with Hugh Jones, alias Hugh John Thomas, of Merion, one of the Merioneth Adventurers, who afterwards removed from Merion to Plymouth, and then died. Hannah Morgan, above referred to, was the daughter of John Morgan, of Vaenor, Radnor. His plantation is now the property of his descendant, Miss Martha Brown, of Radnor.

John Morgan, "gentleman," settled in Radnor very early, and married Sarah Jones, daughter of John Evans, of the Parish of Nantmell, or Nantmele, in Radnorshire, "gentleman," who died in Radnor Township, Pennsylvania, in November, 1707, leaving issue two sons, Rees and Thomas Jones, and a wife Dalila, and daughters, Sarah, aforesaid, wife of John Morgan, Jane, Margaret, wife of Hugh Samuel, and Phœbe, wife of Edward David. John Evans came about 1683, and was born circa 1640.

The Samuel Brooke Branch.

Samuel Brooke, the son of James, the son of the emigrant, John, removed to Radnor in 1771, having purchased of Moses Roberts a tract of land lying about half a mile east of old St. David's Church. He had removed from Limerick to Plymouth in 1758. On going to Radnor they lived for a short time in a log house that was on the property; commencing almost on arrival the building of a substantial house and barn.

The following entries, in the handwriting of Samuel, are on the margins of his almanacs:

"April 10th, 1771, we hauled the first lode to Radnor.

May the 7 day, 1771, Begun the new house at Radnor, that is the masons, the carpenters Began May the 9th day, 1771.

May the first we moved to Radnor, 1771.

August the 16 day, 1771, the masons finished my house.

August 19 day, 1771, we moved in our new house at Radnor. Began the Barn the 17 of the above said month."

The following entry is of the same time: "2730 nails left for the barn." The modern builder would count his nails, not by units, but by kegs; but then each nail was hammered out and headed by hand.

A small forge (tilt mill) was erected on the Radnor place some time before the end of the last century, just when is not known. An old account-book commences January 26th, 1798, at which time the mill was evidently in full blast. The writer has heard his father speak of it as being in operation during the last war with England, at which time certain military equipments were made. The power was obtained from Little Darby Creek, the water being carried nearly half a mile by a large ditch. This ditch is nearly perfect to-day. The foundations of the building, and the pit which was blasted in the rock, for the water-wheel, are easily traced.

The articles manufactured about the end of the last century (at which time John, the son of Samuel, had the forge) appear to have been chiefly skates and spades. The following is an entry in the account-book:

"Thomas Hockley to Jno. Brooke, Dr.

1798	£.	s.	d.
Feby. 2nd, to 20 pairs of Skates 7-6	8.	10.	0
May 19, to 9 doz Spades	33.	15.	0
to 16 pair Skates	6.	04.	0
1799, to 11 pairs Skates	4.	05.	3
Jan'y 8, to 64 pairs Skates	24.	16.	0
Feb'y 2, to 111 pair Skates at 8-	44.	8.	0
May 7, to 3 doz. Spades	11.	5.	0"

The credit side of this account appears curious at the present time. Fifteen cash entries are made in *English currency;* the next is as follows:

"1801, April & May, Jane Clay Rec'd of T. Hockley for me, at 3 different times, 75 dollars and one French crown.

¹The functions performed by John Brooke were various, as will be seen from the following entries:

"Ezra and Gideon Thomas, Dr.

1802	£.	s.	d.
October 22, to Surveying	1.	2.	6.
Do 26, to writing will for Hezekiah Thomas	1.	10.	0."

"Sam'l Stirk to John Brooke, Dr.

1808	£.	s.	d.
Novem'r 28 & 29, to surveying road on the line dividing Easttown and Radnor Townships,	3.	0.	0."

The compass and chain with which these surveys were made are in the possession of the surveyor's grandson. The compass bears the maker's name, David Rittenhouse.

---

¹Cotton gins, or parts of them, were at one time made at the forge. The writer has heard his father speak of one occasion within his recollection when the mill was kept running night and day to complete a gin in time to ship it on a vessel that was to sail from Philadelphia on a given date for Charleston.

Samuel Brooke appears to have abjured the creed of his ancestors, who were Quakers. An entry by him on the margin of a leaf in his Bible states that he "was born April the 15 day, 1717, and Baptised March the Second 1739, and became a member of the Church of England." The Bible referred to is a folio, printed in 1715; where, it is not stated. One of the entries reads: "I Samuel Brooke bought this Bible in Philadelphia November the 17 Day 1747. The price of it was four pounds and ten shillings, but because it was the last the shop keeper had I had it for four pound."

The following entry appears in this Bible. The given name is, unfortunately, illegible: "——— Howell, A Soldier in Colonel Morgan's Riffle, born ———, and was buried May 18, 1778, In Radnor Churchyard, by his son, Vincent Howell."

Samuel Brooke was born April 15, 1717, probably at Limerick, Pa., and died at Radnor, January 18, 1797. He married Margaret Davis April 10th, 1739. She was the daughter, or possibly the granddaughter, of William Davis, at whose house services were held by Rev. Evan Evans, from 1700 to 1704. There also the preliminary services were held on the day on which the corner-stone of the present church edifice was laid, the procession marching thence to the site of the church.

Samuel had four sons: David, born June 17th, 1742; died May 2d, 1811.

John, born June 2d, 1749; died October 21st, 1828.

Samuel, born June 25th, 1752; date of death not known.

Jesse, born January 25, 1760; date of death not known. He was born "in the new stile, all the rest were born in the old stile."

John Brooke inherited the Radnor property and lived on it until his death, when it passed to his son Jesse. Later it was purchased by Benjamin, the son of Jesse, and remained in his possession until 1891. John had two sons and two daughters: Jesse, born October 4th, 1793; died August 14th, 1868. Benjamin, born December 7th, 1795; died (without issue) September 2d, 1817. Margaret, born June 7th, 1799; died September 14, 1841. She became the wife of Adam Siter. Rebecca, born December 17th, 1806; died November, 1841.[1]

Samuel, his son John, and the deceased descendants of the latter in direct line, five generations in all, are buried in the churchyard at old St. Davids.

David probably remained in Plymouth, as it is recorded that he "was buried in Friends' burying-ground in Plymouth."

Samuel, son of Samuel, had four sons and one daughter. John, who operated a large marble quary in Upper Merion;

---

[1] John was contemporary with General Wayne, and knew him well. The wife of John was a Norton, whose ancestors had lived near the Wayne estate in County Wicklow, one of them being a member of Wayne's troop at the battle of the Boyne.

THE MORGAN HOUSE, RADNOR, PA.

Charles, Elijah, well known throughout this portion of the State; Samuel, and Margaret.

Jesse, son of Samuel, established a flour mill on Ithan Creek, near the Haverford line. He had ten children: Davis, Samuel, Alexander, Jesse, John, Margaret, Mary, Eleanor, Elizabeth and Anna.

Jesse succeeded his father at the mill, and was known as "Miller Jesse," in contradistinction from his cousin, who was known as "Church Jesse."

Partly from their near residence to the church, Samuel, John, or the descendants of the latter, were prominent in the affairs of old St. David's for nearly a century. John superintended the reroofing of the church early in the present century, and also the erection of horse-blocks. In one of his account-books there is a charge, dated 1811, against "Radnor church congregation," of the cost of thirty bushels of lime and eight dollars in cash paid a mason, "for work at horse-blocks and chimney tops." The building of the old parsonage, in 1844, was supervised by Jesse. The writer has a distinct recollection of seeing him, Benjamin Brooke, the son of Nathan, and the Rev. Wilie Peck, rector of the church, busily engaged in staking out the foundation lines for the house, and at the same time having a lively discussion on the merits of mesmerism, then a prominent fad.

NOTE.—The author is indebted to Dr. Brooke, U. S. N., for the above data. Dr. Brooke resides at Radnor, near the home of his ancestors.

MILES, EVANS, BROOKE.

"JAMES MILES, daughter of SAMUEL & wife (MARGARET JAMES), was the first white child born in Radnor. She was born on the land now owned by Mary Lewis (widow), where the present house stands, but not in it, on the 21st day of Eighth-month, 1687; married Thomas Thomas, of Radnor; died 27th Eighth-month, 1770. Entered at Radnor on the 28th day of the month; lived in matrimonial covenant with Thomas Thomas 62 years & 3 months. She was known of a Sunday morning to walk a half mile to milk her cows, return, get breakfast for the family, after which she would walk to Philadelphia to Friends' Quarterly Meeting and return home the same day. Her daughter, wife of Nathan Lewis, lived on the property late Eli Lewis's, at this time James Miles lived at the old mansion where the large Holly Tree stands, now Levi Lewis's mill (grist mill, since Tryon Lewis's). She would milk her cows at 5 o'clock of an evening, walk a distance of three miles, always limiting the time to one hour to go on a visit and the same to return. The late Eli Lewis was her grandson. Her visits to her daughter, Margaret Lewis, were as far back as 1731, and known to us as late as 1753.

"This daughter, and the only one, visited Great Britain twice as a public Friend. During one of her visits to a friend in the City of London, was taken into a room to see a sight, which proved to be an ear of Indian corn, when she informed her friends that there was much of it grown in Pennsylvania. Inquiry was made how it was used, when she informed them that the grain ground into fine meal, sifted through a sieve and well boiled, was eaten with milk. Nothing but a trial would satisfy, and Margaret had her son Levi Lewis, who was then miller at his grandfather's, Thomas Thomas, mills (and since known as Levi Lewis's mill), to prepare and send a bag of meal to London friends. How it was cooked and relished the present writer does not recollect any tradition thereof; this took place about 1735. The Holley tree spoken of was found about one mile in a northeasterly course from where it stands on ground General Washington's picket garde occupied during the winter of 1777-8."

James & Ruth Miles were children of Samuel & Margaret Miles, who came from Wales in 1682, with William Penn.

James Miles was borne on the 21st of 8th mo., 1687.

Ruth Miles (wife of Owen Evans and mother of Amos Evans) was born on the 28th of 1st month, 1693.

Amos Evans (who married Elizabeth Lewis) was born in 4th month, 1721.

SAMUEL MILES, the Emigrant, Samuel Miles, of the Parish of Hamhanghobyeholgen in the County of Radnor, Old Wales, Great Britain, married his wife, Margaret James, at the Parish of New Church, in the house of Ann Thomas, on the 25th of 4th month, 1682.

Arrived in Pennsylvania Eight-mo., 1682. (October.)

Form of Samuel Miles' marriage:

The meeting being ready to depart the said Samuel Miles and Margaret James stood up. Samuel spoke these words (in the Welsh tongue): friends and people who or may witness this thing, that is I take Margaret James (taking her by the right hand) to wife in the fear of God before you all, to love her and to comfort her and to live together in what condition soever always God to bring us into as it behoveth a Christian.

And her the said Margaret James in like manner said these words (in the Welsh tongue); likewise friends I take this said Samuel Miles (taking him by the right hand) to be my (here the words differed) husband, to love and obey him as long as it pleases God, giving life and living on this world.

OWEN EVANS, son of Amos & Elizabeth. Evans was born on the 18th of 4th mo., 1746.

Mary Evans was born on the 5th of 10-mo., 1747.

Ruth Evans was born on 28th of 10-mo., 1749.

Ann Evans was born the 2d of 2d mo., 1752; married Dr. Davis, of
Lydia Evans was born 23d of 10-mo., 1754.
Rebecca Evans was born 4th of the 6-mo., 1757.
Hannah Evans was born on the 29th 8-mo., 1759. She married George Brooke, of Limerick, and was my grandmother, they being the parents of Owen Brooke, of Radnor, my father, and it is from her we inherit our Welsh blood. Her sister Roselinda, married a Willing.

H. E. BROOKE.

THE MERION MEETING.

Few Colonial churches in Pennsylvania are of such importance as the Merion Meeting-House of Friends. It is claimed, indeed, that so far as the antiquity of the edifice is concerned no place of worship of any other denomination in this state dates back to such a remote period. The mere precise age of the walls, however, although of passing interest to the local historian, does not compare in real historic value to the study of the influence which the builders of this meeting exerted, and through their numerous descendants have since commanded, in the Judiciary, Legislature, medical science, literature and industrial achievements of this Commonwealth. All of the famous cathedrals of Europe, Reims, St. Denys, the Pantheon, the Valhalla of Germany, Santa Croce in Florence, and the English Abbey of Westminster, are crowded with monuments to the illustrious dead, each stacked with trophies, armorial bearings, and all that grotesque imagination has given to art. Yet all such splendor and boast of heraldry, by very reason of its sumptuous ostentation, often alienates our reverence for the persons thus distinguished. It is not so easy, in any of those majestic churches, to lift the veil which separates us from the past, as it is, whilst standing upon the burial plot of the Merion Meeting, to bring ourselves face to face with the lives of the founders whose bones lie mouldering beneath the leveled turf, in unmarked and unremembered graves.

It would, perhaps, be well, before recording the early story of this place, to consider what manner of men were these who rest here forgotten, but in peace and honor. They were, as you know, the first settlers of all this fine country, the planters of the Great Welsh Barony, the founders of Merion, and of the townships of Haverford and Radnor. They were members of the only organized bodies of colonists on Pennsylvania soil that, without any exception, sprang from gentle blood. They

THE MERION MEETING.

came hither to seek, in the primeval forest, that freedom to worship God which a weak government and fanatical public had denied them at home. They were conscientious and consistent enemies of strife and oppression, humble disciples, according to the inner light, of the ancient Christians, followers of the truth. These were the men who builded here, under the shadow of the vasty oaks, after the manner of their ancestral Druid priests, this monument to Religious Liberty. Think for a moment how bitter, at first, must have been the struggle in the innermost hearts of these Cymric Quakers against the inherent instincts of the fierce and war-like race from whence they sprang.

They were descended from a people to whom battle and murder and sudden death had always been familiar, and even common place. Not a few of their forefathers had been famous soldiers—men, before whose pitiless lance the foeman went down at the waft of death, as drift-wood is whirled before the floods of spring. Yet here, in their Meeting, the early Welsh settlers taught their children the arts of peace, and, unconquered by the old warlike traits, lived and died in love with all men and beloved by them.

It is, however, true that in after years, when the Revolution rolled to the confines of Merion Township, the martial spirit of the ancient Britons stirred the soul of their Quaker descendants, and the trumpet's peal called out the Cymry once more to the squares of battle, for "where Freedom's aid's invoked there will the Briton die." How these sons of Merion and adjoining townships distinguished themselves in the war of Independence is a matter of history, but it is certain that no descendant of the founders is now a member of the old meeting.

That a building, presumably of logs, existed upon the site of the present edifice so early as 1683 cannot for a moment be doubted, nor does the writer find anything to disprove that the first *stone* building was erected in 1695, as currently believed. So far as Friends' Records are concerned the items bearing upon the subject are few and far from satisfactory.

At the recent Bi-Centennial Celebration of the Merion Meeting, Mary J. Walker narrated in a concise manner all that she could gather from papers in the possession of Friends regarding the building of the meeting-house. So far as the archives of the Society go, the writer has found little of additional interest or historic value bearing upon the point in question. After referring to the early history of the township, Miss Walker said:

"From the minutes kept by women Friends, we have 'eight shillings paid for cleaning Merion meeting-house 12th of Twelfth-month, 1695,' and for several successive years there is a similar entry.

"While it is true that the *Monthly* Meeting minutes say certain favors were granted in 1713, for *finishing* Merion Meeting-house, it is also true that as early as 1702 the minutes of the *Preparative* Meeting tell of *finishing* and *furnishing* Merion meeting-house, of providing hinges, locks, shutters, and benches (they seem desirous to 'secure' the meeting-house), and in 1703 Friends are requested to pay their subscription towards building the *addition* to the meeting-house. 'On the 19th day of Third-month, vulgarly called May, in the year *1693*, in a solemn and public assembly, in their (Friends') public meeting-place at Merion,' was solemnized a marriage. May not this 'public meeting-place' have been the temporary log structure, and the present building been commenced in 1695, as the ancient stone in the gable testifies, and finally completed in 1713? That the most of the present building was erected in 1713 is evident from a paper recently found containing the names of subscribers and the amount contributed in *that year, for building* the meeting-house."

In addition to this it may be added that, according to family records, a marriage was performed in Merion Meeting-House 20th of 1st month, 1684. From the above data we gather that there certainly was a meeting-house of logs here so early as 1683, so that the only question to be decided is, when was the stone building erected? The tablet set into the northwest gable, but formerly facing the road now known as Montgomery Avenue, bears the date "*1695.*" Let us see how far actual facts will bear out the statement of this ancient stone.

First, as to the location of the meeting-house, we have a record of the selection of this site for a burial place for Friends, upon report of a committee, soon after April, 1684. This place, was chosen, probably, because several of the earlier settlers, as well as some members of the family of Edward Rees (alias Prees or Price) were already interred at or near this spot. The convenient location was also, doubtless, an element in the consideration of this lot.

It was, indeed, easily reached from various parts of the township, and from Haverford and Radnor.

The old Gulph Road, leading from Philadelphia to the Gulph Mills at Upper Merion, passed by here at a very early date after the first settlement, and could be reached by bridle-paths, then existing, from the principal highways of the adjoining townships. The Welsh were careful, as we have observed elsewhere, to build good roads immediately after their arrival, and the "Towns" of Haverford and Radnor were to be reached from Philadelphia by "Haverford Street," projected in 1683, and "Radnor Street," surveyed in the same year. The Haverford and Darby road was laid out on 7th of 12th month, 1687, and the Radnor and Chester road, 20th of 2nd month, 1691. The old Haverford road leading to John Bevan's plantation, Henry Lewis's, Ralph Lewis's, and others, was established 12th October, 1704.

An early road leading toward Merion from Radnor, was that surveyed in 1694.

The information concerning the highways of Merion is not so exact, but there can be no doubt that the first road, on the bed of the "Old Gulph," was made in 1683.

Entering Merion from Blockley below the Merion Line, this old way extended towards what is now called Libertyville, thence past the plantation of Robert Owen, now the estate of the late Colonel Jones, it wound through Mill Creek, past Wayn Mills, belonging to John Roberts, the miller, and thence north and west by a ford over Mill Creek to the present Pyle's Mill, thence through "Harriton," then Bryn Mawr, Rowland Ellis' plantation, passing near the residences of Robert and Thomas Lloyd, to the Gulph.

What we are accustomed to call Montgomery Avenue or Lancaster Road, extending from High Street, Philadelphia, to Lancaster, was formerly known as the old Conestoga Road, but was not confirmed until 1721, and then only to Brandywine. There was also, at a very early date, a road leading

almost direct from Merion Meeting to Haverford Meeting-House. In 1785 a road was petitioned for, and allowed from Levering's Ford, on the Schuylkill, to the Conestoga Road, with which it connected at the corner of the meeting-house lot. It is said that Haverford Township was in very early days reached from the settlement near Pencoyd by a bridle-path along the line of the Liberty Lands, north of Blockley, on the site of the present City Avenue.

This, doubtless, intersected the Gulph road, and is said to have been originally an Indian trail, but it seems more plausible that it was the old Swede path, leading from the Delaware settlements to those on the Schuylkill, and may even have been one of the roads erected by the agents of the Dutch West India Company at a very early period.

Although some of these roads were not confirmed until late years, yet they all existed at the time of the first settlement as rights of way by mutual consent, and came, by continual use, to be public highways.

We mention these facts in order to show how central and convenient for a Çolonial place of worship was the site selected for the Merion Meeting-House.

It is the opinion of the writer that a shelter of rough logs was immediately erected during the Fall of 1683, and probably prior to Penn's arrival, and continued to serve as a place of worship until the year 1695.

There had then, indeed, been many changes in old Merioneth Township since the day that Dr. Edward Jones landed his company of Quaker Adventurers. Men of standing in their native country had joined the settlement, and their wealth and influence already began to be noticeable. One of these later colonists was Robert Owen, of Fron Gôch, who arrived in 1690 with his wife and family. This man was a minister of recognized ability in Wales, and not only of considerable reputation amongst the Quakers, but also well known to other denominations, by whom, for his integrity and ability, he was much loved and esteemed. Upon his arrival in the Barony he was hailed as a leader in every enterprise undertaken by his countrymen, and is called one of their "chiefs" in documents of that day.

NOTE.—" The following account concerning him was furnished by an ancient worthy Friend, now (1716) living, viz.: Eleanor Evans, daughter of Rowland Ellis and widow of John Evans, of Gwynedd."

" Robert Owen was born near a town called Bala, in Merionethshire, North Wales. He was a man of good natural abilities, and had something so mild, humane and engaging in his temper and disposition that he was beloved and esteemed by all who knew him.

" The first effectual reach he had from God, as he related himself, was on this occasion. His father, whom he dearly loved, being sick, nigh unto death, he often implored God for his recovery; but his father died, and he, taking a walk into the fields to vent his grief, began to query with himself why his prayers were

It is certainly to this man, preëminently, that we owe the present Merion Meeting. By his untiring energy and self-sacrifice the spot became a stronghold of Quakerism in Pennsylvania and the principal place of worship in the Welsh Tract at that time; a position which it continued to occupy for many years.

In 1695 Robert Owen decided to erect a new and commodious dwelling for his family in place of the temporary shelter which, until this year, had served as his residence. The erection of a stone house in those days was a momentous event. Masons and carpenters had to be brought from the city and lodged with the family until the work was completed. Quarries must be opened, and lime hauled from the kilns then in operation further up the Schuylkill; timbers had to be shaped from the giant trees of the forest, and nails and bolts forged at the nearest smith's shop. The stone which Robert Owen used for his dwelling, in 1695, was quarried on his own plantation from a peculiar vein of sandstone which, extending through Merion from the southeast to the northwest, cropped out there. The walls of the oldest part of the Merion Meeting-House, namely the northwest end, are of this stone, and, so far as can be ascertained, under the present modern rough-cast on the outside, the original plaster used is of the same composition as that in the Owen house. The manner of laying the walls and the general workmanship of the oldest part appear to be identical. We should, therefore, conclude that the work was done at the same time as Robert Owen's home, whilst the mechanics were in the neighborhood, and that the other parts were added as the meeting increased in wealth.

---

not heard, his earnest request for his father's life not answered. It presently occurred to him that God heareth not sinners.

"On that he instantly turned his face the way his back was, crying out in the anguish of his soul, 'So I turn, I turn to thee, O God.' A happy turn it proved to him, for some time after he came among Friends, and the testimonies God gave him to lean to his name, dropped as the rain, and distilled as the dew.

"He came with his wife and family to Pennsylvania about the year 1690, and lived there several years, where it was well known his services to the church and his country were of consideration. He lived, died and was buried in Merion."

The above from the Lives of Ministers of the Gospel Among the People called Quakers, Vol. II, MS., in Library of Haverford College, now deposited in the Friends' Library, Philadelphia.

THE RADNOR MEETING, PA.

The Merion Meeting. 371

The first transfer of land recorded, was, it will be remembered, in 1695, 20th of 6th month, from Edward Rees, for one-half acre of land, the consideration being a few shillings. This conveyance was an actual deed, and passed the title to the land, for the uses of the Merion Meeting, and was not a lease, as stated by several writers.

The trustees at that time were Robert Owen, Edward Jones, Cadwalader Morgan and Thomas Jones. Other property was added to the meeting by gift of Joseph Tunis, in 1763, and in 1801 and also in 1804 by John Dickinson. Of late years Joseph and John George and very recently Edward Price, have left liberal bequests for the maintenance of the meeting.

Haverford Meeting-House, says Smith, was built between 1688 and 1700, the deed for the property being executed 7–1–1693.

Radnor Meeting-House (meaning the present structure) was probably not built until 1717, but a log edifice stood here until that date. There is much confusion regarding the exact relations which these three meetings bore to each other in the first instance. As, however, this is a question of more interest to those directly connected with the Society than to others, it will suffice here to explain that for a long time they were practically one and the same meeting, although they separately controlled in turn the Yearly, Monthly and Preparative Meetings of Friends. The records of these meetings, for a number of years, were not entirely separated, a fact that frequently leads to confusion.

In these old books the certificates brought from Wales by the first Cymric settlers were duly recorded. They form a roll to which too much importance cannot be attached, for it is from these settlers that one of the best elements of the Commonwealth of Pennsylvania has sprung. We have given several of these letters in the pages of this work, but to illustrate the character of the founders of the Merion Meeting we give the following abstract from a certificate given to Joshua Owen,[1] of

---
[1] He was son to Owen Humphrey, of Llwyndu, descended from Ednowain ap Bradwn, and from Edward III., King of England.

Llwyndu, in the parish of Llangylnin, in the County of Merioneth, Batchelor. Of him it says: " He is born of an honest Parentage who were careful in his Education from his Childhood & his Conversation among us was accordingly Civil; Peaceable and Industrous in his calling, and his parting is with relations' Consent and orderly in all respects."

This is signed by eleven Friends of Tyddyn y Garreg Meeting, 1783, 27th of 5th month.

What emigrant to a new country could have a better testimonial than this, and where, except in Pennsylvania, can it be equalled?

A public or circulating library was established by the three sister meetings at a very early period. We know, certainly, that it was in operation probably before 1697. About this time it is noted that " Friends think it meet that Friends' books belonging to the Weekly Meeting of Radnor, Haverford and Merion be brought once a week." Soon after this, in 1700, a purchase of twenty-five books is noted. They were divided equally amongst the Meetings. Among these were: *Caleb Pusey's Answer to Daniel Leeds, Joseph Wyeth's Remarks on Dr. Brays, Wm. Shewrn's Epistles, The Christianity of ye Quakers Assured*, and many other light and cheerful works of the same character. Doubtless they afforded much food for thought at that time, but might be considered a trifle dry in this generation.

When anyone within the Welsh Tract misbehaved themselves very scandalously, and failed of reformation by means of soft counsel or the perusal of the aforesaid works, they had a pleasant practice of nailing up an accusation against him upon the door of the meeting-house, but this could not be lawfully done " before he was dealt with according to Gospel order," for we read that upon the 9th of the 2-month, at Haverford:

" David Powell's paper of accusation agt. certain P'sons, being posted upon ye meeting house before ye Said P'sons were dealt with according to Gospel order, David Lawrence, John Roberts and Rees Thomas are ordered to deal with him for this his ungospel like proceeding."

There is but little doubt but they dealt very severely with him, for we find that shortly after, " David Powell doth acknowledge his fault."

Nor were those Quakers who resided upon plantations at distant corners of the Barony permitted to evade their duty, or lust after vain things whilst at their far-off homes, for certain persons were appointed to "visit Friends' families once a Quarter to see that things be in good order answerable to our profession." This was in 1696. The records of the meetings were carefully looked after, and " David Maurice is ordered to make a cupboard or chest," for to keep Friends' books for the use and service of this meeting (i. e. Haverford). After awhile additional reading matter was called for and John Jarmon for Radnor, William Howell for Haverford, and John Roberts for Merion, "are ordered to receive Friends' subscriptions toward buying books."

John Humphrey, in his will, had left the sum of £10 towards printing a Welsh book, which he had written, " if convenience be had for the same in these American parts." In 1702 this money was still unexpended and held by the Quarterly Meeting, and David Lewis and Daniel Humphrey wanting " money to furnish their Haverford Meeting, ask for £10 left by John Humphrey," for that purpose.

There are many other things of interest connected with the three meeting-houses which might be related here did space permit.

Hugh Roberts, prior to his death, presented a very handsome sun-dial to Merion Meeting, which stood on a post in front of the house until the Revolutionary War, when it was confiscated on account of the lead which it contained. It seems rather odd when we reflect, that this kindly gift of peaceful old Hugh Roberts probably ultimately caused the death of many a British trooper.

The old wall around the Merion Meeting ground was built with the bequest of Edward Rees (Price), whilst John Roberts and numbers of other Merion Friends left generous sums to the meeting.

The importance of the influence which the Merion Meeting exerted upon Colonial generations can not well be overestimated when we consider those who descended from the founders. And of these descendants I need barely mention to you the names of John Dickinson, Dr. Thomas Cadwalader, John and Lambert Cadwalader, Clement and Owen Biddle, Edward Roberts, Robert Wharton, Joshua Humphreys and Dr. Lloyd Zachary, to illustrate this point.

During the Revolution, as we have observed, many left the ranks of Friends and joined the Continental army, and after these were expelled it came to pass that in course of time few or none of the descendants of the Cymric Friends were members of this meeting.

In 1829–30 the meeting-house was "repaired." The rough stone work was covered by a thick coat of plaster or rough-cast, destroying, in a great measure, the antique appearance of the building. A picture of the meeting, as it appeared in 1829, before the "improvements" were finished, is given in the text of this article.

ROBERT AND THOMAS LLOYD, OF BRYN MAWR.[1]

ROBERT LLOYD, the owner, in Colonial days, of an extensive plantation to the northward of Rowland Ellis, and of the present Bryn Mawr, arrived in Pennsylvania in 1683. He was born in Merionethshire, probably in one of the Western Parishes about 1669. He spent his youth in Merion, residing for some time at the house of Robert Owen, probably from 1691 to 1697.

By deed, 5 September, 1698, he purchased from William Howell, Edward Jones, John Roberts, Griffith Owen and Daniel Humphrey, 409 acres of land in the location mentioned. This tract had formerly been the property of Thomas Ellis. [Deed Book E 4, Vol. 7, p. 20, etc., Philadelphia.] This tract was confirmed to Robert Lloyd, 12-month 6, 1707–8, by William Howell et al., Robert Lloyd and Lowry, his wife, by deed dated 10 February, 1709, conveyed 154½ acres of this plantation to Thomas Lloyd (Deed Book F 8, page 40, etc., Philadelphia.)

Robert Lloyd was doubtless related to several of the Merion settlers. He was one of the overseers to the will of Robert Owen, dated 1697, and was a very prominent man in township affairs. His will is dated 1714 (Will Book D, p. 112, etc., Philadelphia). He died 3-mo. 29, 1714, at Merion.

Robert Lloyd married Lowry Jones at Merion Meeting 8-mo. 11th, 1698. Their youngest son,[2] Richard Lloyd, was born 1st mo. 15th, 1713–14, at Merion; died 8-mo. 9th, 1755, at Darby, Pa.; married 9-mo. 24th, 1736, at Darby Meeting, Hannah Sellers, born 12-mo. 10th, 1717, at Darby; died there

---

[1] I am indebted to Howard Williams Lloyd, Esq., for data concerning these settlers.

[2] For other lines and issue see page 81.

4-mo. 12th, 1810, as the widow of Lewis Davis and daughter of Samuel Sellers and Sarah (Smith) Sellers. Richard and Hannah Lloyd had issue: Isaac and Hugh.

Hugh Lloyd was born 11th mo. 22d, 1741-2, in Merion; died 3-mo. 20th, 1832, in Kensington, Philadelphia County; married 6-mo. 4th, 1767, at Darby Meeting, Susanna Pearson, born 7th mo. 22d, 1746, in Darby; died there 4th mo. 17th, 1825, daughter of Thomas Pearson and Hannah (Blunston) Pearson.

Hugh Lloyd was one of the representatives from Chester County to the several Conferences or Conventions held at Carpenter's Hall, Philadelphia, prior to the Declaration of Independence, a Colonel of the Third Battalion, Chester County Militia; in the year 1776, a Presidential Elector, and cast his ballot for George Washington for the latter's second term as President of the United States. In 1792 he was appointed one of the Associate Judges of Delaware County, and filled that position until December 31, 1825, when he resigned.

Charles Lloyd, a son of Hugh and Susanna Lloyd, born 6-mo. 20th, 1776, at Crum Creek, Delaware County, died 1-mo. 26th, 1860, at Paschallville, Philadelphia; married 3-mo. 8th, 1798, at Darby Meeting, Frances Paschall, born 2-mo. 24th, 1771, at Kingsessing, Philadelphia; died 8-mo. 27th, 1857, at Paschallville, daughter of Dr. Henry Paschall and Ann (P. Garrett) Paschall. Among other issue of Charles and Frances Lloyd was Henry Paschall Lloyd, born 2-mo. 12th, 1805; died 6-mo. 6, 1886, married 2-mo. 2nd, 1843, in Philadelphia, Annabella Williams, daughter of Howard Williams, and Ann (Heacock) Williams, and had Howard Williams Lloyd.

RICHARD LLOYD, fourth son and youngest child of Robert and Lowry Lloyd, was born 1st mo. 15th, 1713-14, and died 8th mo. 9th, 1755. He married 9th mo. 24th, 1736, at Darby Meeting, Hannah Sellers, daughter of Samuel and Sarah Smith Sellers. They had children as follows:
  I. Samuel, died in infancy.
  II. Isaac, married Ann Gibbons, left issue:

III. Hugh, born 11th mo. 22nd, 1741-2; died 3d mo. 20th, 1832. He married 6th mo. 4th, 1767, at Darby Meeting, Susanna Pearson, daughter of Thomas and Hannah Blunston Pearson.

III. Hugh and Susanna Lloyd had:
1. Thomas, born 6th mo. 24th, 1768; died 12th mo. 11th, 1814. He married Mary Wood and left issue.
2. David, died in infancy.
3. Samuel, died in infancy.
4. Richard Pearson, born 11th mo. 8th, 1773; died 8th mo. 21st, 1814; married Edith Lane, and left issue.
5. Charles (see below).
6. Hannah, born 2nd mo. 15th, 1779; died 8th mo. 7th, 1868; married John Coats Browne, and left issue.
7. Samuel, born 9th mo. 22nd, 1781; died 9th mo. 3rd, 1806, unmarried.
8. Robert, born 9th mo. 30th, 1784; died 2nd mo. 4th, 1875; married Ann Browne, and left issue.
9. Hugh Pearson, born 5th mo. 29th, 1788; died 1876; married Mary Warner and Sidney Steel, and left issue by 2nd wife.

5. Charles Lloyd, son of Hugh and Susanna, born 6th mo. 20th, 1776; died 1st mo. 26th, 1860; married 3d mo. 8th, 1798, at Darby Meeting, Frances Paschall, daughter of Dr. Henry and Ann Garrett Paschall, of Kingsessing. Issue:

Paschall, born 1st mo. 15th, 1799; died 8th mo. 17th, 1884; married Henrietta J. Fitch and Massey Serrill, and left issue.

Charles Washington, died unmarried.

Hannah, born 1st mo. 25th, 1802; died 6th mo. 20th, 1868; married James Andrews, and left issue.

Frances, born 2d mo. 5th, 1803; died 1st mo. 24th, 1871; married William Davis Jones, and left issue.

Henry Paschall, born 2d mo. 12th, 1805; died 6th mo. 6th, 1886; married Annabella Williams, they had:
Ann W., died unmarried.
Howard W.
Charles H., died in infancy.
Martha Hughes, died in infancy.
Susanna, died unmarried.

Charles, born 10th mo. 2nd, 1811; died 11th mo. 30th, 1888; married Mary Humphreys Oakford, and left issue.

Franklin, born 5th mo. 27th, 1814; died 8th mo. 11th, 1884; married Hannah Heacock, and left issue.

NOTE.—Robert Lloyd, son of Robert and Lowry, married Catherine Humphrey, and had Margaret Lloyd, who married Seymour Hart, and had Rebecca Hart, who married Stephen Simmons and had Elizabeth G. Simmons, who married Joseph Price, and had: Stephen Simmons Price, Ann C., Rebecca S., and Thomas C.

THOMAS LLOYD was a brother of Robert Lloyd, of Merion, and probably younger. The exact year of his birth is not known. His name does not appear in the " First Tax List for Philadelphia County, 26th day of September, 1693," but on 3rd mo. 5th, 1696, at the marriage of Robert Roberts and Katherine Jones, at Haverford Meeting, he signs as a witness immediately after his brother Robert. He doubtless arrived in Pennsylvania in the early part of the latter year (1696). He married about 1698, Elizabeth, daughter of William ap Edward.[1] This ceremony was probably performed by a Justice of the Peace, which was occasionally the case among the early Friends. The event would not, therefore, be recorded in the Meeting Books. Under date of 6th mo. 8th, 1700, in Merion Meeting Minutes, is the following: " Thomas Lloyd and wife Elizabeth make acknowledgement for marrying out" [i. e., outside the good and usual order of the Monthly Meeting]. As has been previously stated, Thomas Lloyd purchased from his brother, Robert, one hundred and fifty-four and one-half acres of land. The date of the conveyance[2] is 10th of February, 1709, the consideration being " fforty pounds of lawful money of Pennsylvania," and the location of the land as follows: It was in the Township of Merion, north of Bryn Mawr, and was bounded by land belonging to David Llewellyn, Robert Lloyd, Rowland Ellis, John Williams, and Morris Llewellyn. Thomas Lloyd lived the life of a yeoman farmer, cultivating his plantation and raising his family. Part of the land adjoining, belonging to Rowland Ellis, was sold to Richard Harrison. In 1737 a complaint was made to the Monthly Meeting that Thomas Lloyd and wife were interfering with Richard Harrison's slaves. A committee was appointed to investigate the matter.

On 8-mo. 13th, at a Monthly Meeting held at Haverford, they made the following report: " The Friends appointed to hear the complaint of Richard Harrison against Thomas Lloyd, reports in writing under their hands that the said Richard had

---
[1] For an account of William ap Edward see p.
[2] Philadelphia Deed Book F 8, p. 140, etc.

just cause of complaint. Also that there was a paper brought to this meeting signed by Thomas Lloyd and his wife, acknowledging that they were heartily sorry that they had given the said Richard and wife just cause to be offended in that they had anything to do with their negroes and that they had acted very unadvisedly and foolishly and promised to avoid anything of the kind for the time to come, and Richard Harrison being present at this meeting accepts thereof for satisfaction."

Items of this kind taken from the Meeting Minute-Books give an insight to the social conditions of the early settlers. The keeping of slaves was not then looked upon as being anything out of the way. Where disputes arose between neighbors over supposed trespass on the part of slaves or from other causes, the cases were very properly brought before the Monthly Meeting for settlement.

Thomas and Elizabeth Lloyd had children as follows: Thomas Lloyd, born 7th mo. 1699; married, and removed to and became identified with Bucks County; died prior to 1763 and left issue.

Sarah Lloyd, born 7th mo. 14, 1701; married, 9th mo. 8th, 1721, at Merion Meeting, John Morgan, son of Edward, of Gwynedd.

Jane Lloyd, born 6th mo. 1st, 1703; married 8th mo. 8th, 1725, at Merion Meeting, Lewis Williams, of Gwynedd. Her second husband was named Darkins.

John Lloyd, born 10th mo. 19th, 1704; married, 10th mo 31st, 1731, at Merion Meeting, Eleanor Pugh, daughter of Henry and Catherine, of Merion. His will is dated 3rd mo. 20th, 1769, proved August 11th, 1770, at Philadelphia.

Elizabeth Lloyd, born 8th mo. 29th, 1706; married, 9th mo. 8th, 1728, at Merion Meeting, Joseph Morgan, son of Edward, of Gwynedd.

William Lloyd, born 10th mo. 4th, 1708; probably died young. He is not mentioned in either his father's or mother's will.

Evan Lloyd, born 5th mo. —— 1713; married about 1756, but not under the care of his Monthly Meeting. He, as executor, on February 26th, 1757, enters satisfaction on a mortgage, made by his father on the farm.

Both Thomas and Elizabeth Lloyd lived to an advanced age. He died in 1748. In his will, dated 5th mo. 26th, 1741, and probated at Philadelphia 6th of February, 1748, he appoints his wife executrix. She in her will, dated December 2nd, 1748, proved at Philadelphia February 6th, 1748–9, mentions the fact of "Having been left by my husband executor and being taken sick before the execution," etc., appoints her son, Evan Lloyd, executor. He, therefore, had the settlement of both estates.

SOME NOTES ON THE WARNER FAMILY OF BLOCKLEY.

So many of the Welsh families intermarried, in Colonial times, with the Warners, of Blockley, that some account of the first settlers of that name may not be out of place here.

The founder of the family was one William Warner, who was born at Draycot in the Parish of Blockley, Worcestershire, being the son of John Warner, and was baptized in the Parish Church there 8 July, 1627. The tradition is that he had been a Captain in the Parliamentary Army, and that he left England after 1658. There is certainly nothing improbable in this statement, when we consider that a large numer of men, holding commissions under Cromwell, were subsequently forced to leave England, in order to save their estates from confiscation and themselves from transportation as convicts, and we may accept the story until evidence is produced to overthrow it. From the late investigations of the writer it seems apparent that William Warner settled first in New England, or at least remained there some time. His subsequent movements are somewhat uncertain, but it may be presumed that he drifted into Pennsylvania by way of New Jersey.

He was certainly here sometime before Penn, and purchased lands on the Schuylkill, direct from the Indians, and his titles were confirmed by the Upland Court, and later by Penn's Commissioners.

At a Court at Upland, held 3 April, 1678, he had a grant of 100 acres of land on the west bank of the Schuylkill. On 1 June, 1681, he made application to purchase land from the Indians, and upon the same day he had a grant to take up 400 acres. His purchase from the Indians was probably in common with others, for the Court required that a proportion of the 335 guilders to be paid to the Indians, should be paid.

In 1681 he was appointed a member of Deputy Gov. Markham's Council. The oath of office subscribed by him, 3 August, 1681, is extant. A fac-simile of it is to be found in the Edition of the *Duke of York's Laws*, published by the State of Pennsylvania, 1869.

William Warner was appointed one of the nine Justices, under Markham, 13 September, 1681. (Also sessions of 30 November, same year.)

He was a member of the first Assembly of Pennsylvania, convened at Philadelphia 10 March, 1683. He named his plantation, which extended from the Schuylkill River to above the present Hestonville, or Fifty-second Street, on both sides of the Pennsylvania Railroad, Blockley, from his native place and the township, formerly known by another name, was afterwards so called.

William Warner's wife's name was Anne. He died upon the plantation on the Schuylkill about October, 1706, his will being dated 8 September, 1703, and was proved at Philadelphia 18 October, 1706 [Will Book C, p. 51]. In it he mentions his wife and children.

One of his daughters married James Kite (see Kite family). The eldest son, ISAAC WARNER, had by his father's will the plantation on the Schuylkill, to him during life, and after his decease to the eldest son of Isaac.

Isaac Warner (1st) married Ann Craven, 30 November, 1692, and died in April, 1727. His will is dated 6 April, 1727, and was proved in Philadelphia 26 April, same year (Will Book E, p. 42, etc.). The eldest son of Isaac and Ann Warner was William Warner, who lived upon the plantation in Blockley, and died about the month of September, 1766. His will, dated 19 April, 1762, was proved at Philadelphia, 13 September, 1766 (Will Book O, p. 25, etc.).

This William Warner was the " Baron," and one of the founders of the " State on Schuylkill," in 1732. The Colonial Hall of the Schuylkill Fishing Company was built upon his property. The eldest son of William Warner was Isaac Warner, first Lieutenant-Colonel and then Colonel of the Seventh

Battalion, Philadelphia County Militia, during the Revolution.
This Isaac married, circa 1757, Lydia Coulton, and died in November, 1794. His will, dated 9 July, 1794, was proved at Philadelphia 29 November, 1794 (Will Book D, p. 154, etc.).

His daughter, Lydia, married Algernon Roberts, of Merion (see Roberts family). His son, Joseph C. Warner, born 15 November, 1767; married, 16 April, 1795, Sarah Powell, and died 20 January, 1803, intestate. This Joseph C. Warner had by Sarah, his wife, a daughter, Rebecca Ashton Warner, born 14 September, 1800; married, 26 June, 1823, Henry Erwin, and died 7 August, 1881. Her will is dated 15 June, 1881, proved at Philadelphia. Her son, Joseph Warner Erwin, born 12 September, 1824; married, 23 July, 1850, Caroline A. Borden, and died 27 October, 1890, leaving issue (inter aliä), a daughter, Ida Warner, who married Joseph I. Doran, of Philadelphia, and had issue. There are very many families bearing the name of Warner who are descended from the first William Warner. Amongst these may be mentioned J. Anderson Warner, of Ardmore, and the Warners of Haverford and Rosemont. It may be mentioned that a nephew of the original William Warner died in Philadelphia, and that one Edward Warner, probably a kinsman, died in Wilmington.

APPENDIX.

OWEN, OF DOLSEREY.

Robert Owen, of Dolserey, and Jane, his wife, the latter a daughter of Robert Vaughan, Esq., of Hengwrt, the celebrated Antiquary and Genealogist, came to Pennsylvania on the ship "Vine," Captain Preeson, Master, from Liverpool, which arrived in Philadelphia, or probably Chester, in 1684. The following is abstracted from a part of the original copy of the Register of Arrivals in the possession of the Historical Society of Pennsylvania.

"*William Preeson, Mr. of the Vine, of Leverpoole, arrived the 17th day of the 7-mo., 1684, at Philadelphia From Dolyserne (Dolserey) near dolgues (Dôlgelly in Merionethshire), Robert Owen & Jeane his wife and Lewes their Sone.*" Dr. Griffith Owen also came on this ship, and servants are mentioned.

Edward Owen, another son had previously located on Duck Creek, New Castle County (now Deleware), and Robert and Jane appear to have removed there at once. They were certainly living there in 1865, because Robert Owen and Lewis Owen are witnesses to a deed of Edward Owen, of Duck Creek, to Griffith Owen, for all of the said Edward's right to his share of the Merion purchase. Robert and Jane Owen, being elderly people, died shortly after this. Their descendants continued in New Castle and held property there. Some of their wills are of record.

Robert and Jane Owen had nine sons. The following are known to the writer:

1. Robert Owen, believed to have been eldest son; he inherited Dolserey, near Dôlgelly, having remained in Wales. He married (probably as 2nd wife) Jane ————, and had issue who were baptised in Dôlgelly Church, the records of which event being as follows (it being noted that Robert Owen, Jr., abandoned the Quaker Faith):

   1694.—"*Humphredus filius Roberti Owen de Dolyserrey et Janae vxuris Bapt. fuit decimo tertio Junii.*"
   1699.—"*Hugo filius Roberti Owen de Dolyserre et Janae ux. Bapt. fuit vicesimo octavo die Dacembris Scilicit Festo Innocentium.*"
   1701.—"*Katharina filia Roberti Owen de Dolyserre et Janae ux. Bapt. fuit 1 mo. die Septembris.*"
   1703.—"*Anna, filia Roberti Owen de Dôlyesy et Janae ux. Bapt. fuit nono die Marti.*"
   1705.—"*Gulielmus fil Roberti Owen de Dolyerre et Janae ux. Bapt. fuit duodecimo die Marti.*"

2. Griffith Owen, he appears to have studied medicine and to have practiced at first in England. He died in Philadelphia, having married and had issue.

3. Rowland Owen (doubtful).
4. Edward Owen, of New Castle Co.
5. Lewis Owen, of New Castle Co.
6. Humphrey Owen (doubtful).

This Robert Owen, of Dolserey, was son of Humphrey Owen, descended from Lewis Owen, Baron of the Exchequer of North Wales, who was murdered, 1555. The Arms of this branch of the family, an extended pedigree of which is before the writer, were: a chevron inter three cocks, quartered with the three snakes nowed of Ednowain ap Bradwen. Many descendants of this ancient family are believed to exist in Delaware.

JOHN BEVAN AND HIS NEPHEW REES THOMAS.

In the letter written by Rees Thomas, dated "Ye 29th day of ye 2-mo., 1695," addressed to his father-in-law William Awbrey, is the following: "My unkle John Bevan came over very well and a good voyage he had," etc. If this relationship was the same as we now understand to exist between uncle and nephew it could have been in only one of two ways. Either by Barbara, wife of John Bevan, being sister to the father, or to the mother of Rees Thomas. It could not have been through the father of the latter being a brother of John Bevan. This needs no argument. Rees had cousins whose father used Thomas as a fixed surname. William Thomas, John Thomas and David Thomas of Radnor, the latter afterwards of Gwynedd, were these. (See will of David Thomas of Gwynedd, dated 29th, 4th month, 1732, proved June 11th, 1737, at Philadelphia). Neither could it have been by the mother of Rees Thomas, being sister to John Bevan. The only sister of the latter died young. There could be no possible relationship through Martha, wife of Rees Thomas. He distinctly writes my uncle, not our uncle. Elizabeth, the mother of Martha, was an only child. William, the father of Martha, was of Llanelieu, Breconshire, and son of *Thomas* Awbrey.

Was John Bevan married twice? First to Barbara [perhaps Thomas] of Wenvoe. Second to Catherine, daughter of *William* Awbrey, of Pencoed, near Llaniltern, Glamorganshire. HOWARD WILLIAMS LLOYD.

Thomas and John Wynn were therefore alive 1665 and 1670, and probable later. Both were then thirty or thirty five years old. This would seem to correspond with Dr. Wynne and his brother's age. The result of this research is not given with any idea of building a pedigree, but with the hope that some one in the future may fix positively and correctly, the ancestry of Dr. Thomas Wynne.
HOWARD WILLIAMS LLOYD.

The above note needs some little explanation. Mr. Lloyd seems to be of the opinion that John Bevan was married twice, and that Rees Thomas was his nephew through the Thomas family of Wenvoe. Mr. Lloyd gives his opinion, first, upon the statement of Mr. Clark, in his Glamorganshire families, that John Bevan, senior, of Treverigg, married *Barbara*, of Wenvoe, and the statement by the same authority, in the pedigree of the Awbreys, of Pencoed, that Catherine, daughter of William Awbrey, of that place, married John Bevan, of Treverigg.

Now, in the first place we know positively, from the will of John Bevan, that *he did* marry a daughter of William Awbrey, of Pencoed, and that she did not survive him. We also know that his children named their sons Awbrey before the death of Barbara Bevan, and we have the statement of Rees Thomas, who married Martha Awbrey, a kinswoman to the Awbreys of Pencoed, that his second son was the first of the name in Pennsylvania, implying a possibility of other Awbreys in the near future. We have also pretty trustworthy family tradition upon the subject, coupled with the statement of a person who lived at that time, or soon after. There is little question that *Catherine* is a typographical error for Barbara. William Awbrey, of Pencoed, married a Thomas living near Wenvoe, of a family who had assumed this surname for several generations prior to 1682, and among them the name of *Rees Thomas*, was of frequent occurrence, so that it is probable that Rees Thomas was thus related to John Bevan. The term " uncle " in Wales means any relationship, such as first or second cousin once removed.

T. A. GLENN.

WYNNSTAY, OR WYNNESTAY, BLOCKLEY, AND WYNNSTAY, RUABON.

It has been stated in account of Dr. Thomas Wynne, that his son Jonathan's place in Blockley was called " Wynnstay," probably as early as 1710.

An extensive estate of that name is in Ruabon, Denbighshire, about five miles southwest from Wrexham. As this was the neighborhood in which Dr. Wynne lived for a time prior to his removal to Pennsylvania, the coincidence is certainly curious and it was thought best to make an investigation. Every Wynn will probated in the Prerogative Court of Canterbury, from County Flint, between 1638 and 1688 was examined. Those from Caernarvonshire, Denbighshire and Anglesey partially so, while a rather hasty glance was given those at St. Asaph, prior to 1700. Other sources of information have also been consulted. The result is:

Sir John Wynn, of Gwyder,[1] born 1553, was created a Baronet, 1611; d. 1 March, 1626–7; m. Sydney, daughter of Sir William Gerard, Chancellor of Ireland. She d. 8th June, 1632; buried at Llanrwst, Caernarvonshire. They had a large family. Their sons being:

I. John, who d. before his father, m., but d. s. p. 19 July 1649.

II. Sir Richard, who m., but d. s. p.

III. Thomas, d. infant.

IV. Sir Owen, who d. 13 August, 1660, aged 68 years, leaving a son, Sir Richard, who m. and had: Mary, who inherited Gwydir.

V. Robert, entered holy orders and d. 1617, aged 24 years.

The name of Wynnstay or Wynnestay, for it was written both ways in Pennsylvania and in Wales, seems simply to signify " Wynne's field," or " the home of the Wynnes." I believe that the literal translation of this word is " Wynne's ditch," so called formerly from the fortifications or moats surrounding many dwellings. I do not think that there was any connection between Wynnestay, in Block-

---

[1] The descent of Sir John Wynn was: John ap Morris Wynn ap John Wynn ap Meredith ap Ievan ap Robert ap Meredith ap Howell ap David ap Griffith ap Caradoc ap Thomas ap Rhodri ap Owen Gwynedd.

ley and Wynnstay in Wales, or the families thereof. I am of the opinion that Dr. Thomas Wynne descended from one of the very numerous families of Wynne or Wynn, living in his time in Flintshire, and that neighborhood. It may be stated authoritively here that the Wynne pedigree published some years since in the *Magazine of American History*, and extensively copied, is totally erroneous and without any foundation whatever. It was reproduced in a late publication against my advice. T. A. GLENN.

VI. William.

VII. Maurice, purchased Crogen, county Merioneth, from Morgan Lloyd; he d. 1670, 1 s. p.

VIII. Ellis, who died 20th Nov. 1619, unm. buried at Whitford, county Flint.

IX. Henry.

XI. Roger; there were two of this name, both infants.

The 9th son, Henry Wynn, of the Inner Temple, London; m. Catherine dau. and h. of Ellis Lloyd, of Rhiwgoch, Merionethshire. He d. 27 July, 1671; buried in Temple Church, London. By her he had an only son, Sir John, the last Baronet. This Sir John Wynn m. Jane, dau. and h. of Eyton Evans, of Watstay, the name of which place he changed to *Wynnstay*. He d. s. p. 7, Jan. 1718-19, aged 91. He bequeathed everything that he had acquired both by inheritance and marriage to his relative, Watkin Williams, who assumed the name of Wynn.

Sir Watkin Williams-Wynn giving him his full name, was a son of Sir William Williams, of Glasgoed and Llanvorda, by Jane Thelwall. The latter was dau. of Edward Thelwall, of Plas-y-Ward, county of Denbigh, who died 12 December, 1679, having m. June, 1664, Sidney Wynn, dau. William Wynn, 6th son of Sir John Wynn, of Gwydir. William Wynn was b. about 1600; he m. Jane, dau. of Thomas Lloyd, of Gwern-y-Brechtwyn, m. covenant dated March 20, 1628. He was Prothonotary of North Wales, and purchased Branas, county Merioneth, from Humphrey Branas. At the time of his death, 24 October 1664, he lived at Garthg-y-nan, Llanfair, Dyffryn Clwyd, Denbighshire. His will is dated 21, October 14, Chas. II. (1663). He appoints his brother, Morris Wynn, of Crogen, county Merioneth, his brother Henry Wynn of Inner Temple, London, and John Wynn, of Watstay, county Denbigh, overseers. He bequeaths the profits of the Prothonotary's office for the counties of Anglesey, Caernarvon and Merioneth to be applied to the payment of his debts, and for the benefit of his daughter, Sidney Wynn. He mentions his son, Richard Wynn, of Penheskyn, county Anglesey, and his sons, *Thomas* and *John*. He appoints his wife, Jane Wynn, sole executrix. Proved 25 April 1665. (P. C. C. Hyde 35.)

The Children of [1] *William and Jane Wynn;* 1, Sidney, m. Edward Thelwall, she was the favorite child. 2, Richard, of Penheskyn, at the time of his father's death, was afterward's of Branas and Garthg-y-nan. He inherited these estates as eldest son. He m. Katharine, dau. Viscount Bulkeley. They had: William, Richard and Mary, all of whom died infants; Sidney Thelwall became the heiress

---

[1] In Dwnn's "Heraldic Visitations of Wales there is a pedigree of the Wynn's of Gwydir, and it states that William Wynn was Prothonotary of North Wales. His male descendants became extinct in the second generations."

of her brother, Richard Wynn. 3, William, 4, Mary; both d. young. 5, *Thomas*, 6, *John*.

In a reprint of "The History of the Gwydir Family" is the statement that Thomas Wynn was baptised at King's Vorton, Worcestershire, 1 February, 1636. He was living in 1665, as was John. The latter was alive 1670, for Maurice Wynn of Crogen, in his will, 21, Sept. 1670, mentions nephews, Richard Wynn, of Branas, son and heir of his brother William Wynn, of Garthg-y-nan and John Wynn.

REES THOMAS AND HIS DESCENDANTS.

The children of Rees Thomas have already been given. Rees, the eldest son, was born 1693, of whom presently.

Awbrey, the second son d. s. p. Herbert, the third son, d. s. p. William, the fourth son, was born 1701. He is mentioned in his father's will, 1742, and appears to have been a favorite child. From the Orphans' Court Docket, Philadelphia, it appears that he died in Lower Merion, upon his estate at Rosemont, *prior to* 1787. He left issue: Jonathan, Rees, Martha, m. John Llewelyn, Lydia, m. Peter Evans, Hannah, m. Jonathan Powell, David, Richard. By an order of the Orphans' Court we find that of William Thomas' land, 98 acres were deeded to John Curwin; 73 acres to William Thomas, "a grandson," and 80 acres to John Powell, and 19¾ acres to Michael Cline, whilst Jonathan Thomas purchased 28 acres.

Rees Thomas, second son of William, son of Rees Thomas and Martha Awbrey, married Rebecca Brooke and had issue several children, of whom, Martha Thomas, born 8-7-1770; died 6-26-1810, married John Yocum, whose daughter married an Egbert and had Hamilton Egbert, of Lower Merion, father of Joseph C. Egbert, M. D., of Wayne, Pa. Rees Thomas, eldest son of Rees Thomas first, had a large family. Among the present descendants are persons bearing the name of Perot, Lloyd, Roberts, etc. The writer has in his possession a brief of titles to the property at Rosemont, formerly the plantation of Rees Thomas, and an extended genealogy of this family, but the same is too voluminous for insertion here.

ROWLAND ELLIS, OF BRYN MAWR.

A careful examination of the title to "Harriton," would appear to cast a doubt upon the statement of Mr. Richard Vaux that the house occupied by Charles Thomson, was built by Rowland Ellis in 1704, although 1714 may have been the date. Nor does Mr. Vaux in his article in the Pennsylvania magazine go fully into detail regarding the conveyance to Richard Harrison.

An examination of the deeds of record at Philadelphia shows that on 24 Feb., 1708, Rowland Ellis, of the township of Merion, in the County of Philadelphia, granted and conveyed unto Rees Thomas, of Merion, and William Lewis, of Newtown, Chester, for the consideration of £180, all that messuage and plantation—" wherein the said Rowland now dwells with the tract of land thereunto belonging." The description of this tract, 300 acres, does not seem to include the site of the present mansion.

In 1719 the said Rees Thomas and William Lewis granted and conveyed unto Richard Harrison the said 300 acres, and Rowland Ellis, by a subsequent conveyance (lease and release, 22-23 October, 1719) confirmed the *whole tract* of 718 acres, to the said Richard Harrison, for the consideration of £600. A lot of ground of 20 acres was excepted. The plantation was at that time bounded by lands of Henry Pugh, John Williams, Thomas Lloyd, Owen Roberts, Hugh Evans, Thomas Nicholas, Philip Price, Peter Jones, Philip (Luceds?) These conveyances recite the original deed, 30-31 July, 1681, Richard Davies to Rowland Ellis, of Brin Mawr, in the County of Merioneth, gentleman, for 1100 acres, a part of which was surveyed to him in Merion and part in Goshen.

ROBERTS, OF PENCOYD—PAUL BRANCH.

The following was received too late for insertion in the proper place :

John Roberts, m. Gainor Roberts, 1685, and had Robert Roberts, who married Sydney Rees, 1709, and had, Sydney Roberts, who m. John Paul, 5, 13, 1754, and had, Susanna Paul, who m. Bevan Rakestraw, 1776, and had Martha Bevan Rakestraw, who married Robert Embey Foreman, and had : Mortimer Paul Foreman, who m. Sarah S. Gardner and had Olivia Gardner, who m. John Moses, and has : Howard B., Arthur Gardner, F. J., Walter, Helen Graham, Annie Foster.

HUGH ROBERTS.

Col. William Brooke Rawle has called my attention to an old silver cup or small tankard, in possession of the Vaux family. This ancient piece of plate is *said* to have been the property of Hugh Roberts. According to Col. Rawle's description there are two coats. One of these he thinks similar, if not identical, with the arms of Lloyd of Dolobran, the other, having a scaling ladder in the first and fourth quarters, and a goat passant in the second and third quarters. The crests are described as first, two scaling ladders, second, a goat's head.

LEWIS DAVID'S COMPANY.

It was intended to give a detailed account of the settlers under Lewis David's Patent, and in the opening chapters of this work such a proposed sketch is referred to. As, however, the information upon the subject was incomplete and the material gathered unsatisfactory, the suggested chapter was omitted. The following, however, is a list of grantees under that Patent. The dates of conveyance were: 1682, 1, 9 and 10 May, William Howell, of Castlebigch, Pembrokeshire, Yeoman, 500 acres. Henry Lewis, [1]Parish of Narbarth, Pembrokeshire, 1000 acres·

---

[1]Henry Lewis, who settled in Haverford, was ancestor to Edmund Lewis, now of Haverford.

His will was as follows : Henry Lewis, " of Maencoch[1] in the township of Haverford on the west side of Schookill "; dated 14th 6-mo. 1688. Proved 8th 8-mo. 1705.

250 acres which he "purchased from Lewis David of Landeur, late of the Pembroke in S. Wales, being situate in said township of Haverford."

Sons, Samuel and Henry Lewis.

---

[1]Probably a corruption of Maenclochog, a parish in Pembrokeshire, 9 miles from Narberth.

Rees Rothers, Parish of Lanwenog, Cardiganshire, Yeoman, 500 acres. Evan Thomas, Parish of Lanykeaven, Pembrokeshire, 250 acres. Lewis David, of Llandewy Velfrey, gentleman, retained balance.

GARRIGUES.

Haydock Garrigues descended from the ancient French family of that name, a pedigree of whom, procured in France, is in the possession of the family, was born in Philadelphia, 1805; died in Haverford township 1877. He was the son of Samuel Garrigues, of Haverford, who was interested both in that township and in Merion. The family are descended from the Sharpless family and derive a strain of Cymric blood from Isaac Thomas, of Chester county.

Daughter, Elizabeth.
Wife Margaret, executor.
Overseers: "My friends," Ellis Ellis, Humphrey Ellis, Samuel Rees, John Bevan, John Lewis.
Witnesses: Lewis David, Griffith Owen, Thomas Ellis.

INDEX.

[This is not intended as a complete index, but is merely a reference to considerable or important mention of families and persons.]

A.

	PAGE.		PAGE.
Aiken	304	Ashbridge	82, 83
Allen	141, 233	Aubrey	176
Andreas	103	Awbrey	305 et seq.
Andrews	256		

B.

Bacon	153	Blackford	148
Benade	184	Blair	146
Berg	184	Brooke	355 et seq.
Bell	161	Browning	110
Bevan	34, 35, 155 et seq.	Burr	138
Biddle	134, 136, 145 et seq.		

C.

Cadwalader	130, 131, 138, 144, 147, 252 et seq.	Comfort	153
		Conarroe	145
Carpenter	345, 346, 347, 348	Conner	235, 240
Chambers	183	Corson	151, 152, 153
Chapman	144, 147, 148, 150	Cowpland	83
Cheyney	81	Cresson	152
Clothier	35	Cully	108
Coates	83, 84	Cuthbert	109, 141

D.

Dana	110	Denny	107
Darch	238	DeVinney	182
David	71, 81	Dixon	83
Davies	35	Drexel	84
Davis	82	Duer	141
Day	152	Dunlap	144

E.

Edge	83	Eskens	110
Egbert	314, Appendix	Evans	81, 82, 86, 121, 136, 220, 230, et seq.
Ellet	349		
Ellis	205, et seq.		

F.

Fisher	265	Foulke	82, 92 et seq., 151, 203, 221, 231, 248.
Fornance	283		

Index.

G.

	PAGE.		PAGE.
Garrett	81, 107	Glenn	141
Garrigues	39, Appendix	Gordon	144
George	90, 91, 107	Govett	180, 181
Gibbons	181	Griscom	336 et seq.
Glen	239		

H.

	PAGE.		PAGE.
Haines	153	Hibbard	137
Hale	240	Hoopes	82
Harmer	179	Horn	167, 168
Hayes	139	Hopper	283
Henszey	35	Howell	70, 82, 109
Henri	83	Hubbs	231
Henry	182, 183, 184	Hudson	137, 138, 140
Herbert	305 et seq.	Humphrey	125, 206, 207, 242 et seq.

J.

James	82	Jones	40, 41, 61, 65, 67, 73, 75, 80, 81, 82, 83, 88, 111, 139, 151, 181, 256, 294, 315.
John	72, 73, 122	Jordan	177, 182, 184

K.

Keith	278	Knowles	181
Kite	84, 85, 86	Kuhn	233

L.

Lawlor	178	Lloyd	70, 75, 77, 79, 81, 83, 92 et seq., 167, 181, 321, 375 et seq.
Lea	83	Logan	277
Leacock	107	Loin	103
Levering	303	Lukens	152
Lewis	35, 83, 171, 172, 231, 235		

M.

Mahan	234	Miles	153
Malthen	184	Miller	149
Maris	137	Montgomery	97
Marshall	181	Morgan	87, 88, 355
Mather	83	Morris	136, 233, 260
Mattison	109	Musser	232
Maud	265		

N.

Nancarro	321	Niles	141
Newlin	236, 237 et seq.	Noble	103, 107
Nicholas	77		

O.

Oborn	181	Owen	64, 65, 70, 112 et seq., 158, 131, 137, 249.
Ogden	140		
Osborne	81, 83 et seq.		

P.

	PAGE.		PAGE.
Palmer	108	Philler	148
Parry	291 et seq.	Phillips	340, 148
Parke	83	Pignatelli	148
Paschall	81, 83	Potesdad	148, 150
Pearce	181	Pratt	82
Penn	313	Prees	77, 96
Pennypacker	179	Price	75, 77, 97, 277
Perot	314, Appendix.	Pryor	177

R.

Randolph	240	Roberts	46, 83, 98 et seq., 105, 130, 139, 177, 280, 303, 323.
Rhoads	137		
Rees	77 et seq., 92	Robinson	147
Rettew	81	Rossell	278
Richardson	137, 177, 178	Ruschenberger	278
Ridgway	84	Rutter	147

S.

Scarlet	251	Stacey	178
Sellers	181	Stadelman	107
Shriver	168	Stevenson	277

T.

Tatham	146	Tilghman	277
Thayer	148	Toland	277
Thomas	60, 70, 88, 111, 305 et seq., Appendix.	Townsend	84
		Troth	83

W.

Walker	278 et seq.	Wiltbank	265
Walter	71	Winsor	148
Warner	81, 108, 153, 381	Wistar	153
Webb	83	Wister	276 et seq.
West	137	Wood	182
Wharton	138, 140	Woole	184
Wheeler	103	Wright	85
Wilkins	85	Wynne	250, 261 et seq.; Appendix.
Williams	65, 73, 90, 91		

Y.

Yocum 152

Z.

Zachary 342

www.ingramcontent.com/pod-product-compliance
Lightning Source LLC
Chambersburg PA
CBHW071223290426
44108CB00013B/1271